Financial Markets and
Monetary Policy

Financial Markets and Monetary Policy

Jeffrey A. Frankel

The MIT Press
Cambridge, Massachusetts
London, England

This book was set in Palatino by Asco Trade Typesetting Ltd., Hong Kong and was printed
and bound in the United States of America.

Library of Congress Cataloging-in-Publication Data

Frankel, Jeffrey A.
  Financial markets and monetary policy / Jeffrey A. Frankel.
     p.   cm.
  Includes bibliographical references and index.
  ISBN 0-262-06174-0 (hc.)
  1. Portfolio management. 2. Inflation (Finance) 3. Interest rates.
  4. Monetary policy—United States. 5. Fiscal policy—United States. I. Title.
  HG4529.5.F73   1995
  332.6—dc20   94-37015
                                                                    CIP

To Jessica;
it's not even close

Contents

    Interest Rate Yield Curve along Its Entire Length   117

10 The Power of the Yield Curve to Predict Interest Rates
    (or Lack Thereof)   131

III Uncertainty, Policy Coordination, and Nominal GDP Targeting
Introduction to Part III   147

11 Ambiguous Policy Multipliers in Theory and in Empirical
    Models   153

12 The Implications of Conflicting Models for Coordination between
    Monetary and Fiscal Policymakers   171

13 International Macroeconomic Policy Coordination When
    Policymakers Do Not Agree on the True Model   205

14 International Nominal Targeting (INT): A Proposal for Overcoming
    Obstacles to Monetary Policy Coordination   233

15 The Stabilizing Properties of a Nominal GDP Rule for Monetary
    Policy   253

    Notes   271
    References   297
    Index   317

Preface

This is my second collection of writings. While the first collection dealt exclusively with international financial markets, the subject here is primarily domestic financial markets, including the role of national monetary authorities. The chapters divide neatly into three areas: optimal diversification by investors, commodity prices and the yield curve as two kinds of monetary indicators, and the choice of a regime for monetary policy in the presence of uncertainty. It might help to point out the connections among these three areas from the outset, since they may not be self-evident. This is an aim of the introduction that follows.

The collection is not intended to be a new treatise. Any sense of continuity must come from the logic of the chapters themselves, and the other introductions I have written—one for each of the three parts. As in the earlier volume, however, I have done a bit of neatening up, such as updating the references to the most final known publication and collecting them at the back of the book.

The acknowledgments in the first collection, *On Exchange Rates*, were rather self-indulgently extensive. They apply equally here, but I shall not repeat them. I must, however, thank my collaborators Charles Engel, Kenneth Froot, Anthony Rodrigues, Gikas Hardouvelis, Cara Lown, Horace Brock, Katharine Rockett, and Menzie Chinn.

Introduction

We begin with the behavior of investors in financial markets. It is they who primarily determine the course of those markets and, ultimately, their impact on the real economy.

Changes in the supplies of money and bonds will affect interest rates in ways that depend on the behavior of the investors who must absorb these assets. The theme of part I is optimal portfolio diversification. It should be placed in the context of an attempt that began with James Tobin, to put more structure on the analysis of the asset demands of investors. If investors are risk-averse and therefore treat assets as imperfect substitutes, then changes in relative asset supplies will have effects on required rates of return. An increase in the supply of long-term government bonds, for example, will drive up the long-term interest rate. These essays generally conclude, however, that the degree of substitutability among optimizing investors is relatively high and therefore that portfolio effects are likely to be relatively small. For many purposes, the assumption that expected returns are approximately equalized across assets may not be too bad.

We then turn to problems of monetary policy. The *instruments* of monetary policy directly available to central bankers include open market operations (as well as policy with regard to reserve requirements and the discount window). The ultimate *objectives* of monetary policy are generally agreed to be price stability and maximization of output or employment. In between the instruments and the ultimate objectives are *intermediate targets* and *indicators*. Proclaiming and abiding by targets is a way that a central bank can assure others, both domestic citizens and foreign countries, what its policy is. Monitoring sensitive indicators is a way that a central bank can detect early warnings of deviations from the intended targets or objectives. In simple theories, direct instruments and ultimate objectives are all that matter. Should monetary authorities use intermediate targets and indicators, and if so, what should they be? Part II of the volume explores some possible indicators, and part III some possible targets.

First, let us recall some historical context. Inflation rates rose to alarming levels in the 1970s. By the end of the decade, the United States was ready for a major change in monetary policy. One way of interpreting the source of the shift was a change in the priority that the aggregate national political process placed on low inflation, as compared to low unemployment. Such a shift was symbolized by the victory of the Republicans over the Democrats in the 1980 election campaign, although the key changes in monetary policy had already been made by Paul Volcker after his appointment as Federal Reserve Chairman. Similar shifts took place around the same time in some other major industrialized countries. Another way of interpreting the source of the shift was a new realization that, even if the public would be happy with a few extra points of inflation in exchange for a few less points of unemployment, this trade-off is not in fact available to the economy in the long run.

The specific regime that was adopted by major central banks around the world as a way to commit to low inflation was the monetarist rule: by 1980 most of them were pursuing target rates of growth for the money supply. The subsequent decade, however, left many central bankers disillusioned with monetarism. The question of the optimal nominal anchor is thus in the 1990s still an open one.

Consider two flaws in monetarism. One affects the problem of indicators, the other the problem of intermediate targets. First, monetarism assumed that prices are perfectly flexible, even in the short run. As we shall see, this tended to imply, for example, that high nominal interest rates were necessarily an indicator of high expected inflation. Second, monetarism underestimated the degree of variability of money demand. It argued that if the central bank proclaimed a rigid path of slow but steady growth for the money supply, and stuck to its target, then nominal GNP growth would be stable.

We learned in the 1980s that both of these propositions were wrong. When nominal interest rates rose sharply at the beginning of the decade, it was not because expected inflation was rising. Rather contraction of monetary policy had succeeded in raising the real interest rate. To infer from the high nominal interest rates that expected inflation was still rising and that further tightening was called for would have been to make precisely the wrong inference. Again, when the rate of growth of the money supply persistently broke above the preannounced target range during the period 1983–86, it was not, as the monetarists warned at the time, because monetary policy was becoming inflationary. Rather, there had been a large upward shift in the demand for money. To suggest from the acceleration of the money supply that tightening was called for would again have been to make the wrong inference. Evidently a more subtle framework is required.

Part II of this book looks at two kinds of indicators of expected inflation, which might be of interest to central bankers seeking to gauge whether monetary policy is currently loose or tight. In both cases, we abstract from the portfolio effects considered in part I. Investors are assumed to come close to equalizing the expected returns on different assets.

The first indicator is the price of agricultural commodities and minerals such as gold. The second is the term structure of interest rates. When the real price of commodities is unusually high, or the yield curve is unusually steep, it signals that real interest rates are unusually low, which means that participants in financial markets consider monetary policy to be unusually inflationary. What may be slightly distinctive about these essays is that they rely on a framework in which, because prices of most goods are sticky, changes in monetary policy affect the real interest rate. The model itself is extremely commonplace; but these particular monetary indicators have in the past been largely monopolized by monetarists with overly simplistic flexible-price models.

The question of whether goods prices are sticky or flexible, and the question of whether assets are close substitutes, are just two of the many issues that economics has not settled to everyone's satisfaction. Such ambiguities create important uncertainties regarding the effects of monetary and fiscal policy on the economy. The starting point of part III is a documentation of just how wide is the range of these uncertainties, and how much difficulty it creates for international coordination of macroeconomic policy. The ending point of part III is a brief for focusing on nominal GDP as the most suitable target for monetary policy. Nominal GDP targeting addresses some of the difficulties afflicting the making of policy, such as difficulties created by uncertainty regarding future disturbances.

I

Do Investors Diversify
Optimally?

Introduction to Part I

The theory of optimal portfolio diversification allows the macroeconomist to bring more information to bear on the question of the parameters in investors' asset-demand functions, as compared to general textbook formulations. Indeed, this was the original motivation underlying the research for which James Tobin won the Nobel Prize. That research gave rise to an entire field modern finance as taught, for example, in business schools—from which the macroeconomic motivation surprisingly has largely disappeared.

The essays in part I propose and implement an econometric technique for imposing the constraints of mean-variance optimization on the shares of their portfolios that investors choose to allocate to various assets. Coauthors and I have suggested a name for this technique: the "CASE method," standing for Constrained Asset Share Estimation. (This name does not appear in the earlier papers, however.)

One key advantage of the CASE method is that it allows expected returns to fluctuate freely, an important attribute for macroeconomic applications. Originally the variances and covariances of asset returns were assumed constant, although not the betas or covariances with the market return. Thus the innovation was quite different from that made by Rob Engle's introduction of the ARCH technique (AutoRegressive Conditional Heteroskedasticity) for modeling time-varying variances. Nevertheless, ARCH and its extensions (notably Generalized ARCH) have over the last ten years become a necessary element of modeling financial market behavior, reflecting that variances are in fact empirically observed to vary over time. The last of the chapters in part I applies this ARCHified version of CASE to the U.S. stock market.

Chapter 1 applies the CASE method to the important macroeconomic question of portfolio crowding-out: do increases in the supply of government debt drive up the required rate of return on capital? In general, the answer to this question depends on whether government bonds are closer substitutes for equity than for money. If bonds *are* close substitutes for equity, then an increase in the supply of bonds is much like an increase in the supply of equity, and will drive up the expected rate of return that equity must pay to be willingly held. This higher required rate of return might, in turn, crowd out investment in plant and equipment. Earlier econometric studies had found it very difficult to get precise and plausible estimates of such substitutability parameters, without imposing prior beliefs. This chapter proposes a specific technique for trying to improve the estimates by bringing to bear the information contained in the hypothesis of expected-utility maximization. The striking conclusion to emerge from this approach, if conventional levels of risk aversion are assumed, is that portfolio effects are extremely small. This same conclusion has emerged from the application to other portfolio questions of the hypothesis of expected-utility maximization.[1] In the present context, it seems to suggest, under the assumptions of the model, that portfolio crowding-out of investment is likely to be small. It should be noted that this conclusion, even if accepted, still leaves ample room for other channels whereby government deficits crowd out private capital. One would not want to base conclusions regarding the overall effect of fiscal policy on interest rates on the results of this chapter, especially given the record of the large U.S. budget deficits and high real interest rates that began in the 1980s.

Chapter 2 applies the same approach, the CASE method, to the question of government debt management policy, namely, the term-structure composition of the debt. Would a shift in the government supply of debt from long-term bonds to short-term bonds have a substantial effect on market rates of return? This chapter was originally an invited response to a study of debt management in Sweden. In the United States, the question became more topical in 1993 when a newly elected President Clinton decided to make precisely such a shift in debt management policy. (In the U.S. case, those concerned about the government deficit hoped that the effect of the shift on market interest rates would be small, so the government could take advantage of low short-term interest rates and thereby save on interest payments. Those concerned with private investment hoped that the downward effect on long-term interest rates would be large.) As with the crowding-out question considered earlier, the conclusion of chapter 2 is that small portfolio effects seem to follow from the constraints of optimal portfolio diversification, assuming one chooses to impose those constraints. But one begins to question the levels of risk aversion that are conventionally assumed in such analyses, if not the entire framework of optimal portfolio diversification.

The next several chapters continue to use the same econometric technique, the CASE method, but they switch the emphasis from imposing the constraints of mean-variance optimization in order to test macroeconomic questions, to explicit testing of the constraints themselves. These chapters thus fit into the large literature in the field of finance that tests the Capital Asset Pricing Model (CAPM). Chapter 3 seeks to introduce the test of CAPM in an intuitive way. Most finance specialists would rather avoid explicit focus on asset quantities, distrusting the data, and would prefer to look only at market prices. The chapter, however, points out that the numbers on portfolio shares held by investors are lurking unacknowledged within the famous "betas" of the standard tests, as components of the return on the aggregate market index. An explicit focus on these hitherto implicit portfolio shares yields a better test. The chapter tests the CAPM hypothesis on the same data set as that used in chapter 1: a portfolio of equities, federal government bonds, state and local bonds, corporate bonds, real estate and other tangible assets, and Treasury bills and other short-term assets. The result is a failure to reject the constraints of CAPM, in favor of the more general alternative hypothesis in which asset demands are an unspecified linear function of expected returns.

Chapter 4, coauthored with Charles Engel (not to be confused with Robert Engle), internationalizes the test of CAPM: the portfolio now consists of the assets of six major industrialized countries. The finding is the same as in the previous chapter: a rejection of the constraints imposed by mean-variance optimization.

These early applications of the CASE method were limited in (at least) two ways. Most important, they made the assumption that the variances and covariances of returns on individual assets were constant over time, though not the covariances of individual returns with the overall market return. This assumption grew increasingly difficult to justify. The use of ARCH and the other techniques to model the time-varying variances of returns, mentioned above, is perhaps the most important development of the last decade in empirical finance. One important application of these techniques to testing CAPM is Bollerslev, Engle, and Wooldridge (1988). A number of authors have recently integrated the CASE and ARCH methods: Engel and Rodrigues (1989, 1993), Giovannini and Jorion (1989), and Thomas and Wickens (1993).

Most tests feature a very limited menu of assets—the U.S. stock market, for example. The test in chapter 3 considered a portfolio that was relatively comprehensive in the range of assets included (bills, bonds, equity, real estate, etc.), except that they were all U.S. assets. The test in chapter 4 was relatively comprehensive along a different dimension, including assets from six countries; but they were all bonds. Engel (1994) has recently applied the ARCHified CASE method to a portfolio that is international and that includes both bonds and equities.[2]

In light of the extent to which they share the same questions and the same tools, it is remarkable the extent to which research in finance groups at business schools proceeds independently of finance research in economics departments. My CASE coauthors (Charles Engel, Tony Rodrigues, and Ken Froot) and I felt the need to produce a version of the test targeted for a finance audience. The paper produced here as chapter 5 applied the ARCHified and GARCHified CASE method to a portfolio of U.S. equities, the portfolio most commonly investigated in finance journals. The chapter also describes how the technique relates to important recent contributions to the empirical asset-pricing literature, such as that of Harvey (1989).

It is not possible to allow both expected returns and variances to vary freely over time, in the manner that expected returns are allowed to vary freely in the first four chapters. Either the first or the second moment must be modeled with some degree of ad hoc—ery, such as autoregressively or as a function of other observable economic variables. Harvey (1989) chooses to model expected returns in an ad hoc manner, before testing the constraints of expected utility maximization. We choose to do it the other way: to model the variances in `an ad hoc manner (ARCH or GARCH), before testing the constraints. Our finding for the U.S. stock market, as for the portfolios considered in the preceding chapters, is a rejection of CAPM. Unlike with most tests of CAPM, we can put an explicit interpretation on the alternative hypothesis—it is a general linear Tobin portfolio-choice model. This model is interesting as an alternative, both because it occupies an important place in the development of finance theory and in modern textbooks, and because it does turn out to have some power to explain stock returns in our sample.

A few readers of the original studies have remarked on what they see as an inconsistency in publishing some papers that impose the constraint of mean-variance maximization, such as chapters 1 and 2, while also publishing others that test and reject that same constraint, such as 3, 4, and 5. This is a matter of one's personal philosophy of good research methodology. Let us posit, uncontroversially, that the goal is to contribute to the process whereby economists seek to advance our understanding of how the economy operates. A large number of economists have been busily engaged in testing an important hypothesis, optimal portfolio diversification, while others have been simultaneously engaged in using that same hypothesis in order to look at other important questions. If one can suggest an econometric technique that seems to offer an improvement over the state of the art within both activities, then I think it follows that one should seek to contribute to both literatures simultaneously.

More controversially, perhaps, I suspect that many econometricians have in some ways become too slavish to the outcomes of their own statistical tests. Needless to say, if a large number of studies consistently find that the data are at odds with a given hypothesis, the good scientist should abandon that hypothesis. This does not mean, however, that a given economist should under all circumstances refrain from considering the implications of an appealing hypothesis in one paper, even if a particular test rejects that hypothesis in another paper. To the contrary, if there is an a priori reason to believe in a hypothesis, it should take more than one test to kill it. I worry that recent years have sometimes seen excessively slavish adherence to the rule of throwing out hypotheses that are statistically rejected by the data, and that this trend has given researchers in finance and macroeconomics a strong incentive to develop sophisticated theories that are lacking in empirically testable implications, or to develop sophisticated empirical tests that lack the power to reject. But perhaps such questions of research strategy must be left as a matter of personal taste.

Having said all this, I must confess that when an author publishes both kinds of research (estimation imposing a hypothesis, as well as tests of that hypothesis) in a single place, as I am doing in this volume, there is a greater obligation to tell the reader at some point what his or her own beliefs are. For what it is worth, my own belief, after so many years of repeated statistical rejections of mean-variance optimization and CAPM by many authors, is that most investors do not in practice obey these constraints, at least not with the conventional assumptions about risk aversion, aggregation, and rational expectations. I still believe, however, that the CAPM theory is in some contexts the best we have. I am particularly reluctant to see it lose out to more sophisticated theories of intertemporal optimization or complete securities markets, if the Darwinian virtue of the latter is that they make themselves less subject to serious econometric testing, for example by focusing on unobservable "factors" or "state variables."

1

Portfolio Crowding-Out, Empirically Estimated

There are a number of questions regarding the behavior of portfolio-holders in financial markets that have a long history of study but that never have been answered satisfactorily. Prominent among them is the question of whether federal government debt drives up the rate of return on capital and thus crowds out private investment in plant and equipment. The effect is known as "portfolio crowding-out" to distinguish it from the "transactions crowding-out" effect of government spending itself that is familiar from the textbooks. The framework in which to examine the question is well established, but the crucial parameters elude successful estimation: how close a substitute is government debt for corporate capital in investors' portfolios? This question and many others depend on the parameters in investors' asset-demand functions.

One obvious way to attempt to estimate the parameters in the asset-demand functions is simply to regress actual portfolio shares held by investors against some measure of expected returns by Ordinary Least Squares (OLS) or by some simultaneous-equation method.[1] Alternatively, the returns could be regressed against the actual portfolio shares to estimate the system of asset-demand functions in inverted form.[2] In this form the system can be thought of as a market equilibrium condition; it tells what the expected returns on the assets must be for given supplies of them to be willingly held. For example, consider the hypothesis that two particular assets are perfect substitutes—that the asset demands are infinitely sensitive to the relative expected rate of return on those assets. This hypothesis is more testable when the asset-demand functions are estimated in inverted form. It says that supplies of the various assets have no effect on the expected relative return of the two assets. (In the matrix B^{-1} below, the relevant row consists of zeros.)

Originally published in *Quarterly Journal of Economics* 100 (1985): 1041–65. Reprinted with permission.

The OLS approach is tried out below. The problem with it is that the estimates tend to be imprecise. Many of the parameter estimates are highly implausible, and we cannot have much confidence in tests of portfolio crowding-out. It would be desirable to bring more information to bear on the parameters in the asset-demand functions.

The theory of portfolio optimization constitutes such additional information. If investors maximize expected utility, then the parameters in their asset-demand functions are not determined arbitrarily but rather are related to the degree of variability of ex post returns and to the degree of risk aversion. Under certain assumptions made in this chapter (one-period maximization of expected utility, constant relative risk aversion, and normally distributed returns) the relationship is extremely simple: the coefficient matrix, in its inverted form, is proportional to the variance-covariance matrix of returns. Then the proposition that two assets are close substitutes becomes the hypothesis that the covariance of their returns is high, and that they have similar covariances with third assets.[3]

This train of thought is a common one in the literature. Roley (1982, p. 646) sums up the woeful status of the regression studies: "Despite the theoretical plausibility of significant relative asset supply effects on security yields, virtually all empirical research has been unsuccessful in isolating these effects." The responses in the literature—attempts to bring to bear the additional information contained in the theory of portfolio optimization—fall into two distinct categories. The first group maintains the framework of regressions of asset quantities and rates of return but uses the Theil-Goldberger mixed-estimation technique to bring in a priori beliefs like gross substitutability among the assets. Examples are Smith and Brainard (1976); Backus, Brainard, Smith, and Tobin (1980); and Backus and Purvis (1980).[4] One problem with this approach is that it does not use all the information contained in the portfolio optimization theory. But in another sense it uses too much information: the assumption of gross substitutability among all assets is a strict one that is not particularly likely to be borne out by the true variance-covariance matrix, as Blanchard and Plantes (1977) have argued.

The second category of studies makes no use of time-series data on asset quantities, and instead computes the optimal portfolio from data on ex post rates of return. The difficult question is how to measure expected rates of return. The traditional method is to assume expected returns constant over the sample period. Then they can be estimated by the sample means, and the variance-covariance matrix can be estimated by the second moments around the means. Examples are Roley (1979) and Nordhaus and Durlauf

(1982). The problem here is that the assumption that expected returns are constant seems inconsistent with the fact that nominal interest rates, expected inflation, real interest rates, etc., are observed to vary over time.

Previous studies have, at best, allowed expected returns to change in an ad hoc manner. Some, like Friedman (1983), split the sample into sub-samples. Others, like Bodie, Kane, and McDonald (1983), model the return as an autoregressive process. Still others, like Friedman (1985a), estimate expected returns in a given period as a vector autoregression, using all the data available up to that period to estimate the parameters, as in the technique of rolling regressions. Such approaches are a step forward in that they allow expected returns to change over time. But the expected returns can only change slowly from one period to the next. Thus, these studies are still inconsistent with the framework of the macroeconomic questions we wish to answer, such as the effect of a sudden increase in the supply of government debt on the various expected rates of return.

This chapter estimates the parameters in the asset-demand function and tests hypotheses about them, using a technique that imposes the optimization hypothesis. The essence of this technique is the recognition that the variance-covariance matrix of returns is precisely the variance-covariance matrix of the error term in the system of equations, and that the parameters should be estimated subject to this constraint. The technique dominates the regression studies in that it uses all the information in the optimization hypothesis, and it dominates the optimal portfolio studies in that it allows expected returns to vary freely over time. The striking conclusion that emerges is that portfolio crowding-out is unlikely, and more generally that portfolio effects on expected rates of return are virtually certain to be minor in any case.

1.1 Hypotheses Regarding the Asset-Demand Functions

In this section we present the specification of the asset-demand functions, and discuss in greater detail various hypotheses regarding their parameters. We specify asset demands as a linear function of expected returns:

$$\mathbf{x}_t = \mathbf{A} + \mathbf{B}(E_t \mathbf{r}_{t+1}), \tag{1}$$

where $\mathbf{x}_t$ is a vector $[x_t^T\ x_t^F\ x_t^S\ x_t^C\ x_t^K]'$ of the shares in the total portfolio that are allocated to each of five assets: (1) tangible assets, i.e., real estate and consumer durables; (2) long-term federal debt; (3) long-term state and local debt; (4) long-term corporate debt; and (5) equities. There is a sixth asset that we omit as redundant given that the six shares must sum to one. It is

(6) deposits, which is an amalgamation of a monetary aggregate (basically M3) and short-term corporate and government securities. We aggregate the short-term assets together partly because they all have nominal returns known to the investor with certainty (assuming away default risk), which implies that their only risk comes from a common source, inflation; they should in theory be perfect substitutes with respect to risk. One cannot explain in a risk-return framework why investors would hold money as opposed to short-term securities that pay interest. Furthermore, by now, most assets included in M3 pay variable interest rates, so that the distinction between money and other short-term securities has in any case become thoroughly blurred. We choose a maturity of one year or less as the definition of short-term, not just because that is the accounting definition of short-term, but also because our data on portfolios held by U.S. households are yearly data, and it is convenient (though not essential) that the term of maturity correspond to the frequency of observation.

$E_t \, \mathbf{r}_{t+1}$ is a vector $E_t[r_{t+1}^T \ r_{t+1}^F \ r_{t+1}^S \ r_{t+1}^C \ r_{t+1}^K]'$ of the expected real returns on the five assets, each measured relative to the expected real return on the reference asset, deposits. $\mathbf{A}$ is a vector of five constants. $\mathbf{B}$ is a 5×5 matrix of coefficients that describes the reponsiveness of asset demands to expected returns. Equation (1) is general in form, in that we have not said what determines the parameters in $\mathbf{A}$ and $\mathbf{B}$. But it is restricted somewhat in that we have assumed that wealth enters homogeneously, and that the equation is linear in expected returns. It will turn out that equation (1) is precisely the correct form for asset-demand functions to take, with specific values for $\mathbf{A}$ and $\mathbf{B}$, if investors maximize a function of the mean and variance of their real wealth. We have excluded any transactions demand for assets, and any tax effects, though both could in theory be subsumed in the rates of return if they could be properly measured.

We shall be working with the system of asset demands, equation (1), in inverted form:[5]

$$E_t \mathbf{r}_{t+1} = -\mathbf{B}^{-1}\mathbf{A} + \mathbf{B}^{-1}\mathbf{x}_t. \tag{2}$$

We assume that the financial markets are always in equilibrium: expected rates of return are whatever they have to be for asset supplies to be willingly held by investors.[6]

Within this framework we shall be testing hypotheses concerning the derivatives of particular expected rates of return with regard to particular asset supplies. Presumably the expected rate of return on an asset, say federal bonds, has a positive derivative with respect to the supply of that asset. An increase in the federal debt raises the expected return that must be paid to investors to induce them to hold it. But the effect on the expected returns on alternative assets is not clear a priori.

Here the most interesting question is whether an increase in federal debt drives up the required rate of return on private capital. The "portfolio crowding-out" literature of Blinder and Solow (1973) and Tobin and Buiter (1976) assumed in the tradition of Keynes that all forms of long-term debt and capital were perfect substitutes, so that a ceteris paribus increase in federal debt necessarily raised the required rate of return on capital. Those papers traced out over time the "general equilibrium" effects of cumulating government debt; the issue was only whether the contractionary effects were outweighed by other expansionary effects. As Tobin (1961), Friedman (1978), and Roley (1979) argue, if we relax the unrealistic assumption that government bonds are perfect substitutes for private capital, then an increase in the supply of government bonds will not necessarily drive up the required rate of return on capital at all. It depends on the degree of substitutability. If bonds are relatively close substitutes for capital (the limiting case being that of Blinder-Solow and Tobin-Buiter), then an increase in the supply of bonds will indeed drive up the required return on capital. But if the bonds are relatively close substitutes for money, then it will drive *down* the required return on capital, as if it were an increase in the supply of money. Friedman calls this possibility "portfolio crowding-in."

To consider effects on the expected rate of return on equity, we pick out the relevant equation from the system of five equations represented by equation (2):

$$E_t r^K_{t+1} = c_5 + b_{51}\left(\frac{T}{W}\right)_t + b_{52}\left(\frac{F}{W}\right)_t + b_{53}\left(\frac{S}{W}\right)_t + b_{54}\left(\frac{C}{W}\right)_t$$

$$+ b_{55}\left(\frac{K}{W}\right)_t, \tag{3}$$

where

c_5 is the last element of $-\mathbf{B}^{-1}\mathbf{A}$,

$b_{51} - b_{55}$ is the last row of $\mathbf{B}^{-1}$,

T is the supply of tangible assets,

F is the supply of federal bonds,

S is the supply of state and local bonds,

C is the supply of corporate bonds,

K is the supply of equity,

W is wealth, $\equiv T + F + S + C + K + D$, and
D is the supply of short-term bills and deposits.

The effect of an increase in F without a change in the other variables in equation (3) is given by b_{52}/W_t. Since we are holding wealth constant, the increase in F must come at the expense of the omitted asset, deposits D. Thus, the experiment we are considering has precisely the interpretation of an open-market sale of bonds by the central bank. Since we have aggregated together money and short-term Treasury securities, the experiment can also be interpreted as a shift in the term-structure composition of the national debt, as in studies of debt management policy by Tobin (1963), Friedman (1978), and Roley (1979, 1982). While one might think that a decrease in the money supply would necessarily have the contractionary effects associated with an increase in $E_t r_{t+1}^K$, Tobin points out that a shift from short-term Treasury securities to long-term Treasury securities will have no effect if the two are perfect substitutes. To test whether such an operation raises the expected relative return on equity $E_t r_{t+1}^K$, we would test whether b_{52} is significantly greater than zero.

The effect of an increase in W without a change in the other variables in equation (3) is given by

$$\frac{\partial E_t r_{t+1}^K}{\partial W_t} = \left[-b_{51}\left(\frac{T}{W}\right)_t - b_{52}\left(\frac{F}{W}\right)_t - b_{53}\left(\frac{S}{W}\right)_t - b_{54}\left(\frac{C}{W}\right)_t \right.$$
$$\left. - b_{55}\left(\frac{K}{W}\right)_t \right] \Big/ W_t. \qquad (4)$$

Since we are holding the other asset supplies constant, the increase in wealth must come in the form of an increase in the supply of the omitted asset, deposits D. Thus, equation (4) has precisely the interpretation of the effect of a "helicopter-drop" of money (or of the comparative statics effects of a money-financed government deficit). To test whether it has the negative effect on $E_t r_{t+1}^K$ that one would expect, we test whether $-\mathbf{b}_5 \mathbf{x}_t$ is significantly less than zero, where $\mathbf{b}_5$ is the last row of $\mathbf{B}^{-1}$.

The main event is portfolio crowding-out: the effect of an increase in F, including the wealth effect, on $E_t r_{t+1}^K$:

$$\frac{\partial E_t r_{t+1}^K}{\partial F_t} = \left[-b_{51}\left(\frac{T}{W}\right)_t + b_{52}\left(1 - \frac{F}{W}\right)_t - b_{53}\left(\frac{S}{W}\right)_t - b_{54}\left(\frac{C}{W}\right)_t \right.$$
$$\left. - b_{55}\left(\frac{K}{W}\right)_t \right] \Big/ W_t. \qquad (5)$$

Notice that equation (5) is the sum of the effect of open-market substitution of bonds for money, b_{52}/W_t, plus the effect of an increase in money, the wealth effect of equation (4). An expression greater than zero represents portfolio crowding-out; an expression less than zero represents portfolio crowding-in.

The rate of return on equity cannot be identified perfectly with the cost of capital relevant to a firm's decision to undertake investment in plant and equipment. Perhaps if we had data on the asset holdings of the aggregated private sector, including real capital held by the corporate sector, we could use the profit rate as an unambiguous measure of the return on real capital. But it seems desirable to avoid such an extreme degree of aggregation, and to work with the holdings of the household sector alone. We shall look at the effect on the rate of return on equity because that is what is held by households. We shall also look at the effect of an increase in federal bonds F on the expected rate of return on corporate bonds $E_t r^C_{t+1}$. Since corporate bonds are an alternative to equity as a way of financing investment by firms, this effect is also relevant to the question of portfolio crowding-out.[7] Note that our goal here is nothing more than to examine the effect of the supply of government debt on the expected relative rates of return that various assets must pay to private investors. To answer the more ambitious question of whether an increase in debt has an expansionary or contractionary effect on real activity, we would need to know not just the asset-holding preferences of households, but also those of firms, pension funds, banks, and other financial intermediaries, not to mention what we would need to know about saving behavior and goods markets. The term "portfolio crowding-out" is here used merely as shorthand for certain partial derivatives.

1.2   Estimation of the Asset-Demand Functions, without the Constraints of Mean-Variance Optimization

The frequent stumbling-block to the estimation of asset-demand functions like equation (1), or the inverted form (equation (2)), is the measurement of expected returns, which are not directly observable. As discussed at the beginning of the chapter, we do not want to measure expected returns by the sample average or by an ad hoc ARIMA function of lagged returns, because this would not allow them to fluctuate freely. But the way we have set up equation (2), all that is necessary is to assume that expectations are rational: expectational errors are random, where "random" means uncorrelated with the information set I_t available at time t. Then actual ex post returns are given by

$$\mathbf{r}_{t+1} = E_t\mathbf{r}_{t+1} + \boldsymbol{\varepsilon}_{t+1}, \qquad E_t(\boldsymbol{\varepsilon}_{t+1}|\mathbf{I}_t) = 0. \tag{6}$$

Substituting (2) into (6), we get

$$\mathbf{r}_{t+1} = -\mathbf{B}^{-1}\mathbf{A} + \mathbf{B}^{-1}\mathbf{x}_t + \boldsymbol{\varepsilon}_{t+1}. \tag{7}$$

This system of equations can be estimated by OLS because the left-hand side variable is now observable, and the error term, by the assumption of rational expectations, is uncorrelated with the righthand-side variables x.[8]

The system was estimated on yearly observations from 1954 to 1980. The data are described elsewhere.[9] The OLS results are reported in table 1.1. As previous studies have found, for example, Smith and Brainard (1976) and Friedman (1978, 638), simple OLS estimation of such a system does not yield very satisfactory results. The implausibility of some of the estimates in table 1.1 will become clearer when we turn to our hypothesis testing. But for the moment, one anomaly stands out. Many of the coefficients that we might a priori expect to be positive appear negative. For example, an increase in the supply of federal bonds (in exchange for money) equal to 1.00 percent of investors' portfolios appears to drive the expected relative rate of return on federal bonds *down* by 2.26 percent (226 basis points) rather than up. While that coefficient estimate is not statistically significant, three others are, as follows: the negative coefficient of federal bonds in the equation for the return on state and local bonds, and the negative coefficients of federal bonds and state and local bonds in the equation for the return on corporate bonds. It seems a priori that the three bonds should be substitutes, but the negative signs seem to suggest that the three bonds are complements. It is small wonder that previous authors have considered it necessary to adopt techniques that combine the data with their a priori beliefs.[10]

1.3   The Constraints of Mean-Variance Optimization

The innovation of this chapter is that it estimates the parameters of the asset-demand system, equation (1), using the constraints that come from the hypothesis that investors choose their portfolios so as to maximize a function of the mean and variance of their real wealth. This hypothesis has a distinguished history, consisting notably of the Tobin-Markowitz model (e.g., Tobin 1958) and the Capital Asset Pricing Model (CAPM). Much of the large literature on CAPM is devoted to testing the model, and the

Table 1.1
Unconstrained estimation of inverted asset-demand function. Equation-by-equation OLS: Sample, 1954–80

Dependent variable: Real rate of return on asset relative to short-term bills	$\mathbf{B}^{-1}$: Coefficients on shares of portfolios allocated to						D.W.	SSR	R^2	Log likelihood	$F_{(5,21)}$
	Constant	Tangible assets	Long-term federal debt	State and local debt	Corporate bonds	Equities					
Tangible assets	-0.103 (0.409)	0.251 (0.594)	0.279 (0.562)	-4.755 (2.750)	3.005 (2.838)	0.003 (0.445)	2.06	0.00648	0.52	74.21	4.62*
Long-term federal debt	1.15 (1.19)	-2.071 (1.736)	-2.260 (1.642)	-7.756 (8.040)	22.329* (8.299)	-1.711 (1.300)	2.18	0.005538	0.52	45.25	4.51*
State and local debt	0.979 (1.637)	-2.090 (2.378)	-5.163* (2.250)	-17.020 (11.017)	40.202* (11.372)	-1.635 (1.782)	1.70	0.10399	0.54	36.74	5.01*
Corporate bonds	0.780 (0.931)	-1.565 (1.352)	-3.038* (1.279)	-14.240* (6.262)	30.394* (6.464)	-1.365 (1.013)	1.97	0.03359	0.67	51.99	8.45*
Equities	0.110 (2.600)	-0.612 (3.776)	6.412 (3.573)	-19.562 (17.491)	3.991 (18.054)	0.500 (2.828)	2.08	0.26209	0.32	24.26	1.95

	$-(G-1)(T/2)\log 2\pi$	$-(T/2)\log|\mathbf{\Omega}|$	$-\frac{1}{2}(G-1)T = \log$ likelihood
$\mathbf{B}^{-1}$ unconstrained	-124.06	450.98	-67.50	259.42*
$\mathbf{B}$ constrained to 0	-124.06	412.49	-67.50	220.93

*Significant at the 95 percent level. (Standard errors are reported in parentheses.)

results are often not favorable.[11] However, this approach remains the most attractive way of bringing more structure to bear on simple asset-demand functions.

We now derive in discrete time the correct form for the asset demands of an investor who maximizes a function of the mean and variance of his or her end-of-period real wealth.[12]

Let W_t be real wealth. The investor must choose the vector of portfolio shares $\mathbf{x}_t$ that he or she wishes to allocate to the various assets. End-of-period real wealth will be given by

$$W_{t+1} = W_t[\mathbf{x}_t'\mathbf{r}_{t+1} + 1 + r_{t+1}^D], \tag{8}$$

where $\mathbf{r}_{t+1}$ is still the vector of returns on the five assets relative to the return r_{t+1}^D on the reference asset (deposits). The expected value and variance of end-of-period wealth (equation (8)), conditional on current information, are as follows:

$$E_t W_{t+1} = W_t[\mathbf{x}_t'E_t\mathbf{r}_{t+1} + 1 + E_t r_{t+1}^D]$$

$$V_t W_{t+1} = W_t^2[\mathbf{x}_t'\mathbf{\Omega}\mathbf{x}_t + V r_{t+1}^D + 2\mathbf{x}_t'\operatorname{cov}(\mathbf{r}_{t+1}, r_{t+1}^D)],$$

where we have defined the 5×5 conditional variance-covariance matrix of relative returns:

$$\mathbf{\Omega} \equiv E_t(\mathbf{r}_{t+1} - E_t\mathbf{r}_{t+1})(\mathbf{r}_{t+1} - E_t\mathbf{r}_{t+1})'.$$

The hypothesis is that investors maximize a function of the expected value and variance:

$$\Phi[E_t(W_{t+1}), V_t(W_{t+1})].$$

We differentiate with respect to $\mathbf{x}_t$:

$$\frac{d\Phi}{d\mathbf{x}_t} = \Phi_1\frac{dE_t W_{t+1}}{d\mathbf{x}_t} + \Phi_2\frac{dV_t W_{t+1}}{d\mathbf{x}_t} = 0.$$

$$\Phi_t W_t[E_t\mathbf{r}_{t+1}] + \Phi_2 W_t^2[2\mathbf{\Omega}\mathbf{x}_t + 2\operatorname{cov}(\mathbf{r}_{t+1}, r_{t+1}^D)] = 0.$$

We define the coefficient of relative risk aversion $\rho \equiv -W_t 2\Phi_2/\Phi_1$, which is assumed constant.[13] Then we have our result:

$$E_t\mathbf{r}_{t+1} = \rho\operatorname{cov}(\mathbf{r}_{t+1}, r_{t+1}^D) + \rho\mathbf{\Omega}\mathbf{x}_t. \tag{9}$$

This is just equation (2) with the following constraint imposed:

$$\mathbf{B}^{-1} = \rho\mathbf{\Omega}. \tag{10}$$

(There is also a constraint imposed on the intercept term $\mathbf{A}$. But it is not convenient to impose this constraint in the econometrics. Nor do we need it, since the constraint on the coefficient matrix already gives us twenty-five overidentifying restrictions.)

For economic intuition, we can invert equation (9) to solve for the portfolio shares, the form analogous to equation (1):

$$\mathbf{x}_t = -\Omega^{-1} \operatorname{cov}(\mathbf{r}_{t+1}, r^D_{t+1}) + (\rho\Omega)^{-1} E_t \mathbf{r}_{t+1}. \tag{11}$$

The asset demands consist of two parts. The first term represents the "minimum-variance" portfolio, which the investor will hold if he is extremely risk-averse ($\rho = \infty$). For example, suppose that he views deposits as a safe asset, which requires that the inflation rate is nonstochastic. Then his minimum-variance portfolio is entirely in deposits: the five entries in $\mathbf{A}_t$ are all zero because the covariance in equation (11) is zero. The second term represents the "speculative" portfolio. A higher expected return on a given asset induces investors to hold more of that asset than is in the minimum-variance portfolio, to an extent limited only by the degree of risk aversion and the uncertainty of the return.

A simple way to estimate the system that would be similar to the traditional CAPM literature is as follows. First, expected returns $E_t \mathbf{r}_{t+1}$ are assumed constant over time, and are estimated from the averages of ex post returns realized during the sample period. Second, the variance-covariance matrix Ω is assumed constant over time, and is estimated from the squared deviations of realized returns around those constant expected values. The problem with assuming expected returns constant has already been pointed out, however: it is inconsistent with the framework of changes in asset supplies and consequent changes in expected returns in which we are interested.

The solution is to recognize that the variance-covariance matrix Ω is precisely the variance-covariance matrix of the expectational error, the ε_{t+1} term in equation (2), and that the equation should be estimated subject to that constraint:

$$\mathbf{r}_{t+1} = -\mathbf{B}^{-1}\mathbf{A} + \rho\Omega\mathbf{x}_t + \varepsilon_{t+1} \qquad \Omega = E_t \varepsilon_{t+1}\varepsilon'_{t+1}. \tag{12}$$

Imposing a constraint between the coefficient matrix and the error variance-covariance matrix is unusual in econometrics. It requires nonlinear Maximum Likelihood Estimation (MLE). The appendix to Frankel and Dickens (1984) shows the log likelihood function and its first derivatives and describes the program used to find the parameter estimates that maximize it.)

The coefficient of risk aversion ρ can be estimated along with the other parameters. The MLE results turn out very reasonable in magnitude for the elements of B^{-1}, but the likelihood function is maximized at an implausibly high value for ρ: 110.31 (with an asymptotic standard error of 152.16).[14] This coefficient is conventionally considered to be far lower. The literature appears to have settled roughly on a value of 2.0. (See, for example, the evidence in Friend and Blume 1975.) Since our aim is to obtain the most efficient estimates by imposing a priori information, we here apply the MLE technique subject to the constraint $\rho = 2.0$.

The estimates are reported in table 1.2. In contrast to the OLS results in table 1.1, the MLE results show that the expected returns on the three bonds turn out to depend positively on each others' asset supplies.

Although we have set up our hypothesis testing on the matrix form $B^{-1} = \rho\Omega$, the preinverted form $B = (\rho\Omega)^{-1}$ is of interest because it represents investors' original asset-demand functions. Table 1.3 inverts the 5×5 matrix from table 1.2. Two assets are defined to be substitutes if their off-diagonal entry is negative. Thus, we see formally that each of the three bonds is indeed a substitute for the other two.[15] However, several pairs of assets are complements. For example, an increase in the expected return on corporate bonds *raises* the demand for deposits, as one can tell from the sum of the five elements of the column. Thus, the assumption of gross substitutability among all assets, imposed a priori by some previous studies, does not appear to be borne out.

Before we turn to the hypothesis testing, we should take note of the surprisingly small magnitudes of the estimates in table 1.2. For example, an increase in the supply of federal bonds (in exchange for money) equal to 1.00 percent of investors' portfolios appears to drive up the expected relative rate of return on equity by an infinitesimal 0.0005 percent (0.05 basis points). Even the effect on the expected relative rate of return on federal bonds itself is only 0.0084 percent (0.84 basis points). The inverted estimates in table 1.3 appear correspondingly high.

The apparent implausibility of these estimates is a little-noticed but unavoidable property of the mean-variance optimization theory and the constraint $\rho = 2.0$, not an artifact of the estimation technique. The unconditional variance-covariance matrix of the relative returns around their sample means is of a magnitude not much larger than our $\hat{\Omega}$, so *any* estimate of $\rho\Omega$ is going to be of a magnitude not much larger than the numbers in table 1.2, unless people are far more risk-averse than is usually thought. The MLE results with ρ unconstrained are much more reasonable. For

Table 1.2
Constrained estimation of $\rho\Omega$, inverted asset-demand function. MLE with ρ constrained to 2.0: 1954–80

Dependent variable: Real rate of return on asset relative to short-term bills	Constant	$\mathbf{B}^{-1}$: Coefficients (constrained to $\rho\Omega$) on shares of portfolios allocated to				
		Tangible assets	Long-term federal debt	State and local debt	Corporate bonds	Equities
Tangible assets	−0.00985	0.00099		(symmetric)		
	(0.01246)	(0.00082)				
Long-term federal debt	−0.02728	−0.00056	0.00841			
	(0.03647)	(0.00169)	(0.00493)			
State and local debt	−0.02546	−0.00015	0.00998	0.01689		
	(0.04884)	(0.00232)	(0.00645)	(0.00686)		
Corporate bonds	−0.02523	0.00013	0.00682	0.01007	0.00748	
	(0.02882)	(0.00146)	(0.00404)	(0.00566)	(0.00436)	
Equities	0.05384	−0.00086	0.00050	0.00060	0.00185	0.02889
	(0.05644)	(0.00436)	(0.01002)	(0.00910)	(0.00631)	(0.01346)
$-(G-1)(T/2)\log 2\pi$					$-(T/2)\log|\Omega| - \frac{1}{2}\sum \hat{\varepsilon}'_t \hat{\Omega}^{-1} \hat{\varepsilon}_t = $ log likelihood	
−124.06					352.73	228.67

Table 1.3
Constrained estimate of $(\rho\Omega)^{-1}$, preinverted asset-demand function $\mathbf{B}^{-1}$ in table 1.2 inverted, with ρ constrained to 2.0

The demand for the assets listed below	Tangible assets	Long-term federal debt	State and local debt	Corporate bonds	Equities
Tangible assets	1,398.6	445.0	80.3	−557.0	68.1
Long-term federal debt	445.0	643.2	−86.0	−487.6	35.3
State and local debt	80.3	−86.0	343.1	−390.8	21.9
Corporate bonds	−557.0	−487.6	−390.8	1,133.5	−73.0
Equities	68.1	35.3	21.9	−73.0	40.3
Short-term bills and deposits (= −sum of other rows)	−1,435.0	−549.9	+31.6	+374.9	−92.6

Demand depends on the expected real return (relative to the real return on bills) of

example, an increase in the supply of federal bonds equal to 1.00 percent of investors' portfolios drives up the expected return on federal bonds by 0.462 percent (46.2 basis points). But if the correct value of ρ is indeed on the order of 2.0, the only possible inference is that changes in ex ante relative rates of return are extremely small. Fortunately, the *relative* values of the coefficient estimates in tables 1.2 and 1.3 are very similar to the relative values of the corresponding coefficients estimated with ρ unconstrained. Since the relative values are all that matters for the portfolio crowding-out tests, our findings are not very sensitive to whether the correct value of ρ is 2.0 or much higher.

1.4   Results of Tests of Portfolio Crowding-Out

We now turn to the tests of hypotheses regarding "portfolio crowding-out," or the derivatives of expected rates of return with respect to asset supplies. In each case, after testing the hypothesis on the unconstrained estimates, we then test it on $\mathbf{B}^{-1} \equiv \rho\Omega$, the MLE parameter estimates of table 1.2 that are constrained to come from mean-variance optimization by the investor. Since the matrix is symmetric, there are in effect only fifteen estimated parameters (not counting the intercept terms). Each hypothesis consists of a single linear constraint on the parameters in vector form, β for the unconstrained parameters and Σ for the constrained ones. The test results are reported in table 1.4.[16]

Table 1.4
Test results

Effect	t	OLS: Coefficients not constrained to be optimizing (table 1.1)		MLE: Coefficients constrained to be optimizing (table 1.2)	
		Test-statistic			
		$\mathbf{R}\hat{\boldsymbol{\beta}}$	$(\mathbf{R}\hat{\boldsymbol{\beta}})'[\mathbf{R}V(\hat{\boldsymbol{\beta}})\mathbf{R}']^{-1}(\mathbf{R}\hat{\boldsymbol{\beta}})$	$\mathbf{R}\hat{\boldsymbol{\Sigma}}$	$(\mathbf{R}\hat{\boldsymbol{\Sigma}})'[\mathbf{R}V(\hat{\boldsymbol{\Sigma}})\mathbf{R}']^{-1}(\mathbf{R}\hat{\boldsymbol{\Sigma}})$
1. $\dfrac{\partial Er^K}{\partial K}$	1954	+0.36	0.37	0.0164	4.4*
	1980	+0.58	1.17	0.0192	3.9*
2. $\dfrac{\partial Er^K}{\partial D}$	1954	−0.14	0.13	0.0126	4.7*
	1980	+0.08	0.05	0.0098	5.3*
3. $\dfrac{\partial Er^K}{\partial F}$	1954	+6.3	1.52	0.0120	1.6*
	1980	+6.5	1.59	0.0092	0.8
4. $\dfrac{\partial Er^F}{\partial F}$	1954	−1.1	0.24	0.0076	1.6
	1980	−0.9	0.14	0.0084	2.2
5. $\dfrac{\partial Er^C}{\partial F}$	1954	−2.3	1.6	0.0052	1.7
	1980	−2.1	1.3	0.0060	2.3

*Significant at the 95 percent level. The critical level for a χ^2 with 1 degree of freedom is 3.8.

Hypothesis 1: The supply of equities has a positive effect on the expected relative return on equities.

This is a fairly unexceptionable proposition. We would expect an increase in any of the asset supplies to drive up the own rate of return, in order to induce investors to hold the increased supply willingly. Indeed the diagonal terms of the matrix estimated by MLE are positive by construction, though the wealth effect represented by equation (4) could in theory turn the total effect negative. We begin our testing of the derivatives or "crowding-out" effects with this example in order to get some idea of the power of our tests. In other words, if we cannot find a significant effect here, then the practical usefulness of the technique is in some doubt.

Recall that the wealth effect of an increase in any asset supply depends not only on the coefficients but also on the $\mathbf{x}_t$, the shares of the portfolio already allocated to the various assets. The constraints tested take the form that a linear combination $\mathbf{R}\boldsymbol{\beta}$ of the coefficients $\boldsymbol{\beta}$ is zero, where the weights in $\mathbf{R}$ come from the elements of $\mathbf{x}_t$. Since the $\mathbf{x}_i$ vary over time, the test-statistic will vary somewhat over time. In the 1954–80 sample, there is a pronounced upward trend in the portfolio share allocated to tangible assets (real estate and consumer durables), and there are corresponding

downward trends in the other assets. In the case of each derivative, to
ensure that our results are not sensitive to the point in time that we pick,
we shall try the test once using portfolio shares at the beginning of the
sample period, x_{54}, and once using shares at the end of the sample period,
x_{80}. It is of course the second test that is more relevant for any possible
policy conclusions in the 1980s.

Under the unconstrained OLS estimates, the point estimate of the own-
effect for equities is indeed seen to be positive, in 1954 as well as 1980.
However, the test-statistic is not significant; not even at the 75 percent
level if one should choose to go that low. Under the constrained MLE
estimates, on the other hand, the positive effect is highly significant in
either year. We accept Hypothesis 1; i.e., we reject a zero effect. This case
appears to be a good illustration of the benefit gained by using the extra
information embodied in the constraint of mean-variance optimization.

*Hypothesis 2: The supply of deposits has a negative effect on the expected
relative return on equities.*

As a matter of economics, this proposition is of interest because it says
that an increase in the money supply has a stimulating effect, to the extent
that business fixed investment responds to the required rate of return on
capital. As a technical matter, the derivative with respect to deposits is
of interest because they are the reference asset. The total effect of an
increase in, say, federal bonds (considered in the next hypothesis), is given
by a wealth or "helicopter drop" effect, represented by the derivative
considered here, plus a substitution or "open market operations" effect,
represented by the single relevant element of $\mathbf{B}^{-1}$.

Under the unconstrained OLS estimates the test-statistic is extremely
low in significance. The derivative even changes sign during the sample
period. Under the constrained MLE estimates the derivative is negative, as
hypothesized, and is highly significant. This finding holds in 1954 as well
as 1980. Again we see the benefit of using the information in the constraint
of mean-variance optimization.

*Hypothesis 3: The supply of federal bonds has a positive effect on the expected
relative return on equities.*

This is the derivative that is most easily associated with the controversy
surrounding government deficits and the possibility of portfolio crowding-
out. The unconstrained OLS estimates show positive effects, but they are
not significant at the 95 or 90 percent levels. In this case the constrained
MLE estimates are quite different. The point estimates of the effect are

negative, indicating not portfolio crowding-*out* but portfolio crowding-*in*. This finding may appear surprising, but it is consistent with the fact that equities are not substitutes but *complements* for government bonds in our estimates. To see this, one must look at the preinverted form $\mathbf{B} = [\rho\boldsymbol{\Omega}]^{-1}$ reported in table 1.3. The demand for government bonds is seen to be a positive function of the expected return on equities. The complementarity of these two assets in turn follows from the fact that the rate of return on government bonds has a much lower correlation with the rate of return on equities than with the rates of return on most of the other assets. After all, why should investors treat long-term nominal obligations of the government so very differently from short-term nominal obligations (money and Treasury bills), which we found in Hypothesis 2 to have a negative effect?

The effect is not significantly less than zero at the 95 or 90 percent levels. So we should probably describe the finding as a failure to reject the absence of any effect. On the other hand, if one wanted to describe it more aggressively as a rejection of portfolio crowding-out, one could draw some slight support from the fact that the effect is significantly negative at the 75 percent level, as of 1954. Perhaps it would best to describe the finding by arguing that we are not far from the borderline case in which we can ignore any portfolio effects of debt-financed government deficits on the expected return to capital.

Hypothesis 4: The supply of federal bonds has a positive effect on the expected relative return on federal bonds.

As with Hypothesis 1, a positive own-derivative might seem assured a priori. But it is worth recalling at this juncture the Ricardo-Barro proposition that government debt has no effects because there are implied future tax liabilities that offset it. Government debt is not a true "outside asset."[17]

When estimated by unconstrained OLS, the derivative of Er^F with respect to F appears of the wrong sign and insignificant, a symptom of the negative value estimated for b_{22} in table 1.1. When estimated by constrained MLE, it is positive as hypothesized. It is insignificant, however, except at the 75 percent level. One cannot claim much evidence on the Ricardo-Barro proposition from these results.

Hypothesis 5: The supply of federal bonds has a positive effect on the expected relative return on corporate bonds.

Since much business fixed investment is financed by the issue of corporate debt rather than equity, this proposition may be as relevant to the crowding-out issue as Hypothesis 3. When we use the unconstrained OLS estimates, we get an (insignificant) apparent negative effect, attributable to the estimated negative value for b_{42}. When we impose the optimization constraint, the MLE estimate becomes positive as we would expect: federal bonds and corporate bonds are substitutes because their returns are highly correlated. However, we cannot reject the hypothesis of a zero effect.

1.5   Conclusion

This chapter has introduced an MLE technique to obtain the most efficient estimates of the parameters in investors' asset-demand functions of the portfolio-balance type. The technique itself may be as important as the specific results obtained. It dominates previous OLS attempts to relate asset supplies to rates of return because it brings more information to bear on the question: the information that the parameters are not determined arbitrarily but rather depend on the variances and covariances of real returns, assuming that investors optimize with respect to the mean and variance of real wealth. The technique dominates previous estimates of the optimal portfolio in that it allows expected returns to vary freely, rather than assuming them measurable by a constant sample mean or by a slowly moving ARIMA process.

It might be objected that the assumption of constant expected returns (first moments) is no worse than the assumption of constant variances and covariances (second moments) which *is* maintained in this chapter. It is certainly true that parameters such as the variances in our asset-demand functions can change over time. One could split up the sample period to see whether the parameters shifted, for example, when the Federal Reserve Board switched in 1979 from a policy of targeting the interest rate to a policy of targeting the money supply, as predicted by the famous "Lucas critique." One could also allow the variances to change gradually over time. But this chapter is written under the supposition that fluctuations in expected returns are more of a problem than fluctuations in variances. After all, the former are the variables in the asset-demand functions, and the latter are the parameters. Allowing expected returns to vary was first priority. Allowing the parameters to vary is a subject for future research.

The benefits of using the MLE technique are seen from the test results for the portfolio crowding-out hypotheses. In the cases where the sign of the effect seemed clear a priori, Hypotheses 1, 2, 4, and 5, the results of the MLE technique are much more in conformity than the results of OLS. In the one case in which the sign is a subject of controversy, the effect of government debt on the required expected relative return on equity (Hypothesis 3), the MLE technique changes the point estimate from crowding-out to crowding-in. While the degree of portfolio crowding-in is not significantly different from zero, a 95 percent confidence interval would exclude all but a very small degree of crowding-out. Federal debt is a close, even if not perfect, substitute for money, because the relative return on debt and money has a low variance.

An increase in the supply of federal debt *is* estimated to drive up the expected relative rate of return on corporate *debt*, but only by a very small 0.0060 percent (or 0.60 basis points) for every 1 percent of wealth. With total U.S. household assets at roughly $10 trillion as of 1980, an increase in federal debt of $200 billion (if not absorbed by the Fed, foreigners, or institutional investors) would drive up the expected relative rate of return on corporate debt by roughly 0.0120 percent (1.2 basis points). These numbers are based on given changes in the market value of asset supplies; if a $200 billion increase in debt causes an instantaneous fall in market bond prices and therefore in the value of existing debt, then the effect on expected rates of return will be even smaller.[18] Even if the increased debt supply comes in exchange for money as in Federal Reserve open market sales, the estimated effect on the expected relative rate of return on corporate debt is only 0.0068 percent for every 1 percent of wealth; with household deposits at $1,777 billion as of 1980, that is about 0.0012 percent for evey 1 percent reduction in household deposits.

It bears repeating that the trivial magnitudes of these estimated portfolio effects are a direct outcome of the mean-variance optimization framework, not of the particular estimation technique developed here. Unless the coefficient of risk aversion is much greater than two, or unless we are prepared to abandon the mean-variance framework altogther, we are stuck with the conclusion that asset supplies have effects on expected relative rates of return that, even when statistically significant, are economically insignificant.[19] However, nothing in this chapter precludes significant changes in the expected *levels* of rates of return on all assets in tandem. For example, if the federal government budget deficit uses up much of the flow of saving, it could very well drive up all rates of return and thus crowd out private investment. Other possible channels whereby government deficits could drive up nominal interest rates include a wealth effect on spending, and expectations that monetization will lead to inflation. What is precluded under the assumptions of the model is a meaningful change in expected *relative* returns as a result of portfolio effects.

Acknowledgments

This is an abridged version of NBER Working Paper No. 1205. I would like to thank Alejandra Mizala-Salces for capable research assistance; Paul Ruud for his nonlinear Maximum Likelihood Estimation program; the National Science Foundation under grant No. SES-8218300 for research support; David Backus, Bent Hansen, Bob McDonald, Randy Olsen, and Larry Summers for comments; and the National Bureau of Economic Research for secretarial support.

2

A Comment on Debt Management

The topic of debt management and its possible effects on the stock of real capital via portfolio crowding-out has been relatively overshadowed in recent research, by the more fundamental question of whether debt might be altogether neutral in its effects. But it is still an important topic in the United States, as well as in smaller countries that are only now developing free and open markets in debt. That the literature is of a manageable size is certainly an advantage. The study by Agell and Persson (1991) covers all the relevant issues nicely and makes a good start at trying out the various alternative econometric approaches with which one might address the question.

The portfolio balance framework, the "work-horse" model used to address such questions, is easily stated:

$$\alpha = \pi + \beta r^e, \tag{1}$$

where α represents the shares of the investor's portfolio that he or she allocates to various assets, and r^e represents the expected rates of return on the various assets. The question of whether a change in the maturity composition of debt affects required rates of return on short- and long-term debt is the question of how closely substitutable are the two kinds of debt in investors' portfolios. If the two assets are perfect substitutes, that is, if the relevant element of β is infinite, then the composition of the debt has no effect. For the effect on the required rate of return on real capital, the question is, how closely substitutable are long-term debt and real capital? Effects on the rates of return can be seen more clearly by inverting the equation:

Originally appeared as "Does Debt Management Matter? Comment" in *Does Debt Management Matter*, ed. J. Agell, M. Persson, and B. Friedman (Oxford University Press, 1992), 81–91. Reprinted by permission of Oxford University Press.

$$r^e = -\beta^{-1}\pi + \beta^{-1}\alpha. \tag{2}$$

(This is equation (9) in Agell and Persson.) Now it is clear that, if the relevant element of β is infinite, the corresponding effect on the rates of return will be zero.

There is more than one general approach that can be taken to estimating such a system of equations econometrically.

2.1 Regression of Asset Shares and Expected Returns

The first variant of the regression approach consists of regressing asset shares α against returns, as in equation (1), to estimate the matrix of substitutability coefficients.[1] This may be the better way if one thinks that errors in the asset-demand functions (factors omitted from the simple portfolio balance theory) are large. A major drawback, however, is the large errors one makes in using the observable ex post returns r in place of the correct, but unobservable, ex ante expectations of investors.

The alternative is to run the regression in inverted form, as in equation (2).[2] There are two advantages to doing it this way. First, one can use ex post returns r to measure expectations r^e, under the rational expectations argument that

$$r = r^e + \varepsilon,$$

where ε, the forecasting error made by investors, is assumed to be purely random. Substituting into equation (2) gives us

$$r = -\beta^{-1}\pi + \beta^{-1}\alpha + \varepsilon. \tag{3}$$

This is a suitable equation on which to run a regression, because the rational expectations assumption says that the error term is uncorrelated with all information available at time t, including α. The second advantage is that the inverted system can be thought of as the market equilibrium condition. It tells us what the rate of return has to be for given asset supplies to be willingly held. In particular, perfect substitutability between two assets holds when the relevant element of β is infinite, which is more testable in inverted form: it is simply the condition that the relevant row of β^{-1} consists of zeros.

The best method may be to use simultaneous equation estimation to allow for both kinds of errors, i.e., omitted factors in the portfolio balance equation and the expectational errors that investors make in predicting returns.[3] (The difficulty, as so often, is finding proper instrumental variables.) But however the equation is estimated, the results have always been very imprecise, and often implausible in sign or magnitude. Such difficulties induce one to look around for additional information that can be brought to bear on the subject.[4] A promising source of additional information is the theory of optimal portfolio diversification, which leads us to the second way in which one can go about estimating the parameters.

2.2   Estimation of the Optimally Diversified Portfolio

If investors choose their asset shares, α, optimally to maximize a function of the mean and variance of their wealth, then the parameters of the asset demand equation are bound by the simple constraint

$$\beta^{-1} = c\Omega, \tag{4}$$

where c is the coefficient of relative risk aversion and Ω is the variance–covariance matrix of real returns on the various assets. We can now see that the case when assets are highly substitutable is the case when risk is not very important, either because uncertainty is low (the elements of Ω are small) or because investors are not very risk-averse (c is small).

The traditional way of estimating Ω is to compute the variance-covariance matrix of returns over a particular period of time.[5] This approach has several problems. First, it does not facilitate the testing of the proposition that investors do in fact choose their portfolios optimally, which one would like to be able to do before imposing the proposition. Second, the technique of computing Ω from observed squared deviations of the rate of return around its sample mean does not allow expected returns to vary over time; thus, it is inconsistent with the sort of policy question one is trying to answer, namely, the effect of a change in the composition of assets on the expected rate of return.

A relatively simple way to allow the expected returns to vary over time is to estimate a vector autoregressive (VAR) process on the returns, as Agell and Persson do.[6] Better yet, one can allow the coefficients to change over time with a "moving sample," as in the technique of "rolling regressions," which the authors also try.[7] Although these approaches are a major improvement over the traditional way of estimating Ω, they are based on the assumption that this period's expected returns are determined by last period's returns. Thus, they still do not lend themselves to experiments where expected returns change suddenly because of a contemporaneous change in monetary or debt management policy, or in response to news about future monetary or debt management policy.

2.3   The Constrained Asset Share Estimation Method

Elsewhere, I have proposed a technique for estimating asset-demand functions which I believe combines the best of the previous two approaches
(Frankel 1982b, and chapter 1 in this volume). Substitute equation (4) into
equation (3):

$$r = -\beta^{-1}\pi + (c\Omega)\alpha + \varepsilon. \tag{5}$$

Ω is the variance-covariance matrix of ex post returns as perceived by
investors; that is, it is the variance-covariance term of their forecasting
errors ε. In other terms, $\Omega = \text{var}(\varepsilon)$. Thus, the technique calls for estimating
the equation subject to the constraint that the coefficient on the asset shares
is proportional to the variance-covariance matrix of the error term. Estimating a system of equations subject to a constraint between the coefficient
matrix and the error variance-covariance matrix is unusual in econometrics
(as compared to constraints among the coefficients). But it can be done by
nonlinear maximum likelihood estimation. We now call this the constrained
asset share estimation (or CASE) method. The advantages of the technique
are, first, that one can test the optimization hypothesis (simply by a likelihood ratio test on the constraint (4)), and second, that it allows the
expected returns to vary freely.

The application of the CASE method still leaves one with several basic
questions. The first is whether the assumption of optimal portfolio diversification is in fact justified. Second is the objection that, if one is to make such
a fuss about letting the expectations r^e vary over time (the first moments
of the conditional distribution of asset returns), then should one not also
allow the variance-covariance matrix Ω to vary over time (the *second*
moments)? Third is the question—which applies as much to the regression
method (equation (3) above) as to the CASE method—of whether the
treatment of expectations as forward-looking is correct (i.e., whether one
can infer what investors believe ex ante from what is observed to happen
in a given sample period ex post). I will take the three in reverse order.

I am quite sympathetic to the third point. The rational expectations
methodology is absolutely standard in the modern macroeconomic literature, of course. In both the literature on the foreign exchange risk premium
and the literature on the term structure of interest rates, for example, the
methodology of inferring what investors must have expected from what is
observed to happen ex post is the norm. Yet it can yield strange conclusions. Studies using survey data on the expectations of market participants

give very different results from the rational expectations methodology. The survey data results are more in keeping with simple notions that expectations are in part reflected in the forward discount (in the case of the foreign exchange market) or in the term structure of interest rates.[8] For better or worse, however, the rational expectations methodology continues to reign supreme.

The second point, which some have cited as a limitation of my technique, is not really a problem at all. One can allow the variance-covariance matrix Ω to change over time by using the auto-regressive conditional heteroskedasticity (ARCH) method of Rob Engle, while maintaining the constraint of the CASE method (Engel and Rodrigues 1989; Bollerslev et al. 1988; Engel et al. 1995). While the evidence does support the need to let Ω move over time, the results tend in other regards to be similar to results obtained in the earlier studies, which constrained Ω to be constant.

Another way that one can deal with the need to let the variances change over time is to extract from options prices estimates of what the market thinks the variances are. Assuming that the theoretical option-pricing equation that is used to extract the variances is correct, the technique has a major advantage. It allows the investors' subjective variances to vary freely, not just in the slow-moving manner of ARCH. Agell and Persson do look at options prices, and they find that the implicit variances are generally much smaller than the variances measured from ex post data, but move around more.

The remaining problem with using the CASE method may be thornier, depending partly on one's a priori degree of attachment to the optimizing paradigm. The data appear to be at war with the hypothesis of optimal portfolio diversification. If the coefficient of relative risk aversion c is not constrained, then the estimates can be quite plausible. Consider the example of recent U.S. fiscal deficits in the area of $150 billion. They represent yearly issues of debt of roughly 1 percent of wealth, where we are including corporate assets and real estate in wealth, but not human wealth or the wealth of non–U.S. residents. Some estimates in chapter 1 say that such an increase in Treasury debt drives up the expected relative rate of return on Treasury debt by 0.462 percent, which, though low, is not completely unreasonable. But this is for c estimated at 110.3, which is much higher than conventional estimates of the coefficient of risk aversion like 2 or 4. If c is constrained to 2, then the estimated effect of a debt increase equal to 1 percent of wealth is a very small 0.008 per cent—less than one basis point!

A related difficulty is that tests of the optimization hypothesis in fact reject the constraint. Thus, using the technique, or any other variant of optimal portfolio diversification, requires that one accept the optimization assumption on a priori grounds.

The problem lies not in the estimation technique, but in the inherent nature of the hypothesis of optimal portfolio diversification. In my estimates, the variances of per annum returns on stocks and bonds are in the vicinity of 0.004. Readers are invited to choose their own favorite estimate of the coefficient of relative risk aversion c, and multiply it against 0.004 as in equation (4), to see how small the elements of β^{-1} must be. Agell and Persson, and Friedman before them, get roughly similar variances. For the case of long-term bonds, they estimate the unconditional variance of the per annum return at 0.0145 per cent ($= 4 \times 0.0036$ in their Table 4.2 (a)). The conditional variance is slightly smaller than this (owing to the "shrinkage" of taking out the forecastable component): 0.012 percent ($= 4 \times$ 0.003 in their Table 4.3 (b)). These estimates of the variance are somewhat higher than mine, perhaps for reasons relating to frequency of observation. So they imply an effect of the debt supply on the rate of return on debt ($2 \times 0.012 = 0.024$ percent, or $2\frac{1}{2}$ basis points) that is somewhat higher than mine.[9] And my estimate of the effect on the rate of return on equity is *very* small, because the correlation of the returns on long-term debt and equity was close to zero in my sample period (chapter 1 in this volume). But the important point is that *all* these estimates are exceedingly small judged by the standards of policymaking and observed fluctuations in the financial markets. Even under the largest of the estimates, the effects of debt management on rates of return would appear to be too insignificant to bother with.

At least three reactions to this apparent impasse are possible. The first would be to argue that investors are optimizing in some intertemporal dimension in a more sophisticated manner than is captured in simple mean-variance optimization (which is consistent with maximization of expected intertemporal utility only if either the asset return process is restricted—e.g., to the log-normal—or the utility function is restricted—e.g., to the logarithmic). This point is capable of yielding all manner of theoretical results. The drawback with pursuing it is that it does not lead readily to an alternative approach to empirical estimation, unless one imposes further restrictions, which are typically far more arbitrary than those needed for mean-variance optimization.[10]

The second, quite different, possible reaction is to conclude that investors must be *less* sophisticated than the mean-variance theory supposes.

This response would suggest a return to the unconstrained regression approach above.

The third possible response to the inconvenient quantitative implications of mean-variance optimization is to push and tug a bit at the parameters to come up with estimates that are not too unreasonable. First, one can assume a coefficient of relative risk aversion greater than 2. Second, one can omit real estate from the definition of wealth. The rationale would be similar to the presumed rationale (beyond questions of data availability) for omitting human wealth and foreign wealth: an argument that only some subset of total wealth is available in portfolios that are relevant for the determination of prices in domestic financial markets. What is accomplished is that, when the denominator is made smaller, a given increase in government debt like $150 billion becomes a larger fraction α of the portfolio. Thus, it has a larger effect on expected returns on equations (2) or (5). This is the solution that Ben Friedman has settled on. A sympathetic interpretation would argue that it represents a step in the direction of institutional realism, by recognizing that savings that accumulate with institutional investors like pension funds and mutual funds have more of an immediate impact on financial markets than the broader total of household wealth. Nevertheless, one should keep in mind that, in theory, real estate, foreign wealth, and human wealth should matter too.

As their final exercise, Agell and Persson allow for the endogenous effect on current asset prices when computing the effect of changes in supplies on expected returns. The authors are quite correct about statements regarding "an increase in government debt equal to 1 percent of wealth": the effect on expected returns will be smaller if one takes into account that a $150 billion increase in the supply of one asset out of a total portfolio of $15,000 billion will have some downward effect on the price of the asset, so that the change in α will be less than 1 percent. They calculate effects under the simplifying assumption that the expected future price of the entire asset is tied down, so as not to have to specify and solve an intertemporal general equilibrium model. They find that treating the contemporaneous asset prices as endogenous in this way in fact makes little difference for the effects of asset supply changes on expected rates of return.

They express some surprise that endogenizing asset prices makes little difference. But it seems to me that this is precisely what one might have predicted. The reasoning is as follows. We saw above that, for ordinary estimates of the magnitude of the variances and of the coefficient of risk aversion, the degree of substitutability among assets is very high. We can express this by saying that it takes only small changes in expected rates of return to have large effects on portfolio shares, or that large changes in portfolio shares have small effects on expected rates of return. The important point here is that this high degree of substitutability prevents large fluctuations in expected future capital gains and therefore ties the current asset price closely to the expected future asset price. Since Agell and Persson assume that the expected future asset prices are unchanged, it is not surprising that the contemporaneous asset prices change very little, from which it follows that the change in α is not very different from what it was when changes in contemporaneous asset prices were ruled out of the experiment.

As I said above, the inconveniently high magnitude of the implied degree of substitutability is not the fault of the researchers, but is inherent in the constraints of optimal portfolio diversification. I incline to the view that most investors either use a bigger coefficient of risk aversion in their investment decisions than they do in other aspects of their economic and noneconomic behavior, or else measure the risk of acquiring a given asset against a much smaller frame of reference than their entire wealth. Either way, the implication would be that investors act as if they are less ready to make large changes in their holdings in response to small changes in returns than our optimization theory would suggest.

Acknowledgments

I thank Jonas Agell and Mats Persson for the opportunity to examine their research, and Villy Bergstrom and FIEF for the opportunity to examine Stockholm.

3   Portfolio Shares as "Beta Breakers"

When James Tobin won the Nobel Prize in Economics in 1981, it was in part for his role in laying the foundation of modern portfolio theory.[1] He showed how an optimizing investor will want to allocate his or her portfolio among assets, based not just on their expected returns, but also on their riskiness.

His motivation was primarily to be able to examine macroeconomic questions like the following: When the government increases the stock of debt by a given amount, by how much must the interest rate rise for investors to hold the additional debt willingly? His answer was that the parameter in question depends on the variability of returns and on the investors' degree of risk-aversion. If returns are highly variable, or if investors are highly risk-averse, then they will insist on diversifying their portfolios among different assets to minimize risk. It will require a big change in expected returns to coax them into "going out on a limb," to hold more of any one particular asset.

3.1   How Does the CAPM Deal—or Fail to Deal—with This?

Portfolio theory has come a long way since 1958. The most important development has been the Capital Asset Pricing Model (CAPM). The model is most often represented as a linear relation between the expected return on a given asset Er^i relative to the risk-free rate r^0, and the expected return on the total market portfolio Er^m relative to r^0:

$$Er^i - r^0 = \beta_m^i (Er^m - r^0), \tag{1}$$

Originally published in *Journal of Portfolio Management* 11, 5 (Summer 1985): 18–23. This copyrighted material has been reprinted with permission from the *Journal of Portfolio Management*.

where

$$\beta'_m = \frac{\text{cov}(r^i, r^m)}{\text{var}(r^m)}.$$

The constant of proportionality, the beta, is the coefficient in a regression of the return in question against the market return. It represents the idea that the riskiness of an asset depends not on the variance of its return, but on the covariance of the return with the return on the rest of the market portfolio—because that is how much the asset adds to the overall riskiness of the portfolio.

There is an enormous literature devoted to testing CAPM econometrically.[2] Some progress has been made. For example, the "menu" of assets included has been extended beyond the original narrow category of equities to include various kinds of bonds and tangible assets such as real estate.[3] Also, the analysis has been set up as a likelihood ratio test, which has desirable statistical properties.[4] But some important limitations remain.

For one thing, many tests are in practice predicated on the assumption that expected returns are constant over time. This assumption makes it possible to estimate expected returns from the average returns actually observed over the sample period. It is evident, however, that expected rates of return in fact vary over time. Some studies allow expected returns to change slowly over time, for example by computing a moving average of actual returns, or by splitting the sample period into subperiods. But these ad hoc approaches would not allow us to handle events where expected returns change suddenly because the supplies of money or bonds or other assets change suddenly, or because news comes out about expected *future* changes in asset supplies or other factors.

Before we read out the other counts in the indictment of CAPM tests, let us pause to ask a question. What happened to the portfolios held by the investors? Tobin's original aim was to show what determined the shares of the investors' portfolios allocated to the various assets. But these portfolio shares are nowhere to be seen in equation (1).

One might think that the sensible way of testing whether investors' portfolio decisions are described accurately by CAPM would be to look at actual portfolios held by investors, to compute the optimal CAPM portfolio based on means, variances, and covariances, and then to test whether the two are equal—but there is something of a taboo in the finance field against looking at actual portfolios held by investors.[5] It is argued, plausibly, that data on portfolio holdings are far less reliable than data on asset returns. If asset returns are observed to behave "as if" the market were obeying CAPM, what difference does the specific causal mechanism make? In other words, what difference does it make whether the typical person on the street understands CAPM consciously or explicitly?

3.2 Enhancing the CAPM with Portfolio Shares

One answer to this argument is that we are not in the comfortable position of observing that asset returns do in fact behave this way. There are all sorts of problems with the current methodology, beginning with the difficulty we have already discussed in measuring ex ante expected returns from ex post realized returns without unrealistically assuming the former fixed over time. As is often the case with the "as if" argument, social scientists need all the help they can get and cannot afford to ignore matters of causal mechanism. But a second answer is that the investors' portfolio shares are hiding in equation (1) anyway.

To see this, we must recognize that the return on the aggregate market portfolio r^m is a weighted average of the returns on the individual assets that make up the market portfolio. In some of the early CAPM tests, constant equal weights were used. But it is by now standard to use as weights the actual shares that the individual assets have in the market portfolio, which we will represent by x^j:

$$r^m = \sum_j x^j r^j. \tag{2}$$

When we take the covariance of return r^i with this weighted average to compute β_m^i, equation (1) becomes

$$Er^i - r^0 = \frac{\sum_j x^j \operatorname{Cov}(r^i, r^j)}{\operatorname{Var}(r^m)} (Er^m - r^0). \tag{3}$$

We see that the portfolio shares x^j break the beta up into the covariances with the individual assets. For this reason, we can think of the portfolio shares as "Beta Breakers."[6]

The grounds for the second count in the indictment of standard tests of CAPM can be seen from equation (3). Even if we are willing to assume that the distributions of the individual asset returns are stationary, the portfolio shares x^j undeniably *do* vary over time in practice, and so the betas must also vary over time. But the standard tests treat the betas as constant, or at best as changing slowly over time, even while using the time-varying asset share numbers in the computation of r^m![7]

Let us define ρ to be the market price of risk $(Er^m - r^0)/\mathrm{Var}(r^m)$, equal to the coefficient of relative risk-aversion, which we can assume to be constant. Equation (3) becomes

$$Er^i - r^0 = \sum_j x^j \mathrm{Cov}(r^i, r^j)\rho. \qquad (4)$$

The return on asset i is a linear combination of the covariances with the other assets' returns, where the weights in the linear combination are the portfolio shares.[8] We have one of these equations for each asset i.

We can think of this system of equations as a set of asset demands like those envisioned by Tobin, but the system is in inverted form. That is, instead of showing investors' asset demands as a function of the expected rates of return, the equation turns the relationship around and shows the expected rate of return that a particular asset must pay if the supplies of the various assets that exist in the market are to be willingly held by investors.

For example, if the supply of a particular asset x^j, say, corporate bonds, goes up, then that asset clearly must pay a higher expected return to be willingly held. If the supplies of *other* assets go up, say, government bonds, then that will also raise the required expected return on corporate bonds to the extent that the two assets are close substitutes in investors' portfolios. Equation (4) tells us that two assets will be close substitutes if their returns are highly correlated.

Notice from equations (3) or (4) that the two criticisms of the standard tests that we have made are related to each other. The expected returns vary over time precisely to the extent that the portfolio shares, and therefore the betas, vary over time. From the viewpoint of individual investors, it is changes in the assets' expected returns that cause their demands for the assets to vary. Or, from the viewpoint of market equilibrium, it is changes in the supplies of the assets that cause the required rates of return to change.

3.3   The Alternative Hypothesis

The third and last count in the indictment of standard tests of the CAPM hypothesis is that the alternative hypothesis is not specified. Suppose we reject CAPM. Then where does that leave us?

The alternative hypothesis I am proposing is that asset demands are a function of expected returns alone, not of covariances. Investors do not have an intuitive feel for assets' covariances with the market portfolio, and they either do not believe the betas computed for them by stock market analysts or do not consider them relevant.

We assume that the demand for asset j, as a proportion of an investor's portfolio, is a linear function of the expected returns on the various assets:

$$x^j = A^j + B_1^j(Er^1) + \cdots + B_i^j(Er^i) + \cdots + B_j^j(Er^j) + \cdots + B_d^j(Er^d). \quad (5)$$

We would expect the coefficient on the asset's own return, B_j^j to be positive: An increase in the expected return on asset j raises the demand for asset j. We would expect the coefficient on most of the other assets i to be negative: An increase in the expected return on another asset reduces the demand for asset j.

For econometric estimation, it will help to invert the system of equations, like (5), that are the investors' demands for each asset j. We then derive another system of equations, of which a representative example is:

$$Er^i = c^i + \sum_j x^j D_j^i. \quad (6)$$

The matrix of coefficients D is just the inverse of the matrix B. As in equation (4), we can see how a change in the supplies of the assets, x, must bring about a change in the expected returns in order for the assets to be willingly held. For example, D_i^i is presumably positive: An increase in the supply x^i of asset i raises the expected return Er^i that it must pay.

We knew exactly determined the parameters in the relationship in equation (4)—the covariances of the returns and the coefficient of risk-aversion —but the parameters (A, B, C, and D) in equations (5) and (6) are not specified. They could be anything. Investors might have direct "tastes" for assets that we can only take as given, much as consumers have direct tastes for commodities.

We could probably agree that risk plays *some* role. If investors did not care about risk at all, then all the D coefficients would be zero. In that case, if any asset were to pay a lower return than the other assets, there would be a zero demand for it. In other words, arbitrage would insure that expected returns are equalized across assets. Given this equalization, asset supplies x would then have zero effects on expected rates of return. That is an unlikely special case. Presumably investors do care about risk, they do want to diversify their holdings, and they do pay attention at least to the variance of an asset's return to assess its riskiness. At this point, however, we are assuming that investors do not necessarily compute covariances or use CAPM to determine their holdings.

Measuring expectations is often a stumbling block to empirical work. As mentioned at the outset, we do not want simply to compute average realized returns, because that would require the assumption that expected

returns are constant over time. The way we have set things up, all we have
to do is assume that investors form expectations rationally; then we can
estimate each equation (6) by an Ordinary Least Squares (OLS) regression
of realized returns, r, against the portfolio shares x.[9]

3.4   Some Empirical Results

Table 3.1 reports the results of such regressions for a portfolio of six assets:
real estate, federal bonds, state and local bonds, corporate bonds, equities,
and short-term assets (Treasury bills, commercial paper, and deposits).[10]
The numbers look very large. They say, for example, that it would take a
31.02 percent increase in the expected annual relative return on corporate
debt to induce investors to accept an increase in their holdings of corporate
debt equal to one percent of their portfolio!

We can formally test the hypothesis that investors do not care at all
about diversifying risk by testing whether the coefficients are zero. This
hypothesis is rejected for the first four out of five equations taken one by
one (by F tests), and also for the system as a whole (by a likelihood ratio
test). Investors do diversify.

But this still leaves us with the question whether the coefficients are
determined in precisely the way that CAPM says they should be. CAPM
says that D, the matrix of coefficients in equation (6), is given as in equation
(4): by ρ times the variance-covariance matrix of returns, which we will call
Ω. Recalling from chapter 1 that Ω is the variance-covariance matrix of
the error term, the equation is estimated subject to that constraint, using
Maximum Likelihood Estimation (MLE).[11]

Table 3.2 reports the results of this estimation. The numbers look quite
different from those in table 3.1. If one believes the CAPM hypothesis a
priori, then the difference is simply the result of more efficient estimates.
Indeed, the coefficients seem more plausible.

For example, we now see that it would take a .478 percent (i.e., 47.8
basis-point) increase in the expected annual relative return on corporate
debt to induce investors to accept an increase in their holdings of corporate
debt equal to one percent of their portfolio. To take another example, an
increase in the outstanding stock of federal debt equal to one percent of
the portfolio would drive up the required return on federal debt by .541
percent. It would drive up the required return on state and local debt and
corporate debt by .936 percent and .432 percent, respectively. These two
assets are close substitutes for federal debt because their returns are highly
correlated with its return. On the other hand, the one percent increase in

Table 3.1
Unconstrained estimation of inverted asset-demand function.
Equation-by-equation OLS: 1954–80

Dependent variable: Real rate of return on asset relative to short-term bills	Constant	B⁻¹: Coefficients on shares of portfolios allocated to					D.W.	SSR	R^2	Log likelihood	$F_{(5,21)}$
		Tangible assets	Long-term federal debt	State and local debt	Corporate bonds	Equities					
Tangible assets	−.107	.256	.278	−4.701	2.969	.007	2.06	.00652	.52	74.12	4.51*
	(.410)	(.546)	(.564)	(2.760)	(2.849)	(.446)					
Long-term federal debt	1.272	−2.274	−2.284	−7.847	22.604*	−1.836	2.17	.005476	.54	45.40	4.98*
	(1.188)	(1.726)	(1.633)	(7.995)	(8.253)	(1.293)					
State and local debt	1.185	−2.467	−5.384*	−17.194	41.645*	−1.865	1.67	.11217	.56	35.72	5.43*
	(1.701)	(2.470)	(2.337)	(11.442)	(11.811)	(1.850)					
Corporate bonds	.844	−1.685	−3.136*	−14.340*	31.019*	−1.439	2.00	.03370	.68	51.95	9.06*
	(.932)	(1.354)	(1.281)	(6.272)	(6.474)	(1.014)					
Equities	−.026	−.397	5.445	−18.233	4.301	.619	2.04	.22578	.29	26.27	1.75
	(2.413)	(3.504)	(3.316)	(16.234)	(16.757)	(2.625)					

$\mathbf{B}^{-1}$	$-(G-1)\frac{T}{2}\log 2\pi$	$-\frac{T}{2}\log|\mathbf{\Omega}|$	$-T(G-1)/2$	= log likelihood
unconstrained	−124.06	448.75	−67.50	257.19*
constrained to 0	−124.06	410.35	−67.50	218.79

Table 3.2
Constrained estimation of inverted asset-demand function.
MLE (ρ unconstrained): 1954–80

Dependent variable		B^{-1}: Coefficients (constrained to $\rho\Omega$) on shares of portfolios allocated to:					
Real rate of return on asset relative to short-term bills:	Constant	Real estate and consumer durables	Long-term federal debt	State and local debt	Corporate bonds	Equities
Tangible assets (Real estate and consumer durables)	−.023 (.069)	.061 (.049)	−.038 (.099)	−.010 (.186)	.010 (.097)	−.019 (.164)
Long-term federal debt	−.031 (.162)	−.038 (.099)	.541 (.446)	.639 (.640)	.432 (.411)	−.031 (.435)
State and local debt	−.047 (.266)	−.010 (.186)	.639 (.640)	1.131 (.850)	.648 (.647)	−.046 (.541)
Corporate bonds	−.073 (.149)	.010 (.097)	.432 (.411)	.648 (.647)	.478 (.436)	.041 (.290)
Equities	−3.99 (.485)	−.019 (.164)	−.031 (.435)	−.046 (.541)	.041 (.290)	1.121 (.500)

ρ: coefficient of risk-aversion
125.72 (156.92)

$-5\frac{T}{2}\log 2$	$-\frac{T}{2}\log|\Omega| + \frac{1}{2}\sum \varepsilon' \varepsilon \Omega \varepsilon$	= log likelihood
−124.06	354.82	230.76

the stock of federal debt would *reduce* the required return on real estate and equities by .038 percent and .031 percent respectively. These two assets are complements of federal debt, not substitutes, because their returns are not highly correlated with its return.

The one implausible number in table 3.2 is the estimate for the coefficient of risk aversion, 129.72. This coefficient is normally thought to be much lower.[12]

In any case, I have chosen to emphasize the use of the technique to test the CAPM hypothesis, rather than the use of the technique to impose the hypothesis. Any time one imposes a constraint on estimates, the fit to the data (the sum of squared residuals) must worsen relative to the case of unconstrained OLS. Nevertheless, the log likelihood reported in table 3.2 indicates that the fit has worsened a lot. The data consider the CAPM constraint to be very onerous; they yearn to breathe free. In other words, the likelihood ratio test rejects the hypothesis that CAPM holds.

3.5   Conclusion

How could CAPM fail to hold? Do our results imply that investors are irrational?

There are a number of assumptions that we have necessarily tested at the same time as CAPM, assumptions that: the assets can be aggregated into six, investors' expectations are rational, the variances and covariances of individual asset returns (as opposed to the market return) are constant over time, all households are alike and so their holdings can be added together, and the data are accurately measured. The failure of any one of these assumptions could explain the results of our test.

My own feeling is that it is indeed the failure of CAPM that explains the results. It should be emphasized that we have tested the hypothesis that investors' asset demands are determined exactly as CAPM says they should be. Asset demand functions might be equal to those given by CAPM plus some other factor that would explain our results and would at the same time leave open the possibility that CAPM still has something useful to tell us about investor behavior.

Appendix 3A

The main source for data on supplies of six assets held by households was the Federal Reserve Board's *Balance Sheets for the U.S. Economy* (October 1981), Table 702. This source was used in place of the Fed's *Flow of Funds*

Accounts, Assets and Liabilities Outstanding, to which it is closely related, because only the *Balance Sheets* include data for tangible assets, i.e. real estate and consumer durables (see page iii of the *Flow of Funds* for an explanation). The variables used in the econometrics are shares of wealth, the supply of the asset in question divided by the sum of all six asset supplies.

The asset supplies were taken from the *Balance Sheets* as follows. Total tangible assets are line 1. Deposits are the sum of lines 13, checkable deposits and currency; 14, small time and savings deposits; 15, money market fund shares; 16, large time deposits; 20, short-term U.S. government securities; and 25, open market paper. Long-term federal debt is line 18 (U.S. government securities) minus line 20. State and local debt is line 23. Private bonds are line 24 (corporate and foreign bonds) plus line 26 (mortgages held). Finally, equities are line 27 (corporate equities) plus line 32 (noncorporate business equity).

For three of the asset supplies—long-term federal debt, state and local bonds, and private bonds—the numbers represent book value and must be multiplied by some measure of current market prices to get the correct measure of market value. The very large decline in prices of bonds over the postwar period make this correction a crucial one. (Equities and tangible assets are already measured at market value, while capital gains and losses are irrelevant for the short-term asset.) Measures of the current market bond prices are reported by *Standard and Poor's Trade and Security Statistics Security Price Index Record* (1982); see p. 235 for U.S. government bond prices, p. 233 for municipal bond prices, and p. 231 for high-grade corporate bond prices. Standard and Poor's computes the price indexes from yield data, assuming a 3 percent coupon with fifteen years to maturity for the federal bonds and a 4 percent coupon with twenty years to maturity for the other two.

Among the rates of return (all in log form for this paper, as opposed to the level form), the most problematical is that on real estate and durables, taken here as the percentage change in the home purchase component of the CPI reported in the *Economic Report of the President* 1982 (p. 292). There exist better measures of housing prices, and unpublished estimates of imputed service returns on housing and durables, but they are not available for the entire sample period.

The Treasury bill rate is used for the rate of return on deposits and short-term securities. The source is the Federal Reserve Board: 9–12 month issues from *Banking and Monetary Statistics 1941–1970* (certificates of indebtedness and selected note and bond issues; the one-year bill market yield is not available before 1960); and the one-year bill secondary market rates from *Annual Statistical Digest 1970–1979*, Table 22A, and *ASD 1980*, Table 25A. Note that in aggregating non-interest-paying money together with interest-paying accounts and securities, we are assuming that the former performs an implicit liquidity service that brings its return up to the explicit return of the latter.

Each of the long-term assets entails a yield plus capital gains. For each of the three kinds of bonds, capital gains are percentage change in the same bond prices from Standard and Poor's Trade and Securities Statistics that were discussed above. The yields are from the same source: respectively, the median yield to maturity of a number of government bonds restricted to those issues with more than ten years to maturity, p. 234, an arithmetic average of the yield to maturity of fifteen high grade municipal bonds, p. 232, and an average of the AAA Industrial and Utility bonds, p. 219. (The yields are also available from the Fed sources: *BMS 1941–1970*, Table 12.12; *ASD 1970–1979*, Table 22A; and *ASD 1980*, Table 25A.) For equities, capital gains are percentage change in Stanford and Poor's index of common stock prices from *BMS 1941–1970*, Table 12.16; *ASD 1970–1979*, Table 22A; and *ASD 1980*, Table 26A. To capital gains we add the dividend price ratio on common stock from *BMS 1941–1970*, Table 12.19; *ASD 1970–79*, Table 22A; and *ASD 1980*, Table 25A.

The foregoing are all nominal returns. To convert to real returns when computing percentage returns on levels, we use the percentage change in the CPI from the *Economic Report of the President 1982*. To be precise, we divided one plus the nominal return by one plus the inflation rate. Subtracting the inflation rate from the nominal return would give approximately the same answer, and when we computed real returns relative to the numeraire asset the two inflation rates would conveniently drop out, but this answer would differ from the correct one by a convexity term. When computing the percentage relative returns in logs, the inflation rates drop out in any case.

Absent from the calculations is any allowance for differences in tax treatment. In particular, the returns on state and local bonds, and to some extent on tangibles, are here understated relative to the other assets because they are tax-free. The unconstrained constant term that we allow for in the econometrics should capture most of this effect (and any other constant omitted factors such as the service return from tangibles, as well). But it would be desirable to compute after-tax real returns instead.

Acknowledgments

This chapter is an informal exposition of the technique developed in NBER Working Paper No. 1113, April 1983: "Are Asset Demand Functions Determined by CAPM?" I would like to thank Paul Ruud for access to his nonlinear Maximum Likelihood Estimation program; Bill Dickens for programming assistance; Alejandra Mizala-Salces for valor and perseverance in a six-month safari over the high peaks and low valleys of the likelihood function; Ross Starr for access to necessary data; the Institute of Business and Economic Research at U.C. Berkeley and the National Science Foundation under grant no. SES-8218300 for research support; and Charles Engel and Richard Startz for important suggestions.

4

Do Asset-Demand Functions Optimize over the Mean and Variance of Real Returns? A Six-Currency Test

Global investors are thought to balance their portfolios among the assets of various countries as functions of the expected rates of return. What determines the parameters in these functions? The most promising source of enlightenment is finance theory. Under the hypothesis that investors optimize with respect to the mean and variance of end-of-period wealth, the parameters are seen to depend in a simple way on the variance-covariance matrix of returns and on the degree of risk aversion.[1]

The hypothesis of mean-variance optimization has not been adequately tested empirically. A number of studies have taken the empirical techniques for estimating the Capital Asset Pricing Model (CAPM) that have been developed for other financial markets, and have extended them to foreign currencies.[2] But, as noted by Dumas (1982), many of these studies are not set up as tests of the hypothesis that actual asset-demand functions are in fact of the mean-variance optimizing form. This chapter uses international data on net asset supplies to test the hypothesis explicitly.

As mentioned in the preceding chapters, another problem with most early empirical finance studies is that they made the assumption that the expected returns perceived by investors are constant over time. This assumption was made, often implicitly, in order to be able to estimate the expected returns from the unconditional ex post sample mean. But the assumption is not appropriate for a macro model. It would imply that the *arguments* of the asset-demand functions, as opposed to the parameters of the functions, are constant over time. It is an essential element of most macro models that expected returns be allowed to vary, for example in response to central bank intervention or to other new information.

With Charles Engel, originally published in *Journal of International Economics* 17 (December 1984): 309–23. Reprinted with permission.

A few studies do allow expected returns to change over time, but only gradually, as a function of past returns. Two estimates of the optimal portfolio, von Furstenberg (1981) and de Macedo, Goldstein and Meerschwam (1982), estimate expected returns from the time series of actual returns as in the technique of "rolling regressions." Hansen and Hodrick (1983) resembles this chapter in that they explicitly test the optimization hypothesis. But they consider the market or "benchmark" portfolio to be unobservable, so instead of trying to measure the return directly, they use as instrumental variables lagged values of the relative returns on the various currencies.

In this chapter expected returns are allowed to vary freely. Ex post rates of return are related to the asset supplies by an equation in which the error term is identified as the market's expectational error.[3] The hypothesis that the functions are optimizing can be implemented by imposing the by now familiar constraint that the coefficient matrix is proportional to the variance-covariance matrix of the error term, and estimating by maximum likelihood (MLE). If the optimizing hypothesis were true, the constrained MLE estimates would be the most efficient estimates of the parameters. Moreover, one can test the hypothesis by comparing the likelihood when the parameters are estimated subject to this constraint to the likelihood when they are estimated unconstrained. Our finding is that a likelihood ratio test *rejects* the constraint of mean-variance optimization. As discussed in chapter 2, this suggests that market agents are either not sophisticated enough to maximize their end-of-period wealth with regard to mean and variance, or else are *more* sophisticated than this, maximizing instead a more complicated intertemporal function.

This chapter continues past work by the authors. There are two important new features. First, we extend the test of mean-variance optimization to an international portfolio of six nominal assets: marks, pounds, yen, French francs, Canadian dollars, and U.S. dollars. Dumas (1982, p. 5) and many other authors have emphasized the importance of looking at "a reasonably complete list of individual assets available across the world." Of course, it would be desirable to include equities and all other assets, but data difficulties inevitably put a limit on the number of assets we can consider.

Second, we use price data to measure real returns explicitly, thus allowing for inflation risk, rather than treating the exchange rate as the only stochastic variable.[4] As Kouri and de Macedo (1978, p. 118) have emphasized, "rational lenders and borrowers are presumably concerned with the *real* values of their assets and liabilities, and hence the purchasing power of a currency over goods and services available in the world economy is the

appropriate standard of its value." The price for allowing stochastic inflation rates is that we are not able to allow consumption preferences to differ
among investors residing in different countries. We assume, rather, that all
investors have the same preferences and thus can be aggregated together.[5]

Section 4.1 of this chapter shows how asset-demand functions can be
estimated, *without* imposing the constraint of mean-variance optimization.
Section 4.2 derives theoretically the optimizing form of the functions. Section 4.3 estimates the asset-demand functions subject to the constraint that
they are indeed of this form, and does the likelihood ratio test. Section 4.4
draws conclusions. Details of the data calculations are available in an
appendix to Frankel (1982b).

4.1   Estimation of Unconstrained Asset-Demand Functions

In this chapter we assume that investors allocate their portfolio among
assets denominated in six currencies. We define a column vector of five
portfolio shares:

$$x_t' \equiv [x_t^{DM}\ x_t^{\pounds}\ x_t^{Y}\ x_t^{F}\ x_t^{C\$}].$$

The residual is the share allocated to U.S. dollars: $(1 - x_t'\iota)$, where ι is a
column vector of five ones. The asset-demand function gives us the demands as a function of the expected rates of return on the assets relative to
the numeraire asset, the dollar:

$$x_t = \alpha + \beta(E_t r_{t+1} - \iota E_t r_{t+1}^s), \tag{1}$$

where $E_t r_{t+1}^s$ is the expected real return on dollar assets, $E_t r_{t+1}$ is a column
vector of the expected real returns on the other five assets, β is a matrix of
coefficients, and α is a vector of intercepts. We will show in the next section
that the linear form (equation 1) is correct if agents are mean-variance
optimizing. But the important point is that at this stage we are not constraining the parameters in α and β to be anything in particular. They could
be based on investors' arbitrary "tastes" for assets as easily as on mean-
variance optimization. Of course we have already restricted the function
somewhat; for example, many macroeconomic models include real income
levels, representing a transactions demand for the assets.

As discussed earlier, the stumbling block in past econometric estimation
of portfolio-balance equations has been the measurement of expected returns. The solution adopted here is to invert equation (1), so that expected
returns depend on asset supplies:

$$E_t r_{t+1} - \iota E_t r_{t+1}^s = -\beta^{-1}\alpha + \beta^{-1}x_t. \tag{2}$$

To deal with the unobservability of expectations, we make the assumption that investors form them rationally. The ex post relative return $(r_{t+1} + \iota r_{t+1}^\$)$, which *is* observable, is assumed equal to the expected return plus a random error term ε_{t+1}. By "random," we mean uncorrelated with all information I_t available at the beginning of the period over which the return is measured:

$$r_{t+1} - \iota r_{t+1}^\$ = E_t r_{t+1} - \iota E_t r_{t+1}^\$ + \varepsilon_{t+1}, \qquad E(\varepsilon_{t+1}|I_t) = 0. \tag{3}$$

Substituting equation (2) into equation (3):

$$r_{t+1} - \iota r_{t+1}^\$ = -\beta^{-1}\alpha + \beta^{-1}x_t + \varepsilon_{t+1}. \tag{4}$$

The parameters of equation (4) can now be estimated by regression. The regression error is simply the expectational error ε_{t+1}, which we know to be uncorrelated with the right-hand-side variables by the assumption of rational expectations.

At first thought, it might seem that the components of the right-hand-side variables—the asset quantities or, at least, the asset prices—must be endogenous. But the existence of other equations that determine these variables does not in itself mean that the error term is correlated with the variables. Owing to the special nature of the rational expectations assumption, the error term will still be uncorrelated with the right-hand-side variables, as long as the asset-demand function specified in equation (1) holds exactly. The assumption that there are no omitted variables or measurement error in equation (1) is admittedly a strong one.[6]

Table 4.1 reports regressions of the system of equations (4). Only one or two coefficient estimates in each equation are significantly different from zero. Of those, the two diagonal elements, which are the only ones on which we have a priori information, are of the incorrect sign: an increase in the supply of Canadian dollars or marks appears to induce a decline, rather than an increase, in the expected future returns on these two assets. On the other hand, we are able to reject with a likelihood ratio test the constraint that all coefficients are zero. The log-likelihood for the five unconstrained equations taken together is 1086.49, whereas the constrained log-likelihood is only 1057.11. (Twice the difference is distributed χ^2 with 25 degrees of freedom.)

One assumption that we have already made is borne out. The absence of serial correlation in the error term is established by Durbin-Watson statistics and Box-Pierce Q statistics for lag lengths of twelve months

Table 4.1
Unconstrained asset-demand functions, OLS

Dependent variable: $r_{t+1} - r_{t+1}^{\$}$, real rate of return on national currency relative to the dollar.[a]
Independent variable: x_t, shares of asset supplies in the world portfolio, with total wealth computed as the sum of the asset supplies, each evaluated at its respective exchange rate.

Sample: June 1973 to August 1980 (87 observations).

National currency	$-\beta^{-1}\alpha$, constants	β^{-1}, Coefficients on					Log lik.	R^2	D.W. Q(12)	S.E.R.	$F_{(5,81)}$
		$x_t^{C\$}$	x_t^F	x_t^{DM}	x_t^Y	$x_t^{\$}$					
Canadian dollar	0.125[b] (0.060)	-1.466[b] (0.692)	-0.020 (0.322)	0.384 (0.243)	-0.120 (0.082)	0.150 (0.087)	251.87	0.09	2.04 25.32[b]	0.01338	1.63
French franc	0.014 (0.138)	1.770 (1.584)	-1.132 (0.737)	-0.710 (0.557)	0.311 (0.188)	-0.159 (0.199)	179.87	0.08	2.37 6.86	0.03061	1.37
Deutsche mark	0.153 (0.145)	1.324 (1.669)	-0.818 (0.776)	-1.773[b] (0.587)	0.361 (0.198)	-0.211 (0.210)	175.30	0.13	2.20 14.58	0.03226	2.48[b]
Japanese yen	0.289[b] (0.130)	0.319 (1.494)	-1.309 (0.695)	-2.213[b] (0.525)	0.271 (0.177)	-0.141 (0.188)	184.98	0.21	2.04 12.26	0.02887	2.04
British pound	0.028 (0.121)	1.772 (1.389)	-0.938 (0.646)	-0.993[b] (0.488)	0.419[b] (0.165)	-0.182 (0.175)	191.27	0.15	2.02 13.12	0.02685	2.86[b]

a. The real return on assets denominated in currency j is computed as follows:

$$1 + r_{t+1}^j \equiv \frac{1 + i_t^j}{(P_{t+1}^{\$}/P_t^{\$})(S_{t+1}^j/S_t^j)},$$

where i^j is the one-month Eurocurrency interest rate; S^j is the price of the dollar in terms of currency j (equal to one for $j = \$$); and $P^{\$}$ is a worldwide price index expressed in dollars, computed according to a Cobb-Douglas formula:

$$P^{\$} \equiv \prod_{i=1}^{6} (CPI^i S^i)^{\alpha_i},$$

α_i being the weight of country i's goods in world consumption as measured by its GNP. Note that if any α_i is one, the denominator collapses to one plus the inflation rate in country i.

(reported) and fewer (not reported). The absence of serial correlation supports the hypothesis of rational expectations.

The main lesson to be drawn from table 4.1 is the low degree of precision that plagues estimation of general portfolio-balance equations, and the need to bring additional information to bear. This provides the motivation for considering the constraints placed on the parameters by the hypothesis of mean-variance optimization. If one believes this hypothesis, then the resulting estimates will be more precise.

4.2 Estimation of Asset-Demand Functions Constrained to be Optimizing

In chapter 1 we derived the correct form for the asset demands of an investor who maximizes a function of the mean and variance of his end-of-period real wealth, W_{t+1}.[7] Restating that result,

$$E_t z_{t+1} = \rho \, \text{cov}_t(z_{t+1}, r_{t+1}^\$) + \rho \Omega x_t, \tag{5}$$

where we have defined the vector of returns on the five assets relative to the dollar:

$$z_{t+1} \equiv r_{t+1} - \iota r_{t+1}^\$,$$

and the variance-covariance matrix of relative returns:

$$\Omega \equiv E_t(z_{t+1} - E_t x_{t+1})(z_{t+1} - E_t z_{t+1})'.$$

For economic intuition, we invert equation (5) to solve for the portfolio shares, the form analogous to equation (1):

$$x_t = -\Omega^{-1} \text{cov}_t(z_{t+1}, r_{t+1}^\$) + (\rho \Omega)^{-1} E_t z_{t+1}. \tag{6}$$

Recall that the first term represents the "minimum-variance" portfolio. If an investor is extremely risk-averse ($\rho = \infty$) and views the dollar as a safe asset (which requires not only that he consume only U.S. goods but also that U.S. prices are nonstochastic when expressed in terms of dollars), then his minimum-variance portfolio is zero in each of the other five assets. The second term represents the "speculative" portfolio. A higher expected return on a given asset induces investors to hold more of that asset than is in the minimum-variance portfolio, to an extent limited only by the degree of risk aversion and the uncertainty of the return.

We now estimate the system (equation 4) subject to the constraint implied by mean-variance optimization:[8,9] $\beta^{-1} = \rho \Omega$. As explained in chapters 1 and 2, Ω is the variance-covariance matrix of the error term: $\Omega \equiv$

$E_t \varepsilon_{t+1} \varepsilon'_{t+1}$. Imposition of a constraint between coefficients and variances, as opposed to a constraint among coefficients, requires maximum likelihood estimation.[10] Appendix 4A derives the first-order conditions for the maximization of the likelihood function and describes the program used.

If the aim, under the a priori constraint of mean-variance optimization, is to use the information to get the most efficient possible estimates of the parameters, then one might wish not only to impose the constraint that the coefficient matrix is proportional to the variance-covariance matrix Ω, but to impose as well an a priori value for the constant of proportionality, which is the coefficient of relative risk aversion ρ. De Macedo (1980) and Krugman (1981) refer to the "Samuelson presumption" that $\rho = 2.0$. Table 4.2 reports the estimated parameters for the case $\rho = 2.0$. The results look quite different from those in table 4.1.[11] If one believes in the constraints, then the difference is simply the result of more efficient estimates. One would have to invert the coefficient matrix in order to recover the original β matrix and see which assets are close substitutes for which other assets.

In this chapter, however, we use our technique to test explicitly the hypothesis of mean-variance optimization rather than to impose the hypothesis. The log-likelihood for the estimates in table 4.2 is 1057.05, a decrease from the unconstrained log-likelihood 1086.49. In other words, the fit has worsened considerably. Twice the difference is 59.0, which is above the 5 percent critical level of 37.7. This constitutes a clear rejection of the optimization hypothesis.

Perhaps 2.0 is not the correct value for the constant of risk-aversion ρ. We used the MLE program to find simultaneously the values of ρ and Ω

Table 4.2
Constrained asset-demand functions, MLE

Dependent variable: $r_{t+1} - r^{\$}_{t+1}$, real rate of return on national currency relative to the dollar.

Sample: June 1973 to August 1980 (87 observations).

| National currency | Constants | β^{-1} constrained to $\rho\Omega$, with $\rho = 2.0$ | | | | |
		$x_t^{C\$}$	x_t^F	x_t^{DM}	x_t^Y	$x_t^£$
Canadian dollar	−0.00103	0.00037	0.00010	0.00021	0.00002	0.00009
French franc	0.00140	0.00010	0.00188	0.00169	0.00099	0.00100
Deutsche mark	0.00050	0.00021	0.00169	0.00223	0.00106	0.00107
Japanese yen	0.00193	0.00002	0.00099	0.00106	0.00196	0.00081
Pound sterling	0.00211	0.00009	0.00100	0.00107	0.00081	0.00158

Log-likelihood = 1057.05.
See table 4.1 for definitions of variables.

that maximize the likelihood. The log-likelihood at this point is 1057.96. (The MLE estimate of ρ is $-67.0!$) The value of ρ makes almost no difference; we are still able to reject the hypothesis easily.

4.3 Conclusions

The theory of expected utility maximization, and in particular the simple framework of mean-variance optimization, is a very attractive way to bring more structure to the problem of asset-demand functions. The reader who is a priori inclined to accept that framework can view the numbers reported in table 4.2 as efficient estimates of the parameters in an international asset-demand function. The estimates are efficient because they use the information that, if investors indeed optimize, the coefficient matrix should be proportional to the error variance-covariance matrix. At the same time, the estimates can be argued to be superior to those in previous studies of the optimal portfolio because they use data on asset supplies and thus allow expected real returns to change from period to period.

However, the primary aim of this chapter is to test explicitly the validity of the hypothesis of mean-variance optimization. The likelihood ratio test rejects the constraints imposed by the hypothesis. Thus, if we are to believe these results, the unconstrained parameter estimates reported in table 4.1, as imprecise as they are, are the best we can do.

How could investors fail to optimize with respect to the mean and variance of their real wealth? It is possible that they are simply not sophisticated enough. The literature on equity markets, for example, cannot be said to have found good empirical evidence for the CAPM theory.[12] Of course it is possible that agents are rational, but optimize subject to constraints such as imperfect capital markets. A corporation may use as its measure of risk the variance of its own dollar profits, as opposed to the covariance with the market portfolio that the finance theory says it should use; and yet this may be rational if the corporation finances its projects internally and has to pay a penalty whenever an unexpected fall in earnings forces it to borrow externally. The same could be true of an individual.[13]

On the other hand, investors may be *too* sophisticated to optimize (merely) with respect to the mean and variance of their real end-of-period wealth. Stulz (1981), Hodrick (1981), and Hansen and Hodrick (1983) argue that investors maximize a more complicated intertemporal utility function. Unfortunately, their theoretical results are not as conducive to empirical testing as is the one-period mean-variance framework.[14]

The theory tested in this chapter is one commonly discussed in the literature. The theory requires many assumptions: one-period expected utility maximization, a normal distribution for underlying returns, a constant variance-covariance matrix,[15] constant relative risk aversion, homogeneous investors, rational expectations, asset supplies that are properly measured from variables like government debt and foreign exchange intervention, and perfect capital markets. The failure of any one of these assumptions would explain the test result, the rejection of the theory.

Appendix 4A

The parameters of the model were estimated by a maximum likelihood routine based on Berndt et al.'s (1974) maximizing algorithm for nonlinear models. The program makes use of the likelihood function, and its first derivatives. The log of the likelihood, under the normality assumption, is

$$L = -\frac{GT}{2}\log(2\pi) - \frac{T}{2}\log|\Omega| - \tfrac{1}{2}\sum_{t=1}^{T}\varepsilon_{t+1}'\Omega^{-1}\varepsilon_{t+1}, \tag{A1}$$

where

$$\varepsilon_{t+1} = z_{t+1} - E_t z_{t+1}$$

$$= z_{t+1} - c - \rho\Omega x_t,$$

and G is the number of equations (five) and T is the number of observations (eighty-seven).

In standard econometric problems the symmetry of the variance-covariance matrix Ω can safely be ignored in deriving the first-order conditions, because the ijth element and the jith element of Ω enter the likelihood function symmetrically. In our problem, this is not true because of the restriction that Ω be proportional to the coefficient matrix, so care must be taken to allow properly for the symmetry. First, we derive $\partial L/\partial \Omega$ for an arbitrary (nonsymmetric) Ω:

$$\frac{\partial L}{\partial \Omega} = -\frac{T}{2}\frac{\log|\Omega|}{\partial \Omega} - \tfrac{1}{2}\sum_{t=1}^{T}\frac{\partial \varepsilon_{t+1}'\Omega^{-1}\varepsilon_{t+1}}{\partial \Omega}$$

$$= -\frac{T}{2}\Omega'^{-1} + \tfrac{1}{2}\sum_{t=1}^{T}[\Omega'^{-1}\varepsilon_{t+1}\varepsilon_{t+1}'\Omega'^{-1}$$

$$+ \rho(\Omega^{-1}\varepsilon_{t+1} + \Omega'^{-1}\varepsilon_{t+1})x_t']. \tag{A2}$$

Now, imposing symmetry, we let

$$Q = [q_{ij}] = -\frac{T}{2}\Omega^{-1} + \frac{1}{2}\sum_{t=1}^{T}[\Omega^{-1}\varepsilon_{t+1}\varepsilon'_{t+1}\Omega^{-1} + 2\rho\Omega^{-1}\varepsilon_{t+1}x'_t]. \qquad \text{(A3)}$$

Then, if ω_{ij} is the ijth element of Ω,

$$\partial L/\partial\omega_{ii} = q_{ii} \qquad \text{(A4)}$$

and

$$\partial L/\partial\omega_{ij} = q_{ij} + q_{ji}, \, i \neq j. \qquad \text{(A5)}$$

We also have

$$\partial L/\partial\rho = \sum_{t=1}^{T} \varepsilon'_{t+1}x_t \qquad \text{(A6)}$$

and

$$\partial L/\partial c = \sum_{t=1}^{T} \Omega^{-1}\varepsilon_{t+1}, \qquad \text{(A7)}$$

where Ω has been assumed symmetric.

Acknowledgments

This is a slightly revised verion of NBER Working Paper No. 1051, December 1982. We would like to thank Paul Ruud for making available his Maximum Likelihood Estimation program, and Robert Hodrick and Steven Kohlhagen for comments and suggestions. We would also like to thank the Institute of Business and Economic Research at U.C. Berkeley, and the National Science Foundation for research support under grant numbers SES-8007162 and SES-8218300.

5

The Constrained Asset Share Estimation (CASE) Method: Testing Mean-Variance Efficiency of the U.S. Stock Market

This chapter uses Constrained Asset Share Estimation (CASE) to test the conditional mean-variance efficiency (MVE) of the U.S. stock market. The CASE technique is useful in time-series tests of simple asset pricing models because it allows estimated expected returns to vary in an unrestricted way. It was first applied in a macroeconomic context in which the "market" portfolio included not only equities, but also money, bonds, and real estate.[1] It has since been applied more widely to other portfolios and has been extended to allow for variation in conditional second as well as first moments.[2]

The CASE technique nests MVE in a more general, but economically meaningful, theory of portfolio determination. In contrast, most tests of the null hypothesis of MVE have no clear alternative hypothesis. This feature is particularly important because many tests do in fact reject MVE. When one rejects the null hypothesis, it is good to have some idea of what the alternative is. In the central tests below, the alternative to MVE is that investors' portfolio shares are linearly related to expected returns, but that investors' asset demands are not determined in the precise way that MVE would imply they should be. The alternative hypothesis is the more general portfolio-balance approach to asset demands that was first introduced by Tobin (1958, 1969). The problem he was addressing was the relationship between expected returns and the demand for bonds and other assets. Sharpe's (1964) CAPM grew out of an attempt to place more structure on Tobin's portfolio-balance model by modeling the behavior of individuals as mean-variance optimizers (as in Markowitz, 1952, and Tobin, 1958). However, most modern testing of CAPM has departed from this original context.

With Charles Engel, Kenneth A. Froot, and Anthony P. Rodrigues, to appear in *Journal of Empirical Finance* 2 (1995). Reprinted with permission.

The CASE method allows expected returns to vary freely, as they must, for example, whenever new information that may not be observed by the econometrician becomes available to the investor. In addition, in many of the tests below we allow second moments to vary according to an ARCH or GARCH process.[3] Allowing for such variation in conditional moments is essential for a properly specified test of MVE. There is considerable evidence that both the conditional expectation and conditional variance of excess returns contain important predictable components.[4]

Our tests below emphasize the nested nature of the hypotheses we consider. We pay special attention to the importance of ARCH versus MVE versus the asset shares themselves, in explaining risk premia. The broad findings can be summarized as follows. First, we find that stock-market shares by themselves have statistically significant power in predicting monthly excess stock returns. This is what we would expect if the stock market is mean-variance efficient and if required returns change over time. However, we reject the restrictions implied by constant-variance MVE. Moreover, the predictive ability of the asset shares disappears when the constant-variance version of MVE is imposed.

However, the constant-variance version of MVE can be rejected in favor of a version of MVE in which the covariance of the asset returns follows a GARCH process. Furthermore, the GARCH version of MVE does have statistically significant ability to predict stock prices. This model produces an estimate of the coefficient of risk aversion of about 3.0, with a standard error of about 1.4. Thus a version of MVE in which market betas vary conditionally both because of changes in asset shares and time variation in the variances of individual asset returns has explanatory power and produces plausible parameter estimates. This finding may be relevant to the recent findings of Fama and French (1992) that betas based on unconditional covariances have no predictive ability once size is included as an explanatory variable. Although we do not address that issue directly, our findings suggest that the CAPM might have performed better in the Fama and French setting if the betas were conditional on contemporaneous information. Nonetheless, we reject the restrictions that this version of MVE imposes on a GARCH version of the Tobin portfolio-balance model.

In short, the unrestricted linear Tobin asset pricing model has predictive power under both of our specifications (with the GARCH specification doing better than the constant-variance version). The MVE-constrained model itself also has predictive power under the GARCH specification. However, the restrictions that MVE places on the Tobin model can be rejected in all cases.

Sections 5.1 and 5.2 briefly describe the model and the data, respectively. Section 5.3 tests for constant-variance MVE. We introduce our ARCH specifications in section 5.4. Section 5.5 summarizes our general nesting procedure for the hypotheses of interest and offers our conclusions.

5.1 The Model

Mean-variance efficiency implies that the vector of conditional risk premia is a linear combination of the asset shares in the portfolio, with the weights proportional to the conditional variance of asset returns:

$$E_t(r_{t+1}) = \rho_t \Omega_t \lambda_t, \tag{1}$$

where $E_t(r_{t+1})$ is the expected return above the riskless rate on an $N \times 1$ vector of assets conditional on all information available at time t, Ω_t is the conditional variance of returns between t and $t + 1$, λ_t is the $N \times 1$ vector of portfolio weights, with $\Sigma_{i=1}^{N} \lambda_{t,i} = 1$, and ρ_t is the price of risk equal to $E_t(m_{t+1})/\mathrm{Var}_t(m_{t+1})$, where m_{t+1} is the return on the aggregate portfolio. If the aggregate stock portfolio is the "market" portfolio, MVE is equivalent to CAPM, and the parameter ρ is to be interpreted as the coefficient of relative risk aversion. Note that the right-hand side of (1) is equivalent to the risk-adjusted conditional expected return on the aggregate (or market) portfolio,

$$E_t(r_{t+1}) = \beta_t E_t(m_{t+1}), \tag{2}$$

where

$$\beta_t = \frac{\mathrm{cov}_t(m_{t+1}, r_{t+1})}{\mathrm{var}_t(m_{t+1})} = \frac{\Omega_t \lambda_t}{\mathrm{var}_t(m_{t+1})}.$$

This expression makes it clear that the vector of subportfolio β_is varies both with the shares of assets in the portfolio, λ_t, and the conditional covariance matrix, Ω_t, and thus may move substantially over short time intervals.

Proceeding along a familiar route, the assumption of rational expectations allows us to replace the vector of expected excess returns with the actual returns by including a prediction error that is orthogonal to all information at time t:

$$r_{t+1} = \rho_t \Omega_t \lambda_t + \varepsilon_{t+1}, \tag{3}$$

where $\varepsilon_{t+1} = r_{t+1} - E(r_{t+1})$. Information about the conditional covariance matrix of returns can be obtained from the error terms, because

$$\Omega_t = E_t(\varepsilon_{t+1}\varepsilon'_{t+1}). \tag{4}$$

MVE therefore imposes a set of restrictions that are highly nonlinear in that they constitute proportionality between the coefficient matrix and the variance-covariance matrix of the error term in equation (2).

To evaluate equation (4), we must take a position on how Ω_t changes over time. In sections 5.3 and 5.4 below, we assume first that Ω_t is constant and then that it follows an ARCH or GARCH process, respectively. We test the hypothesis that MVE holds against more general alternatives in which investors forecast excess returns as a function of asset shares and past prediction errors (as in the Tobin model).

The portfolio-balance model of Tobin (1958, 1969), representing a general relationship between asset demands and expected returns, can be written as

$$\lambda_t = \mathbf{B}_t E_t(r_{t+1}), \tag{5}$$

where $\mathbf{B}$ is an $N \times N$ matrix of coefficients. By inverting the system of equations in (5), we obtain an expression for expected excess returns,

$$E_t(r_{t+1}) = \mathbf{A}_t \lambda_t, \tag{6}$$

where $\mathbf{A}_t = \mathbf{B}_t^{-1}$. This system of equations representing the portfolio-balance model is a generalization of MVE. MVE imposes the restriction that the matrix of coefficients $\mathbf{A}_t$ be proportional to the variance of the forecast error, ε_{t+1}.

Hence an insight of the CASE method: MVE can be viewed as the null hypothesis in a test where the alternative hypothesis is the more general unconstrained portfolio-balance model. Using ex post returns, equation (6) can be written as follows:

$$r_{t+1} = \mathbf{A}_t \lambda_t + \varepsilon_{t+1}. \tag{7}$$

Although the values of the equities are endogenous variables in an economic sense, they are still uncorrelated with the prediction errors, which under rational expectations are uncorrelated with all information available at time t.[5]

We also test the MVE hypothesis above, as well as the more general alternatives, against an even more restrictive null hypothesis: that investors expect conditional excess returns to be zero. The results of our tests are discusssed in sections 5.3 and 5.4. Section 5.5 presents a diagram which makes it easy to see the results of our nested hypothesis tests.

It is interesting to contrast our test of MVE with two closely related tests. A detailed comparison of our test to that of Harvey (1989) would consume much space, but the essence of the comparison is simple. The MVE of equation (1) or (2) implies a relation between expected returns and covariances of returns. The model is not testable until some auxiliary assumption is imposed. Our auxiliary assumption is a model of the covariance matrix Ω_t—it is alternatively modeled to be constant, or to follow a GARCH process. Given the model for Ω_t, the MVE model determines the behavior of expected returns. Harvey, however, makes his auxiliary assumption about the expected returns rather than the covariances. He assumes that expected returns are linear in observable economic data such as dividend yields. This model, combined with MVE, then determines the behavior of the covariance of returns. The two approaches are similar in that they both test the cross-equation restrictions imposed by MVE while maintaining an auxiliary assumption. One advantage of our approach is that, in making the auxiliary assumption about the covariances rather than the means, our alternative to MVE is explicit and economically meaningful.

Ng (1991) estimates a constrained version of MVE that is in most respects identical to our constrained model. However, her alternative hypothesis differs from ours. She tests the restriction that the intercept term in equation (1) is zero. Our test is more analogous to that of Harvey (1989), in the sense that we test cross-equation restrictions.

5.2   The Data

Our tests use monthly stock returns from the New York and American Stock Exchanges from January 1955 to December 1984. To ease the computational burden in estimating equation (3), we aggregate the stocks into $N = 11$ (and sometimes 7) industry portfolios.[6]

Table 5.1 describes the aggregation of stocks into industry portfolios. The returns for each portfolio are value-weighted average returns. The $N \times 1$ vector of portfolio shares, λ_t, is the value of the stocks in the portfolios as a fraction of the total value of all stocks. Because it is desirable to group together equities that have highly correlated returns, we tried to put similar industries into the same portfolio.[7] Stambaugh (1982) aggregates into twenty industries, roughly by type of final output. We further aggregate into eleven industries, combining some of Stambaugh's categories. Table 5.1 shows Stambaugh's twenty industries, as well as the

Table 5.1
Industry portfolios and S.E.C. codes (Stambaugh 1982)

Industry	S.E.C. codes
1. Mining	10, 11, 12, 13, 14
2. Food and Beverages	20
3. Textile and Apparel	22, 23
4. Paper Products	26
5. Chemical	28
6. Petroleum	29
7. Stone, Clay and Glass	32
8. Primary Metals	33
9. Fabricated Metals	34
10. Machinery	35
11. Appliances, Electric Equipment	36
12. Transportation Equipment	37
13. Miscellaneous Manufacturing	38, 39
14. Railroads	40
15. Other Transportation	41, 42, 44, 45, 47
16. Utilities	49
17. Department Stores	53
18. Other Retail Trade	50−52, 54−59
19. Banking, Financial, Real Estate	60−67
20. Miscellaneous	1, 4, 15−17, 21, 24, 25, 27, 30, 31, 46, 48, 70, 73, 75, 78−80, 82, 89, 99

11 Portfolios (combinations of the 20 portfolios)

Portfolio	Industry portfolios
1	1, 20
2	2, 3, 4
3	5
4	6
5	7, 8, 9
6	10
7	11
8	12−15
9	16
10	17, 18
11	19

7 Portfolios (combinations of the 20 portfolios)

Portfolio	Industry portfolios
1	1, 2, 3, 4, 20
2	5, 7, 8, 9
3	6
4	10, 11
5	12−15
6	16
7	17−19

eleven-industry aggregation that we use to perform our maximum likelihood tests of MVE. Table 5.1 also reports the seven-industry aggregation
that we use for the ARCH estimation in section 5.3.

The value shares, λ_t, are used to predict excess returns between time t
and $t + 1$. The shares are measured monthly from the last day of January
1955 to the last day of November 1984 (359 observations), while the
returns are calculated as the dividend plus appreciation over the previous
month beginning the last day of February 1955 and ending the last day of
December 1984. All returns are nominal excess returns above the return on
the one-month Treasury bill recorded by Ibbotson Associates (1986).

5.3   Tests of MVE with Constant Conditional Variances

Table 5.2 reports the results from estimating the unconstrained system of
equations (7), when the matrix A is treated as constant over time. Few of
the coefficients individually are significantly different from zero. Not surprisingly, the R^2s are not very high, and none exceeds .10. We can, however, reject at the 95 percent level the hypothesis that the asset shares have
no explanatory power for excess stock returns. The value of the chi-square
statistic (121 d.f.) is 233.56 compared to a critical value of 147.39.[8,9]

Under the MVE hypothesis, this unconstrained system of inverted asset
demand equations is not estimated efficiently. If we impose more structure
on the system we can hope to improve the precision of our parameter
estimates. Hence we estimate the system of equations (3) which impose the
MVE constraints that $A = \rho\Omega$. For now, the variance matrix Ω is assumed
constant over time.

As in earlier applications of the CASE method, the N-equation system
(equation (3)) must be estimated by maximum likelihood techniques. Note
that the assumption that Ω is constant is not the same as the assumption of
constant betas and expected returns. As we saw in the previous section,
even with a constant covariance matrix, the betas, and hence the expected
returns on all securities including the aggregate or "market" portfolio, will
vary over time in a general way. Table 5.3 reports the maximum likelihood
results of equation (3).

We can report a chi-square statistic for the restrictions implied by equation (3). This is the CASE test of the MVE hypothesis against the more
general portfolio-balance model. We impose 120 restrictions on the unconstrained (121 coefficients are constrained to be proportional to their corresponding elements in the variance matrix). The test statistic has a value of
231.34, so we easily reject the hypothesis of MVE at the 99 percent level.

Table 5.2
Estimated coefficients from unconstrained OLS regressions

Dependent variable: Excess rate of return on asset j
Independent variable: Shares of asset j in total portfolio

	λ^1	λ^2	λ^3	λ^4	λ^5	λ^6	λ^7	λ^8	λ^9	λ^{10}	λ^{11}
Equation 1	−0.14	0.19	0.26	−0.06	−0.11	0.14	−0.70	0.80	0.21	−0.35	0.26
	(0.12)	(0.82)	(0.30)	(0.26)	(0.32)	(0.25)	(0.44)	(0.22)	(0.32)	(0.25)	(0.44)
$R^2 = .023$							Breusch-Godfrey statistic (20 lags) = 42.79*				
Equation 2	−0.11	−2.29*	0.64*	−0.29	−0.28	0.44	−1.12*	0.16	0.59*	0.83	2.06
	(0.13)	(0.86)	(0.32)	(0.27)	(0.34)	(0.26)	(0.46)	(0.23)	(0.22)	(0.57)	(1.24)
$R^2 = .050$							Breusch-Godfrey statistic (20 lags) = 23.38				
Equation 3	−0.20	−1.05	0.12	−0.04	−0.32	0.14	−1.20*	−0.02	0.46*	1.16	2.05
	(0.13)	(0.89)	(0.33)	(0.28)	(0.35)	(0.27)	(0.47)	(0.24)	(0.23)	(0.59)	(1.29)
$R^2 = .047$							Breusch-Godfrey statistic (20 lags) = 16.99				
Equation 4	0.15	−0.55	0.74	−0.82*	−0.81*	0.14	−1.01	0.44	−0.01	−0.60	2.79
	(0.16)	(1.09)	(0.40)	(0.34)	(0.43)	(0.33)	(0.57)	(0.29)	(0.28)	(0.72)	(1.57)
$R^2 = .027$							Breusch-Godfrey statistic (20 lags) = 21.74				
Equation 5	−0.25	−1.00	0.83*	−0.25	−0.81	0.18	−1.68*	0.50	0.41	−0.02	2.20
	(0.16)	(1.07)	(0.39)	(0.34)	(0.42)	(0.33)	(0.57)	(0.29)	(0.28)	(0.71)	(1.55)
$R^2 = .044$							Breusch-Godfrey statistic (20 lags) = 30.71				

Equation 6
-0.10	-0.19	0.46	-0.40	-0.68	-0.45	-0.28	0.37	0.18	-0.06	1.99
(0.15)	(1.04)	(0.38)	(0.33)	(0.41)	(0.32)	(0.56)	(0.28)	(0.27)	(0.69)	(1.51)

$R^2 = .046$ Breusch-Godfrey statistic (20 lags) = 20.41

Equation 7
-0.17	-2.72*	0.83*	-0.26	0.71	0.44	-2.15*	0.37	0.75*	1.21	3.15
(0.17)	(1.13)	(0.41)	(0.36)	(0.44)	(0.35)	(0.60)	(0.30)	(0.29)	(0.75)	(1.63)

$R^2 = .066$ Breusch-Godfrey statistic (20 lags) = 17.38

Equation 8
-0.14	-0.85	0.25	-0.10	-0.43	0.08	-1.41*	-0.04	0.62	0.94	1.80
(0.14)	(0.93)	(0.34)	(0.39)	(0.36)	(0.29)	(0.49)	(0.25)	(0.24)	(0.62)	(1.34)

$R^2 = .067$ Breusch-Godfrey statistic (20 lags) = 21.10

Equation 9
-0.09	-0.77	0.50	-0.10	-0.12	0.18	-0.64	-0.04	0.30	0.07	0.82
(0.12)	(0.80)	(0.30)	(0.25)	(0.31)	(0.25)	(0.43)	(0.21)	(0.21)	(0.53)	(1.16)

$R^2 = .032$ Breusch-Godfrey statistic (20 lags) = 35.07*

Equation 10
-0.11	-0.38	0.20	-0.10	-0.27	0.01	-0.56	0.06	0.41	-0.02	1.05
(0.16)	(1.06)	(0.39)	(0.33)	(0.42)	(0.33)	(0.56)	(0.28)	(0.28)	(0.70)	(1.53)

$R^2 = .027$ Breusch-Godfrey statistic (20 lags) = 44.68*

Equation 11
-0.04	-0.25	0.13	0.19	0.09	0.24	0.13	0.19	0.54	-0.20	-1.31
(0.14)	(0.95)	(0.35)	(0.30)	(0.37)	(0.29)	(0.50)	(0.25)	(0.25)	(0.63)	(1.37)

$R^2 = .027$ Breusch-Godfrey statistic (20 lags) = 42.42*

* = significant at 5% level. (standard errors in parentheses)

Table 5.3
CAPM estimation, constant Ω, 11 assets

$$r_{t+1} = \rho(P'P)\lambda_t + \varepsilon_{t+1}$$

$$Var_t(\varepsilon_{t+1}) = P'P$$

The estimate of the coefficient ρ:

2.0319
(1.6130)

The estimate of the upper triangular matrix P:

.0398	.0322	.0334	.0385	.0411	.0346	.0404	.0331	.0257	.0317	.0374
(.0018)	(.0021)	(.0023)	(.0028)	(.0026)	(.0026)	(.0030)	(.0025)	(.0022)	(.0029)	(.0023)
	.0274	.0197	−.0033	.0166	.0198	.0223	.0189	.0089	.0252	.0047
	(.0011)	(.0015)	(.0023)	(.0019)	(.0025)	(.0022)	(.0019)	(.0017)	(.0025)	(.0015)
		.0204	.0042	.0044	.0097	.0097	.0078	−.0046	.0015	.0000
		(.0008)	(.0024)	(.0015)	(.0019)	(.0019)	(.0014)	(.0018)	(.0018)	(.0018)
			.0360	−.0029	−.0019	−.0032	−.0017	.0018	−.0073	.0125
			(.0014)	(.0016)	(.0021)	(.0019)	(.0015)	(.0018)	(.0019)	(.0016)
				.0276	.0058	.0102	.0090	−.0046	.0003	.0051
				(.0011)	(.0019)	(.0019)	(.0013)	(.0017)	(.0017)	(.0016)
					.0304	.0068	.0050	−.0025	.0021	−.0009
					(.0011)	(.0016)	(.0015)	(.0017)	(.0018)	(.0014)
						.0272	.0063	.0000	.0063	.0020
						(.0011)	(.0014)	(.0017)	(.0019)	(.0017)
							.0214	.0020	.0094	.0027
							(.0010)	(.0018)	(.0018)	(.0017)

.0272	.0032	.0050
(.0011)	(.0017)	(.0014)
	.0287	.0006
	(.0013)	(.0013)
		.0219
		(.0007)

(standard errors in parentheses)

If one were nevertheless willing to accept the MVE estimates on the basis of prior beliefs, they yield asset pricing equations that are much more plausible in some ways. Recall that in the unconstrained regressions we frequently found that an increase in an asset share would actually decrease that asset's expected return. That is not possible with the constrained MVE estimates. Also, the point estimate of ρ, which can be interpreted as the coefficient of relative risk aversion under the assumption that λ_t are shares of the complete market portfolio, is very plausible—2.03. This is very close to the "Samuelson presumption" of a likely value—2.0—for average risk aversion. The coefficient is not estimated precisely, however, as it is not statistically different from zero at the 95 percent level. But its 95 percent confidence interval ranges only up to about 5.3—still a believable estimate for average risk aversion.

On the other hand, the constrained model does a very poor job of predicting excess returns. The failure to reject the hypothesis that $\rho = 0$ implies that asset shares provide no statistically significant explanatory power for risk premia under the MVE restrictions, because the coefficients on the shares are all multiples of ρ.[10] In other words, MVE vitiates the predictive power of the asset shares alone.

For the estimates reported in tables 5.2 and 5.3, the shares are calculated as a fraction of total equity investment. If, however, there are positive net holdings of the riskless asset, then the shares should properly be calculated as a fraction of total equity investment plus the total net value of the riskless asset. The riskless asset could have a positive net value if the government issues riskless short-term bonds, and investors consider government bonds to be additions to net wealth (so that they do not fully discount future tax liabilities) or if the government issues money. We estimated the model under the assumption that the relevant measure of the net supply is the value of all government bonds (which is calculated by Cox, 1985), and again under the assumption that the value of outstanding Treasury bills measures the net supply of the riskless asset. In both cases, the estimates hardly changed.

We considered two other formulations that apply when ρ is interpreted as the coefficient of relative risk aversion, besides assuming that it is constant. In the first, we assumed constant *absolute* risk aversion. In that case, $\rho_t = bW_t$ where b is the coefficient of absolute risk aversion and W_t is the value of all equities at time t. In the second, we considered a more general formulation consistent with the HARA class of utility functions, $\rho_t = a + bW_t$. If $b = 0$, we have the constant relative risk aversion case, and if $a = 0$ we have the constant absolute risk aversion case. Again, however, these versions of the model failed to improve the constrained model's performance.[11]

Maximum likelihood estimation of MVE is difficult because of the constraints imposed between the coefficients and the variance. The entire system must be estimated simultaneously, which in the case of the eleven-asset system means simultaneously estimating 122 coefficients.

If we are interested in testing MVE, but not in actually obtaining the constrained coefficient estimates, we do not need to estimate the constrained set of equations. A Wald test can be performed using only the unrestricted model. In this case, the unconstrained model (6) is particularly easy to estimate, because it requires only equation-by-equation ordinary least squares. Engel and Rodrigues (1993) provide an expression for the Wald statistic for the MVE restrictions. The Wald statistic is not difficult to compute even for large collections of assets. We tested the MVE restrictions for the entire set of twenty industry portfolios composed by Stambaugh, and again rejected MVE restrictions easily. The test statistic was distributed chi-square (19 d.f.), and had a value of 58.99, well above the 99 percent critical value.[12]

The estimates of this section provide little support for MVE of the stock market. In all of the test performed, the restrictions that MVE places on a more general asset demand model are strongly rejected.

5.4 Tests of MVE with ARCH Conditional Variances

In the estimates reported in section 5.3, we assumed that the return covariance matrix, Ω_t, was constant over time. Because it has become clear in recent years that conditional variances of financial variables show a considerable amount of variation, we turn next to a model of time-varying conditional variances.

In simple regression models, the presence of heteroskedasticity often does not affect the consistency of coefficient estimates, although it does cause standard calculations of test statistics to be inconsistent. When the MVE restrictions are imposed, however, changes in variances imply changes in coefficient estimates, which in turn imply changes in expected excess returns. The coefficient on the asset shares in the constrained model must move over time if Ω_t does, so holding Ω_t constant leads to inconsistent coefficient estimates.

Inspection of equation (2) makes it easy to see why it is important to allow for variation in Ω_t. There are two possible sources of variation in expected returns if ρ is constant: changes in asset shares, λ_t, and changes in

Ω_t. Suppose, for example, that favorable news about a stock is announced. One could easily think of cases in which the price is pushed up, increasing the stock's share in the aggregate portfolio, even though its expected return is now lower with the news. If the market is mean-variance efficient, this can happen when the riskiness of the asset declines—its own variance falls, or its covariance with other assets declines. But, for the jth asset, this is exactly a change in the jth row of Ω_t.

We choose to model variances empirically following Engle's (1982) ARCH process. The ARCH takes the conditional variance of this period's forecast error to be a function of past forecast errors. It is not based on any theoretical notion of how the general equilibrium of the economy works. It is an ad hoc model that seems to work well in practice.

In this section, we apply a multiequation version of ARCH to the MVE problem. Because of the difficulty in estimating large ARCH systems, we have further aggregated the assets into the seven portfolios described in table 5.1. Even with only seven equations to estimate, the dimension of the ARCH problem can be quite large. For example, even if we restrict ourselves to first-order ARCH in which the variances and covariances in this period are related only to the squares and cross products of forecast errors in the previous period, the problem is unmanageably large. There are twenty-eight independent elements in the covariance matrix. If each element were linearly related to the twenty-eight lagged squares and cross products of the forecast errors, there would be 812 parameters to estimate.

Given the complexity of estimating the MVE-ARCH system, and given the limited amount of data, it is helpful to lower the number of ARCH coefficients. Our test of MVE uses a parsimonious version of ARCH, in which the model has return variances given by

$$\Omega_t = P'P + G\varepsilon_t\varepsilon_t'G. \tag{8}$$

We treat as parameters the upper triangular matrix P, and the diagonal matrix G. Under this formulation, each element of Ω_t is linearly related to its corresponding component in the matrix of cross products of lagged forecast errors. There are only thirty-five coefficients to estimate. This formulation enforces positive semidefiniteness on the covariance matrix Ω_t.

The unrestricted form of the inverted system of asset-demand equations is given by equation (7). MVE imposes the restriction that $A_t = \rho\Omega_t$, where Ω_t is the conditional variance of r_{t+1}. In practice, if MVE is to be nested in the general system of asset demands, then the elements of A_t in the general system might be related to the same variables to which Ω_t is assumed to be related. More specifically, we assume that in the unrestricted model, the coefficient matrix A_t evolves according to

$$A_t = Q'Q + F\varepsilon_t\varepsilon_t'F, \tag{9}$$

where Q is upper triangular and F is diagonal, and the conditional covariance matrix of returns, Ω_t, is given by equation (8). The MVE constraint, that $A_t = \rho\Omega_t$, imposes thirty-four constraints on the unconstrained asset-demand equations in equation (7).

Before turning to the results of the ARCH estimates, it is useful to examine the constrained MVE estimates of the seven-equation system when Ω_t is constrained to be constant, as in the previous section. Table 4 in the original paper (omitted here to save space) shows that the seven-equation system performs much like its eleven-equation counterpart. The estimate of ρ is close to 2.0. However, it is still not statistically different from zero, which indicates that the asset share data with the MVE constraints imposed still do a poor job of explaining expected returns. In this case, MVE imposes twenty-seven constraints on the general system. The test statistic is distributed chi-square (27 d.f.) and is estimated to be 70.00. The MVE constraints can be rejected strongly at the 99 percent level.

Table 5.4 reports the results of the MVE restrictions imposed on the ARCH system. There are two hypotheses to test here. The first asks whether we can reject the constant-variance MVE model in favor of the ARCH–MVE. A rejection would imply that time-varying variances statistically reduce the distance between the stock-market portfolio and the mean-variance efficient frontier. Such a rejection would lead us to the other interesting question: can we reject the restrictions implied by MVE on the unrestricted ARCH cum portfolio-balance system in equations (7) and (9)?

The constant-variance version of MVE is a special case of the ARCH–MVE model, in which the G matrix from equation (8) is constrained to be zero. This imposes seven constraints on the ARCH system. Our test statistic is 30.82 and is distributed chi-square (7 d.f.). We reject the constant-variance restrictions at the 99 percent level. ARCH therefore improves significantly on the constant-variance form of MVE.

However, only four of the seven ARCH coefficients (elements of the G matrix) are significantly different from zero at the 95 percent level. These coefficients are all quite small in magnitude. The square of each element gives the coefficient relating the variance in each equation to its own lagged squared forecast error. Only one of the squared components of G is greater than .10.

The point estimate of ρ is 1.91—again close to the Samuelson value of 2.0. Once again, the estimate is not statistically different from zero at the 95 percent level (although it is now significant at the 80% level).

Table 5.4
CAPM estimates, ARCH, 7 assets

$$r_{t+1} = \rho \Omega_t \lambda_t + \varepsilon_{t+1}$$
$$\mathrm{Var}_t(\varepsilon_{t+1}) = \Omega_t = P'P + G\varepsilon_t\varepsilon_t'G$$

The estimate of the coefficient ρ:

1.912

(1.477)

The estimate of the upper triangular matrix P:

.03714	.03883	.03364	.04036	.03738	.02700	.03700
(.00152)	(.00189)	(.00274)	(.00213)	(.00204)	(.00191)	(.00200)
	.02050	−.00278	.01648	.01486	−.00395	.00494
	(.00077)	(.00233)	(.00150)	(.00158)	(.00160)	(.00130)
		.03541	−.00285	−.00127	.00084	.00082
		(.00116)	(.00157)	(.00124)	(.00182)	(.00128)
			.02405	.00687	−.00140	.00308
			(.00095)	(.00138)	(.00160)	(.00122)
				.02118	.00253	.00747
				(.00096)	(.00158)	(.00109)
					.02779	.00391
					(.00109)	(.00112)
						.01971
						(.00082)

The estimates of the diagonal elements of G:

.19819	.13305	.31874	.06267	−.03718	.15481	.17706
(.03953)	(.04684)	(.06162)	(.04517)	(.04355)	(.09843)	(.04668)

(standard errors in parentheses)

The next step would be to compare the performance of the ARCH model with the MVE constraints imposed (equations (1) and (8)) to that of the ARCH model with the more general Tobin model of asset demands (equations (7) and (9)). However, given the unsatisfactory performance of the ARCH-MVE model in forecasting returns, we instead first see if the ARCH model of equation (8) can be improved. Specifically, we replace equation (8) with a multivariate GARCH specification, based on the model of variances proposed by Bollerslev (1986). We have

$$\Omega_t = P'P + G\varepsilon_t\varepsilon_t'G + H\Omega_{t-1}H. \tag{10}$$

This formulation modifies equation (8) by adding the term $H\Omega_{t-1}H$, where H is diagonal, to the model of the variance.

Table 5.5
CAPM estimates, GARCH, 7 assets

$r_{t+1} = \rho\Omega_t\lambda_t + \varepsilon_{t+1}$

$\text{Var}_t(\varepsilon_{t+1}) = \Omega_t = P'P + G\varepsilon_t\varepsilon_t'G + H\Omega_{t-1}H$

The estimate of the coefficient ρ:

3.043

(1.407)

The estimate of the upper triangular matrix P:

.01075	.01314	.01078	.01227	.01039	.00716	.00824
(.00126)	(.00175)	(.00172)	(.00156)	(.00106)	(.00112)	(.00088)
	.00625	−.00006	.00424	.00338	−.00099	.00102
	(.00073)	(.00123)	(.00088)	(.00100)	(.00071)	(.00085)
		.01087	−.00050	.00011	.00046	.00084
		(.00148)	(.00072)	(.00070)	(.00077)	(.00071)
			.00679	.00134	−.00045	−.00020
			(.00110)	(.00074)	(.00053)	(.00073)
				.00519	.00057	−.00004
				(.00076)	(.00069)	(.00077)
					.00663	.00071
					(.00092)	(.00067)
						.00194
						(.00102)

The estimates of the diagonal elements of G:

.18916	.13561	.25085	.11798	.08263	.22818	.12647
(.02024)	(.02459)	(.04273)	(.02997)	(.02781)	(.03748)	(.01812)

The estimates of the diagonal elements of H:

.94234	.93786	.92592	.95185	.96264	.94444	.97392
(.01117)	(.01424)	(.01969)	(.01252)	(.00724)	(.01272)	(.00328)

(standard errors in parentheses)

There are several interesting aspects to these GARCH estimates, which are reported in table 5.5. First, since the ARCH model is nested in the GARCH model, we can test for the joint significance of the GARCH coefficients in the matrix **H**. That test statistic is chi-square (7 d.f.) and its value is 76.22. The hypothesis that H is zero is overwhelmingly rejected.

In fact, the elements of the matrix **H** are all quite large, as opposed to the elements of the **G** matrix. They all exceed .9, and are statistically significant individually. The square of these coefficients would serve as a measure of the persistence of the diagonal elements of the variance matrix.

There is evidently a great deal of persistence, which in turn implies that the risk premia on these assets are highly serially correlated.

The coefficient ρ is estimated to be 3.04, with a standard error of 1.41. If we make the additional assumptions required to obtain CAPM from MVE, ρ has the interpretation of being the coefficient of relative risk aversion. A value of 3 seems quite plausible, and does not imply the excessive risk aversion that some other asset pricing models require in order to accord reasonably well with the data (see, for example, Mehra and Prescott, 1985).

Moreover, the fact that the t-statistic $(= 2.16)$ is significantly different from zero implies that the constrained MVE model with GARCH has a statistically significant power in explaining equity returns ex ante. That is, the model is useful in predicting the excess returns on equities.

The next step is then to compare the GARCH model with the MVE constraints imposed, in the Tobin portfolio-balance model given by equation (7). We modify the model of A_t in equation (9) by adding terms relating A_t to lagged values of the variance matrix:

$$A_t = Q'Q + F\varepsilon_t\varepsilon_t'F + K\Omega_{t-1}K. \tag{11}$$

Here, the matrix K is diagonal.

Rather than estimate the full-blown unconstrained model, consisting of equations (7) and (11), we test the restrictions that the MVE system, equations (1) and (10), put on this model using a Lagrange multiplier (LM) test. The LM test is useful in this context because it requires estimation only of the constrained model by maximum likelihood. The hypothesis that A_t is proportional to Ω_t imposes forty-two constraints on the general Tobin portfolio-balance model. The test statistic is distributed chi-square (42 d.f.) and has a value of 81.90. The constrained M.V.E. model is easily rejected at the 99 percent level.[13]

We conclude that while letting the variance change over time is important in improving the explanatory power of MVE, it does not improve it enough relative to an unconstrained system of asset-demand equations.

5.5 Summary of Conclusions

Figure 5.1 provides a graphical summary of our nested hypothesis test. At the top of the figure is the most unrestricted model we consider, the unrestricted GARCH model in equations (7) and (11). At the bottom of the figure is the most restrictive model, that asset shares are of no help in explaining required returns, or equivalently, that risk aversion is zero. For

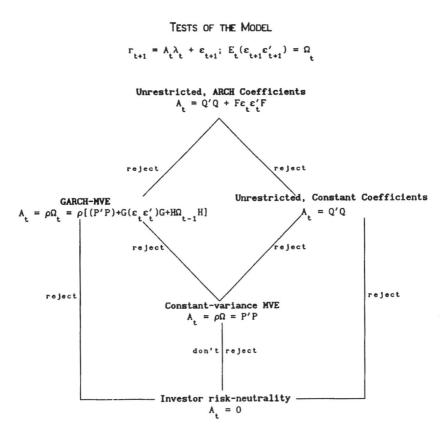

Figure 5.1
Summary of nested tests of portfolio-diversification hypotheses.

each pair of models, the line connecting them reports the results of a test of whether the lower model (the null hypothesis) can be rejected in favor of the upper model (the alternative hypothesis). It is easy to see that both of the MVE formulations—the constant-variance case and the GARCH case—are rejected when compared with any more general alternative hypothesis. This is our most important finding.

It is also apparent that allowing variances to be time-varying significantly improves the explanatory power for both the constrained and unconstrained models. In section 5.4, we reported that the ARCH–MVE model significantly outperformed the constant variance MVE model, but that the ARCH–MVE model was in turn bettered by the GARCH–MVE model. It is also the case that the unconstrained portfolio-balance model with GARCH coefficients significantly outperforms the portfolio-balance model with contant coefficients.[14]

All of the models estimated, with the exception of the constant-variance version of MVE, have significant predictive power for expected excess returns. That is, the model of investor risk neutrality ($A_t = 0$) can be rejected.[15]

In particular, it is interesting that the GARCH version of MVE has power in explaining equity returns. Allowing the covariances of asset returns to be time-varying significantly improves the predictive power of the constrained MVE model. Fama and French (1992) suggest that covariances, as reflected in a measure of an asset's unconditional beta, essentially have no power to predict returns when size is included as an explanatory variable. It seems unlikely that the predictive power in our model occurs because our betas are correlated with size, because it is unlikely that the GARCH effects are related to firm size. Though we do no formal test of our model with size included as an explanatory variable, it appears that the covariance of asset returns does help predict the mean of asset returns, as CAPM would have it.

Still, we always reject MVE in favor of the Tobin portfolio-balance model. There are several ways to rationalize this rejection. One would be that the true asset pricing model is not the CAPM, but rather a multifactor CAPM, the APT, a version of the intertemporal CAPM, or perhaps a version of the one-period CAPM that allows for more investor heterogeneity in either tastes or information sets. A second explanation for the results would rely on the Roll (1977) critique. If the stock market is very unlike the true "market" portfolio, we would not expect to find MVE, even if the CAPM holds.[16] Indeed, under this explanation, the asset shares and ARCH processes cannot be accurately observed.

A third explanation of the results would be that the residuals in equation (2) lead to poor measures of the conditional variances. If "peso problems" affect stock market returns, the estimated residuals will be biased. Imposing the MVE restrictions only compounds the problems. For example, in the five years following the stock-market boom of August 1982, the market rose at an average annual rate of 22 percent. Few would argue in retrospect that it is possible to obtain from this period ex post, valid measures of ex ante expected risk and return.

One could imagine other reasons as well why the MVE model may fail to describe the asset price movements of a given sample as well as the generalized Tobin portfolio-balance model. The CASE approach allows us to see how the MVE model, while successful in its GARCH formulation at predicting excess returns, is still not as successful as the unrestricted model.

Acknowledgments

We thank the Alfred P. Sloan Foundation and the Division of Research at Harvard Business School for research support. The views expressed here are those of the authors and do not necessarily reflect those of the Federal Reserve Bank of New York, or of the Federal Reserve System.

II

Two Monetary
Indicators: Commodity
Prices and the Interest
Rate Term Structure

Introduction to Part II

In this part of the book, we consider some economic variables that are readily observed in the marketplace, and that might be useful as sensitive early indicators of the perceived state of monetary policy. Any indicators that are available in advance of the actual inflation numbers are useful. Furthermore, market perceptions of whether monetary policy is excessively easy are an important determinant of actual inflationary pressure. In particular, the demand for goods in many sectors of the economy responds to the perceived real interest rate.

We assume here that risk premiums are not very large or variable. Thus it is assumed that the degree of investor substitutability among different assets is sufficiently great, and the speed of adjustment of asset markets is sufficiently rapid, that expected returns are equalized across assets. This is quite a different thing, however, from assuming that real interest rates are constant. That proposition would require an additional order of magnitude of greater freedom from frictions. For example, we shall see that if nominal interest rates are determined by a conventional demand-for-money equation, then the proposition that the real interest rate is constant would require that goods prices are free to adjust instantaneously. In other words, goods markets would have to adjust as quickly as asset markets. This is unlikely to be the case.

Even though the prices of most goods and services adjust only slowly, there are some that adjust as quickly as the prices of assets do. These rapidly adjusting "auction goods" include certain agricultural and mineral products. Chapter 6 exposits the "overshooting" model for determining the prices of such goods. When monetary policy is perceived to have loosened and the real interest rate has fallen, the prices of agricultural and mineral products overshoot their long-run equilibrium. Thus, high real commodity prices signal inflationary monetary policy. The theoretical model is a direct steal from Dornbusch (1976), with the price of commodities substituted for the price of foreign exchange.[1]

Chapter 7 offers an empirical application of the model, to the subject of weekly money announcements by the Federal Reserve Board in the late 1970s and early 1980s. This paper was coauthored with Gikas Hardouvelis.[2] The patterns of reaction to reports of unexpected increases in the money supply (during the week prior to the announcement) are striking: in the 1980s commodity prices tended to fall in reaction to such reports, whereas in the late 1970s they tended to rise. The conclusion is that the Fed's proclaimed commitment to a monetary rule was believed by the financial markets in the 1980s, but was not believed in the 1970s. Another conclusion is confirmation of the overshooting model. This follows from the tendency of interest rates in the 1980s to rise in response to money announcements, at the same time that the commodity prices fell.

Chapter 8 develops an analogous model for the term structure of interest rates. When monetary policy loosens and the short-term real interest rate falls, the short-term nominal interest rate falls by more than the long-term rate. In other words, the yield curve steepens. The chapter shows how to derive a measure of inflation expectations from the term structure. The framework is more subtle than simply assuming that nominal interest rates reflect expected inflation on a one-for-one basis, just as the framework of the preceding two chapters was more subtle than simply assuming that changes in nominal commodity prices reflect inflation one for one. In both case, the additional step of subtlety is the recognition that monetary policy can affect the real interest rate.

Focus on the yield curve as a monetary indicator is greater now, among some economists, than it was in the early 1980s. Its slope is said to be an indicator of future changes in the inflation rate. Chapter 9 (coauthored with Cara Lown) applies the framework of chapter 8 to the problem of forecasting year-ahead changes in the inflation rate. The framework is found to do a slightly better job than does the naive strategy of looking at the spread between the one-year interest rate and a very short-term interest rate.

Chapters 8 and 9 presuppose the expectations hypothesis of the term structure of interest rates, namely, that long-term rates equal the average of expected future short-term interest rates (or at least that the difference, a risk premium or liquidity premium, is constant or unimportant). Many economists will think that this hypothesis is inconsistent with a wide body of evidence that long-term interest rates are biased predictors of expected short-term rates. To assume that long-term rates reflect investors' forecasts is not necessarily, however, the same thing as to assume that they reflect statistically optimal forecasts. The distinction is explored in chapter 10, which is a survey of the question of whether the term structure's ability to predict interest rates is optimal, nil, or something else. It must be confessed that the original readership intended for this essay was a group of portfolio managers who might be interested in "beating the market." The motivation for including the chapter here, however, is to elaborate on the expectations hypothesis that is the foundation of the preceding two chapters.

6

Expectations and Commodity Price Dynamics: The Overshooting Model

When considering the determination of agricultural commodity prices, it is increasingly difficult to ignore the role of macroeconomic and financial factors. Schuh (1974) first pointed out the importance of these factors. But in many of the papers that followed, the exchange rate was the sole mechanism of transmission from monetary policy to agricultural commodity prices. (Besides Schuh 1974, 1976, see Chambers and Just 1981, 1982.) The importance of the exchange rate, especially clear in recent years, should not obscure the point that monetary policy has effects on the real prices of agricultural commodities even in a closed economy. An increase in the expected economy-wide inflation rate due, for example, to an increase in the money growth rate, causes investors to shift out of money and into commodities. As a consequence of the increased demand for commodities, expected future inflation has a positive effect on commodity prices in the present. On the other hand, an increase in the nominal interest rate in excess of the expected inflation rate (that is, an increase in the real interest rate) due, for example, to a decrease in the level of the money supply or to a fiscal expansion, causes investors to shift out of commodities and into bonds. It thus has a negative effect on commodity prices.

This chapter lays out a simple model which captures these effects. The model is a very direct application of the overshooting model of exchange rates developed by Dornbusch (1976). Dornbusch emphasized the distinction between the prices of foreign currencies, which are free to adjust instantly in response to changes in supply or demand, and the prices of most goods and services, which are not. In this chapter we simply substitute the prices of basic commodities for the prices of foreign currencies. We also allow for changes in the trend rate of money growth, in addition to the changes in the money supply level that were considered by Dornbusch.

Originally published in *American Journal of Agricultural Economics* 68, 2 (May 1986): 344–48. Reprinted with permission.

Bosworth and Lawrence (1982, pp. 77–87), Frankel (1984, pp. 560–63), and—the classic reference—Okun (1975) discuss the implications of, and possible reasons for, the tendency of commodities to have flexible prices much like assets while other goods and services have sticky prices. Bordo (1980) has shown empirically that the prices of raw goods indeed respond more quickly to changes in the money supply than do prices of manufactured goods.

Consider first an unanticipated one percent drop in the money supply that is expected to be permanent. In the long run we would expect all prices, manufactured goods as well as commodities, to fall by one percent in the absence of new disturbances. But in the short run manufactures prices are fixed. Thus, the reduction in the nominal money supply is a reduction in the real money supply. To equilibrate money demand, interest rates of course rise. But we have an arbitrage condition that must hold in the commodity markets: since commodities are storable, the rate of return on Treasury bills can be no greater than the expected rate of increase of commodity prices minus storage costs. This means that the spot price of commodities must fall today and must fall by more than the one percent that it is expected to fall in the long run. In other words, commodities prices must overshoot their long-run value. Only then can there be a rational market anticipation of future capital gain that is sufficient to offset the higher interest rate.

Consider now an alternative experiment: an unanticipated increase in the expected long-run rate of money growth with no change in the current actual money supply. Of course the rate of increase of all prices, manufactured goods as well as commodities, will in the long run be equal to the new rate of money growth in the absence of new disturbances. (We are taking secular growth in real income and in velocity as exogenous and, for simplicity, equal to zero.) In the long run the inflation rate will be built into a high nominal interest rate.[1] But in the short run the nominal interest rate does not rise fully to reflect the higher inflation rate. The real interest rate falls. Now recall the arbitrage condition that precludes a difference between the interest rate and the expected rate of increase of commodity prices less storage costs. At the moment of the increase in the expected rate of money growth, commodity prices must jump up above their long-run equilibrium path. Only then can there be a rational market anticipation of future depreciation (relative to the long-run inflation rate in the economy) that is sufficient to offset the lower (real) interest rate. Thus we have overshooting of equilibrium in this case as well.

We now turn to the model of determination of commodity prices that formalizes this notion of overshooting in response to changes in the expected level or growth rate of the money supply.

We define two prices, the price of basic commodities, p_c in log form, and the price of manufactures, p_m in log form. For simplicity we are aggregating all commodities together. Commodities are homogenous and storable and thus subject to the condition that their expected rate of change $\dot{p}_c^e$ minus storage costs sc, is equal to the short-term nominal interest rate i:

$$i = \dot{p}_c^e - sc. \tag{1}$$

(We assume that the risk premium is either equal to zero or is subsumed in the storage costs, which are assumed constant.) It will turn out that the level of p_c is determined by equation (1) together with the rest of the model and the assumption that expectations are rational.

Unlike the commodities, the level of manufactures prices is fixed by its own past history. It can adjust in response to excess demand only gradually over time, in accordance with an expectations-augmented Phillips curve:

$$\dot{p}_m = \pi(d - \bar{y}_m) + \mu \tag{2}$$

where d is the log of demand for manufactures, $\bar{y}_m$ is the log of potential output in that sector, and μ is a term representing the expected secular rate of inflation. Here we can think of μ as the expected rate of money growth.[2] Excess demand is in turn defined as an increasing function of the price of commodities relative to manufactures and a decreasing function of the real interest rate:[3]

$$d - \bar{y}_m = \delta(p_c - p_m) - \sigma(i - \mu - \bar{r}). \tag{3}$$

We can think of $\bar{r}$ as any constant term. But our definition of long-run equilibrium will be zero excess demand ($\bar{d} = \bar{y}_m$). Thus, in long-run equilibrium the relative price of the two commodities ($p_c - p_m$) settles down to a given value ($\bar{p}_c - \bar{p}_m$), for convenience normalized at zero in log form, and the real interest rate ($i - \mu$) settles down to the given constant value $\bar{r}$.

We substitute (3) in (2):

$$\dot{p}_m = \pi[\delta(p_c - p_m) - \sigma(i - \mu - \bar{r})] + \mu. \tag{4}$$

The last sector of our model is the money market. We assume a simple money demand equation:

$$m - p = \phi y - \lambda i \tag{5}$$

where m is the log of the nominal money supply, p is the log of the overall price level, y is the log of total output, ϕ is the elasticity of money demand with respect to output, and λ is the semielasticity of money demand with respect to the interest rate. The overall price level is an average of manufactures prices, with weight α, and commodity prices, with weight $(1 - \alpha)$:

$$p = \alpha p_m + (1 - \alpha)p_c. \tag{6}$$

Substituting in (5),

$$m - \alpha p_m - (1 - \alpha)p_c = \phi y - \lambda i. \tag{7}$$

We now consider the long-run equilibrium version of the money demand equation:

$$\bar{m} - \alpha \bar{p}_m - (1 - \alpha)\bar{p}_c = \phi \bar{y} - \lambda \bar{i},$$

$$= \phi \bar{y} - \lambda(\bar{r} + \mu) \tag{8}$$

where we have used our result that the long-run real interest rate $\bar{i} - \mu$ is $\bar{r}$.

We take the difference of the two equations (7) and (8),

$$\alpha(p_m - \bar{p}_m) + (1 - \alpha)(p_c - \bar{p}_c) = \lambda(i - \mu - \bar{r}), \tag{9}$$

where we have assumed that there are no expected changes in the money supply ($m = \bar{m}$) other than the expected rate of constant growth, and we have for simplicity here taken output to be fixed at the level of potential output:[4] $y = \bar{y}$.

Now we bring the different components of our model together. We combine equations (1) and (9):

$$\dot{p}_c^e = \frac{\alpha}{\lambda}(p_m - \bar{p}_m) + \frac{(1 - \alpha)}{\lambda}(p_c - \bar{p}_c) + \mu + \bar{r} + sc. \tag{10}$$

We also combine equations (4) and (9) (and use the normalization $\bar{p}_c - \bar{p}_m = 0$):

$$\dot{p}_m = \pi\{\delta[(p_c - \bar{p}_c) - (p_m - \bar{p}_m)] - \sigma/\lambda[\alpha(p_m - \bar{p}_m)$$

$$+ (1 - \alpha)(p_c - \bar{p}_c)]\} + \mu$$

$$= -\pi[\delta + \sigma\alpha/\lambda](p_m - \bar{p}_m) + \pi[\delta - \sigma(1 - \alpha)/\lambda](p_c - \bar{p}_c) + \mu. \tag{11}$$

We close the model by assuming that expectations are formed rationally: $\dot{p}_c = \dot{p}_c^e$. Equations (10) and (11) can be represented in matrix form:

$$\begin{bmatrix} \dot{p}_m \\ \dot{p}_c \end{bmatrix} = \begin{bmatrix} -\pi(\delta + \sigma\alpha/\lambda) & \pi(\delta - \sigma(1-\sigma)/\lambda) \\ \alpha/\lambda & (1-\alpha)/\lambda \end{bmatrix} \cdot \begin{bmatrix} (p_m - \bar{p}_m) \\ (p_c - \bar{p}_c) \end{bmatrix}$$

$$+ \begin{bmatrix} \mu \\ \mu + \bar{r} + sc \end{bmatrix}. \tag{12}$$

The characteristic roots for (12) are the solutions $-\theta_1$ and $-\theta_2$ to

$$[-\pi(\delta + \sigma\alpha/\lambda) + \theta][(1-\alpha)/\lambda + \theta] - (\alpha/\lambda)\pi[\delta - \sigma(1-\alpha)/\lambda]$$

$$= 0 \tag{13}$$

$$-\theta = [-(1-\alpha)/2\lambda + \pi(\delta + \sigma\alpha/\lambda)/2]$$

$$\pm \sqrt{[-(1-\alpha)/2\lambda + \pi(\delta + \sigma\alpha/\lambda)/2]^2 + \delta\pi/\lambda}.$$

The solutions for the expected future paths of the two prices in level form, as τ goes from 0 to ∞, are

$$p_m(\tau) - \bar{p}_m(\tau) = \exp(-\theta\tau)[p_m(0) - \bar{p}_m(0)] \text{ and}$$

$$p_c(\tau) - \bar{p}_c(\tau) = \exp(-\theta\tau)[p_c(0) - \bar{p}_c(0)] \tag{14}$$

where $-\theta$ is the negative root from (13). (We have thrown out the positive root to ensure stability.)

In rate-of-change form the equations are

$$\dot{p}_m = -\theta(p_m - \bar{p}_m) + \mu$$

$$\dot{p}_c = -\theta(p_c - \bar{p}_c) + \mu + \bar{r} + sc. \tag{15}$$

Notice that the secular inflation term in $\dot{p}_c$ exceeds that in $\dot{p}_m$ by $\bar{r} + sc$. How can commodity prices on average rise permanently relative to prices of manufactures? This is a general problem with the commodity arbitrage condition (1). There are several possibilities. First, for an agricultural commodity, $\bar{p}_c$ may gradually increase relative to $\bar{p}_m$ (monetary conditions aside) during most of the year, as long as some of the previous harvest peak is being stored, and fall discontinuously when the new harvest comes in. In anticipation, the stocks held would dwindle to zero before the harvest. Thus there is no long-run trend in $(\bar{p}_c - \bar{p}_m)$.[5] Alternatively, for a nonperishable, nonrenewable commodity such as gold or oil, there may indeed be a long-run trend in $(\bar{p}_c - \bar{p}_m)$, à la Hotelling. These explanations are examples of the sort of exogenous real factors that have been excluded from the formal monetary model. A third possibility is that sc should really be defined as storage costs plus any risk premium *minus a possible convenience yield,* this last representing flow value derived from holding inventories, either in the form of the ability to respond to unexpected developments (precautionary demand) or in the form of direct utility (e.g., in the case of gold). This is my preferred possibility.

Most of the preceding was simply to establish that the rationally expected rate of change of commodities prices takes the simple regressive form of (15). Combining with the arbitrage condition (1),

$$p_c = \bar{p}_c - \frac{1}{\theta}(i - \mu - \bar{r}). \tag{16}$$

Notice that if a change in macroeconomic policy has raised (lowered) the real interest rate $i - \mu$ above (below) its long-run equilibrium level $\bar{r}$, then commodity prices p_c have fallen below (risen above) their long-run equilibrium path $\bar{p}_c$. It is necessary that commodities be currently "undervalued" (overvalued) so that there will be an expected future rate of increase (decline) in the price sufficient to offset the high (low) real interest rate. Notice further that the higher the speed of adjustment θ, the less will p_c react. It is a slow speed of adjustment in manufactured goods markets (π, to which θ is directly related) that adds to overshooting in the commodity markets.

What determines the long-run equilibrium path $\bar{p}_c$? In the long run, relative prices are determined by exogenous real factors, so

$$\bar{p}_c = \bar{p}_m = \bar{p} = \bar{m} - \phi\bar{y} + \lambda(\bar{r} + \mu) \tag{17}$$

where we have used the long-run money demand equation (8). Substituting into (16),

$$p_c = \bar{m} - \phi\bar{y} + \lambda(\bar{r} + \mu) - \frac{1}{\theta}(i - \mu - \bar{r}). \tag{18}$$

We see that, in addition to the effect of the real interest rate just discussed, an unanticipated increase in the expected long-run rate of money growth μ increases the current $\bar{p}_c$ and therefore the current p_c. We thus have what we wanted, a model of commodity prices that shows both the negative effect of the real interest rate and the positive effect of the expected long-run money growth rate.

To quantify the immediate impact of a change in the level or growth rate of the money supply, we take the change in equation (1), then use equation

(15) to get the change in the rationally expected rate of appreciation and use equation (17) to get the change in $\bar{p}_c$:

$$\Delta i = \Delta \dot{p}_c^e$$

$$= -\theta \Delta(p_c - \bar{p}_c) + \Delta\mu$$

$$= -\theta\Delta p_c + \theta\Delta m + (1 + \theta\lambda)\Delta\mu. \tag{19}$$

Finally, we take the change in equation (5), keeping in mind that only i and p_c, not p_m, are free to respond to a monetary disturbance,

$$(1 - \alpha)\Delta p_c - \Delta m = \lambda\Delta i;$$

we combine with equation (19) to obtain our result:

$$\Delta p_c = \frac{1 + \lambda\theta}{1 - \alpha + \lambda\theta}\Delta m + \lambda\frac{1 + \lambda\theta}{1 - \alpha + \lambda\theta}\Delta\mu. \tag{20}$$

We can see that when there is a change in the level of the money supply, p_c initially overshoots its long-run equilibrium because the coefficient of Δm is greater than unity. In the limit as θ goes to infinity, the coefficient goes to unity and there is no overshooting.

A change in the rate of growth μ changes the long-run equilibrium price by $\lambda\Delta\mu$. The degree of initial overshooting is then the same as for the change in the level.

To summarize, monetary policy has an effect on real agricultural commodity prices even though they are flexible in nominal terms, because the prices of other goods are sticky. A decline in the level of the money supply in the short run raises the real interest rate, which depresses commodity prices. Commodity prices will fall more than proportionately to the change in the money supply; they overshoot their new long-run equilibrium. For commodities to be willingly held, they must be sufficiently undervalued that there is an expectation of future price increases large enough to offset the higher real interest rate. This expectation will subsequently turn out to be rational, as the general price level rises over time, and the reduction in the real money supply and its effects on the real interest rate and real commodity prices disappear over time. A decline in the rate of growth of the money supply has similar overshooting effects on commodity prices. An implication is that macroeconomic policy may be as important a source of fluctuations in agricultural prices as the traditional microeconomic factors.

Acknowledgements

Thanks are due to Julia Taylor for pointing out that the limit of θ as $\pi \rightarrow \infty$ is not infinite, as implied in an earlier version; and to Rudiger Dornbusch, Peter Berck, and Rakia Moalla-Fetini for discussion regarding the problem of commodity prices on average rising permanently relative to prices of manufactures.

7   Commodity Prices, Money Surprises, and Fed Credibility[1]

Strict monetarist theory holds that excessive money growth, or the expectation of future money growth, shows up immediately in the rapid inflation of goods prices. However, it is widely argued that, for most goods, prices are in fact sticky in the short run and reflect money growth only in the long run. If one seeks a sensitive market measure of the perceived looseness or tightness of monetary policy, one must look elsewhere than at the general price level.

Interest rates, being determined in quickly adjusting financial markets, *are* free to respond immediately to expectations regarding monetary policy. In 1981 and 1982, every Friday at 4:10 P.M. Eastern Standard Time the Federal Reserve Board would announce the money stock for the week ending nine days previously. If the announced money stock was different from what the market had been expecting, interest rates generally jumped in the same direction. Clearly they were responding to revisions of the expected future path of the money stock. But nominal interest rates are an ambiguous indicator of expectations. On the one hand, an announced increase in the money stock may be received by the market as indicating a higher Fed target money growth rate. The higher expected growth rate would then imply a higher expected inflation rate, and the rise in interest rates would then be explained as an inflation premium. On the other hand, the market may have confidence in the Fed's commitment to stick to its money growth target and may interpret the money stock change as an unintended fluctuation originating in money demand or the banking system. The market would then expect the Fed to contract the money supply in the near future to get back to the target path. The rise in nominal interest rates would be explained as an increase in *real* interest rates, without any necessary change in expected inflation.

With Gikas A. Hardouvelis, originally published in *Journal of Money, Credit and Banking* 17, 4 (November 1985, Part I): 427–38. Reprinted with permission.

Arthur Okun (1975), among others, drew a distinction between manufactured goods (and other "customer goods" and services) and basic
commodities (or "auction goods"). The former have sticky prices: they are
differentiated products traded in imperfectly competitive markets where
there is no instantaneous arbitrage to ensure perfect price flexibility.
But the latter have flexible prices: they are homogenous products traded
in competitive markets where arbitrage does ensure instantaneous price
adjustment. Commodities are more like assets in this respect. Since their
prices are free to adjust from day to day, and even from minute to minute,
they offer a potential measure of the market's perception of current
monetary policy. And, unlike interest rates, they are an unambiguous
indicator of the direction in which monetary expectations are revised. If
expectations are revised in the direction of faster future monetary growth,
and consequently higher inflation, investors to protect themselves will
instantly shift out of money and into commodities, thus driving up current
commodity prices. If expectations are revised in the direction of slower
future monetary growth, and consequently lower inflation, investors will
instantly shift into money and out of commodities, thus driving down
commodity prices.[2]

In this chapter we look at the reactions to money supply announcements
in the prices of nine commodities (gold, silver, sugar, cocoa, cattle, feeders,
wheat, soybeans, and corn), to assess the degree of market credibility that
the Fed enjoys in its commitment to money growth targets. Several papers
have looked at the reactions in bond markets, stock markets, and foreign
exchange markets, but none to our knowledge has looked at the reactions
to the weekly money announcement in commodity markets.[3]

7.1   The Theory Relating Market Prices to Monetary Expectations

In this section we develop a model of commodity prices in discrete time,
suitable for empirical testing. It is analogous to the overshooting model
that was developed in continuous time in the preceding chapter.

We begin with a simple money demand equation:

$$m_t - p_t = a_t - \lambda i_t, \tag{1}$$

where m_t and p_t are the logs of money supply and price level, respectively;
i_t is the very short-term interest rate; and a_t represents the influence of real
income and other exogenous shifts in money demand. The market in storable commodities will be subject to the condition that the expected rate of
change of commodity prices $E_t(cp_{t+1} - cp_t)$, minus storage costs sc, is equal

to the short-term interest rate:

$$E_t cp_{t+1} - cp_t - sc = i_t. \tag{2}$$

We assume that the risk premium is either zero or is subsumed in the storage costs, which are assumed constant.[4]

Imagine for a moment that the prices of all goods in the consumption basket are perfectly flexible, not just those of basic commodities, and that as a consequence the relative price of commodities and other goods is invariant with respect to monetary factors. The general price level in this hypothetical case, $\bar{p}_t$, is proportional to the price of commodities. Of course, real commodity prices are determined by weather and a whole host of other factors—most of them peculiar to the commodity in question—that probably overwhelm the monetary factors considered here. Our monetary model is intended to be nothing more than a model of how commodity prices move *relative* to their real equilibrium. As long as such real factors do not change at 4:10 P.M. on Fridays, our model will be appropriate for the study of money announcements.[5]

Equating $\bar{p}_t$ with cp_t and substituting equation (2) into equation (1) gives

$$m_t - \bar{p}_t = a_t - \lambda(E_t\bar{p}_{t+1} - \bar{p}_t - sc). \tag{3}$$

Solving for $\bar{p}_t$,

$$\bar{p}_t = \left(\frac{1}{1+\lambda}\right)(m_t - a_t) + \left(\frac{\lambda}{1+\lambda}\right)(E_t\bar{p}_{t+1} - sc). \tag{4}$$

Rational expectations imply

$$E_t\bar{p}_{t+1} = \left(\frac{1}{1+\lambda}\right)E_t(m_{t+1} - a_{t+1}) + \left(\frac{\lambda}{1+\lambda}\right)(E_t\bar{p}_{t+2} - sc). \tag{5}$$

We substitute (5) into (4), then substitute for $E_t\bar{p}_{t+2}$, and continue recursively:

$$\bar{p}_t = (1/(1+\lambda)) \sum_{\tau=0}^{\infty} (\lambda/(1+\lambda))^{\tau} E_t(m_{t+\tau} - a_{t+\tau}) - \lambda sc. \tag{6}$$

Thus $\bar{p}_t$ should be viewed as the present discounted sum of the entire expected future path of the money supply, relative to money demand.

If one believes literally the hypothesis that prices of all goods are perfectly flexible and move alike in response to monetary developments, then equation (6) can be used directly to interpret the reactions of commodity prices to monetary announcements. In this case the rationale for looking at the prices of standard commodities, as opposed to the other goods and services in the CPI, would presumably be that they are the only ones measured frequently enough to be observed before and after the weekly money announcements.

We now consider the more general case in which the prices of most goods and services are believed to be sticky in the short run. Equation (6) cannot be used to indicate the reaction of either the general price level p_t (which will be zero except to the extent that commodity prices—or other perfectly flexible prices such as those of imports—directly enter the consumption basket) or of commodity prices cp_t. We assume instead that p_t adjusts gradually over time to eliminate excess demand, and in the long run moves with $\bar{p}_t$. Then it can be shown that cp_t will react in the same direction as $\bar{p}_t$, but will move more than proportionally in the short run:

$$\Delta cp_t = \left(1 + \frac{1}{\theta\lambda}\right)\Delta\bar{p}_t \tag{7}$$

(where θ is defined as the fraction of the deviation from long-run equilibrium $\bar{p}_t$ that p_t can be expected to close each period). In the special case of instantaneous adjustment of all prices, θ is infinite and (7) reduces to the case considered above, $\Delta cp_t = \Delta\bar{p}_t$.

Equation (7) was developed by Dornbusch (1976) in a continuous-time context, to show how the spot price of foreign currency (in place of cp_t) reacted more-than-proportionally to a sudden permanent change in the money supply, that is, how the exchange rate overshot its long-run equilibrium. In the case of a sudden permanent change in m, equation (6) in difference form reduces to $\Delta\bar{p}_t = \Delta\bar{m}_t$. But the celebrated "overshooting" result is easily generalized to include any sort of discrete-time monetary process. Equations (6) and (7) are derived in Engel and Frankel (1983, 1984b) for a general money supply process, with the purpose of studying the reactions to the weekly money announcements in the spot price of the deutschemark.[6] Applying that derivation to the present problem is a simple matter of replacing the price of foreign exchange with the price of commodities.[7]

7.2   The Relationship between Revisions in Monetary Expectations and the Weekly Announcements

We combine equations (6) and (7) to obtain

$$\Delta cp_t = \left(1 + \frac{1}{\theta\lambda}\right)\Delta[(1/(1 + \lambda)) \sum_{\tau=0}^{\infty} (\lambda/(1 + \lambda))^\tau E_t(m_{t+\tau} - a_{t+\tau})]. \tag{8}$$

We assume that the Friday revision in the expected future monetary path, as represented by the term in brackets, is linearly related to the unanticipated money announcement. Mussa (1975) shows that this linear form is the rational one for market expectations to take, in a money supply process with permanent disturbances to the trend and transitory disturbances to the level. (The effects of the announcement on the estimates of the trend and level depend on the relative variances of the two kinds of disturbances.) Thus the reaction in commodity prices is linearly related to the money announcement. Before we attempt to verify this relationship empirically, several observations are in order.

The first observation is that to get a negative relationship it is not sufficient that the change in the money supply that is announced to have taken place in the preceding week be believed to be transitory. It is necessary also that the change in the money demand term a_t, which includes real income and exogenous shifts in money demand, is believed to be at least partly permanent. This point, which has been made by Engel and Frankel (1983) and Nichols, Small, and Webster (1983), is easily seen as follows. Assume that the money demand equation (1) holds instantaneously and that i_t is contemporaneously observable. Then market participants always know $m_t - a_t$. But in a week when the interest rate is observed to be low, they do not know whether that is due to a high m_t or a low a_t. They find the answer the following Friday. When they learn that the week's m_t was high, they simultaneously learn that a_t was high (or else they find out that m_t and a_t were both low). If the change in m_t is thought to be more transitory than the change in a_t, then the revision in $\bar{p}_t$, that is, the bracketed expression in equation (8), will be negative. In the polar case where the change in m_t is thought to be purely transitory, and the change in a_t to be permanent, the revision in $\bar{p}_t$ reduces to $-\lambda/(1 + \lambda)$ times the unanticipated money announcement. (In the opposite polar case in which the announced change in m_t is thought to signal a one-for-one increase in the Fed's targeted growth rate, the revision in $\bar{p}_t$ reduces to $+\lambda$ times the unanticipated money announcement.)

The second point to be emphasized is that it is only the unanticipated component of the announcement that matters. If markets are efficient, whatever component of the announcement that was predictable will already have been incorporated into the financial market prices. The market's expectations are determined not only by past money stock figures, but by official pronouncements and many other factors as well. Any attempt to measure expected money growth by, for example, an *ARIMA* model of the money stock times series, is unlikely to be accurate. Fortunately, a convenient measure of market expectations is provided by the weekly survey conducted by Money Market Services, International, of sixty individuals who make predictions of what the week's money announcement will be.[8] We measure the market reaction as the change in the futures price from the close (3:00 P.M. E.S.T.) of the market just before the Friday announcement to the open on Monday.[9] We have grounds to hope that relatively little will happen in between to affect market prices, other than the money announcement. Of course there will always be an error term consisting of neglected factors, notably other relevant news that comes out over the weekend. But these other factors will be far less important than they would be in a context of week-to-week or month-to-month changes. Furthermore, there is good reason to believe that the money surprise is predetermined, that is, that the error term arising from other weekend news will be independent of the money surprise: both the money announcement and the expectations survey are committed to paper before the Friday market close. Thus simultaneity problems vanish.

7.3 Empirical Results

In this section we discuss the results of regressing various market prices against the money surprise for the period from July 1980 to November 1982. The money surprise is defined as the logarithmic difference between the newly announced money supply and the level predicted by the survey. The latter is the change predicted by the survey plus the money supply announced one week previously. The dependent variable is the logarithmic change in the market price, times 100, to express the change in percentage terms.[10] The period was chosen to coincide with a new monetary regime: the Fed announced a change in operating procedures on October 6, 1979, and (in cooperation with the Carter Administration) imposed credit controls from March to July 1980, in an effort to get the money growth rate under control.

We begin with the results (not shown here) for bond and foreign exchange markets, territory that has also been covered in other papers.[11] A highly significant negative coefficient on the price of three-month Treasury bills illustrates once again the well-documented fact that the interest rate reacts positively to a money surprise. The dollar prices of all five foreign currencies also react negatively to the money surprise (the Swiss franc, Deutschemark, Pound sterling, Japanese yen, and Canadian dollar). The unweighted average of the percentage changes in the five currency prices also shows a significant negative reaction. These results in themselves constitute evidence that the market expects the Fed to correct deviations

Table 7.1
Reactions of commodity prices to money surprises: 1980–82

Variable	Coefficient	t-statistic	p-value[a]	D–W	R^2
Corn	−0.0695	−0.35	.727	2.11	0.1%
Feeders	−0.2533	−1.90	.060	2.28	2.9%
Gold	−0.5254	−1.60	.122	2.11	2.1%
Live Cattle	−0.2145	−1.12	.265	2.09	1.0%
Soybeans	−0.1566	−0.75	.455	2.12	0.5%
Wheat	−0.1366	−0.63	.530	2.14	0.3%
Cocoa	−0.5039	−0.74	.461	1.87	0.5%
Silver	−0.6330	−1.52	.131	2.23	1.9%
Sugar	−1.1806	−3.25	.001	1.97	8.0%
Stacked	−0.4082	−3.57	.0009	2.01	1.1%

Notes: Dependent variables: Percentage change in market price from close Friday to open Monday.
Independent variable: Percentage difference between the actual and expected level of the money supply announced each Friday.
Sample: July 7, 1980–November 5, 1982 (123 observations).
a. The one-tailed probability of finding a t-statistic this large or larger.

from its money growth rate target; the anticipation of future money contraction reduces the price of foreign exchange, or raises the value of the dollar.

The new results are those for the nine commodities, reported in table 7.1. In each case the reaction is again negative. Only the reaction of sugar is significant at the 95 percent level, though feeders are significant at the 90 percent level. An average (not shown here) of the changes in all nine commodity prices is highly significant. Again the result suggests that positive money growth surprises cause expectations of future money growth reductions.

To get more efficient estimates, we stacked the observations for different commodities in a single regression. In other words, we constrained the reaction coefficients to be the same. This constraint comes out of the theory. Equation (7) implies that a change in monetary expectations causes commodity prices to react to an extent determined only by θ, the speed of adjustment of the sticky manufacture prices, and by λ, the semielasticity of the money demand with respect to the interest rate—not by any characteristic of the individual commodities. Only if some commodity prices were sticky, or if a change in the steady-state inflation rate implied a change in the relative price of commodities in the long-run equilibrium, that is, if money were nonneutral even in the long run, would expected inflation have more effect on some commodity prices than on others.[12]

The same constraint applies to the effects on foreign exchange prices. The original version of this article reported a regression for all five exchange rates stacked. The joint negative reaction was highly significant. The last row in table 7.1 reports the regression for all nine commodities stacked.[13] The joint negative reaction is again highly significant. Overall the evidence strongly supports the proposition that announcements of high money growth induce market expectations of future contractions.

It is of some interest to see what happens Monday *after* the opening. If the commodity prices were to continue to move in the same direction during the course of trading on Monday, this would constitute evidence of less-than-perfect efficiency in the market and an opportunity for speculative profits. A sharp movement in the opposite direction would constitute evidence of the same.[14] The coefficients reported in the original paper showed little systematic pattern. When the total reactions from the close of the market on Friday to the close on Monday were computed, the extra noise from the within-Monday movements reduced the significance levels of most of the coefficients though their signs were still all negative. Even the stacked regressions for the foreign currencies and a subset of commodities were no longer significant at the 95 percent level. This illustrates the importance of observing the market prices as close as possible, before and after, to the Friday money announcements, in order to minimize noise.

It is also of interest to see how the markets reacted to money growth surprises in earlier periods. The *Wall Street Journal* only began reporting the necessary market prices for agricultural commodities in November 1978. Table 7.2 shows the reactions of commodity prices to the money surprises for the period before the Fed's change in operating procedures on October 6, 1979. (The money supply announcements were made on Thursday afternoons during this period. The market reactions are reported from Thursday close to Friday open.) This was, of course, a period dominated by fears of inflation. As one might expect, a majority of the commodities now react *positively* to the money surprises, though only silver is significant at the 95 percent level.

On the whole, the evidence suggests that the market during this period did not have faith in the Fed's commitment to achieve its preannounced yearly money growth targets. Unanticipated announcements of increases in the money supply were interpreted as indicating more of the same in the future. However, the evidence is not as strong as it was for the contrary finding during the later period.

Table 7.2
Reactions of commodity prices to money surprises: 1978–79

Variable	Coefficient	t-statistic	p-value[a]	D–W	R^2
Corn	−0.2258	−0.72	.443	2.23	1.1%
Feeders	−0.1684	−0.74	.463	2.04	1.2%
Gold	1.5080	1.33	.190	2.17	3.7%
Live Cattle	0.0463	0.14	.989	2.09	0.0%
Silver	0.4192	2.04	.047	1.88	8.3%
Soybeans	0.4342	0.86	.394	2.19	1.6%
Sugar	−0.5123	−1.38	.174	1.72	4.0%
Wheat	−0.0803	−0.26	.796	2.72	0.1%
Cocoa	0.4915	1.66	.104	1.94	5.7%
Stacked	0.2125	1.25	.211	1.97	0.4%

Notes: Dependent variables: Percentage change in market price from close Thursday to open Friday.
Independent variable: Percentage difference between the actual and expected level of the money supply announced each Thursday.
Sample: November 3, 1978–October 4, 1979 (48 observations).
a. The one-tailed probability of finding a t-statistic this large or larger.

The period of regime transition began October 6, 1979, and ended in July 1980 with the removal of the last of the credit controls.[15] Reactions of the foreign exchange and commodities markets during this transition period, as one might expect, show no clear sign pattern and no coefficients are significant (reported in Frankel and Hardouvelis 1983).

To sum up, there is a contrast between the pre-October 1979 results and post-July 1980 results. The switch from positive to negative in the majority of the coefficients tends to support the proposition that commodity (and foreign exchange) prices are indicators of Fed credibility.

7.4   Conclusions

The reactions of the various markets to the money announcements can be used for two distinct purposes: (1) they support the proposition that during the 1980–82 period, the market had confidence in the Fed's commitment to correct deviations from money growth rate targets; and (2) they support the proposition that movements in the nominal interest rate during this period were primarily movements in the real interest rate rather than the expected inflation rate, as in the overshooting model cited in section 7.1.

The reactions in the prices of foreign exchange and commodities support the first proposition, whether one believes in an overshooting model or not. If one believes that all prices are perfectly flexible, even those of manufactured goods, then monetary policy should be instantly reflected in all prices. If one believes that some prices are sticky in the short run, then monetary prices should be reflected in the prices of foreign exchange and commodities that much more. Either way, the negative reaction of commodity prices to positive money announcements, documented in table 7.1, indicates that during the 1980–82 period the market expected the Fed to correct deviations from its targets. Similarly the positive reaction before October 1979, documented in table 7.2, indicates that the market was more inclined to attribute money surprises to revisions in the Fed's target rate of growth during this period.

The second proposition above follows from the first proposition *together* with the observed reactions of interest rates to the money announcements. During the 1980–82 period, interest rates reacted positively to money announcements, as documented in many other papers and in the original version of this article (in the form of a negative reaction of the price of Treasury bills). If one did not know about the reactions of the foreign exchange and commodity markets, one could conceivably interpret the positive reactions in the nominal interest rate as increases in the expected rates of money growth and inflation. But given our finding that the market has confidence in the Fed's commitment to stick to its money growth rate target during this period, that avenue is not open. If increases in the expected inflation rate are ruled out as an explanation for increases in the nominal interest rates, as a matter of definition that leaves only increases in the real interest rate. Hence the second proposition. The overshooting model of section 7.1 offers a specific explanation for the changes in the real interest rates. When the general price level is not free to respond fully to market expectations, a contraction in the nominal money supply is a contraction in the real money supply. It has the real effects of tightened liquidity, in particular an increase in the real interest rate and overshooting of commodity prices. Recall that within the framework of equation (7), the model in which there is no variation in the real interest rate is the special case in which θ, the speed of adjustment of sticky goods prices, is infinite. Engel and Frankel (1983, 1984b) explain at greater length how the observation that interest rates and foreign exchange prices (or commodity prices) react to money announcements in opposite directions constitutes a rejection of the special case of flexible prices in favor of the more general sticky price model.

Acknowledgements

We thank Richard Just and Gordon Rausser for providing commodity data, Money Market Services, International, for providing their survey data on money stock expectations, Andreas Fisher for research assistance, Dominique van der Mensbrugghe for programming assistance, and Rudiger Dornbusch, Bent Hansen, Richard Meese, William Poole, Ken Rosen, and Robert Shiller for useful discussion and comments.

8

A Technique for Extracting a Measure of Expected Inflation from the Interest Rate Term Structure

Introduction

Few macroeconomic variables are as crucial to so many policy controversies, and yet as hard to measure in empirical work, as the expected inflation rate. Each of the proxies that are often used for the expected inflation rate has serious drawbacks. Public opinion survey data are not based on observed economic behavior. Future values of the actual inflation rate differ from the expected inflation rate by large expectational errors, even though they have mean zero if expectations are rational. Lagged values of the actual inflation rate, or other relevant macroeconomic variables, cannot hope to capture all the information that enters into the formation of expectations—for example, the latest government announcements of money growth.

One proxy sometimes used for the expected inflation rate is the nominal interest rate (minus a constant) under the hypothesis that the real rate of interest is constant. This proxy has the advantages that it is based on observed economic behavior and that it is capable of capturing the latest information available in financial markets. The disadvantage lies in the questionableness of the hypothesis that the real rate of interest is literally constant.

Much has been written on both sides of this issue. The controversy began when Fama (1975) accepted the joint hypothesis that the real rate of interest was constant and that expected inflation was an unbiased predictor of actual inflation. Fama's tests were subsequently attacked by Hess and Bicksler (1975), Joines (1977), and Nelson and Schwert (1977).[1]

Originally published in *Review of Economics and Statistics* 64, 1 (February 1982): 135–40. Reprinted with permission. Appears here with a new appendix.

Most economists probably would not agree with the claim that the real rate of interest is literally constant in the short run.[2] But a majority perhaps would agree that, in the absence of new disturbances (such as unexpected monetary expansions), the expected inflation rate will become increasingly incorporated into the nominal interest rate with the passage of time. Since long-term interest rates are known to reflect expected future short-term interest rates, an important implication is that long-term interest rates reflect the expected inflation rate more fully than do short-term interest rates. This principle is recognized in financial markets. For example, when President Carter announced a more restrictive monetary policy in late 1978, in an effort to combat inflation and the depreciation of the dollar, the long-term interest rate fell below the short-term interest rate for the first time in several years. The *Wall Street Journal* characterized the reaction in bond markets as follows:

Although analysts painted a bleak outlook for short-term interest rates, many said the dollar-defense program could help to lower longer-term bond yields. That's because investors might feel more convinced the government is determined to fight inflation. Indeed, prices on bonds jumped sharply yesterday, pushing yields down.[3]

This chapter suggests a precise technique for extracting a measure of expected inflation from the term structure of interest rates. Briefly, the procedure is as follows. For a given term of maturity, the interest rate can be regarded as a weighted average of an instantaneously short-term interest rate that is sensitive to the current tightness of monetary policy, and an infinitely long-term interest rate that reflects only the expected inflation rate. The weights in the average depend, first, on the speed with which the system converges to the steady-state inflation rate (in expectation), and, second, on the length of maturity of the bond in question. At any point in time, we can look at two maturities and extrapolate to infer the infinitely long-term interest rate that reflects only the expected inflation rate. The result is a time series that represents the market's expected inflation rate, up to a constant.

8.1 Theory

We assume a world in which at every point there exists a commonly held expectation, π^e, as to what the long-run inflation rate is. The natural interpretation is that π^e is the public's best guess as to the central bank's current target rate of monetary growth, corrected for any trend in real income or velocity.[4] It is this π^e that we try to measure.

We do not assume that the real rate of interest is constant in the short run. But we do assume that, in the absence of future disturbances, the real rate of interest will converge to a constant in the long run. Specifically, the public, at time 0, expects the gap to be closed at a certain rate δ:

$$di_t/dt = -\delta(i_t - \pi_0^e - \bar{r}), \tag{1}$$

where i_t is the (instantaneously) short-term interest rate, π_0^e is the long-run inflation rate expected at time 0, and $\bar{r}$ is the long-run real interest rate, all three of which are not directly observable.

The argument is that adjustment takes time because goods prices are sticky. For example, when an increase in the expected rate of future monetary growth raises the expected rate of inflation, if the short-term interest rate were to rise instantly, real money demand would fall, which is not possible when the price level and thus the real money supply are fixed. Over time, however, prices rise in response to excess goods demand; the real money supply is free to fall and, thus, the short-term interest rate is free to rise. A model formalizing this argument is specified in the appendix to this chapter. It is demonstrated in this model that rational expectations will take precisely the form of (1).[5]

Equation (1) implies that, at time 0, the public expects the short-term interest rate at time t to be a weighted average of the long-run interest rate ($\pi_0^e + \bar{r}$) and the current short-term interest rate (i_0):

$$i_t = (1 - \exp(-\delta t))(\pi_0^e + \bar{r}) + (\exp(-\delta t))i_0. \tag{2}$$

The entire analysis that follows hinges on equation (2), representing the tendency of the interest rate to approach $\pi_0^e + \bar{r}$ as time passes, in the absence of new disturbances. It cannot be tested empirically, because the expected inflation rate cannot be directly observed. It must be accepted as plausible, based on the argument that is made above and formalized in the appendix.

We need only one additional assumption: i_0^τ, defined as the interest rate on τ-maturity bonds (issued at time 0), is the average of the expected instantaneously short-term interest rates between time 0 and time τ, plus a possible constant liquidity premium term:[6]

$$i_0^\tau = \frac{1}{\tau} \int_0^\tau i_t \, dt + k_\tau. \tag{3}$$

The liquidity premium k_τ may or may not be a smoothly rising function of τ.[7]

By integrating (2), we find that the τ-maturity can be represented as another weighted average:

$$i_0^\tau = (1 - \omega_\tau)(\pi_0^e + \bar{r}) + (\omega_\tau)(i_0) + k_\tau, \tag{4}$$

where the weights are given by $\omega_\tau = [1 - \exp(-\delta\tau)]/\delta\tau$.

For any given point in time, we can obtain the Treasury bill rate for two (or more) maturities, $\tau 1$ and $\tau 2$ (say, 3 months and 12 months). Thus, for any given point in time, we have two (or more) equations like (4), which we could solve for the two unknowns, π^e and i (up to constants),[8] if only we knew the parameter δ, and thus the weights $\omega_{\tau 1}$ and $\omega_{\tau 2}$. The reduced-form equations for π^e and i (up to constants) in terms of the observable long-term and short-term interest rates are

$$\pi^e = \frac{\omega_{\tau 1}(i^{\tau 2} - k_{\tau 2}) - \omega_{\tau 2}(i^{\tau 1} - k_{\tau 1})}{\omega_{\tau 1} - \omega_{\tau 2}} - \bar{r}$$

$$i = \frac{(\omega_{\tau 1} - 1)(i^{\tau 2} - k_{\tau 2}) - (\omega_{\tau 2} - 1)(i^{\tau 1} - k_{\tau 1})}{\omega_{\tau 1} - \omega_{\tau 2}}. \tag{5}$$

For example, if $\tau 2$ were sufficiently large, $\omega_{\tau 2}$ would be close to zero and π^e would be close to $i^{\tau 2} - k_{\tau 2} - \bar{r}$.

The relationship is illustrated schematically in figure 9.1 (in the next chapter). At any point in time, the short-term and long-term nominal interest rates, $i^{\tau 1}$ and $i^{\tau 2}$, are each weighted averages of i and $\pi^e + \bar{r}$, with the long-term rate giving greater weight to $\pi^e + \bar{r}$. We can extrapolate from the observed $i^{\tau 1}$ and $i^{\tau 2}$ to infer the value of $\pi^e + \bar{r}$. (For simplicity, the figure omits the possible liquidity premium.)

Thus, if we knew the parameter δ, we would know the weights, and we could compute the series for the right-hand sides of equation (5) and thus the series for π^e and i. On the other hand, if we knew the series for π^e and i, and we were willing to assume that the public's estimate of δ is equal to the true value of δ (i.e., expectations are rational), we could estimate the parameter δ as follows. We would regress the "real interest rate" $i - \pi^e$ against its own lagged value to ascertain the speed with which the system tends to equilibrium.[9] Equation (1) implies that the coefficient in such a regression, β, is equal to $\exp(-\delta/n)$, where n is the number of observations per year (or $1/n$ is the length of the observation interval).

It might appear that we are trapped, unable to estimate the parameter δ without the series i and π^e, and unable to estimate the series i and π^e without the parameter δ. But there is an easy solutuion. From equation (5), the reduced form for the real interest rate is[10]

$$i - \pi^e = \bar{r} + \frac{(i^{\tau 1} - k_{\tau 1}) - (i^{\tau 2} - k_{\tau 2})}{\omega_{\tau 1} - \omega_{\tau 2}}. \tag{6}$$

If we are interested only in regressing this expression against its own lagged value, we will get the same estimate for the coefficient regardless of the weights $\omega_{\tau 1}$ and $\omega_{\tau 2}$. Thus, we can estimate β simply by regressing the interest rate spread $i^{\tau 1} - i^{\tau 2}$ against its own lagged value.

8.2 Estimation

Table 8.1 reports the estimates of β from such regressions, along with the implied values for δ, $\omega_{\tau 1}$, and $\omega_{\tau 2}$. Each regression represents a different pair of terms of maturity. If the theory held perfectly, the estimates of β would be the same.[11] The discussion will concentrate on the three-month and ten-year interest rates, as they constitute the greatest spread.

The estimates of β and δ are interesting statistics in their own right. They can be interpreted as the speed (in discrete time and continuous time, respectively) with which the macroeconomic system adjusts to long-run equilibrium. For example, an estimate of $\beta = 0.964$ indicates that when a monetary or other disturbance raises the short-term interest rate above its long-run level, 96.4 percent of the effect remains one month later and 64.1 percent (which is 0.964^{12}) remains one year later.

However, the primary purpose for estimating β and δ was as a means of estimating $\omega_{\tau 1}$ and $\omega_{\tau 2}$ and computing a time series for $\hat{\pi}$. From equation (5), we have

$$\pi^e + \bar{r} + \frac{\omega_{\tau 1} k_{\tau 2} - \omega_{\tau 2} k_{\tau 1}}{\omega_{\tau 1} - \omega_{\tau 2}} = \frac{\omega_{\tau 1} i^{\tau 2} - \omega_{\tau 2} i^{\tau 1}}{\omega_{\tau 1} - \omega_{\tau 2}}. \tag{5'}$$

Now, computing π^e up to a constant is a simple matter of computing the appropriate linear combination of $i^{\tau 2}$ and $i^{\tau 1}$. Notice that the weights in this linear combination add up to unity, but that the weight on $i^{\tau 1}$ is negative, representing the fact that we are extrapolating beyond $\tau 2$.

The resulting time series, the main end product of this chapter, appears as appendix 2 in the original version of this paper. The interest rates used are those on securities of maturity three months and ten years. (This series is highly correlated with the two based on other maturities.) The estimate of expected inflation rises fairly steadily from 1959 to 1979.

As can be seen from equation (5'), the constant by which this time series differs from π^e has two components: the long-run real rate of interest, $\bar{r}$, and a term representing the liquidity premium spread, which may be very small.

Table 8.1
Estimation of speed of adjustment
$(i_t^{\tau 2} - i_t^{\tau 1}) = \alpha + \beta(i_{t-1}^{\tau 2} - i_{t-1}^{\tau 1}) + u_t$

Terms of maturity		Regression results				$\hat{\delta} = -12 \log \hat{\beta}$	Implied parameter estimates	
$\tau 1$	$\tau 2$	$\hat{\alpha}$	$\hat{\beta}$	R^2	D.W.		$\hat{\omega}_{\tau 1} = -\dfrac{1-\beta^{\tau 1}}{\tau 1 \log \beta}$	$\hat{\omega}_{\tau 2} = -\dfrac{1-\beta^{\tau 2}}{\tau 2 \log \beta}$
3 mo.	10 yr.	.002 (.0002)	.9636 (.0186)	.92	1.78	0.4444	.9845	.2224
3 mo.	12 mo.	.0008 (.0002)	.8452 (.0341)	.72	1.92	2.0178	.7853	.4297
1 yr.	10 yr.	.0001 (.0001)	.9628 (.1899)	.92	1.46	0.4554	.8033	.2173

Note: $i^\tau = \log(1 + \text{yield}$ on U.S. Treasury securities of term τ months). Estimated standard errors are reported in parentheses. The technique is ordinary least-squares. The sample is August 1958–December 1978, monthly.

The only obvious way to estimate this constant is to assume that public expectations of inflation were, on average, correct during this period, and to compute the constant as the average of the difference between the actual inflation rate and the value of the time series in Appendix 2 of the original paper. A drawback of this procedure is that the public may have underestimated the actual inflation rate during the latter part of this period. The mean of the difference over the period was 0.0132. Since this number seems too low to be the sum of the long-run real interest rate and a liquidity premium term, it suggests that the market, on average, did indeed underpredict the inflation rate.[13] However, the decision whether or not to subtract 0.0132 off to get our final estimate of the time series is not a crucial decision, because many purposes to which one would want to put the series require only that it be accurate up to a constant.

One obvious and immediate application for the measure of expected inflation is to use it to test the hypothesis of rational expectations (jointly with the hypothesis that the model is valid, i.e., that the technique for extracting expected inflation from the term structure is an accurate one). Such tests showed significant autocorrelation of prediction errors, rejecting the null hypothesis. The results are not reported, in the interest of brevity.

8.3 A Comparison with Survey Data

Another proxy that is sometimes used for the expected inflation rate is survey data, such as the semiannual Livingston survey of price expectations.[14] One possible way of evaluating different proxies is to compare their ability to predict actual inflation, though this procedure assumes a degree of rationality in expectations.

Table 8.2 reports the mean squared prediction error of several alternative proxies. Because the new term structure measure is only meaningful up to a constant term, its mean squared prediction error is calculated as the variance of its prediction error; in other words, it is normalized on the mean actual inflation rate. If we compare this number (4.716×10^{-4} for the three-month to ten-year spread) to the mean squared error of the Livingston survey data (7.671×10^{-4}), we find that the survey data do a much worse job of predicting the one-year inflation rate.[15] However, one might argue that, for purposes of in-sample prediction of inflation, it is not a fair comparison to give the new measure a degree of freedom without also giving the survey data a degree of freedom. This suggests comparing 4.716×10^{-4} with the *variance* of the survey data prediction errors,

Table 8.2
Ability of expected inflation proxies to predict inflation

Expected inflation proxy	One-year inflation rate		Five-year inflation rate	
	Mean squared error $\times 10^4$	Number of observations	Mean squared error $\times 10^4$	Number of observations
Measure extracted from term structure (normalized on mean inflation rate) $\tau 1 = 3$ months; $\tau 2 = 10$ years	4.716	225	3.261	177
Livingston price expectations survey data:				
Normalized on mean inflation rate	5.009	37	2.813	29
Not normalized	7.671		12.301	
Three-month Treasury bill yield (normalized on mean inflation rate)	3.634	225	3.399	177

5.008×10^{-4}. The new measure still does a better job than the survey data—but only slightly.

Since the term structure measure is constructed to reflect the long-term inflation rate, not the one-year inflation rate, table 8.2 also reports mean squared errors using the five-year inflation rate.[16] (The last five years of observations must be sacrificed to do this.) The difference between the mean squared error of the term structure measure and that of the non-normalized survey data is even greater than before, but the term structure measure no longer does as well as the normalized survey data.

Table 8.2 also reports the mean squared error of the three-month Treasury bill yield, which does better at predicting one-year inflation than the term structure measure but does worse at predicting five-year inflation.

8.4 Summary

To summarize the procedure of this chapter, a plausible model—in which monetary policy can create short-run variations in the real interest rate due to sticky prices, but in which the real interest rate tends to a constant in the long run—was shown to imply that the nominal interest rate for a given term of maturity can be expressed as a weighted average of the instantaneously short-term interest rate and the infinitely long-term interest rate that fully reflects the expected long-run inflation rate. The weights depend on a parameter representing the speed of adjustment of the system, which is estimated. Thus, the interest rates for any two maturities can be extrapolated to infer the expected long-run inflation rate. A comparison of the resulting time series with the time series of actual inflation suggests that the market underestimated inflation in the 1970s. However, the new measure of expected inflation does a slightly better job of predicting actual inflation, in terms of mean squared error, than do survey data.

Appendix 8A: A Simple Macroeconomic Model of Adjustment in the Price Level and Interest Rate

Equation (1) embodies the proposition that the real interest rate has a tendency to adjust over time toward a constant. This proposition would follow from a wide variety of macroeconomic models that included a money-demand equation and price-adjustment equation. This appendix specifies one such model, of textbook familiarity, demonstrating that the rationally expected path of the nominal interest rate is of the same form as equation (1). We need to assume three equations:

$$y - \bar{y} = -\gamma(i - \pi^e - r), \tag{A.1}$$

$$m - p = \phi y - \lambda i, \tag{A.2}$$

$$\frac{dp}{dt} = \rho(y - \bar{y}) + \pi^e, \tag{A.3}$$

where y is the log of output, $\bar{y}$ is the log of normal or potential output, i is the short-term nominal interest rate, π^e is the expected long-run inflation rate, m is the log of the money supply, and p is the log of the price level.

  Equation (A.1) is an IS relationship; it says that the output gap is related to the current real interest rate through investment demand.[17] We note immediately that, in the long run, when $y = \bar{y}$, we have

$$\bar{i} = \pi^e + r.$$

  Equation (A.2) is an LM relationship; it says that real money demand depends positively on income, with an elasticity of ϕ, and negatively on the interest rate, with a semielasticity of λ. In the long run, $dm/dt = dp/dt = \pi$.

  Equation (A.3) is a supply relationship; it says that the rate of price change is given by the sum of an excess-demand term and the expected steady-state inflation rate.

Differentiating equation (A.2), we find

$$\frac{dm}{dt} - \frac{dp}{dt} = \frac{\phi\, dy}{dt} - \frac{\lambda\, di}{dt}. \tag{A.2'}$$

Differentiating equation (A.1), we have

$$\frac{dy}{dt} = -\gamma\frac{di}{dt}. \tag{A.1'}$$

We substitute equations (A.1') and (A.3) into equation (A.2'):

$$\pi - [\rho(y - \bar{y}) + \pi^e] = -(\phi\gamma + \lambda)\frac{di}{dt}.$$

Finally, we substitute in equation (A.1), assume perfect foresight ($\pi = \pi^e$), and solve for the expected rate of change of the interest rate:

$$\frac{di}{dt} = -\delta(i - \pi^e - r), \tag{1}$$

where $\delta \equiv \rho\gamma/(\phi\gamma + \lambda)$. This is equation (1) in the text.

The foregoing perfect-foresight formulation can be transformed to a stochastic one by introducing future disturbances to the level (m) and trend (π) of the money supply. As long as these disturbances have expectation zero, equation (1) will describe the rationally expected path of i. We could even allow for purely transitory disturbances in m.

Acknowledgments

I would like to thank Matthew Canzoneri, Stanley Fischer, and Dale Henderson for comments on Federal Reserve Board International Finance Discussion Paper No. 148, of which this chapter is a condensed version. I would also like to thank the Institute of Business and Economic Research of the University of California, Berkeley, for research support.

9

An Indicator of Future Inflation Extracted from the Steepness of the Interest Rate Yield Curve along Its Entire Length

The idea that the slope of the term structure of interest rates can be used as an indicator of whether monetary policy is currently tight or loose is not new. But the idea has generated some new research since 1988 when Manuel Johnson, then vice-governor of the Federal Reserve System, announced that the term structure was one of three indicators that he thought might be useful to gauge whether monetary policy was expansionary or not.[1] Frederic Mishkin (1988, 1990a, 1990b, 1990c, 1991, 1992), in particular, has written on this subject.

We learn two things from Mishkin's results. Rejecting the null hypothesis that the coefficient on the term spread is zero, we learn that the term structure has explanatory power for predicting changes in inflation. At the same time, rejecting the null hypothesis that the coefficient is one in the same equation, we learn that the real interest rate is not constant. Thus we would like to proceed with a model of the term structure that does *not* require the real interest rate to be constant. But Mishkin's equation is not suitable, derived as it is from the assumption that the real interest rate is constant.[2] This chapter derives the appropriate alternative hypothesis to both of the null hypotheses rejected by Mishkin, appropriate, at least, for thinking about the term structure when monetary policy is thought to affect the real interest rate.

The intuitive argument is the same as in the preceding chapter: when short-term interest rates are high relative to longer-term interest rates (as in an "inverted yield curve"), monetary policy is tight, and the inflation rate will eventually fall. The reason for looking at the slope of the yield curve (rather than, for example, at just the one-year interest rate, as an indicator of expected one-year inflation) is that an inverted yield curve means that

---

With Cara Lown, originally published in *Quarterly Journal of Economics* 109, 2 (May 1994): 517–30. Reprinted with permission.

monetary policy is tight in *real* terms—namely, that the *real* interest rate is high and that this will have a negative effect on the real demand for goods. The role of the short-term interest rate is not simply to reflect expected inflation over the short term in the same way that the long-term interest rate reflects expected inflation over the long term. Rather, the long-term interest rate is thought to reflect expected inflation more *fully* than does the short-term interest rate. Thus the slope of the yield curve can be thought of as an inverse indicator of the real interest rate. A more expansionary monetary policy, for example, is widely thought of as lowering short-term real interest rates, even if long-term interest rates simultaneously rise due to an increase in expected inflation. This argument is formalized below.

The chapter shows that the Mishkin approach, while a useful first step, is an unnecessarily restrictive way of inferring the expected future path of inflation from the term structure of interest rates. It shows that the appropriate indicator of expected inflation can make use of the entire length of the yield curve, in particular by estimating the steepness of a specific nonlinear transformation of the curve, rather than being restricted to a spread between two points. The resulting indicator, besides having a theoretical foundation more consonant with reality, does a better job of predicting the inflation rate over the period 1950–91.

9.1   A First Illustration

Let π^{12} be the inflation rate over the next twelve months, π^3 be the inflation rate over the next three months, i^{12} be the twelve-month interest rate and i^3 be the three-month interest rate. Mishkin (1988, 1990a, 1990c, 1991) runs the following regression:

$$(\pi^{12} - \pi^3) = a + b(i^{12} - i^3) + u. \tag{1}$$

He finds two principal results. First, the coefficient b is significantly greater than zero, showing that the term structure does contain information useful for predicting the path of the future inflation rate. Second, b is significantly less than 1. This is a rejection of the null hypothesis that real interest rates are constant: if the twelve-month $(i^{12} - E\pi^{12})$ and three-month $(i^3 - E\pi^3)$ real interest rates were both constant (where E is used to identify the *expected* inflation rate), then b should equal 1.

The statistical rejection of the hypothesis that the real interest rate is constant is consistent with current conventional wisdom, and with the earlier results of Mishkin (1981). But then we are left with no alternative hypothesis, no theoretical framework with which to interpret equation (1) for the relevant case where b is greater than 0 while less than 1. Fortunately, we already have the simple framework developed in chapter 8 for thinking about the slope of the term structure, which allows for variation in the real interest rate.

Only two assumptions are required by this framework: (1) The long-term interest rate reflects expected future short-term interest rates (up to a possible risk premium or liquidity term that does not vary over time).[3] (2) Market participants expect that the steady-state inflation rate will be increasingly incorporated into the nominal interest rate with the passage of time (in the absence of new disturbances such as unexpected changes in monetary policy).[4] This second assumption will hold, for example, if short-run variation in the real interest rate arises because the price level is sticky and, consequently, changes in the nominal money supply have real effects in the short run. The two assumptions together imply that the long-term interest rate reflects expected inflation more fully than does the short-term interest rate. This in turn implies that the slope of the term structure can be used to extract indicators of the real interest rate, the current tightness of monetary policy, and the expected future path of the inflation rate.

The purpose of this chapter is not solely to present the appropriate framework for thinking about the term-structure indicator of monetary ease. The appropriate framework has important practical consequences. It suggests a way of extracting a measure of expected future inflation that is superior to Mishkin's equation (1), regardless of whether his coefficient b in that equation is constrained to 1. The suggested technique makes use of points all along the yield curve, rather than restricting the analysis to the two points of maturity that correspond to the maturity of inflation in which we are interested.

The first part of table 9.1 offers a simple first-pass illustration, for the sample period 1960–91, of the benefits of making use of the extremities of the yield curve, even when the goal is only to forecast the path of inflation over the coming year as in several articles by Mishkin (1990a, 1990c, 1991). As in those papers, the dependent variable is the spread in the future inflation rates, $(\pi^{12} - \pi^3)$. The first column shows the Mishkin approach: the explanatory variable is the interest rate spread $(i^{12} - i^3)$, which corresponds precisely to the maturities of the inflation rates, as we would want if our theoretical rationale were the hypothesis that real interest rates were constant. The finding is the same as in Mishkin: the coefficient on the term spread is positive and statistically significant. In other words, the term spread does contain information useful for predicting the path of inflation.

Table 9.1
Forecasting the inflation spread (12 month–3 month)

Monthly Observations, January 1960–November 1991
$(\pi^{12} - \pi^{3})_{t} = a + b(yield\ curve\ measure) + u_{t}$

Interest rates expressed in log form. In estimating B1, each interest rate is first expressed as a deviation from the sample mean for its term, as an estimate of the liquidity premium, k_{r}.

Measure of slope of yield curve	Mishkin approach 12-month minus 3-month spread	Alternative approach	
		5-year minus fed funds spread	Nonlinear measure of steepness B1
Jan. 1960–Nov. 1991			
Constant term	−0.32	−0.09	0.14
	(−1.51)	(−0.62)	(0.90)
Coefficient of slope	76.15	29.91	24.71
	(2.25)	(3.03)	(2.98)
R^{2}	.035	.065	.065
adjusted R^{2}	.032	.062	.062
Jan. 1960–Sept. 1979			
Constant term	0.06	0.16	0.26
	(0.21)	(0.84)	(1.38)
Coefficient of slope	44.13	21.40	11.53
	(0.87)	(1.64)	(0.96)
R^{2}	.010	.038	.014
adjusted R^{2}	.005	.033	.009
Oct. 1979–Nov. 1991			
Constant term	−0.86	−0.48	0.30
	(−2.65)	(−2.16)	−(1.42)
Coefficient of slope	106.90	39.08	33.98
	(2.34)	(2.78)	(3.20)
R^{2}	.084	.104	.135
adjusted R^{2}	.077	.098	.129

t-statistics are in parentheses and are corrected for the moving average error process (introduced by overlapping monthly observations of year-ahead forecasts). The uncorrected t-statistics are biased upwards.

The second column of the top panel shows the simplest possible version of the alternative approach: the explanatory variable is the spread between two relatively more extreme points on the yield curve, the five-year interest rate minus the overnight interest rate. The results show a stronger relationship for the alternative approach than for the Mishkin approach. The t-statistic is higher, and the R^2 is more than twice as high.[5]

Table 9.2 presents similar results, with the difference that the inflation spread is constructed from the adjusted CPI, which treats housing costs on a rental-equivalence basis throughout the sample period. The results, while not identical, are qualitatively similar.

The results in table 9.1 suggest that the spread between the five-year and overnight interest rates gives us a better measure of the overall steepness of the yield curve, and so does a better job of predicting the path of inflation, than does the spread between twelve-month and three-month interest rates. This possibility is consistent with the results in Fama (1990), Mishkin (1990b, 1992) and Jorion and Mishkin (1991), despite the absence in those papers of any theoretical framework that would predict the finding that the longer-term part of the yield curve reflects expected inflation better than the shorter-term part does.

Mishkin (1990b) looks at the long-term spread *as a predictor of the future change in the inflation rate over the long term*, and finds a closer relationship than that between $(\pi^{12} - \pi^3)$ and $(i^{12} - i^3)$ shown in equation (1):

The evidence indicates that there is substantial information in the longer maturity term structure about future inflation.... For maturities of six months or less, the term structure contains no information about the future path of inflation, but it does contain a great deal of information about the term structure of real interest rates.

But Mishkin does not consider using the longer term spread to forecast $(\pi^{12} - \pi^3)$. The reason is that the equation originates in a theoretical framework in which the real interest rate is constant, so that the nominal interest rate of any given term is only thought useful for predicting inflation over the same term.

Similarly, Fama (1990, p. 60) finds that "when the forecast horizon is extended, the information in the spread about the real return decays relative to the information about inflation." The model in this chapter provides a simple explanation for such findings.

If the spread between the five-year and overnight interest rates is useful for predicting the path of inflation, it seems logical that one might obtain a still better indicator by using multiple points along the yield curve to get a

Table 9.2
Forecasting the inflation spread (12 month–3 month)

Monthly Observations, January 1960–November 1991
$(\pi^{12} - \pi^{3})_t = a + b(yield\ curve\ measure) + u_t$

Interest rates expressed in log form. In estimating B1, each interest rate is first expressed as a deviation from the sample mean for its term, as an estimate of the liquidity premium, k_r.

Measure of slope of yield curve	Mishkin approach 12-month minus 3-month spread	Alternative approach 5-year minus fed funds spread	Nonlinear measure of steepness B1
Jan. 1960–Nov. 1991			
Constant term	−0.18	−0.05	0.09
	(−1.09)	(−0.40)	(0.70)
Coefficient of slope	46.49	18.95	14.04
	(1.72)	(2.36)	(2.06)
R^2	.020	.040	.032
adjusted R^2	.018	.038	.029
Jan. 1960–Sept. 1979			
Constant term	0.02	0.14	0.20
	(0.07)	(0.92)	(1.32)
Coefficient of slope	43.78	15.41	6.78
	(1.04)	(1.41)	(0.77)
R^2	.013	.027	.006
adjusted R^2	.009	.023	.002
Oct. 1979–Nov. 1991			
Constant term	−0.53	−0.34	−0.24
	(−2.15)	(−1.88)	(−1.37)
Coefficient of slope	56.35	22.67	18.53
	(1.62)	(2.04)	(2.17)
R^2	.040	.061	.068
adjusted R^2	.034	.054	.062

t-statistics are in parentheses and are corrected for the moving average error process (introduced by overlapping monthly observations of year-ahead forecasts). The uncorrected t-statistics are biased upwards.
*The inflation spread is constructed from the adjusted CPI (obtained from Mishkin) which treats housing costs on a rental-equivalence basis throughout the sample period.

better estimate of its overall steepness. A brief inspection of an actual yield curve, however, reveals that the appropriate estimate of the steepness is unlikely to be the slope in a simple linear relationship between the interest rate and its term of maturity: there is more information in the spread between the one-year rate and the two-year rate than there is between the twenty-nine-year rate and the thirty-year rate. The alternative theoretical framework examined here shows the appropriate nonlinear transformation to apply to the yield curve before estimating its slope, which is another attraction of the model.

The remainder of the chapter is organized as follows. First an alternative framework that allows the real interest rate to vary is presented. Then the technique suggested by this framework for extracting a measure of the steepness of the yield curve using points from its entire length, rather than from only two maturities, is described. (The chapter thus pursues the extension to chapter 8 that is suggested there in note 11.) Finally, the technique is shown to offer a predictor of the path of inflation over the year that performs well relative to the approach illustrated in the first column of table 9.1.

9.2 A Framework that Lets the Real Interest Rate Vary over Time

Assume that the short-term real interest rate, though not constant, is expected by market participants to converge to a constant in the long run in the absence of future disturbances. Specifically, assume that the short-term nominal interest rate is expected to adjust to the steady-state inflation rate according to a first-order continuous-time stochastic differential equation as follows:

$$di_t = -\delta(i_t - \pi_0^e - r)\,dt + \sigma\,dw, \qquad dw \sim N[0, \sqrt{t}], \tag{2}$$

where i_t is the (instantaneously) short-term interest rate, π_0^e is the exogenous long-run inflation rate expected at time 0, and r is the constant long-run real interest rate—all three of which are not directly observable. The expected speed of adjustment is δ. The special case where the real interest rate is constant can be considered the limiting case $\delta = \infty$.

Equation (2) can be taken on its own, as a natural parameterization of how the interest rate adjusts. The equation is intended to be a way of specifying, as simply as possible, the notion that the real interest rate is not constant in the short run but has a tendency in that direction in the long run.

It is also possible to make an economic argument to illustrate a reason the interest rate might follow the path indicated by equation (2). The argument—by now familiar from the preceding chapters—is that adjustment takes time because the interest rate is determined by money-demand equilibrium and goods prices are sticky. Recall the example of an increase in the expected rate of future monetary growth that raises the expected rate of inflation. If the short-term interest rate were to rise instantly, real money demand would fall, which is not possible when the price level and thus the real money supply are fixed. But over time, prices rise in response to demand for excess goods. Thus over time the real money supply is free to fall and the short-term interest rate is free to rise to reflect expected inflation. This argument is formalized in the model in the appendix to chapter 8. That model demonstrates that rational expectations will take precisely the form of equation (2). The model, however, is only intended as an example to help motivate the equation.

We take the expectation of equation (2), looking forward from time 0. It follows that market participants expect the short-term nominal interest rate at time t to be a weighted average of the long-run nominal interest rate $(\pi_0^e + r)$ and the current short-term nominal interest rate i_0:

$$E_0 i_t = [1 - \exp(-\delta t)](\pi_0^e + r) + [\exp(-\delta t)]i_0. \tag{3}$$

The entire analysis that follows hinges on equation (3), representing the tendency of the nominal interest rate to approach $(\pi_0^e + r)$ as time passes, in the absence of new disturbances.

We need only one other assumption: i_0^τ, defined as the interest rate on τ-maturity bonds (issued at time 0), is the average of the expected instantaneously short-term interest rates between time 0 and time τ, plus a possible liquidity premium term k_τ:[6]

$$i_0^\tau = \frac{1}{\tau} \int_0^\tau E_0 i_t \, dt + k_\tau. \tag{4}$$

By integrating (3), we find that the τ-maturity interest rate can be represented as another weighted average

$$i_0^\tau = (1 - w_\tau)(\pi_0^e + r) + (w_\tau)i_0 + k_\tau, \tag{5}$$

where the weights are given by $(w_\tau) = (1 - \exp(-\delta\tau))/\delta\tau$. Equation (5) can also be written as

$$i_0^\tau = k_\tau + i_0 + (\pi_0^e + r - i_0)(1 - w_\tau). \tag{5'}$$

For any given point in time, we can observe the Treasury security rate for two or more maturities, τ_1 and τ_2 (say, 3 months and 5 years). Then (given an estimate of δ) we can solve for the unknown $(\pi_0^e + r - i_0)$, which is the appropriately calculated slope of the yield curve at that point in time. The relationship is illustrated schematically in figure 9.1. The lower half of the graph illustrates the nonlinear relationship between the term τ and the weight $(1 - w_\tau)$; the upper half illustrates the linear relationship between $(1 - w_\tau)$ and the interest rate i_0^τ of the corresponding term. At any point in time, for instance, $t = 0$, the τ-term nominal interest rate is a weighted average of $(\pi_0^\tau + r)$, the hypothetical infinitely long-term interest rate, and i_0, the hypothetical infinitely short-term interest rate. The longer the term of maturity, the greater the weight given to the former and the less to the latter. Although any two points would be sufficient to construct an appropriate estimate of the difference between the extremities $(\pi_0^e + r)$ and i_0 that reflects the steepness of the yield curve, a better technique would be to apply OLS regression to however many points along the curve are available. One can see from equation (5') that the coefficient in a regression of i_0^τ against $\{1 - [1 - \exp(-\delta\tau)]/\delta\tau\}$ is the appropriate measure of $(\pi_0^e + r - i_0)$, the overall steepness of the yield curve. (If we want to allow for a liquidity premium or risk premium that—although constant over time—varies with the term to maturity, then we have to subtract from the interest rate i_0^τ the time-series average of i_t^τ for all t, as an estimate of the corresponding premium term k_τ.[7])

Appendix 9A develops the point that the slope of the yield curve, as a measure of the current looseness of monetary policy, reflects the likely future path of inflation. It shows that the difference between the expected twelve-month and three-month inflation rates, the variable examined by Mishkin, is proportional to $(\pi_0^e + r - i_0)$.

9.3   Empirical Results

We now turn to the estimation. We begin by adopting the value of δ, the parameter governing the speed with which the nominal interest rate incorporates the expected inflation rate, estimated in chapter 8: $\delta = .4$. For each monthly observation over the period January 1960–December 1991, we then estimate the steepness of the yield curve at that point in time by running the regression

$$i_t^\tau = B0_t + B1_t\left[1 - \frac{1 - \exp(-\delta\tau)}{\delta\tau}\right]. \tag{6}$$

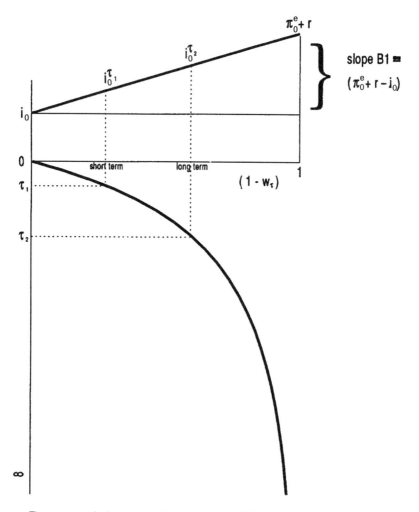

The upper graph shows the relationship between interest rates along the yield curve and the weight $[1-w_\tau]$, as in equation (5'), $i_0^\tau = k_\tau + i_0 + (\pi_0^e + r - i_0)[1-w_\tau]$.

The lower graph shows the nonlinear relationship between the term to maturity τ, and the weight, given by

$$[1-w_\tau] = [1 - (1 - e^{-\delta\tau})/\delta\tau].$$

Figure 9.1
Extrapolation from interest rates to the expected inflation rate.

The coefficient $B1_t$ is the appropriate estimate of the measure of steepness $(\pi_t^e + r - i_t)$.[8] Then we see whether the time series $B1_t$ can help forecast the difference between the future twelve-month inflation rate and the future three-month inflation rate.[9] Finally, we iterate over δ to obtain the estimate of that parameter that minimizes the sum of squared residuals (1.175).[10] (The data are described in appendix B.)

The results of the second stage of this procedure are reported for the period 1960–91 in the last column of table 9.1. The table shows the most proper case, where the k_t premiums, estimated as the average term structure over time, have been subtracted from the interest rates (in log form) before running the regressions at each point in time to estimate $B1_t$. (We also estimated the regressions assuming that the liquidity or term premiums were 0 and so dispensing with subtracting off the means; those results are reported in Table 2b in the working paper version of this chapter.[11])

The t-statistic is significant at the 99 percent level, indicating that the steepness of the yield curve does contain useful information regarding the future path of inflation. Only a relatively small fraction of the variation in the inflation path is predicted, as one would expect. The series are plotted in figure 9.2. Both the t-statistic and the R^2, when compared to those in the first column of table 9.1, indicate that our measure, extracted from the interest rate yield curve along its entire length, is a considerably better indicator than the simple term spread used by Mishkin.

It is often suggested that the change in Federal Reserve operating procedures of October 1979 marked a structural break in relationships among the money supply, inflation, and interest rates. For this reason we tried testing the term structure equations separately on the two subperiods before and after that date. The middle panel in the table shows the subperiod January 1960–September 1979. Our approach again beats the Mishkin approach, with an adjusted R^2 almost twice as great.

The bottom third of the table shows the same exercise for the second subperiod, October 1979–November 1991. There is a change in the results between the two sample periods, though only the downward shift in the constant term is statistically significant. (The upward shift in the coefficient on $B1_t$ is not significant, once the proper correction for the moving average error process is applied.[12]) The alternative approach again beats the Mishkin approach.

We also compare the simplest version of the alternative approach, which uses the spread between the five-year and overnight interest rates, and the more sophisticated version, which uses the nonlinear estimate of the

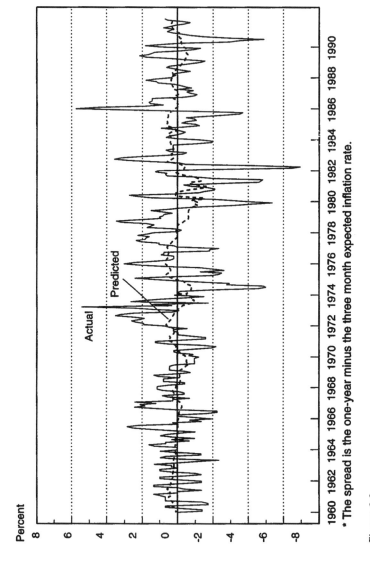

Figure 9.2
Actual and predicted inflation spreads.

steepness of the entire length of the yield curve. In the first subperiod, the sophisticated form of the alternative approach does not do as good a job of forecasting the inflation spread as the simple form, even though both do better than the Mishkin approach. In the more recent subperiod, the more sophisticated version dominates the simpler version as well as dominating the Mishkin approach.

In short, in addition to being based on a theoretical framework that allows the real interest rate to vary, our technique appears to have the advantage of doing a relatively good job of forecasting the course of inflation over the coming year. Most of the benefit can be obtained from simply looking at a wide long-short spread.

Appendix 9A: The Relationship between the Inflation Spread and the Steepness of the Yield Curve

We combine two equations from the appendix in chapter 8, equation (A3) and the first equation in note 17, to get

$$\frac{dp}{dt} = \pi_0^e - \gamma\rho(i_t - r). \tag{A1}$$

Expected inflation over the term τ is then given by the expectation of

$$\pi_0^\tau = \frac{p_\tau - p_0}{\tau}$$

$$= \frac{1}{\tau}\int_0^\tau \frac{dp}{dt}\,dt$$

$$= \frac{\tau}{\tau}\pi_0 - \frac{\gamma\rho}{\tau}\int_0^\tau (i_t - r)\,dt$$

$$= \pi_0 - \gamma\rho\left[\frac{1}{\tau}\int_0^\tau i_t\,dt - r\right]$$

$$= \pi_0 - \gamma\rho[i_0^\tau - k_\tau - r] \qquad \text{from equation (4) in this chapter}$$

$$= \pi_0 - \gamma\rho[i_0 + (1 - w_\tau)(\pi_0 + r - i_0) - r] \qquad \text{from (5')}$$

$$= \pi_0 + \gamma\rho[r - i_0] - \gamma\rho(1 - w_\tau)(\pi_0 + r - i_0). \tag{A.5}$$

This is the expression for the τ-period inflation rate. Following Mishkin, however, we wish to predict the *difference* between the τ_2-period and τ_1-period inflation rates:

$$\pi_0^{\tau_2} - \pi_0^{\tau_1} = \gamma\rho(w_{\tau_2} - w_{\tau_1})(\pi_0^e + r - i_0). \tag{A.6}$$

This shows that the expected change in the inflation rate is simply proportionate to $(\pi_0^e + r - i_0)$, which is the steepness of the yield curve. This is the proposition claimed at the end of section 9.2 and implemented in section 9.3.

Appendix 9B: Data Description and Sources

The interest rates used in this paper are monthly averages of daily figures and are from the Citibase data bank. The data also appear in the Federal Reserve System Release G.13, and in the Federal Reserve Bulletin, Table 1.35. The following rates are used, based on availability:

1960:01–1969:06: federal funds rate (adjusted to be comparable to bond rates), the three- and six-month Treasury bill rates from the Secondary Market (adjusted to be comparable to bond rates), the one-year, three-year, five-year, ten-year, and twenty-year Treasury bond rates;

1969:07–1976:05: all of the above plus the seven-year Treasury bond rate;

1976:06–1977:02: all of the above plus the two-year Treasury bond rate;

1977:03–1986:12: all of the above plus the thirty-year Treasury bond rate;

1987:01–1991:11: all of the above minus the twenty-year Treasury bond rate.

The inflation rates used in this paper are constructed from the seasonally adjusted consumer price index, which can be obtained from the Citibase data bank or from the U.S. Department of Labor, Bureau of Labor Statistics.

Acknowledgments

We thank Thomas Fomby for helpful advice, Joe Abate, Mark Flaherty, and D'Ann Peterson for effective research assistance. We also thank David Romer, other members of the Berkeley Macroeconomics seminar, Olivier Blanchard, Larry Katz, Angelo Melino, Frederic Mishkin, and other members of the NBER Financial Markets group for useful comments on earlier drafts.

The Power of the Yield Curve to Predict Interest Rates (or Lack Thereof)

The simple expectations theory, in combination with the hypothesis of rational expectations, has been rejected many times in careful econometric studies. But the theory seems to reappear perennially in policy discussions as if nothing had happened to it. It is uncanny how resistant superficially appealing theories in economics are to contrary evidence. We are reminded of the Tom and Jerry cartoons that precede feature films at movie theaters. The villain, Tom the cat, may be buried under a ton of boulders, blasted through a brick wall (leaving a cat-shaped hole) or flattened by a steamroller. Yet seconds later he is up again plotting his evil deed.

—Shiller, Campbell, and Schoenholtz, "Forward Rates and Future Policy"

The term structure theory of forecasting future interest rates is attractive because it offers a simple way of forecasting that requires no information beyond the yield curve itself.[1] As the epigraph suggests, the empirical evidence has for some time been strongly against the theory. Much confusion reigns on this score, however. The issue is of great interest, because the theory's failure would seem to offer traders and investors a valuable opportunity to make money in financial markets. Indeed, confusion among traders and investors about what ought to hold in theory, what is observed to hold in practice, and the implications of the discrepancy, is probably what keeps traders and investors from fully exploiting the opportunity and thereby allows it to persist.

10.1 The Term Structure Hypothesis

Unbiasedness

The term structure hypothesis (henceforth TSH) could also be called the "unbiasedness hypothesis," because the theory says that the forecasts of

Originally published in *Forecast and Risk Assessment*, ed. Horace W. Brock (Strategic Economic Decisions, February 1994), III.1–III.21. Reprinted with permission.

the future path of the interest rate implicit in the term structure are optimal or unbiased. In simple terms, the TSH says that if the yield curve slopes steeply upward (if today's long-term rates are *unusually* high relative to today's short rates), interest rates are likely to rise in the future. If the yield curve slopes downward (an "inverted" yield curve, i.e., today's long-term rates are below today's short rates), interest rates are likely to fall in the future. The forecasts apply both to future short-term interest rates and to future intermediate and long-term interest rates. If the yield curve follows a more complicated pattern, then a correspondingly more complicated path for future interest rates is forecast.

It is easy to state the TSH mathematically in the special case in which one compares a short-maturity interest rate to an interest rate of a maturity exactly twice (or any other integer-multiple) as long. Consider the spread between three-month and six-month Treasury bill interest rates. If the TSH holds (and the yield curve incorporates no liquidity premium or risk premium of any kind), today's six-month T-bill rate should be a simple average of today's three-month T-bill rate and the optimal forecast of what the three-month T-bill rate will be three months from today. This is because investors can choose today whether to buy a six-month T-bill, or to buy a three-month bill instead and plan to roll it over three months from now at the interest rate prevailing then. If the six-month T-bill strategy were more profitable, all investors would want to buy the six-month bill, and none the three-month, putting downward pressure on the six-month interest rate and upward pressure on the three-month rate. In other words, arbitrage should drive the longer-term rate to the appropriate level.

It follows that when today's six-month–three-month spread is observed to be positive, the optimal forecast of the future three-month rate is that it will rise proportionally above today's three-month rate:

$$E_t i_{t+3}^{3m} - i_t^{3m} = 2(i_t^{6m} - i_t^{3m}). \tag{1}$$

This equation will be derived below. To take a numerical example, if $i_t^{3m} = 3$ percent, and $E_t i_{t+3}^{3m} = 5$ percent, then i_t^{6m} should be determined as the average of the two, or 4 percent. Observing today's spread, we would use equation (1) to forecast the future change in the three-month rate as $2(4 - 3)$, or $+2$ percent.

We give two illustrations from the early 1990s. On one hand, the U.S. yield curve had a relatively steep upward slope over the period 1990–93. The Federal Reserve temporarily pushed short-term rates down in response to the recession that began in 1990, but long-term rates did not fall nearly as much. It follows from the TSH that U.S. interest rates could be expected to rise in the near future.

On the other hand, the German yield curve was relatively flat; indeed, over the period 1990–93, the term structure was often inverted. German government expenditure in connection with the absorption of the Eastern *lander* in 1990—undertaken simultaneously with a firm monetary policy on the part of the Bundesbank—drove up German short-term interest rates; long-term rates never rose as much. It follows from the TSH that German interest rates could be expected to rise. Below, we consider whether reality has matched the theory.

Rational Expectations and the Expectations Hypothesis of the Term Structure

If we are most interested in predicting future interest rates, then we are interested in the TSH per se. Nevertheless, before turning to the empirical evidence, it is important to note that the TSH conceptually conflates two specific hypotheses: the rational expectations hypothesis and the expectations hypothesis of the term structure. There has been much confusion on this score. Many people say "expectations hypothesis" when they mean "term structure hypothesis" (or "unbiasedness hypothesis"), and think "term structure hypothesis" when they read or hear "expectations hypothesis." To make sense of the existing tests, or to apply their results to a successful investment strategy, an understanding of the different definitions is necessary.

The first component of the joint hypothesis is the rational expectations hypothesis (REH), which says simply that investors' forecasts are determined so as to equal the optimal forecasts. The rather demanding form of this hypothesis that usually appears in empirical work is that investors' forecasts are assumed to be in-sample optimal. In other words, any systematic patterns observed in a given data sample (provided they are statistically significant) must have been anticipated by investors.[2] Mathematically, REH is stated as follows:

$$(i_{t+3}^{3m})_t^e = E_t i_{t+3}^{3m}, \tag{2}$$

where the left-hand side denotes observers' forecasts, even if kept private, and the right-hand side denotes the optimal forecast, given available information.

The second component of the joint hypothesis is the expectations hypothesis of the term structure (EHTS). It says that variation in interest rates of various maturities solely reflects variation in investors' forecasts of future rates (of shorter maturities). In other words, regardless of whether investors' private forecasts are optimal, arbitrage ensures that they are fully reflected in the observed term structure. Mathematically,

$$i_t^{6m} = [(i_{t+3}^{3m})_t^e + i_t^{3m}]/2 \tag{3}$$

or, equivalently,

$$(i_{t+3}^{3m})_t^e - i_t^{3m} = 2(i_t^{6m} - i_t^{3m}).$$

The logic behind this equation is of course the arbitrage argument made above.

In fact, riskless arbitrage is not possible in this context, because one can never be sure of the price at which one will be able to buy or sell a security in the future. This introduces a complication: the *term premium*. The yield curve is observed to slope upward more often than not, even though interest rates are not always expected to rise. This pattern is evidence of a term premium that investors must be paid to induce them to expose themselves in longer maturities. This is why we originally used the words "if the yield curve slopes *steeply* upward" or "if today's long-term rates are *unusually* high relative to today's short-term rates" in stating the TSH. On average, investors clearly require some extra expected rate of return to be willing to hold longer-term securities, which they cannot be as sure of selling at the predicted price as they can with, say, three-month securities. Equation (3) should really be written:

$$i_t^{6m} = [(i_{t+3}^{3m})_t^e + i_t^{3m}]/2 + p^{6m} \tag{3'}$$

where p^{6m} is the six-month term premium.

The term premium is commonly interpreted in either of two (related) ways. One concerns the *risk* associated with future interest rates or bond prices. Regardless of whether investors can forecast optimally, there is a lot of uncertainty in any interest rate forecast. If the term premium is compensation for the greater risk that goes with holding longer-term securities, then it is a risk premium. The other interpretation is associated with *liquidity*. Short-term U.S. Treasury bills are virtually the most liquid investment in the world. If the term premium is compensation for the lesser liquidity of longer-term securities, then it is a liquidity premium. Whether one adopts the risk premium or liquidity premium interpretation, the EHTS and TSH are little affected by the premium's existence, *provided* it is constant over time. We merely measure the slope of the yield curve relative to the average slope over time. But if, in reality, the premium varies over time (a definite possibility given that the compensation that risk-averse investors require may vary over time), then the EHTS fails.

Together, equations (2) and (3) imply equation (1). (To allow for a constant term premium as in equation (3′), equation (1) must be modified by adding the term p^{6m}.) That is, if investors' forecasts are optimal *and* there are no time-varying liquidity or risk premia preventing their forecasts from being fully reflected in market-determined interest rates, then it follows that one can obtain optimal forecasts from the observed term structure. If we discover that the TSH does not seem to hold in practice, we cannot be sure whether the EHTS fails or the EMH fails.

Before discussing the empirical evidence on the term structure hypothesis or its constituent parts, we note that, if the hypothesis held, the implications for investors would be simple, if unexciting. They could rely on the market for forecasts of future interest rates. It would not make much difference what an investor did: her expected returns would be the same on all assets, long and short.

10.2 Empirical Findings: TSH (or Unbiasedness) Is Almost Always Rejected

As indicated in the opening quote from Shiller, Campbell, and Schoenholtz (1983), many empirical studies have rejected the term structure hypothesis (TSH), finding evidence of bias in the yield curve's implicit forecasts of future interest rates. The bias appears to be smaller for the predictions implicit in short-term Treasury bill rates than for those implicit in long-term bond prices.

In the case of the hypothesized ability of Treasury bill spreads to predict changes in short-term interest rates (as in equation (1)), the news is not uniformly bleak. Several authors have found evidence of *some* degree of predictive power: Campbell and Shiller (1987, 1989), Fama (1984), Fama and Bliss (1987), and Hardouvelis (1988). Other studies have found no statistically significant predictive ability: Shiller, Campbell, and Schoenholtz (1983), Mankiw (1986), Froot (1989), Fama (1990) and Evans and Lewis (1994). The findings appear to be sensitive to the sample period.

The studies agree in one important respect, however. None finds that the ability of the term structure to predict short-term interest rates is as great as the TSH says it should be. The optimistic studies find only a slight tendency for future interest rates to rise when the term structure is steep and to fall when it is flat or inverted. Thus, even in these cases, the term structure predictor is biased. For example, if the spread predicts an increase of 1.00 percentage points, the actual increase might be 0.25 percentage points.[3] This implies a bias of 0.75 percentage points.

A typical test at the long end of the spectrum looks at the spread between the interest rates on a twenty-year bond and a six-month Treasury bill, and tests its ability to forecast changes in long-term bond rates. The usual finding here is a particularly devastating rejection of the TSH. Long-term rates often move in the *opposite* direction from that which is forecast by the term structure, falling when the yield curve's slope is steep, and rising when it is flat. Examples are Mankiw and Summers (1984), Shiller, Campbell, and Schoenholtz (1983), Campbell and Shiller (1987, 1989), Froot (1989), and Jones (1992).

The failure of the TSH suggests that, on average, one can make money by following a simple set of strategies that go by names such as "riding the yield curve" and "the Yield Spread model."[4] The strategies are summed up by the prescription "Go long when the slope is steep, and short when it's not."

There is some evidence of gains to playing this game at the short end of the spectrum. When the one-year (or six-month) T-bill rate is unusually high relative to the three-month (or one-month) rate, an investor should buy the longer-term bills. When it is below the short-term bill rate, she should buy the short-term bills.

The greatest gains, however, appear to be available at the longer end of the spectrum, where the prescription becomes "When bond yields are high above bill rates, buy bonds; when they are below, sell bonds and buy bills." Why are the gains greater at the longer end? As already noted, there is greater evidence of bias in the term structure of bonds than of bills. Another reason is the prospect of capital gains on bonds. Consider an investor who observes a steep yield curve, and buys long-term bonds rather than bills. If interest rates move in the expected direction (i.e., the opposite of what the term structure forecasts under the TSH) within, say, the twelve-months that the bond is held, the lucky investor will reap a capital gain in the form of higher bond prices, in addition to receiving the higher coupon payment from the beginning. Needless to say, such strategies will not make money every time, but a decade and more of research seems to suggest, on average, they will.

Investors making asset-allocation decisions will naturally want to enact a different version of this strategy than will speculators or traders who expect to close out their positions rapidly. The strategy says that, whenever the yield curve is steep, investors who have a longer-term horizon should allocate a high percentage of their portfolios to bonds; when it is flat, a somewhat lower proportion to bonds and more to bills; and when it is inverted, a relatively high proportion to short-term bills. There are also implications for borrowers. When the yield curve is steep, corporate borrowers should delay issuing bonds, and homeowners should opt for the more favorable rates offered by floating-rate mortgages, as opposed to borrowing at fixed rates.

Traders or speculators, who are willing to expose themselves to more risk, can enhance their expected returns by making pure "term structure plays." In other words, when the yield curve is steep, they can finance temporary purchases of long-term bonds by borrowing short-term, or, more simply, they can buy T-bill futures (or call options). When the yield curve is flat or inverted, they can go short in longer-term securities, or sell T-bill futures (or options).

In sum, the strategy is no more than common sense: "When yields on short-term T-bills are high, buy them; when yields on bonds are high, buy *them* instead." As Shiller, Campbell, and Schoenholtz (1983, p. 197) observe, "It is perhaps surprising only to students of the expectations theory that this is what a naive person might have done without the guidance of a sophisticated model."

It is worth recalling why the finding is surprising. In theory, investors should have followed the activist strategy already, responding in the prescribed way to unusually steep or flat yield curves, and, in so doing, restoring the curve to its usual shape. Among academic economists, however, a priori belief in this theoretical argument was so strong that it took more than a decade of statistical findings before they would consider the possibility that the hypothesis failed, and that its failure might be evidence of a serious market imperfection.

10.3   What Explains the Bias in the Term Structure?

There are a number of possible explanations for the failure of the TSH: transactions costs, liquidity premium, risk premium, changes in Federal Reserve operating regimes, and stupidity on the part of investors. Several of these explanations fall under the rubric of the "term premium;" others suggest a failure of the rational expectations methodology. As noted earlier, the hypothesis that has been rejected is really a joint hypothesis. Hence its failure could reflect the failure of either the EHTS or the REH. The difference is important for investor strategy. If the TSH fails because of the existence of a liquidity or risk premium, then the investor will have to ask herself whether she is willing to pay a price, in the form of giving up some expected return, to gain greater liquidity or lower risk. In this case, statements made in the preceding section about opportunities to "make money on average" would remain true, and yet the risk-averse investor might not wish to take advantage of them.

Testing the source of the breakdown, namely, finding out whether it is a failure of EHTS or REH, is much harder than testing the TSH itself. The reason is that we cannot measure investors' forecasts directly. Nevertheless, there is some empirical evidence on each of the possible explanations.

In theory, the failure of the TSH could be due to substantial brokerage costs or bid-ask spreads. In practice, however, transactions costs in modern financial markets are too small to explain the finding. Several studies, such as that of Grieves and Marcus (1990), take transactions costs into account explicitly. To use the estimate based on the findings of Fama (1984), a bias of 0.75 percentage points is easily large enough, even if divided by 4 to reflect a strategy of holding for only one quarter, to outweigh transactions costs.

Conventional Tests for Liquidity or Risk Effects

Most economists have interpreted the bias in the term structure, not as evidence of a failure of the REH or Efficient Markets Hypothesis, but rather as evidence of a term premium, and therefore of a failure of the EHTS. This interpretation is based, however, solely on a priori belief in the REH. Attempts to test directly for liquidity or risk effects, and thereby distinguish explicitly between the two halves of the joint hypothesis, have usually been unable to find such effects. Conventional tests ask what variables the liquidity premium or risk premium ought, in theory, to be determined by, and then test whether such variables are in fact statistically related to the observed term structure bias. We consider several of these variables in turn.

If the bias is a risk premium, as many observers assume, then it should be related to observable variables that theory tells us are determinants of the risk premium. One such variable is volatility. Modern econometric techniques such as ARCH and GARCH, for example, model uncertainty as a function of the variance in the recent past. Is the term structure bias related to volatility as modeled by these techniques? Jones and Roley (1983), Engle, Lilien, and Robins (1987), and Engle and Ng (1990) have shown some success for maturities less than one year.[5] Such studies are typically more successful at modeling volatility as an ARCH process, however, than in showing that variation in volatility is of the nature and magnitude necessary to explain the bias as a risk premium. At the long end of the spectrum, results are bleaker. Mankiw (1984, pp. 84–85) uses an ex post measure of volatility and finds no significant positive relationship to the yield spread. Indeed, for Germany, Canada, and the United States, he gets the wrong sign.

An alternative way to measure risk is to use the forecasts of volatility implicit in options prices. In theory, this approach is superior to the ARCH methods because it measures investors' degree of uncertainty directly, rather than relying on any particular model of how they form their expectations of volatility. Agell and Persson (1992, pp. 60–79) have tried this approach, but with little success in explaining the term structure bias.

The true risk facing an investor in long-term bonds depends not only on the volatility of bond yields, but also on the covariance with the overall risk of the investor's portfolio. Most important, it should depend on the covariance, or beta, with the stock market. Thus the risk premium, in theory, should depend on these covariances. Yet there is little evidence that the term structure bias behaves this way. Mankiw (1986) finds that the estimated relationship between the yield spread and the stock market covariance is of the correct sign, but not statistically significant. He also finds that, even if one takes the estimate at face value, one would need to assume that investors were extremely risk-averse to explain why they react so little to an opportunity for expected profit. Similarly, Grieves and Marcus (1990, p. 2) argue that the coefficient of relative risk aversion would have to be in excess of 260 to explain the observed bias, whereas it is usually believed to be in the neighborhood of 2.[6]

A truly complete theory of the risk premium would include not just the covariances with returns on all stocks and bonds, but also real estate and many other assets that are components of total wealth but are difficult to measure. One technique in use is to exploit the theoretical proposition that consumption, which is measurable, should be proportionate to total wealth, if households are intertemporal optimizers, and to see if the term structure bias is related to the covariance with consumption. This is the approach of Hansen and Singleton (1983), Shiller (1982), and Grossman and Shiller (1982). The findings are not very encouraging. Mankiw (1986, p. 88) statistically rejects the theoretical relationship between the yield spread and consumption covariance and in fact finds the wrong sign.

Yet another approach, appropriate for testing for bias that is either a risk premium or a liquidity premium, is to look for an effect of the relative supplies of long-term bonds versus shorter-term securities. The logic is as follows. We want to test whether investors care only about expected returns (which would give us the EHTS), or whether they also care about liquidity and risk. If they also care about liquidity and risk, then they treat long-term and short-term bonds as imperfect substitutes. Hence they will require an especially high expected return on long-term bonds when they have a lot of them in their portfolios, because they are already heavily exposed; they will require less compensation when they do not hold so many. In market equilibrium, investors' aggregate demand for bonds must equal the supply. Thus an exogenous increase in the supply of long-term bonds, for example, because the government is selling large quantities of them, should drive up the required rate of return. The question of whether this is so in practice, or whether on the other hand the EHTS holds, is often referred to as "the question of debt management policy." For example, the gradual shortening of the maturity structure of the federal debt between 1950 and 1975 should in theory have allowed a reduction in the term premium, while the lengthening of the maturity structure between 1975 and 1990 should have driven it back up again.

There is a long history of testing whether the relative supply of long-term bonds versus short-term bonds has an effect on their expected rates or return, including Tobin (1963), Friedman (1978, 1992), and Roley (1979, 1982). These studies tend to find either no effects, or very small ones. More recent studies have tested whether expected returns depend on a particular combination of asset supplies, variances, and covariances, as they should in theory if investors diversify their portfolios optimally, as in the CAPM. Again, these factors are found to have little ability to explain the observed magnitude of the term structure bias.[7]

The Clinton administration in 1993 began a new experiment in debt management that may turn out to shed light on the EHTS. When President Clinton took office, he announced a plan to shift the composition of the federal debt away from long-term bonds toward shorter-term debt, thus reversing the trend of the preceding fifteen years. A principle motive was to shave a few billion dollars off the federal government's interest bill by taking advantage of the currently steep term structure, as private corporations do.

If the EHTS is correct, then the change in debt maturity should have no effect on the term structure. The EHTS relies on the assumption that investors view long-term securities and short-term securities as perfect substitutes—investors are indifferent as to which they hold, as long as both pay the same expected rate of return. Therefore, there should be no reaction in the markets. On the other hand, if the EHTS does not hold, because there is a liquidity premium or risk premium, then there should be some effect. Investors will not willingly absorb the greater quantity of short-term securities except at higher short-term interest rates. Correspondingly, the reduction in the relative supply of long-term securities will allow their expected rate of return to fall.

A Test Using Survey Data

Froot (1989) has adopted an approach to the question of disentangling the EHTS and REH components of the joint hypothesis that is very different from that of other researchers. He uses data from surveys of market participants regarding their expectations of future exchange rates, in order to measure the term premium directly. His paper is both important, and widely misinterpreted. Some have read the title, "New Hope for the Expectations Hypothesis of the Term Structure of Interest Rates," and erroneously concluded that Froot is offering new hope for *the ability to forecast interest rates*—namely, for the hypothesis that the term structure is unbiased, or what we have called the term structure hypothesis. His results offer no such hope, and he is clear on this point.

Rather, Froot's results offer hope that the failure of the TSH is due to the failure of the REH rather than to the failure of the EHTS, or, in other words, that the observed bias is due to systematic prediction errors rather than to a term premium. This finding applies only to the longer end of the maturity spectrum. (At the shorter end, he finds the reverse: the bias is due to a term premium on short maturities, i.e., a failure of the EHTS.) His conclusions are thus consistent with the inability of earlier researchers to use conventional risk or liquidity determinants to explain the bias in the bond-bill spread.

Violations of the Rational Expectations Hypothesis?

We are thus left with the conclusion that the term structure bias is due to a violation of the rational expectations methodology. How could this be? Several possible explanations have been suggested. A popular one is that the Federal Reserve occasionally switches its procedures for setting monetary policy, and in particular, that during some periods the Fed has targeted short-term interest rates, and during others it has not.[8]

Mankiw and Miron (1986), for example, argue that there was no term structure bias in the years before the founding of the Federal Reserve in 1914, and that it only developed subsequently, as the Fed began to target short-term interest rates. Hardouvelis (1988) tests the Mankiw and Miron theory for the period 1972–85, by testing whether the term structure bias is statistically related to the contemporaneous degree of interest-rate targeting on the part of the Fed. He finds no connection.

More generally (i.e., even in theory), it is important to realize that Fed targeting of short-term interest rates does not necessarily imply bias in the term structure. Recall the a priori argument for the EHTS. If investors make optimal forecasts of future interest rates, their actions will drive long-term rates into line with those forecasts. Nothing about this argument necessarily changes when one of the forces driving short-term interest rates is the Fed's behavior. It just means that investors should be trying to forecast Fed behavior instead of, or in addition to, other forces such as oil shocks, recessions, or Treasury funding operations. Balduzzi, Bertola, and Foresi (1993), for example, find that the market's failure to predict optimally the policy-induced component in the movement of federal-funds interest rates is indeed the source of the term structure's bias, but they point out that this does not rescue the REH.

Yet there is one circumstance where changes in Federal Reserve regime might explain the econometric findings of bias. If such changes are rare and sudden, they might invalidate the assumed probability distribution of the test statistic. The same is true, for that matter, of large sudden changes in *any* determinants of interest rates. The econometrician might be led to believe that she has enough data to answer the question at hand at conventional levels of statistical significance when in reality she does not. This difficulty that large sudden changes can create for econometric inference is known as the "peso problem." Lewis (1991) considers a model in which investors perceived a probability that, after 1979, the Fed would revert to interest rate targeting. She fails statistically to reject this model as an explanation of observed term structure bias. But this is not the same as finding statistical evidence that the apparent bias was in fact an artifact of the possibility of regime shift. Most changes in Fed policy are not large and sudden. On the whole, the peso problem does not seem able to explain the many findings of bias.

Another possible explanation for the bias is that people are so irrational that they repeatedly make easily avoidable perception errors. It seems unlikely that most people are quite this stupid. If the structure of the world were unchanging over long periods of time, most people would eventually figure it out. The problem arises when the structure changes, and people have to learn the new structure. They could be reasonably intelligent, and yet have no way of figuring out *before the end of a given sample period* the parameters of the model that holds during that period.[9] For example, just because the term structure bias has held for the last four decades is no guarantee that it will also hold in the next.

A final explanation is that people are just a little lazy. They suffer from inertia. They do not willfully make forecasting errors. Rather, they do not react sufficiently—in speed or degree—to unusual patterns in the term structure by making the corresponding changes in their portfolio. More generally, they do not react rapidly enough to hard analytical findings (such as those described in this survey) by making changes in their world view. Perhaps they take their cue from market trends to a greater extent than they should, instead of relying a little more on their own judgment.

To recapitulate the bottom line, one can expect on average to make money from the strategy of going long when the yield curve is especially steep and going short when it is inverted. While there is a lot of risk to any given trial of this strategy, as to any purchase or sale of securities, estimates suggest that one would have to be extremely risk-averse to turn down the opportunity. In fact, Grieves and Marcus (1990) find that during part of their data sample (1969–88), the bias was so strong that the activist strategy dominated a simple strategy of buying and holding T-bills *regardless of how risk-averse the investor is.*

The other conclusion to note is the strategy appears to be far more attractive at the longer-term end of the spectrum. One should focus on the spread between bonds and bills, more than on the spread between the twelve-month interest rate and the one-month interest rate. There are three reasons for this. (1) The econometric findings that interest rates move in the opposite direction are stronger for the bond-bill spread. (2) One reaps capital gains on changes in bond prices, in addition to the up-front difference in coupon yields. (3) There are bits of evidence that the observed bias at the short end of the spectrum may be due to a liquidity premium or risk premium; there exists very little of such evidence at the long end of the spectrum.

Acknowledgments

A version of this chapter appeared in *Forecast and Risk Assessment*, ed. H. W. Brock. Menlo Park, Calif.: Strategic Economic Decisions, Inc., 1994. I would like to thank Woody Brock for the inspiration to write this chapter, and for many comments and suggestions on it.

III

Uncertainty, Policy
Coordination, and
Nominal GDP Targeting

Introduction to Part III

Macroeconomic policymaking is more difficult in practice than in theory. It is complicated by the existence of political constraints, shifting expectations, lags, and most of all uncertainty. Uncertainty in turn can take the form of uncertainty about the future baseline path of the economy in the absence of policy changes, uncertainty about the appropriate objectives such as employment and inflation, and uncertainty about the true model that connects policy instruments to the objectives.

Chapter 11 explores uncertainty regarding the true model. It considers theoretical ambiguities in the effects of monetary and fiscal policies, and then examines the predictions of the effects in twelve large established econometric models of the world economy. Both in theory and in the econometric models, there is a wide variation in predictions. In some cases, such as the effect of a monetary expansion on the trade balance and on income in foreign countries, the models are heavily divided even on the sign of the effect.[1] More surprisingly, the nature of the disagreements among the econometric models is generally quite different than the disagreements among the theories.

Next we turn to implications for coordination among policymakers. Global policymaking is naturally decentralized among the national governments responsible for their citizens' welfare, and even policymaking within a given country is partly decentralized among various government agencies. Yet decentralized policymakers often work at cross-purposes. There is the potential for them to raise economic welfare by coordinating, namely, by setting their policy instruments as part of a cooperative bargain, as compared to the Nash noncooperative equilibrium in which each sets its policies independently. The application of game theory to such problems has been a major academic growth area.[2]

Here we examine the difficulties that model uncertainty creates for policy coordination. In chapter 12, I examine the implications of the existence of conflicting models for coordination between the U.S. monetary authorities and the U.S. fiscal authorities. I was originally inspired in the early 1980s in part by the spectacle of a Volcker Fed and a Reagan Treasury that were operating with very different world views. The disagreement may have led to excessively high real interest rates. The question is whether better coordination between the two agencies could have fixed this. The issue remains live in the 1990s (Nordhaus, 1994).

In chapter 13, I examine the implications of the existence of conflicting models for coordination between the U.S. government and foreign governments. This chapter, coauthored with Katharine Rockett, was inspired by the spectacle of different world views in the U.S. and foreign governments in the 1980s, and at a time when many economists thought that only political stubbornness stood in the way of successful international coordination of policies. This chapter, like the earlier one, begins by making the simple theoretical point that policymakers who use different models may still be able to agree on a coordinated policy package, but that the package may in fact make things worse. It then simulates the range of outcomes that would occur if U.S. and foreign governments in fact coordinated while subscribing to the various econometric models that were explored in chapter 11. The possibility that coordination might make things worse turns out to be not just a theoretical curiosum, but a fairly common occurrence.[3]

With the September 1985 Plaza Accord among G-5 finance ministers and subsequent Summit Meetings among G-7 leaders, governments officially adopted a regime of international coordination. About the same time, economists were developing a list of doubts as to whether coordination was so desirable after all. Chapter 14 surveys the obstacles to successful coordination. The obstacles can be classified under three "c" rubrics, for ease of expression: (1) lack of compliance, (2) lack of credibility, and (3) lack of certainty. In other words, the obstacles concern (1) problems of enforcement of cooperative bargains, (2) problems of public expectations of inflation, and (3) problems of uncertainty. The chapter tries to take the constructive tack of asking what could make coordination more likely to succeed. It suggests that the antidote for the first and second problems is some degree of commitment by G-7 governments (preferably quite a low one), perhaps on an annual basis, to some intermediate nominal target. This way citizens within each country and other governments can monitor compliance with the proclaimed policy. The question is in terms of what nominal variable the ex ante intermediate target should be phrased. In the presence of uncertainty, this choice will usually turn out ex post to make a great difference. The chapter argues that nominal GNP would make a more suitable intermediate target than would the money supply and the other variables on which the G-7 have decided to base their discussions.

The case for coordinated international nominal GDP targeting (INT) in the presence of uncertainty is made verbally in that chapter, rather than mathematically or econometrically. The problem is rather complex to handle with a simple general theoretical model. There has been some progress on the choice of intermediate targets for international monetary coordination.[4] There is room for a lot more research, however. I suspect that it may have to take the form of simulations with specific multicountry models.[5]

An important part of the case for international nominal targeting is the same as that for nominal GDP targeting in the domestic context. This case has been already made by many others. Here the issue is setting an intermediate target under uncertainty in order to make the commitment credible to domestic citizens (rather than to foreign countries, as in the problem of international coordination). The final chapter in the book seeks to contribute to the literature on the choice of nominal anchors. To place it in context requires a brief review of the debate on rules versus discretion.

The last twenty-five years of research on the use of monetary policy to affect output and inflation has followed a distinct logical progression. First, Friedman (1968) and Phelps (1967, 1968, 1970) introduced expected inflation into the Phillips curve. They pointed out that a monetary expansion to raise output would come at the expense of ever accelerating inflation, so that the increase in output could not persist in the long run. Second, Barro (1977, 1978), Lucas (1972, 1973, 1976), Sargent (1971, 1973), and Sargent and Wallace (1975, 1976) made the expectations rational. The implication was that policymakers could not have a systematic effect on output even in the short run. They might as well give up on the idea of affecting output, and simply aim for zero inflation. Third, Fischer (1977), Taylor (1980), and others introduced contracts that made wages and prices sticky.[6] The result was to return some effectiveness to monetary policy in responding to disturbances, but again only in the short run.

The next ten years of relevant research brought the debate on "rules vs. discretion" to the center stage of monetary theory. Rational expectations in itself did not imply that the government should abandon all discretionary policy; as noted above there was still scope for responding to disturbances in the short run, provided that policymakers acted with sufficient humility and awareness of the long-run implications. There appeared to be no formal basis to arguments such as Milton Friedman's that the government should completely renounce discretion in favor of rules. How could the country benefit from voluntarily giving up a policy tool?

Calvo (1978) and Kydland and Prescott (1977) introduced the notion of time consistency, a precommitment that would bind government policy-makers and enter private expectations. In the case of monetary policy, a binding precommitment to slow money growth would cause workers and others to reduce their expectations of inflation; the result would be a lower actual inflation rate for any given level of output. At first it seemed that such a precommitment could only improve welfare if discretionary monetary policy were subject to political pressures that aimed for a point on the short-run output/inflation trade-off that was higher than optimal. (Such pressures could result because those who dominated the political process either did not understand the longer-run inflationary effects, or put a lower value on price stability than was in the national interest, or had a higher discount rate than was in the national interest.) Such arguments for insulating monetary policy from populist pressures have some validity in their own right. But Barro and Gordon (1983) showed that discretion could lead to excessive expansion even when the policymakers sought to maximize the "correct" objective function, namely, the correct quadratic loss function in output and inflation. The key to this result is the assumption that the loss function, shared by the policymakers and the country as a whole, is centered around a level of output that is greater than potential output.

This assumption dramatically expanded the boundaries of the existing models. The recognition that any country would like a higher level of output if it could have it sounds simple. Previous authors had felt bound to rule it out on the grounds that, in the long run, it is not attainable. But just because the bliss point is not attainable does not mean that the correct objective function is not centered around it. Technically it requires the existence of some other distortion, such as the existence of unemployment compensation, that artificially raises the natural rate of unemployment or lowers potential output. But there are plenty of those.

The superiority of this framework is shown immediately by its ability to explain the fact that virtually all countries, lacking as most of them do truly binding commitment mechanisms, experience average inflation rates above zero. In the traditional theory, where potential output and optimal output were assumed to coincide, it followed that positive inflation rates (in the aftermath of positive shocks) were no more frequent than were negative ones (in the aftermath of negative shocks). This implication was clearly at variance with reality.

The conclusion from the Barro-Gordon model was that countries should not merely announce their intention to aim for zero inflation and ignore output fluctuations, but should actually be bound in such a way as to prevent them from straying from this commitment even if subsequent events seem to call for it. This result was the long missing formal justification for rules over discretion. But what, exactly, should be the rules?

The final chapter in the book compares four possible rules: a money rule, nominal GDP rule, price level rule, and exchange rate (or price of gold) rule. It argues that the nominal GDP rule dominates the money rule in its ability to stabilize real GDP and the price level, and for plausible parameter values is likely to dominate the others as well.

The conclusion that annual targeting of nominal GDP targeting could be a useful way to conduct monetary policy still leaves important issues unexamined. None of the chapters here address the shorter-term issue of how to move the monetary policy levers, such as unborrowed reserves or the federal funds rate, to achieve the specified nominal GDP target. If nominal GDP seems to be overshooting the target range during the first quarter of the year, by how much should the authorities tighten the controls to try to bring it back into the target range during the rest of the year? Fortunately that topic has been extensively explored by others. Bennett McCallum (1987, 1988a, b) develops possible rules for how the monetary base or federal funds rate should respond to deviations of nominal GNP from the target. Two recent contributions that demonstrate the feasibility of nominal GDP targeting are Feldstein and Stock (1994) and Hall and Mankiw (1993).

In practice, the monetary authorities would have to respond to a whole array of available information, not just to the quarterly nominal GDP reports. The latter are available only with a lag and are always subject to revision. Among the many indicators of monetary ease that they might want to take into account in forecasting the likely future path of nominal demand are commodity prices and the term structure of interest rates, which are available instantaneously. In this way, the results of part II of this volume might be of some help in implementing the sort of scheme proposed in part III.

11 Ambiguous Policy Multipliers in Theory and in Empirical Models

A project undertaken under the auspices of the Brookings Institution asked twelve leading world econometric models to perform simulations for some carefully specified macroeconomic policy experiments. Opinion may vary on whether the twelve models are surprisingly similar or surprisingly dissimilar in their estimates of the effects of macroeconomic policy changes. But this chapter takes the mischievous tack of examining disagreement where it is at its greatest: where the models give answers of opposite sign. I consider the reduced-form policy multipliers of both fiscal policy and monetary policy. My discussion of how the multipliers are determined includes (1) the divergent multipliers one would expect to get from the standard theoretical models that appear in the literature, (2) the divergent multipliers that emerge from the simulations in the Brookings modeling simulation exercise, and (3) an attempt to interpret the second pattern in terms of the first.

The twelve models with their abbreviations are as follows: MCM—the Federal Reserve Board's Multi-Country Model; EC—the European Community Commission's COMPACT model; EPA—the Japanese Economic Planning Agency's model; LINK—Project Link, which put together the various models of national economies that had already been built in the respective countries; LIVERPOOL—the Liverpool model of Patrick Minford, a "new classical" British economist who advised Prime Minister Margaret Thatcher; MSG—the McKibbin-Sachs Global model (which assumes rational expectations, but is otherwise somewhat Keynesian), built by Jeffrey Sachs of Harvard University and Warwick McKibbin of the Brookings Institution; MINIMOD—a smaller approximation of the MCM, built by Richard Haas and Paul Masson of the International Monetary

Originally published in *Empirical Macroeconomics for Interdependent Economies*, ed. Ralph Bryant et al. (The Brookings Institution, 1988), 17–26. Reprinted with permission.

Fund; VAR—estimates by Christopher Sims and Robert Litterman obtained by Vector AutoRegression (a technique that uses no economic
theory, but merely looks for regular patterns in the data); OECD—the
Interlink model built by staff members at the Organisation of Economic
Cooperation and Development (an agency with a membership of twenty-
four industrialized countries and a Secretariat in Paris); TAYLOR—a
rational expectations model built by John Taylor of Stanford University,
a former advisor to President George Bush; WHARTON—a generally
Keynesian model, originally built by Nobel Laureate Lawrence Klein of the
University of Pennsylvania; and DRI—the model of Data Resources, Inc.,
a firm that sells economic forecasts to many corporations, as well as government agencies, from Lexington, Massachusetts.

I examine the models' conflicting implications for the effects of a change
in government expenditure and the effects of a change in the money
supply. In each case, all other policy variables, domestic and foreign, are
held constant.

The well-known ambiguity in the basic two-country Mundell-Fleming
model is the question whether a fiscal expansion causes the domestic currency to appreciate or depreciate. This ambiguity is also a feature of more
general theoretical models. The other ambiguity that appears most commonly in the theoretical literature is the effect of the exchange rate, and
therefore of domestic policy, on foreign income. Somewhat surprisingly,
neither of these issues is the one on which the simulations show the most
conflict. Most of the models show a fiscal expansion appreciating the domestic currency and raising foreign output. The models are in much greater
disagreement on a question that much of the literature considers unambiguous: the negative effect of a domestic *monetary* expansion on the current
account of foreign countries and, through the trade linkage, on foreign
output.

11.1   The General Two-Country Model

Since the generalized Mundell-Fleming model is so familiar, I circumscribe
the algebra tightly. And though I specify the equations in a quite general
form, I then proceed to consider only special cases.

$$M/P = L(Y,i) \qquad \phi \equiv L_y > 0 \qquad \lambda \equiv L_i < 0 \tag{1}$$

$$M^*/P^* = L^*(Y^*,i^*) \qquad \phi^* \equiv L_{y^*}^* > 0 \qquad \lambda^* \equiv L_{i^*}^* < 0 \tag{2}$$

$$Y = A(Y,i; SP^*/P) + G + TB \qquad A_y > 0 \qquad A_i < 0 \tag{3}$$

$$Y^* = A^*(Y^*, i^*; SP^*/P) + G^* - (P/SP^*)TB \qquad A_{y^*}^* > 0 \qquad A_{i^*}^* < 0 \quad (4)$$

$$TB = X(SP^*/P) + \mu^*Y^* - \mu Y \qquad X_S > 0 \tag{5}$$

$$TB = -KA = -K(i - i^*; S/\bar{S}) \qquad k \equiv K_{i-i^*} > 0 \tag{6}$$

$$Y/\bar{Y} = (P/\bar{P})^\sigma \tag{7}$$

$$Y^*/\bar{Y}^* = (P^*/\bar{P}^*)^{\sigma^*}, \tag{8}$$

where

$M \equiv$ money supply

$P \equiv$ price level (domestic goods, unless otherwise stated)

$Y \equiv$ output

$i \equiv$ interest rate

$S \equiv$ exchange rate (home currency cost of foreign currency)

$G \equiv$ government expenditures

$TB \equiv$ trade balance

$KA \equiv$ net capital inflow.

Equations (1) and (2) give the money market equilibrium equations for the domestic and foreign countries, respectively. Equations (3) and (4) show the demands for goods. I allow for the possibility of a Laursen-Metzler effect, that a worsening of the terms of trade would raise expenditure measured in domestic units, by including the real exchange rate after the semicolon. Equation (5) gives the trade balance. Equation (6) gives net capital outflow as a function of the nominal interest differential, and possibly of expected depreciation, where the latter is assumed to be a decreasing function of the spot rate relative to its equilibrium level. Under floating exchange rates the trade balance and net capital outflow are equal. Finally, in equations (7) and (8) the supply of output is seen to be a function of the price level relative to an equilibrium value, which can be thought of as either the expected price level or as the cost of labor and other variable factors of production.

This model leaves out many factors, notably the stocks of government and international indebtedness.[1] Such omissions might be justified by an appeal to the short run, over which the stocks cannot change much;[2] my focus in the simulations is on the effects in the second year after a policy change (possibly just long enough for the trade balance to get past the negative part of the J-curve). In models with forward-looking expectations, such as MSG, LIVERPOOL, MINIMOD, and TAYLOR, long-run effects can be passed back through time to the short run. But even then, the difference is usually quantitative rather than qualitative. The sign of an effect is less likely to be influenced by the omission of such factors as stocks of indebtedness.[3]

I consider first the case in which supply is infintely elastic ($\sigma = \sigma^* = \infty$), so that the price levels P and P^* are fixed in the short run, and all the variables that appear after the semicolons are omitted. This is the basic Mundell-Fleming model.[4] Equation (6) can be used to eliminate the trade balance in equations (3) and (4); these two together with equations (1) and (2) determine four endogenous variables, Y, Y^*, i, and i^*, as a function of the four policy variables, G, M, G^*, and M^*. (Equations (5) and (6) then determine the trade balance and the exchange rate.)[5]

A fiscal expansion in the basic Mundell-Fleming model has the following well-known effects. It increases domestic income Y and therefore the domestic interest rate i.[6] The differential between the domestic and foreign interest rates attracts a capital inflow that, ex post, corresponds to a trade deficit. If capital mobility is sufficiently high (if the slope of the balance-of-payments equilibrium curve μ/k is less than the slope of the LM curve ϕ/λ), the balance of payments will improve at an unchanged exchange rate. This implies that the domestic currency appreciates under floating rates. The currency appreciation may be as important a cause of the trade deficit as the increase in income is. The counterpart foreign trade surplus increases foreign income Y^*.

The primary ambiguity in this scenario is whether capital mobility is high enough (or the LM curve steep enough) for the fiscal expansion to appreciate the currency; the reverse appears as a prominent possibility in textbooks and in many of the large econometric models. Some of these models have been said to exhibit an asymmetry: fiscal expansion in the United States appreciates its currency but—whether because of lower capital mobility, a flatter LM curve, monetary accommodation, or other factors—fiscal expansion in Europe or Japan depreciates their currencies.

A monetary expansion has unambiguous effects in the Mundell-Fleming model. It reduces the domestic interest rate and therefore increases domestic income. The differential between domestic and foreign interest rates induces a capital outflow. The currency unambiguously depreciates, all the more if capital mobility is high. As a result, the trade balance improves, notwithstanding the higher level of income, as seen by the ex post net capital outflow. The stimulus to net foreign demand—that is, to the trade balance—may constitute a larger amount of the increase in output than the stimulus to domestic demand—that is, investment and other interest-sensitive sectors. The corresponding worsening in the foreign trade balance reduces foreign income. Thus the classic Mundell-Fleming result of inverse transmission occurs: a contractionary monetary policy like the one the United States adopted in 1980–82 is expansionary for Europe, via the trade balance.

The theoretical literature features at least five ways the foregoing transmission results can be reversed, each of them through effects of the exchange rate on variables *other than* the trade balance.[7] The exchange rate S can enter the saving-expenditure decision through the terms of trade in equation 4, enter money demand through the price level in equation (2), enter expenditure through real wealth in equation (4), enter supply through the price of imported inputs in equation (8), and enter supply through the nominal wage rate, also in equation (8). I consider each possibility briefly.

First, according to the Laursen-Metzler-Harberger effect, a worsening in the terms of trade—that is, an increase in SP^*/P—should affect the saving-expenditure decision similarly to any other decline in real income. In the traditional Keynesian literature, this means a reduction in saving to protect living standards, as measured in domestic terms: $A_S > 0$.[8] The point of the original Laursen-Metzler (1950) article was that, when a domestic expansion depreciates the domestic currency, the foreign country will respond to the improvement in its terms of trade by decreasing expenditure, resulting in negative transmission under floating exchange rates.

In a monetary expansion, because the Mundell-Fleming model's introduction of capital flows gave the negative transmission result anyway, the Laursen-Metzler effect changes little. But in a fiscal expansion (with low capital mobility, so that the domestic currency depreciates), this negative effect on foreign output could conceivably reverse the standard transmission result. Such a result seems less likely under modern conditions of high capital mobility. For example, in the U.S. fiscal expansion of 1983–85 the dollar appreciated strongly. To simplify the following discussion of the remaining four effects, I assume that a fiscal expansion appreciates the currency.

As previously defined, the price levels P and P^* refer only to goods produced in the domestic and foreign countries, respectively. For the money demand functions, however, they could as easily be replaced by the consumer price indexes, CPI and CPI^*, defined as a Cobb-Douglas weighted average of own goods and imports:[9]

$$CPI = P^\alpha (SP^*)^{1-\alpha} \tag{9}$$

$$CPI^* = (P/S)^{\alpha^*}(P^*)^{1-\alpha^*}. \tag{10}$$

A depreciation of the foreign currency ($S\downarrow$) will lower the foreign real money stock M^*/CPI^*, exerting a contractionary effect on that country's output.

If the depreciation of the foreign currency originates from a domestic fiscal expansion, this effect can reverse the standard Mundell-Fleming result of positive transmission to the foreign country. In a domestic monetary expansion, on the other hand, the domestic currency depreciates, the foreign currency appreciates, CPI^* falls, the foreign real money stock rises, and Y^* can increase: transmission can be positive. Thus both the standard positive transmission of fiscal policy and the standard negative transmission of monetary policy can be reversed. The effect on the real money stock was one argument open to those Europeans who believed that the U.S. policy mix of the early 1980s—tight money and a loose budget, resulting in a strong dollar—had adverse effects on European growth.

Similar to the negative effect of the exchange rate on the real money stock is the negative effect on the real stock of government bonds. A depreciation can be contractionary if real wealth enters the expenditure function. The exchange rate also has a negative effect on expenditure if the country in question is in debt to foreigners in foreign currency, as are many developing countries. Either of those effects is capable of reversing the effect on income through the trade balance; that is, turning the positive transmission of fiscal policy into negative transmission, and vice versa for monetary policy.

Until now I have assumed, for the short run, infinitely elastic supply ($\sigma = \sigma^* = \infty$), so that the output prices P and P^* are fixed (in their own currencies). Relaxing this assumption does not in itself change qualitative conclusions about movements in output, assuming the equilibrium price levels $\bar{P}$ and $\bar{P}^*$—whether interpreted as expected price levels or as markup functions of input costs—are constant in the short run. Where expansionary effects on Y were previously noted, they are replaced by increases in P and, as a result, smaller increases in Y. To be precise, only $\sigma/(1 + \sigma)$ of an increase in aggregate demand will be reflected in higher output. All contractionary effects are similarly reduced. In a well-specified model the changes in P should in the long run be large enough to eliminate any effects on Y. I am concentrating on the short run, however, in which most models show increases in both P and Y.[10]

The last two ways that the standard transmission results can be reversed operate through the equilibrium price levels in the supply relationships. Assume that $\bar{P}$ and $\bar{P}^*$ in the supply functions are determined as markups over input costs; that is, their rate of change is a linear function of the rate of change of the prices of oil and other inputs, the rate of change of wages, and the long-run rate of productivity growth. An increase in input prices will shift the supply relationship adversely, reducing output. Thus insofar as the price of oil is determined in dollars, an appreciation of the dollar is contractionary for non-U.S. countries. This effect of the exchange rate, like the effects on real money balances and real wealth, runs in the reverse direction from the standard trade balance effect in the Mundell-Fleming model: fiscal expansions that appreciate the currency can be transmitted negatively and monetary expansions transmitted positively, rather than the other way around. Thus this argument too was open to those who believed the strong dollar of the early 1980s hurt Europe.

The final variable that might depend on the exchange rate is the wage rate. For simplicity, let $\bar{P}$ equal the wage rate. If wages are fixed, or determined by the unemployment rate, the standard results are not affected. On the other hand, if wages are fully indexed to the domestic price level, equations (7) and (8) become $Y = \bar{Y}$ and $Y^* = \bar{Y}^*$: policy can have no effect on output in either country. The interesting case is when wages are indexed to the consumer price index, including import prices as in equations (9) and (10), because the exchange rate can open a gap between CPI and P. Equations (7) and (8) then become

$$Y/\bar{Y} = (P/SP^*)^{(1-\alpha)\sigma} \tag{11}$$

$$Y^*/\bar{Y}^* = (P^*S/P)^{(1-\alpha^*)\sigma^*}. \tag{12}$$

It is clear that one country's output can go up only if the other country's output goes down. In a domestic fiscal expansion that appreciates the domestic currency (reduces S), there is a contractionary effect on foreign income similar to those effects obtained through real money, real wealth, and oil prices. All four work to reverse the Mundell-Fleming result of positive transmission. One might expect that a domestic monetary expansion, because it increases S in equation (12), would have the opposite transmission effect from a fiscal expansion—that it would increase foreign income. But from equation (11) the monetary expansion would then have to reduce domestic income. This perverse result can be ruled out by the recognition from equation (3) that Y cannot fall unless i rises and reduces A or the currency appreciates and reduces TB, neither of which will follow from a monetary expansion. The only possible solution is that P rises by the same proportion as S (which is the same proportion as the increase in the money supply) and that there are no real effects, either on domestic or foreign income.[11] Table 11.1 summarizes the various possible transmission effects of the exchange rate.[12]

Table 11.1
Theoretical transmission effects of domestic fiscal and monetary expansions

Item	Fiscal expansion with low capital mobility	Fiscal expansion with high capital mobility	Monetary expansion
Domestic currency	Depreciates	Appreciates	Depreciates
Effects on foreign output			
Through trade balance = capital outflow			
Interest differential	Positive	Positive	Negative
Regressive exchange rate expectations	Positive	Negative	Positive
Through domestic demand			
Laursen-Metzler effect	Negative	Positive	Negative
Real money stock	Positive	Negative	Positive
Real wealth	Positive	Negative	Positive
Through supply			
Imported inputs	Positive	Negative	Positive
Wage indexation	Positive	Negative	Positive

11.2 Fiscal Policy Multipliers in the Simulations

Table 11.2 summarizes the effects of a fiscal expansion, an increase in government spending equal to 1 percent of GNP, according to the twelve models in the Brookings simulations. The variables shown are output, the consumer price index, the short-term interest rate, the exchange rate, and the current account. The left columns show the variables in the region originating the fiscal expansion, and the right columns the foreign region. For simplicity, the table shows the effects only in the second year after the policy action.

As one would expect, all the models show a positive effect of fiscal expansion on domestic output. The numbers in the first column can be read as fiscal multipliers, because $(\Delta Y/Y)/(\Delta G/Y) = \Delta Y/\Delta G$. They are mostly in the range of 1 to 2. Almost all the models show increases in the price level and the interest rate, from which presumably follows some amount of crowding out of construction and other interest-sensitive sectors.

The best-known theoretical ambiguity, the effect on the exchange rate, turns out to generate relatively little disagreement. In a U.S. fiscal expansion, ten models show an appreciation of the dollar. The only exceptions are the LINK and WHARTON models, which report a depreciation, evidently attributable to little or no capital mobility. In an ROECD fiscal expansion, there is more divergence. But six out of eleven models still show the standard high capital mobility result, a domestic appreciation against the dollar. The exceptions now also include the EEC, EPA, and VAR models.

The asymmetry between the exchange rate effects of U.S. fiscal expansion and European or Japanese expansion, which here shows up only in these three models, has been attributed to various causes. One of them, a greater tendency to monetize government deficits abroad than in the United States, should have been ruled out by the careful specification in the Brookings experiment that money supplies be held constant. Another reason suggested, lower capital mobility, can explain econometric findings for individual non-U.S. countries but cannot explain the asymmetry in a well-specified two-country Mundell-Fleming model: capital mobility into the United States cannot be higher than capital mobility out of the rest of the world. The same applies to the argument that ROECD countries are more open to trade than the United States. Because the ROECD economy is larger than the U.S. economy, it is less open in the aggregate. One explanation that works is a steeper LM curve in the United States, so that U.S. interest rates are more easily driven up.[13]

For either U.S. or ROECD fiscal policy, the simulations show that in all but one of the structural models changes are transmitted positively to the rest of the world. This is not surprising. Including even the few cases in which a fiscal expansion depreciates the currency, the domestic current account is observed to worsen in all the structural models. (This is necessarily the result in standard theory: it is the worsening of the trade balance, if it is big enough, that is the *cause* of any downward pressure on the currency.) The foreign current account and foreign income therefore increase.[14] In the majority of cases, where a fiscal expansion appreciates the currency, the positive transmission to foreign output provides a preliminary indication that the four theoretical contractionary effects of a currency depreciation discussed in the preceding section (through money balances, real wealth, imported input prices, or wages, respectively) either are not operating or at least are not powerful enough to reverse standard transmission results.

The one exception to positive transmission among the eleven structural models is LIVERPOOL. Though it lines up with the majority on the positive effect of a fiscal expansion on the value of domestic currency, the negative effect on the domestic current account, and the positive effect on the foreign current account, the LIVERPOOL model nevertheless produces

Table 11.2
Simulation effects in second year of an increase in government expenditure of 1 percent of GNP
(Percent, except for interest rates in percentage points and current account in billions of dollars)

Fiscal expansion	Originating region					Foreign region			
	Output	Consumer price index	Short-term interest rate	Currency value	Current account	Current account	Short-term interest rate	Consumer price index	Output
In the United States[a]									
DRI	2.1	0.4	1.6	3.2	−22.0	0.8	0.4	0.3	0.7
EEC[b]	1.2	0.6	1.5	0.6	−11.6	6.6	0.3	0.2	0.3
EPA[c]	1.7	0.9	2.2	1.9	−20.5	9.3	0.5	0.3	0.9
LINK	1.2	0.5	0.2	−0.1	−6.4	1.9	n.a.	−0.0	0.1
LIV	0.6	0.2	0.4	1.0	−7.0	3.4	0.1	0.6	−0.0
MCM	1.8	0.4	1.7	2.8	−16.5	8.9	0.4	0.4	0.7
MINIMOD	1.0	0.3	1.1	1.0	−8.5	5.5	0.2	0.1	0.3
MSG	0.9	−0.1	0.9	3.2	−21.6	22.7	1.0	0.5	0.3
OECD	1.1	0.6	1.7	0.4	−14.2	11.4	0.7	0.3	0.4
TAYLOR[d]	0.6	0.5	0.3	4.0	n.a.	n.a.	0.2	0.4	0.4
VAR[d]	0.4	−0.9	0.1	1.2	−0.5	−0.2	−0.0	−0.0	−0.0
WHARTON	1.4	0.3	1.1	−2.1	−15.4	5.3	0.6	−0.1	−0.2
In Rest of OECD (ROECD)									
DRI	n.a.	n.a.	n.a.	n.a.	n.a.	n.a.	n.a.	n.a.	n.a.
EEC[b]	1.3	0.8	0.4	−0.6	−9.3	3.0	0.0	0.1	0.2
EPA[c]	2.3	0.7	0.3	−0.7	−13.1	4.7	0.6	0.3	0.3
LINK	1.2	0.1	n.a.	−0.1	−6.1	6.3	0.0	0.0	0.2
LIV	0.3	0.8	0.0	3.3	−17.2	11.9	0.8	3.1	−0.5

MCM	1.4	0.3	0.6	0.3	−7.2	7.9	0.5	0.2	0.5
MINIMOD	1.6	0.2	0.9	0.6	−2.2	3.2	0.3	0.2	0.1
MSG	1.1	0.1	1.4	2.9	−5.3	10.5	1.3	0.6	0.4
OECD	1.5	0.7	1.9	0.9	−6.9	3.3	0.3	0.2	0.1
TAYLOR[d]	1.6	1.2	0.6	2.7	n.a.	n.a.	0.4	0.9	0.6
VAR[d]	0.5	−0.3	−0.2	−2.4	1.7	−2.6	0.2	−0.1	0.3
WHARTON	3.2	−0.8	0.8	−2.4	−5.5	4.7	0.1	−0.0	0.0

Source: Reference tables in Bryant et al. (1988), supplemental volume.
n.a. Not available.
a. Simulation B, with all signs reversed.
b. ROECD short-term interest rate not available; long-term reported instead.
c. ROECD current account is Japan, Germany, the United Kingdom, and Canada.
d. CPI not available; GNP deflator reported instead.
e. Stimulation G.

the unique result of a negative effect on foreign output. The reverse transmission holds both from the United States abroad (weakly) and in the
opposite direction (more strongly). Evidently one or more of the four
contractionary exchange rate effects is operating. Minford (1984, eq. 2, pp.
88–89) specifies an adverse supply effect from depreciation, apparently
justified along the lines of the last of the four effects enumerated above: an
increase in wages in nominal or own-product terms.[15] The LIVERPOOL
simulations show a sharper increase in the CPI of the country not undertak-
ing the fiscal expansion, presumably as a result of the depreciation of its
currency, than the other models do. This could explain the strength of the
adverse supply effect in that model.

Not surprisingly the one model that shows the most dissimilar results
is nonstructural: Sims-Litterman VAR. Like the LIVERPOOL model, it
shows no positive transmission from U.S. fiscal policy to ROECD output.
(The effect appears to be inverse in the first two years, but insignificant to
the third digit.) More anomalously it shows a fiscal expansion in either
country reducing the price level P in both countries (GNP deflator).[16]

To sum up the results of fiscal expansion, all structural models show
negative effects on the domestic current account. All but one show positive
effects on both domestic and foreign output. All but one show positive
effects on the domestic price level. Several show a negative rather than
positive effect on the value of the currency, especially when it is the
ROECD that is expanding. But the one case of negative transmission to
foreign output is not one of the few, like the WHARTON model, in which
the domestic currency depreciates, which one would expect to weaken the
transmission link through the trade balance. Rather, it is the LIVERPOOL
model, in which the domestic currency appreciates, raising the other
country's CPI sharply, with adverse effects on supply.

These conflicts regarding the exchange rate and transmission effects of
fiscal policy are relatively few and within the bounds of standard theoretical results. (This does not include the VAR model, which features anoma-
lous effects on price levels, interest rates, and current accounts.)

11.3   Monetary Policy Multipliers in the Simulations

Table 11.3 presents the effects of a monetary expansion equal to 4 percent
of the money supply, phased in over the first year (simulation D for the
United States in Bryant et al. (1988), and simulation H for the ROECD).
The simulation findings for the effects of monetary policy show more
conflict among the models, and with the conflict less in line with well-

known theoretical ambiguities, than do the findings for the effects of fiscal policy. They all agree that the monetary expansion drives down the interest rate and thereby stimulates domestic output. Yet the models divide almost evenly on the question of positive or negative transmission of a U.S. monetary expansion to the rest of the OECD.

All models show a clear depreciation of the dollar. The MCM, EPA, LINK, LIVERPOOL, MINIMOD, TAYLOR, and DRI models exhibit the standard Mundell-Fleming result: the appreciation of foreign currencies causes foreign incomes to decline. However, only the MINIMOD shows the complete Mundell-Fleming story, in which the domestic current account improves, the foreign current account worsens, and, as a result, foreign output declines. The EEC, VAR, MSG, OECD, and WHARTON models show positive transmission instead. When the monetary expansion originates in the ROECD, positive transmission occurs not only in those five models but also in EPA, LINK, and LIVERPOOL. In other words, the Mundell-Fleming transmission result is reversed in eight out of eleven models.

The obvious explanation for a rise in foreign income in response to a domestic increase in the money supply and exchange rate is that the appreciation of the foreign currencies has one or more of the four expansionary effects: an increase in the real money supply or real wealth or a decrease in wages or imported input costs. If any of these expansionary effects is strong enough to dominate the change in the trade balance, a positive transmission should occur. The main obstacle to attaching this interpretation to the models is that in the Brookings simulations for a nonpolicy depreciation of the dollar (simulation F), eight of the ten models show a clear negative effect on foreign income. The only one to show a clear expansionary effect, despite the worsening in the foreign trade balance, is the MINIMOD, which does not show a positive transmission of monetary expansion. This suggests that the observed positive transmission of a U.S. monetary expansion to foreign income occurs through some channel other than the exchange rate.

For the EEC, OECD, and WHARTON models, the channel of the transmission of a U.S. monetary expansion is easily identified: despite the depreciation of the dollar, the U.S. current account worsens and the foreign current account improves. Puzzlingly, the worsening in the U.S. current account occurs not only in the three models in which ROECD output rises, but also in five of the models in which ROECD output falls: MCM, EPA, LINK, LIVERPOOL, and DRI.[17] In the MCM and EPA models, the ROECD current account worsens even though the U.S. current account

Table 11.3
Simulation effects in second year of an increase in the money supply of 4 percent
Percent except for interest rates in percentage points and current account in billions of dollars

Monetary expansion	Originating region					Foreign region			
	Output	Consumer price index	Short-term interest rate	Currency value	Current account	Current account	Short-term interest rate	Consumer price index	Output
In the United States[a]									
DRI	1.8	0.4	−2.3	−14.6	−1.4	14.5	−1.1	−1.3	−0.6
EEC[b]	1.0	0.8	−2.4	−4.0	−2.8	1.2	−0.5	−0.4	0.2
EPA[c]	1.2	1.0	−2.2	−6.4	−1.6	−10.1	−0.6	−0.5	−0.4
LINK	1.0	−0.4	−1.4	−2.3	−5.9	1.5	n.a.	−0.1	−0.1
LIV	0.1	3.7	−0.3	−3.9	−13.0	0.1	−0.1	−0.0	−0.0
MCM	1.5	0.4	−2.2	−6.0	−3.1	−3.5	−0.5	−0.6	−0.7
MINIMOD	1.0	0.8	−1.8	−5.7	2.8	−4.7	−0.1	−0.2	−0.2
MSG	0.3	1.5	−0.8	−2.0	2.6	−4.4	−1.2	−0.7	0.4
OECD	1.6	0.7	−0.8	−2.6	−8.4	3.1	−0.1	−0.1	0.3
TAYLOR[d]	0.6	1.2	−0.4	−4.9	n.a.	n.a.	−0.1	−0.2	−0.2
VAR[d]	3.0	0.4	−1.9	−22.9	4.9	5.1	0.3	0.1	0.4
WHARTON	0.7	0.0	−2.1	−1.0	−5.1	5.3	−1.3	−0.1	0.4
In ROECD[c]									
DRI	n.a.	n.a.	n.a.	n.a.	n.a.	n.a.	n.a.	n.a.	n.a.
EEC[b]	0.8	1.0	−1.0	−2.3	−5.2	1.9	0.0	0.1	0.1
EPA[c]	0.0	0.0	−0.1	−0.1	−0.1	0.1	−0.0	−0.0	0.0
LINK[f]	0.8	−0.6	n.a.	−2.8	−1.4	3.5	0.0	−0.0	0.1
LIV	0.4	2.8	−0.9	−8.4	7.1	−8.2	−1.1	−3.4	1.6

MCM	1.5	0.6	−2.1	−5.4	3.5	0.1	−0.2	−0.2	−0.0
MINIMOD	0.8	0.2	−1.8	−4.8	3.6	−1.4	−0.6	−0.5	−0.3
MSG	0.2	1.5	−0.7	−1.4	−15.9	12.0	−1.2	−0.6	0.3
OECD	0.8	0.3	−1.3	−2.1	−1.6	2.3	−0.2	−0.1	0.1
TAYLOR[d]	0.8	0.7	−0.3	−3.5	n.a.	n.a.	−0.2	−0.5	−0.1
VAR[d]	0.7	−0.5	−3.0	−5.5	5.2	−10.0	0.6	−0.7	1.2
WHARTON	0.2	−0.1	−0.8	0.2	2.6	0.5	0.0	0.0	0.0

Source: Reference tables in Bryant et al. (1988), supplemental volume.
n.a. Not available.
a. Simulation D.
b. ROECD short-term interest rate not available; long-term reported instead.
c. ROECD current account is Japan, Germany, the United Kingdom, and Canada.
d. CPI not available; GNP deflator reported instead.
e. Simulation H.
f. Appreciation of non-U.S. currency not available; depreciation of dollar reported instead.

also worsens,[18] while in the other three, ROECD output falls even though the ROECD current account improves. Either breaking of the trade transmission link seems difficult to explain.

The puzzling fact in the deterioration of the U.S. trade balance in eight out of eleven of the models is not that the dollar depreciates. Higher U.S. income accounts for higher imports, and simulation F, the nonpolicy exogenous depreciation of the dollar, reveals that several of the models have such a prolonged J-curve that the trade balance does not respond positively to the exchange rate until the third or fourth year (WHARTON, OECD, and LINK). The puzzle from the viewpoint of the Mundell-Fleming model is rather how the net capital inflow, which must equal the trade deficit under floating exchange rates, can increase after a monetary expansion. The monetary expansion should decrease the U.S. interest rate (except in models where there are no lags in either expectations or price adjustment). In the simulations the interest rate does indeed decrease.[19] The Mundell-Fleming theory under floating exchange rates says that the lower interest rate should induce a capital outflow, which implies a strong enough currency depreciation to improve the current account correspondingly.[20] The models in the simulations seem to behave more like models of fixed (or managed) exchange rates, where an increase in the money supply flows out of the country through a trade deficit financed out of foreign exchange reserves, than like models that assume no intervention in the foreign exchange market.

Helliwell and Padmore (1985, pp. 1130–31) and Helliwell (in Bryant et al., 1988) have explained why some of the large econometric models show that a monetary expansion causes a net capital inflow. Capital flows respond not only to interest rates but also to expectations of future changes in the exchange rate. If the instantaneous depreciation of the currency, which results from a monetary expansion, generates expectations of future appreciation toward long-run equilibrium, it will have a positive effect on the attractiveness of domestic assets that runs counter to the effect of lower interest rates. In Helliwell's terms, speculative capital flows fulfill the stabilizing "buffer stock" role that official intervention would play under a system of fixed or managed exchange rates. This regressive type of expectation has been found to be rational in the Dornbusch (1976) overshooting model and some other versions of the asset market approach to exchange rate determination. How it alters the Mundell-Fleming approach to the capital account is somewhat less well known, though stated by Mussa (1979, p. 191).[21] Clearly many as yet unresolved research issues continue to fall under the heading of understanding expectations and the capital account.

If the only modification to the Mundell-Fleming model were the addition of regressive expectations about exchange rate changes, positive transmission to foreign income would imply that the foreign interest rate must rise in order for the foreign money market equilibrium condition (equation (2)) to continue to hold with no change in the foreign money supply, because foreign prices would be constant. However, in most of the empirical models that show positive transmission, the foreign interest rate (sensibly) falls with the domestic rate.

Making the Mundell-Fleming model consistent with both an increase in foreign output and a fall in the foreign interest rate requires not only adding regressive expectations to the model of capital flows, but also incorporating a second modification. The foreign money market equilibrium condition (equation (2)) must continue to hold with no change in the foreign money supply. If the foreign interest rate falls, the foreign price level must fall despite the rise in foreign real GNP. The foreign CPI and GNP deflator both do fall in most of the model simulations because of the appreciation of foreign currencies.[22] Indeed, in half the models in which foreign real GNP rises, foreign *nominal* GNP nevertheless falls.

To sum up the results of monetary expansion, almost as many models show positive transmission to the rest of the OECD as show negative transmission, and most show positive transmission from the rest of the OECD to the United States. This reversal of the Mundell-Fleming result is usually due to a shift in the trade balance in favor of the foreign country, not to effects of the exchange rate on foreign income through possible routes outside the trade link.

In terms of target variables of interest to the domestic country, the effect of a monetary expansion on the trade balance is the issue on which the models disagree the most. Several models feature a non-interest-rate-related capital flow into the domestic country—contrary to basic Mundell-Fleming—which allows the monetary expansion to worsen the trade balance. Such simulation results are strikingly different from the outcome emphasized in the theoretical literature.

Acknowledgments

I am grateful to Ralph C. Bryant, Rudiger Dornbusch, John F. Helliwell, Dale W. Henderson, Bert G. Hickman, Gerald Holtham, Patrick Minford, and Warren Trepeta for their useful comments.

12

The Implications of
Conflicting Models
for Coordination
between Monetary and
Fiscal Policymakers

An easy way for an outsider to tell when an academic discipline has not yet
ascertained "the truth" is when its practitioners each give different answers
to the same question. As macroeconomists we know we have not yet
ascertained the truth—if there was previously any doubt on that score—
when we see that the twelve models included in the Brookings simulation
exercise forecast quite different effects for carefully specified policy
changes. The probability that a given model is correct is small when the
number of models giving different answers is large. Furthermore, it is unlikely that we will ever discover the true model. This pessimistic view is
consistent with both the fact that there are now a large number of different
models and the fact that these models keep changing over time.

There are three ways in which research can proceed. The first is for the
researcher to maintain that he or she has now discovered the one true
model and that all other models are wrong. The second is for the researcher, while continuing to speak the language that suggests his or her
model is the true one, to recognize implicitly that this language is merely a
convenient shorthand. The third is for the researcher to focus explicitly on
the coexistence of conflicting models, which this chapter does.

The second research strategy is the best one to pursue for most economic problems. The econometrician knows that his parameter estimates
are not exactly correct. More generally, all modelers know that their
models must be incomplete and misspecified. Nevertheless, if the economist is good, the errors in his model will not be disabling. That is, even if
they could be correctly handled, they would not much change his forecasts
(in the case of an econometric forecasting model) or the conceptual point
he is trying to make (in the case of a theoretical model). Though it may be

Originally published in *Empirical Macroeconomics for Interdependent Economies*, ed. Ralph
Bryant et al. (The Brookings Institution, 1988), 238–54. Reprinted with permission.

useful for the modeler to have explored as many extensions as possible in appendixes and the like, he does not need to be able to claim that he has exhausted the truth. Nor does he need to make overly frequent disclaimers; the readers will understand that the model is not to be taken as literal truth.

These issues become most salient when, as in most modern macroeconomic models, agents in the proposed model must make decisions based on expectations formed from some model of their own. The rational expectations assumption is, of course, the assumption that the model used by the agents is the same as the proposed larger model. As soon as one admits that the proposed larger model may not be perfectly true, one cannot claim that agents' models must be literally identical to the proposed larger model. But, again, for many economic problems, especially those involving the microeconomic decisions of private agents, one can make a case that little is gained by explicitly focusing on divergent models. The assumption that the agents know the one true model will continue to be an attractive modeling strategy.

When the decisionmakers are governments and the decision variables are macroeconomic policies, the case for assuming that all decision makers know the one true model is less compelling. In the first place, there is no powerful force like the marketplace to discipline governments that use incorrect models. In the second place, the Federal Reserve Board's MCM model, the Japanese EPA model, the OECD INTERLINK model, and so on, are the best that these government agencies have, and one can see that these models conflict. One can argue that microeconomic agents have access to specific knowledge of a common model unavailable to the macroeconomist. It would be more difficult for a macroeconomist at a government agency to argue that policymakers at his or her own agency have access to knowledge of a common model unavailable to the macroeconomist himself.[1]

It is a general principle of the existing literature on macroeconomic policy coordination that when the actions of two policymakers affect variables that each cares about, they can do better by cooperating than they would do in the Nash competitive equilibrium, in which each acts to maximize his own welfare function, taking the actions of the other as given. This principle has led economists to propose two kinds of increased coordination: between different domestic policymaking agencies and between domestic and foreign policymakers. An example of the first kind is the argument that the Federal Reserve should agree to follow a looser monetary policy than it did in the early 1980s in return for an agreement by the administration (and Congress) to reduce the federal budget deficit.

The point would be to reduce interest rates, the value of the dollar, and the trade deficit without losing anything on the output-inflation trade-off. An example of the second kind is the argument that the United States should agree to follow a tighter budget policy in return for an agreement by Europe and Japan to move in the opposite direction.[2] The point, again, would be to reduce the trade imbalance without causing a world recession.

The existence of conflicting models gives the literature on international coordination an air of unreality. To begin with, even among economists who agree on the broad outline of the correct model, the issue of the gains from coordination is subtle enough for small differences to lead to opposite recommendations on the direction in which policy settings must be moved to reap the gains from coordination. In domestic U.S. policymaking, for example, movement toward a tight monetary policy and a loose fiscal policy, far from being the outcome of a destructive lack of coordination between the monetary and fiscal authorities, might be thought desirable from the national point of view: the high value for the dollar reduces the U.S. consumer price index and thereby allows an improvement over the regular output-inflation trade-off.[3] Examples in the international context abound. OECD countries are often urged to undertake a coordinated expansion; the argument is that each country is reluctant to expand on its own for fear of worsening its trade balance or currency value.[4] On the other hand, economists have talked about the need for coordinated monetary discipline (particularly in the 1970s) and coordinated budgetary discipline (particularly in the 1980s). Every possible combination seems to have been suggested: the Nash noncooperative equilibrium is variously thought to result in competitive currency appreciation, competitive currency depreciation ("beggar-thy-neighbor"), insufficient expansion, or excessive expansion. It has even been suggested that the gains from international coordination lie in an agreement that one country will expand whenever others are contracting and vice versa.

If such contradictions are possible within the standard models of mainstream macroeconomists,[5] the situation is even worse once the more widely scattered views of policymakers are acknowledged. In the context of 1983–84, there was little point in trying to convince the U.S. Treasury that, to correct the exchange rate and trade imbalance, the United States should reverse its fiscal expansion in exchange for European and Japanese fiscal expansion. The Treasury took the view that there had been no U.S. fiscal expansion to begin with; that fiscal expansion causes currencies, if anything, to depreciate; that the strength of the dollar was instead attributable to other factors (the "safe-haven" effect); that the trade deficit was not attributable to the strong dollar, but rather primarily to rapid U.S. growth); and—most relevant—that the administration did not want Europe and Japan to undertake fiscal expansion.

The purist scholar will argue that if policymakers have different "information," they should share it with one another and agree on a common model. The proposition about gains from coordination holds regardless of which model is correct.[6] In practical terms, then, the purist is urging on economists a research strategy of first discovering and agreeing on the true model, and only then convincing policymakers that it is the true model (a task that would surely be less difficult if macroeconomists agreed among themselves) and pointing out the gains from coordination based on this true model.

Research will, and should, proceed with the aim of developing models that more closely reflect economic reality. Most of this research will, and perhaps should, proceed under the assumption that agents within the model act on the basis of the model itself. But there is also a need for doing research under the assumption that agents have different models. These are the only circumstances under which policymaking is likely to take place in practice.

In this chapter I consider the domestic problem in which the two policymakers are the monetary authority and the fiscal authority. Chapter 13 considers the international problem, in which the policymakers are the U.S. authorities and European and Japanese authorities. The findings in the international context are similar to those reported here. In both problems the twelve models that participated in the Brookings simulations are used to illustrate the conflicting beliefs that policymakers could have and the implications of such beliefs for coordination.

In order to focus on the role of divergent models in policy conflict and coordination, I consider here what happens when the monetary and fiscal authorities have identical welfare functions. In the case of international coordination the policymakers clearly have different welfare functions,[7] but that is not necessarily true in the domestic case.

12.1 The Theory of Coordination When Policymakers Disagree Only about the Model

I begin by showing that if the monetary and fiscal authorities subscribe to different models, they will prefer a cooperative equilibrium to the Nash noncooperative one even though their welfare functions are the same. I also show that if neither policymaker happens to have the correct model,

the cooperative equilibrium could as easily be inferior to the Nash equilibrium as the other way around; that is, it could result, by the light of the true
model, in a lower value of the agreed-upon welfare function.

When international coordination is studied, each country must have
more than two goals; otherwise it can use its two instruments, domestic
monetary and fiscal policy, to attain both goals regardless of what the
other country does, and no interesting issue of coordination arises. But here
I consider domestic coordination and limit the welfare function to two
goals for simplicity: y is the log of domestic output and x is the current
account as a share of GNP, both expressed as deviations from their desired
or sustainable long-run levels. (In computations of the sort performed in
this chapter, I have also tried the exchange rate and the consumer price
index for the second goal.) The framework shared by all the policymakers
is the familiar linear one of targets and instruments:

$$y = A + Cm + Fg \qquad (1)$$

$$x = B + Dm + Gg, \qquad (2)$$

where y is the log of income, x is the current account as a fraction of output,
m is the log of the money supply, and g is government expenditure as a
fraction of output.

Subscripts on the uppercase letters, the policy multipliers, will be used to
indicate the different values they can take depending on the model: a c to
represent the perceptions of the central bank, and an f to represent the
perceptions of the fiscal authority. I adopt the conventional assumption
that policymakers seek to minimize a quadratic loss function w:

$$w = y^2 + \omega x^2. \qquad (3)$$

To ascertain the behavior of the central bank, I differentiate the loss function with respect to m, with subscripts on the multipliers. The first-order
condition is

$$m = -I_c - J_c g, \qquad (4)$$

where

$$I_c \equiv \frac{C_c A_c + \omega D_c B_c}{C_2^2 + \omega D_c^2}$$

and

$$J_c \equiv \frac{C_c F_c + \omega D_c G_c}{C_2^2 + \omega D_c^2}.$$

To ascertain the behavior of the fiscal authority, I take the derivative with respect to g. The first-order condition is

$$g = -K_f - L_f m, \tag{5}$$

where

$$K_f \equiv \frac{K_f A_f + \omega G_f B_f}{F_f^2 + \omega G_f^2}$$

and

$$L_f \equiv \frac{C_f F_f + \omega D_f G_f}{F_f^2 + \omega G_f^2}.$$

If both policymakers knew the true model, all subscripts could be dropped. The optimal solution in terms of the true parameters would then follow by solving the two equations simultaneously for g and m. The issue of conflict or coordination would not arise; each agency would simply do its agreed-upon part.

But if the policymakers believe in different models, the subscripts must remain. Equation (4) gives m as a function of g, and equation (5) gives g as a function of m. They represent the two authorities' reaction functions. The Nash noncooperative equilibrium is

$$m^n = \frac{-I_c + J_c K_f}{1 - J_c L_f} \tag{6}$$

$$g^n = \frac{-K_f + L_f I_c}{1 - J_c L_f}. \tag{7}$$

Assume that the central bank believes in model 1. Its reaction function is CB1 in figure 12.1. CB1 is downward sloping (a positive J_c) when, as in many of the models, m and g both have positive effects on income and negative effects on the current account. The central bank's perceived indifference curves radiate out from its perceived optimum, point 1. They are intersected by CB1 wherever they are flat, because along CB1 the central bank is optimizing with respect to m for a given g, which means it chooses the obtainable point that is closest to point 1 in the indifference mapping.

If the fiscal authority also believed in model 1, its reaction function FA1 would also pass through point 1. But suppose the fiscal authority believes in model 2. Its reaction function FA2 might slope upward (a negative L_f), as in figure 12.1, if, for example, model 2 differs from model 1 by featuring a positive current account multiplier for the money supply, D_f. This param-

Government expenditure (g)

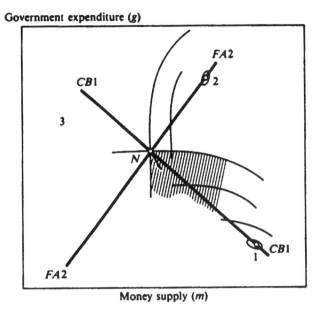

Money supply (m)

Figure 12.1
The Nash competitive equilibrium.

eter is indeed positive for U.S. monetary policy in the MSG, MINIMOD, and VAR models, and for non-U.S. monetary policy in the MCM, LIVER-POOL, MINIMOD, VAR, and WHARTON models.[8]

The fiscal authorities' perceived indifference curves radiate from its perceived optimum, point 2. They are intersected by FA2 wherever they are vertical, because along FA2 the fiscal authority is optimizing with respect to g for a given m. The Nash noncooperative equilibrium is where the two reaction functions intersect, point N. I assume here that the two policymakers know what each other's beliefs are, so that they jump directly to equilibrium at N.[9] If the two policymakers happen to have the same model, then point 1 = point 2 = point N.

It is easy to see that the Nash solution represented by equations (6) and (7) is not the optimum. (One would need $I_c = I$, $K_f = K$, $J_c = J$, and $L_f = L$, where the unsubscripted letters are defined analogously to the subscripted ones so as to represent parameter values in the true model, for the Nash solution to be the optimum.) Neither policymaker will be happy with this equilibrium, each cursing the stupidity of the other for not moving in the desired direction. In the situation shown in figure 12.1, the fiscal authority wishes that the central bank would increase money growth, so as to depreciate the currency and improve the current account. But the central bank's perception is different, that increasing money growth would *worsen* the current account. It wishes that the fiscal authority would decrease government spending.

One might think that when two policymakers have conflicting views on the effects of any proposed package of policy changes, they would simply fail to come to an agreement to coordinate. But even assuming that neither one is willing to revise his beliefs, the policymakers can in general make a bargain that will raise the perceived welfare of each. In figure 12.1 the authorities' indifference curves at N have slopes of zero and infinity, respectively, from which it follows that they are not tangent. They can both agree to move in the southeast direction. There is an entire range of points—those in the shaded lens—that dominate N for both policymakers. Which point will they actually agree on? Much of the literature singles out the Nash bargaining solution, at which the product of the two agents' welfare gains is maximized relative to what perceived welfare would be at the Nash competitive solution $N12$.[10] The bargaining solution is represented by a point on the contract curve like the one labeled $B12$ in figure 12.2. The policymakers would choose m and g to maximize

Government expenditure (g)

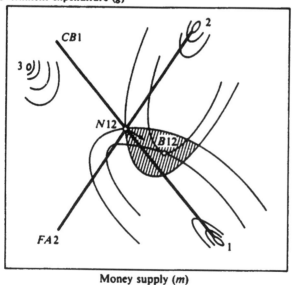

Money supply (m)

Figure 12.2
Policy coordination between central bank and fiscal authority.

$$[W_c(m, g) - W_c(m'', g'')][W_f(m, g) - W_f(m'', g'')]$$

$$= \{[(A_c + C_c m + F_c g)^2 + \omega(B_c + D_c m + G_c g)^2]$$

$$- [(A_c + C_c m'' + F_c g'')^2 + \omega(B_c + D_c m'' + G_c g'')^2]\}$$

$$\times \{[(A_f + C_f m + F_f g)^2 + \omega(B_f + D_f m + G_f g)^2]$$

$$- [(A_f + C_f m'' + F_f g'')^2 + \omega(B_f + D_f m'' + G_f g'')^2]\}. \tag{8}$$

The analytics of finding the Nash bargaining solution are the same as in the standard coordination problem. One could not tell from equation (8), if one did not know, that the parameters refer to different perceptions of the same multipliers rather than to similar perceptions of different multipliers.

The usual enforcement problems exist as well: each would prefer to cheat on the bargain. But for the purposes of this chapter I ignore issues of repeated games, credible commitment, and the like, and simply compare the static cooperative and noncooperative solutions.

One possible alternative to the Nash bargaining point as a cooperative solution for the problem of conflicting models would be for the policymakers to bargain over what is the correct model. In the event of widely diverging Bayesian prior beliefs, it would probably take a prohibitively large amount of new data for the two policymakers to reach a genuine convergence of opinions. But for the sake of compromise, in trying to improve on the competitive equilibrium $N12$, they could agree to base their policy actions on a version of equations (1) and (2) in which the parameter estimates are taken as a weighted average of their individual parameter estimates. If one wished to preserve the symmetry that characterizes the Nash bargaining solution (equation (8)), the weights could be equal.

A possibility for future research is to compare the implications of a strategy of averaging the parameter estimates to the implications of the usual Nash bargaining point. As a positive, rather than normative, solution concept, it has the disadvantage that it could lie outside the shaded lens; that is, it could result in one policymaker's perceived level of welfare being less than it would be at point $N12$. But if the average of two parameter estimates is a better estimator of the true parameter value than either alone, as is often true in statistics, it might be possible to show that the averaging solution would result in a higher expected value of welfare, as judged by the true model, than the Nash bargaining solution. The prescriptive conclusion would be that officials in interagency meetings should spend less time telling one another how to change their policies and more time discussing the basic assumptions underlying their views of the world.

The major question here is whether movement of the policy settings in the direction that raises each policymaker's perceived welfare—for example, movement to the bargaining point $B12$—does indeed affect y and x in such a way as to improve welfare. The answer of course depends on the true model. If one or the other of the policymaker's models (1 and 2) happens to be the true model, cooperation will necessarily improve welfare; otherwise that policymaker would not have agreed to the change. But, as argued earlier, that is unlikely. More likely, reality is represented by some third model, say point 3 in figures 12.1 or 12.2. The true welfare levels produced by various combinations of m and g are represented by the indifference curves radiating from point 3. As the figure is drawn, cooperation turns out to reduce welfare, though the reverse is equally plausible.

To see what other outcomes are possible, the models can be swapped. Figure 12.3 shows the possibilities. If the central bank believes model 3 instead of model 1, its reaction function is given by line $CB3$. If the fiscal authority believes model 1, the reaction line is given by $FA1$. The Nash competitive point is now $N31$ instead of $N12$. The two policymakers can raise the perceived welfare of each by agreeing to move in the northeast direction. If reality is represented by the same model 3, cooperation neces-

Government expenditure (g)

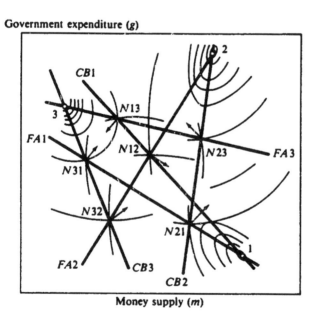

Money supply (m)

Figure 12.3
Possible combinations of three models.

sarily improves welfare. But if reality is represented by model 2 instead of model 3, the Nash point $N31$ must be judged by the standard of the indifference curves radiating from point 2. As the figure is drawn, cooperation turns out to raise true welfare with this combination of models.

Altogether there are 27 ($3 \times 3 \times 3$) combinations: the fiscal authority can believe any of the three models, the central bank can believe any of the three, and reality can be represented by any of the three. In the nine combinations in which the two agencies happen to share the same model, coordination is not an issue. Out of the remaining eighteen combinations there are twelve in which one of the two agencies' models coincides with the true model; here coordination necessarily improves welfare. The other six combinations could go either way; when all three models are distinct, coordination could reduce welfare (as from point $N12$) as easily as improve it (from point $N31$). This case, the three models being distinct, becomes more important as the number of models becomes larger. If there are q models, there are $q(q - 1)(q - 2)$ combinations in which three different models are featured, out of a total of q^3 combinations. The limit as q goes to infinity, in which the probability of divergent models goes to 1, seems to describe the actual state of affairs.

12.2   Evidence from the Simulations

How important is the issue of conflicting models likely to be in practice? For example, is the case in which coordination reduces welfare, as judged by the true model, merely a pathological counterexample? In what follows I use the simulation results of the twelve international macroeconometric models included in the Brookings exercise to see what might happen. If I used all the models there would be 1,728 (12^3) combinations. To keep the problem more manageable,[11] I first concentrate on six models (giving 216 combinations): the MCM, EPA, LINK, LIVERPOOL, VAR, and OECD models. The models were chosen to be representative of the full range of models both with respect to geography—MCM might be associated with U.S. beliefs, the EPA with Japanese beliefs, and the OECD with European beliefs—and with respect to philosophy—the LINK model might be considered the most Keynesian of the twelve, LIVERPOOL the most monetarist or new classical, and VAR the only nonstructural model.

This study follows the path blazed by Oudiz and Sachs (1984). Indeed they listed uncertainty (though not disagreement) over the correct model as one of the topics remaining for future research (p. 56):

A second difficulty in our treatment is the implicit assumption that the "true" model of the world is known with certainty and that exogenous shocks are absent during the planning period.... We have not yet investigated the implications of such uncertainty for the logic of policy cooperation, but it is important to do so. We think Feldstein is correct when he says that such uncertainty is a major practical impediment to greater policy coordination.

Oudiz and Sachs calculated the effects of international coordination by taking the policy multipliers alternately from the MCM and EPA models. They noted differences between the econometric models but maintained the usual assumption that the models used by the two policymakers coincided with each other and with reality.

I take policy multipliers from the simulation results reported in tables 11.2 (government expenditure) and 11.3 (money supply) in the preceding chapter of this volume. These are the effects in the second year, chosen to represent the relatively short run but with enough time allowed perhaps to get past the negative part of the J-curve. For any experiments that envision the policymakers acting in real time, one can imagine using dynamic multipliers—that is, the entire time profile of policy effects that was produced in the simulations—but this complication is left for future research. Table 13.1 will report the policy multipliers for an increase in government spending equal to 1 percent of GNP and a 1 percent increase in the money supply: the effect on the level of GNP and the effect on the current account, both expressed as percentages of GNP.[12]

Computing the reaction functions (equations (4) and (5)) requires knowing not only the perceived policy multipliers but also the relative welfare weight (ω) placed on the trade balance, and the perceived optimums for the income and trade-balance targets.[13] Even though I decided here to attribute the same ω to both policymakers, in order to concentrate solely on conflicts in models, the value judgment remains a difficult and arbitrary task. The calculation of the location of the Nash point can apparently be as sensitive to the choice of welfare weights and constant terms as to the choice of policy multipliers. Oudiz and Sachs (1984) made their choices based on the calculation of what the walfare weights would have to have been for policymakers, optimizing in the Nash equilibrium, to produce the values of output, inflation, and the trade balance actually observed in the 1980s. This methodology has problems. To use it in this context would require the computation of different weights not only for the two policymakers, but for every possible combination of models; the effects of coordination on welfare would then not be comparable. Instead I simply take weights from the EPA case of Oudiz and Sachs and apply them uniformly to all models so as to have a common standard of evaluation.[14] The relative weight on the current account is 0.47, and on output, 0.07. The target optimums are also taken from Oudiz and Sachs: a current account and GNP gap both equal to zero.

One point regarding the constant terms can easily escape notice. In assuming that the policymakers react directly to each other's policy settings g and m rather than to the target variables y and x, I have implicitly assumed that they ignore observed deviations of y and x from what they would have expected on the basis of their models, or that they treat them as purely random disturbances.[15] An alternative would be to assume that they treat such observed discrepancies as following a random walk; that is, as permanent revisions in the constant terms A and B. This would be equivalent to a perpetual updating of the intercepts of the reaction functions to ensure that they will always pass through the target optimum $y = x = 0$.

Table 12.1 reports the results for the Nash equilibrium when the two goals are output and the current account balance, under thirty-six possible combinations of models to which the monetary and fiscal authorities can subscribe. If one chooses, one can think of the policymakers as taking turns in real time. The first row in each section reports whether the Nash equilibrium is stable, and the second reports the number of iterations required to reach convergence (of both target variables, to within a tolerance of 1.0 percent).[16] However, one may choose instead to think of the policymakers as instantly jumping to the Nash equilibrium. The third and fourth rows in each section give the equilibrium values for the money supply and government expenditure, expressed relative to the baseline used in the simulations. The other rows give the values of the target variables and the welfare function that would follow under each of the two models in question.

In general, however, the policymakers believe that by cooperation they can achieve a better outcome than the Nash equilibrium. Table 12.2 shows the type of coordination that the two policymakers view as desirable under each combination of models. The first two rows in each section indicate the change, relative to the Nash equilibrium, that they can agree to make in the money supply and government expenditure in order to maximize the product of the two perceived gains in welfare. The next four rows show the effects that the two agents perceive such a package of policy changes will have on the target variables. The last two rows in each section show how much the central bank and fiscal authority think the country has to gain in

Table 12.1
Noncooperative Nash equilibrium, six models
(Changes in percent; welfare gains in percent of output, squared)

Model subscribed to by fiscal authority	Model subscribed to by central bank					
	MCM	EPA	LIVERPOOL	VAR	OECD	LINK
MCM						
Nash Point						
Stable?	Yes	Yes	Yes	Yes	Yes	Yes
Steps required[a]	99	99	8	3	4	5
Nash change in policy						
Money supply	56.44	827.02	−115.34	7.56	2.46	−1.22
Government expenditure	−9.00	−136.06	19.33	−0.94	−0.10	0.51
Perceived change in targets						
Central bank						
Output	4.97	18.22	9.43	5.67	1.84	1.38
Current account	2.68	62.32	5.92	0.24	−0.42	−0.19
Fiscal authority						
Output	4.97	65.22	−8.46	1.15	0.75	0.46
Current account	2.68	41.00	−5.87	0.25	−0.01	−0.19
Perceived gain for						
Central bank	0.7275	−226.2441	2.2383	0.3251	−0.0328	0.0331
Fiscal authority	0.7275	−134.1217	−5.9732	0.1852	0.0660	−0.0273
EPA						
Nash Point						
Stable?	Yes	Yes	Yes	Yes	Yes	Yes
Steps required[a]	15	19	6	3	5	9

Nash change in policy						
Money supply	53.41	70.84	−87.25	8.77	14.66	26.05
Government expenditure	−7.56	−9.58	8.68	−2.41	−3.09	−4.41
Perceived change in targets						
Central bank						
Output	4.90	4.97	3.24	5.65	2.51	1.29
Current account	2.49	4.29	5.64	0.30	0.32	−0.27
Fiscal authority						
Output	3.16	4.97	−11.43	−1.47	−0.86	0.32
Current account	3.41	4.29	−3.65	1.17	1.47	2.04
Perceived gain for						
Central bank	0.7251	1.4811	2.4094	0.3475	0.3111	−0.0151
Fiscal authority	1.3970	1.4811	−5.4355	0.4151	0.6076	0.9260
LIVERPOOL						
Nash Point						
Stable?	No	No	Yes	Yes	Yes	Yes
Steps required[a]	99	99	11	4	12	99
Nash change in policy						
Money supply	−2592.02	−276.47	−95.12	12.54	75.41	731.08
Government expenditure	511.19	48.49	12.25	−9.27	−21.83	−152.85
Perceived change in targets						
Central bank						
Output	−54.01	−1.12	4.97	5.59	5.81	−1.00
Current account	−163.74	−22.36	5.72	0.51	3.99	−2.53
Fiscal authority						
Output	241.91	22.18	4.97	−5.25	−11.21	−73.43
Current account	124.00	14.31	5.72	0.62	−2.36	−33.42
Perceived gain for						
Central bank	−1892.2482	−46.5560	2.4398	0.4137	0.8096	−1.6697
Fiscal authority	−1497.7557	−5.4740	2.4398	−0.3490	−4.5577	−161.8109

Table 12.1 (cont.)

Model subscribed to by fiscal authority	Model subscribed to by central bank					
	MCM	EPA	LIVERPOOL	VAR	OECD	LINK
VAR						
Nash Point						
Stable?	No	No	No	Yes	No	No
Steps required[a]	99	99	99	99	99	99
Nash change in policy						
Money supply	4.79	5.13	26.33	52.95	6.07	5.94
Government expenditure	2.05	1.42	−37.71	−86.86	−0.31	−0.08
Perceived change in targets						
Central bank						
Output	3.82	3.82	−21.81	4.97	2.04	1.36
Current account	−0.57	−0.75	4.52	2.75	−0.20	−0.21
Fiscal authority						
Output	4.41	4.42	4.66	4.97	4.43	4.43
Current account	0.12	0.14	1.30	2.75	0.19	0.19
Perceived gain for						
Central bank	0.0078	−0.2385	−4.8265	0.7528	0.0773	0.0205
Fiscal authority	0.2882	0.2946	0.6108	0.7528	0.3124	0.3101
OECD						
Nash Point						
Stable?	No	No	Yes	Yes	Yes	No
Steps required[a]	99	99	14	4	99	99
Nash change in policy						
Money supply	−50.69	−29.85	−190.71	9.36	60.01	−33.72
Government expenditure	12.87	7.19	51.04	−3.50	−17.30	8.25

Perceived change in targets						
Central bank						
Output	2.58	3.21	26.05	5.64	4.97	1.49
Current account	−4.06	−3.44	6.66	0.33	3.06	−0.08
Fiscal authority						
Output	−6.12	−4.03	−20.14	−0.10	4.97	−4.42
Current account	−1.95	−1.01	−8.29	0.77	3.06	−1.18
Perceived gain for						
Central bank	−2.3696	−2.5562	−2.0622	0.3583	0.8746	0.0890
Fiscal authority	−2.0379	−1.0444	−14.0644	0.2649	0.8746	−1.2135
LINK						
Nash Point						
Stable?	No	No	Yes	Yes	Yes	Yes
Steps required[a]	99	99	9	3	5	99
Nash change in policy						
Money supply	−104.61	−18.95	−143.05	7.65	1.63	−1101.93
Government expenditure	23.46	5.40	31.56	−0.21	1.06	233.71
Perceived change in targets						
Central bank						
Output	1.38	3.40	15.54	5.67	1.80	4.97
Current account	−7.44	−2.60	6.19	0.24	−0.47	3.34
Fiscal authority						
Output	2.00	1.74	2.11	1.66	1.68	4.97
Current account	0.11	−0.17	0.23	−0.26	−0.24	3.34
Perceived gain for						
Central bank	−6.2719	−1.7294	1.3078	0.3267	−0.0592	0.9933
Fiscal authority	0.2059	0.0648	0.2654	0.0186	0.0292	0.9933

a. 99 indicates more than 20 steps required for convergence.

Table 12.2
The movement from the noncooperative solution to the cooperative solution: Nash equilibrium and coordination, six models
(Changes in percent; welfare gains in percent of output, squared)

Model subscribed to by fiscal authority	Model subscribed to by central bank					
	MCM	EPA	LIVERPOOL	VAR	OECD	LINK
MCM						
Bargaining change in policy						
Money supply	0.00	−765.71	30.23	1.16	35.39	0.33
Government expenditure	0.00	126.45	−8.13	−0.74	−7.80	0.15
Perceived change in targets						
Central bank						
Output	0.00	−14.75	−4.12	0.57	5.57	0.26
Current account	0.00	−58.35	−1.06	0.05	0.93	−0.04
Fiscal authority						
Output	0.00	−59.54	−3.30	−0.90	−0.78	0.39
Current account	0.00	−38.16	2.83	0.29	2.59	−0.07
Perceived gain for						
Central bank	0.0000	2.2770	0.0015	0.0000	0.0041	0.0000
Fiscal authority	0.0000	1.3484	0.0171	0.0001	0.0041	0.0001
EPA						
Bargaining change in policy						
Money supply	4.01	0.00	2.00	1.22	23.71	0.34
Government expenditure	−0.73	0.00	0.81	−0.83	−5.01	0.15
Perceived change in targets						
Central bank						
Output	0.18	0.00	0.54	0.58	3.97	0.27
Current account	0.23	0.00	−0.31	0.05	0.55	−0.04
Fiscal authority						
Output	−0.05	0.00	1.99	−1.05	−1.41	0.36
Current account	0.34	0.00	−0.45	0.42	2.38	−0.08

Perceived gain for						
Central bank	0.0000	0.0000	0.0001	0.0000	0.0022	0.0000
Fiscal authority	0.0003	0.0000	0.0012	0.0002	0.0034	0.0001
LIVERPOOL						
Bargaining change in policy						
Money supply	2558.50	209.76	0.00	−0.43	−20.80	−1017.32
Government expenditure	−505.17	−41.86	0.00	−1.03	6.29	214.84
Perceived change in targets						
Central bank						
Output	50.14	−8.24	0.00	−0.74	−1.40	3.47
Current account	162.36	19.77	0.00	0.00	−1.17	3.23
Fiscal authority						
Output	−239.14	−19.87	0.00	−0.63	3.25	103.47
Current account	−122.29	−9.95	0.00	0.22	0.60	46.12
Perceived gain for						
Central bank	18.9109	0.4280	0.0000	0.0000	0.0006	0.0214
Fiscal authority	14.9907	0.0772	0.0000	0.0002	0.0158	1.5469
VAR						
Bargaining change in policy						
Money supply	3.85	4.78	0.70	0.00	5.14	0.30
Government expenditure	−2.89	−5.10	0.45	0.00	−4.90	0.19
Perceived change in targets						
Central bank						
Output	−3.76	−7.24	0.29	0.00	−3.34	0.30
Current account	1.14	2.62	−0.14	0.00	1.50	−0.04
Fiscal authority						
Output	1.73	1.54	0.70	0.00	1.89	0.30
Current account	0.16	0.21	0.02	0.00	0.22	0.01
Perceived gain for						
Central bank	0.0018	0.0062	0.0013	0.0000	0.0020	0.0000
Fiscal authority	0.0004	0.0006	0.0000	0.0000	0.0006	0.0000

Table 12.2 (cont.)

Model subscribed to by fiscal authority	Model subscribed to by central bank					
	MCM	EPA	LIVERPOOL	VAR	OECD	LINK
OECD						
Bargaining change in policy						
Money supply	88.31	67.99	140.74	1.94	0.00	0.31
Government expenditure	−20.08	−15.67	−42.80	−1.58	0.00	0.17
Perceived change in targets						
Central bank						
Output	−3.03	−6.24	−22.16	0.82	0.00	0.28
Current account	6.72	7.51	−4.04	0.08	0.00	−0.04
Fiscal authority						
Output	13.23	9.96	9.21	−0.97	0.00	0.31
Current account	2.55	2.04	7.98	0.47	0.00	−0.08
Perceived gain for						
Central bank	0.0280	0.0339	0.0385	0.0001	0.0000	0.0000
Fiscal authority	0.0246	0.0163	0.1165	0.0002	0.0000	0.0001
LINK						
Bargaining change in policy						
Money supply	−0.66	−0.72	−0.64	0.00	−0.74	0.00
Government expenditure	−0.08	−0.09	−0.08	0.00	−0.06	0.00
Perceived change in targets						
Central bank						
Output	−0.40	−0.37	−0.06	0.00	−0.36	0.00
Current account	0.05	0.06	0.07	0.00	0.06	0.00
Fiscal authority						
Output	−0.27	−0.29	−0.26	0.00	−0.26	0.00
Current account	0.04	0.04	0.04	0.00	0.04	0.00
Perceived gain for						
Central bank	0.0004	0.0004	0.0001	0.0000	0.0000	0.0000
Fiscal authority	0.0000	0.0000	0.0000	0.0000	0.0000	0.0000

terms of the welfare function (equation (3)) by the movement of the policy settings in the indicated direction. If the policymakers happen to believe the same model, there is no scope for coordination. This is why the entries are all zero in the diagonal cells. It is a result of ruling out conflicting welfare functions; each policymaker thinks that the country is at the optimum.

Otherwise, there will be scope for coordination. Consider the case in which the central bank subscribes to the MCM model and the fiscal authority to the OECD model. Each perceives that it can accomplish relatively large welfare gains by altering the mix in favor of more expansionary monetary policy and more restrictive government spending. That kind of coordination was suggested frequently for the United States in the 1980s; the Nash noncooperative solution consists of monetary policy that is too tight and fiscal policy that is too loose, resulting in a too high level of interest rates, value of the dollar, and size of the trade deficit. That solution shows up in fifteen instances in table 12.2. But all other combinations appear as well. Coordination could call for contractionary monetary policy and expansionary fiscal policy (3 cases, in 2 of which the fiscal authority subscribes to the LIVERPOOL model), or expansion on both fronts (6 cases, in all of which the monetary authority subscribes to the LIVERPOOL or LINK models), or contraction on both fronts (5 cases, in most of which the fiscal authority subscribes to the LINK model).

To find out whether a given plan for policy coordination raises welfare in reality, rather than only in the perceptions of the policymakers, one would have to know the true model. That cannot be done. But one can get an idea of the range of possibilities by judging the plan by the standard of each of the other models. The thirty-six cells in table 12.3 correspond to the same 6×6 combinations of subscribed-to models as in table 12.2. Each gives the true welfare gains, under six possible models of reality.

Consider again the example in which the central bank subscribes to the MCM and the fiscal authority to the OECD model. If either the MCM or OECD model coincides with the true model, there will necessarily be a true welfare gain, equal to 0.0280 or 0.0246, respectively, just as the central bank or fiscal authority thought there would be. (The change in welfare is measured in terms of percentage points of output squared.) It turns out that if the EPA or VAR model is the true model, there will also be a welfare gain. But if the LIVERPOOL or LINK model is the true model, there will be a welfare loss. In those models, the coordination plan moves policy settings in the wrong direction, and everyone would have been better off staying with the Nash competitive equilibrium. One can see why by consulting tables 12.4 through 12.7, which give the actual effects on the target

Table 12.3
True gains from coordination, six models
(Percent of output, squared)

Model subscribed to by fiscal authority	Model subscribed to by central bank					
	MCM	EPA	LIVERPOOL	VAR	OECD	LINK
MCM						
Model representing reality						
MCM	0.0000	1.3484	0.0171	0.0001	0.0041	0.0001
EPA	0.0000	2.2770	0.0546	0.0015	0.0119	-0.0003
LIVERPOOL	0.0000	2.0602	0.0015	-0.0001	-0.0190	-0.0004
VAR	0.0000	31.7657	0.2946	0.0000	-0.0384	0.0003
OECD	0.0000	3.1227	0.0235	0.0008	0.0041	-0.0001
LINK	0.0000	0.2490	-0.0041	-0.0000	-0.0007	0.00000
EPA						
Model representing reality						
MCM	0.0000	0.0000	0.0077	-0.0011	0.0009	0.0003
EPA	0.0003	0.0000	0.0012	0.0002	0.0034	0.0001
LIVERPOOL	-0.0030	0.0000	0.0001	-0.0002	-0.0137	-0.0004
VAR	-0.0180	0.0000	0.0245	0.0000	-0.0381	-0.0008
OECD	-0.0011	0.0000	0.0091	0.0004	0.0022	-0.0003
LINK	-0.0002	0.0000	0.0042	-0.0004	-0.0004	0.0000
LIVERPOOL						
Model representing reality						
MCM	18.9109	0.2028	0.0000	-0.0091	0.0248	1.1951
EPA	41.0267	0.4280	0.0000	-0.0076	0.0366	2.5755
LIVERPOOL	14.9907	0.0772	0.0000	0.0002	0.0158	1.5469
VAR	309.6838	3.5307	0.0000	0.0000	0.0943	19.6586
OECD	24.6334	0.3501	0.0000	-0.0029	0.0006	1.1995
LINK	0.2288	0.0048	0.0000	-0.0032	0.0045	0.0214

VAR

Model representing reality						
MCM	0.0018	−0.0032	0.0172	0.0000	−0.0081	0.0001
EPA	0.0076	0.0062	0.0167	0.0000	−0.0001	−0.0003
LIVERPOOL	0.0003	0.0012	0.0013	0.0000	0.0001	−0.0004
VAR	0.0004	0.0006	0.0000	0.0000	0.0006	0.0000
OECD	0.0035	0.0041	0.0079	0.0000	0.0020	−0.0002
LINK	0.0003	−0.0014	0.0064	0.0000	−0.0030	0.0000

OECD

Model representing reality						
MCM	0.0280	0.0116	0.2626	−0.0038	0.0000	−0.0002
EPA	0.0699	0.0339	0.5784	−0.0016	0.0000	−0.0009
LIVERPOOL	−0.0352	−0.0307	0.0385	−0.0003	0.0000	−0.0003
VAR	0.1135	0.0269	1.5194	0.0001	0.0000	0.0017
OECD	0.0246	0.0163	0.1165	0.0002	0.0000	0.0001
LINK	−0.0015	−0.0017	0.0101	−0.0014	0.0000	0.0000

LINK

Model representing reality						
MCM	0.0004	−0.0001	0.0005	0.0000	−0.0002	0.0000
EPA	0.0013	0.0004	0.0016	0.0000	0.0001	0.0000
LIVERPOOL	0.0002	0.0005	0.0001	0.0000	0.0005	0.0000
VAR	−0.0081	−0.0021	−0.0104	0.0000	−0.0005	0.0000
OECD	−0.0010	−0.0001	−0.0013	0.0000	0.0000	0.0000
LINK	0.0000	0.0000	0.0000	0.0000	0.0000	0.0000

Table 12.4
True deviation of output from target for the United States, six models
(Percent of output, squared)

Model subscribed to by fiscal authority	Model subscribed to by central bank					
	MCM	EPA	LIVERPOOL	VAR	OECD	LINK
MCM						
Model representing reality						
MCM	0.0000	0.7128	−16.7317	−4.7164	−4.9969	−4.1153
EPA	−1.9079	−1.4990	−10.0432	−3.7777	−5.6204	−2.6894
LIVERPOOL	−8.2416	−8.4920	0.3354	−5.0423	−8.0487	−3.8808
VAR	34.1267	37.5387	−63.9532	1.2696	20.6262	−5.0050
OECD	8.6729	9.9423	−25.7322	−2.3604	2.4443	−3.6351
LINK	−0.5815	−0.1063	−11.7360	−3.7257	−3.9127	−3.3250
EPA						
Model representing reality						
MCM	0.1146	2.8462	−21.3645	−8.5678	−6.6785	−4.2402
EPA	−1.8529	0.0000	−14.4107	−7.4841	−7.2366	−4.2853
LIVERPOOL	−8.3017	−8.7332	−1.1943	−6.4534	−8.6608	−6.6509
VAR	34.8074	44.3613	−65.0792	1.2619	20.5965	13.1571
OECD	8.9109	12.8728	−28.5881	−4.4966	1.5048	0.9497
LINK	−0.5051	1.3159	−14.8245	−6.2933	−5.0338	−3.4083
LIVERPOOL						
Model representing reality						
MCM	−8.8435	−20.2104	−20.7404	−21.1082	−14.6059	−2.8765
EPA	−5.3873	−14.3254	−13.2871	−19.4424	−15.6035	13.9371
LIVERPOOL	−2.1934	−2.6645	−0.0000	−10.8451	−12.9277	25.0673
VAR	−27.8120	−52.4570	−71.5160	−0.1141	29.6644	−194.9638
OECD	−12.0996	−24.7141	−29.8917	−11.7987	−0.5646	−51.6255
LINK	−6.4772	−14.0551	−14.4085	−14.6536	−10.3187	−2.4991

VAR

Model representing reality						
MCM	-4.9133	-9.5370	-63.5687	-143.1262	-11.8082	-4.0977
EPA	-3.9595	-8.3949	-60.3521	-136.8941	-10.6102	-3.0590
LIVERPOOL	-5.1002	-6.7680	-26.4905	-55.6022	-7.6548	-4.5880
VAR	1.1738	0.9901	0.3962	0.0000	1.3504	-0.2471
OECD	-2.4940	-5.1034	-35.1982	-79.3878	-6.2697	-2.4062
LINK	-3.8570	-6.9395	-42.9606	-95.9990	-8.4536	-3.3133

OECD

Model representing reality						
MCM	-5.4155	-7.5070	-10.4543	-11.4562	-15.1923	-3.9277
EPA	-6.0030	-8.0072	-6.0178	-10.2830	-16.4499	-0.7507
LIVERPOOL	-8.1646	-8.9151	-1.0859	-7.5471	-13.6635	-0.5662
VAR	20.3758	20.2664	-39.1329	1.4925	33.1360	-26.6433
OECD	2.1482	0.9611	-15.8933	-6.0382	0.0000	-9.0760
LINK	-4.1918	-5.5862	-7.5510	-8.2190	-10.7097	-3.2000

LINK

Model representing reality						
MCM	-3.9851	-4.4057	-3.7985	-4.0885	-4.4494	0.8722
EPA	3.0879	-1.9465	5.3447	-3.1268	-3.1016	61.6607
LIVERPOOL	6.6012	-2.0996	10.5046	-4.7261	-4.1706	107.8856
VAR	-74.5666	-17.5891	-100.1328	0.6962	-3.8895	-737.9225
OECD	-21.3881	-7.0207	-27.8361	-2.1593	-3.5344	-188.6813
LINK	-3.2382	-3.5186	-3.1138	-3.3071	-3.5478	0.0000

Table 12.5
True deviation of the current account from target for the United States, six models (Percent of output, squared)

Model subscribed to by fiscal authority	Model subscribed to by central bank					
	MCM	EPA	LIVERPOOL	VAR	OECD	LINK
MCM						
Model representing reality						
MCM	0.0000	0.1651	−5.7120	−2.1420	−0.0940	−2.9369
EPA	−0.5957	−0.3207	−9.7174	−3.9392	−0.9795	−5.0637
LIVERPOOL	−9.0121	−9.3068	−0.8578	−6.3553	−7.6628	−5.9744
VAR	−0.8906	−0.7312	−5.5423	−2.4652	−1.4817	−2.7933
OECD	−3.1406	−3.1773	−2.8723	−3.2364	−2.5410	−3.5683
LINK	−4.1431	−4.2261	−2.0962	−3.5376	−3.6181	−3.5576
EPA						
Model representing reality						
MCM	0.0400	0.3133	−4.6365	−1.1530	0.3351	−1.0509
EPA	−0.5319	−0.0000	−8.3848	−2.6938	−0.4396	−2.3314
LIVERPOOL	−9.0686	−9.9557	−0.3901	−6.0303	−7.5191	−7.2129
VAR	−0.8583	−0.4253	−5.5146	−2.3952	−1.4524	−1.8730
OECD	−3.1422	−3.3984	−1.9416	−2.4322	−2.1908	−2.9448
LINK	−4.1572	−4.4560	−1.6718	−3.1899	−3.4662	−3.6456
LIVERPOOL						
Model representing reality						
MCM	−4.0499	−3.6446	−5.4539	1.9291	3.2979	−22.6456
EPA	−6.9138	−6.8876	−9.5409	1.1611	3.4702	−33.6198
LIVERPOOL	−4.0077	−1.3554	−0.0000	−4.8794	−7.4750	6.9849
VAR	−3.8597	−4.8977	−5.8513	−2.2356	−0.8492	−12.4174
OECD	−3.3310	−1.7675	−2.2837	0.1419	−0.2367	−10.0759
LINK	−3.0060	−1.8450	−1.6929	−2.0502	−2.8000	−2.6306

VAR

Model representing reality						
MCM	-2.1011	-0.9317	12.8925	33.2964	-0.3113	-2.4558
EPA	-3.8897	-2.4204	14.9796	40.6707	-1.6319	-4.3642
LIVERPOOL	-6.3321	-5.9300	-1.3380	5.3905	-5.7635	-6.3031
VAR	-2.4664	-2.3912	-1.4338	-0.0000	-2.3315	-2.5532
OECD	-3.1984	-2.2387	9.0274	25.6317	-1.7524	-3.4155
LINK	-3.5193	-3.1009	1.7804	8.9652	-2.8978	-3.5852

OECD

Model representing reality						
MCM	-0.0120	0.5143	-4.7916	-0.3872	3.8029	-5.1939
EPA	-0.8811	-0.2203	-8.0704	-1.7247	4.1746	-8.3316
LIVERPOOL	-7.6103	-7.4266	-3.0934	-5.8029	-7.6643	-4.5021
VAR	-1.4867	-1.4540	-4.4025	-2.3308	-0.6631	-3.8905
OECD	-2.4618	-2.0286	-3.3669	-1.8213	-0.0000	-4.3193
LINK	-3.5790	-3.3895	-2.7986	-2.9303	-2.7661	-3.4562

LINK

Model representing reality						
MCM	-10.0710	-4.1468	-12.7286	-2.3618	-2.7372	-79.0324
EPA	-15.4161	-6.8349	-19.2659	-4.2274	-4.7903	-115.3088
LIVERPOOL	-1.2015	-5.0845	0.5410	-6.3687	-6.0229	44.0089
VAR	-6.3117	-3.4241	-7.6074	-2.5056	-2.7308	-39.9298
OECD	-5.8838	-3.9216	-6.7638	-3.3864	-3.4618	-28.7198
LINK	-3.1889	-3.4625	-3.0660	-3.5912	-3.5335	-0.0000

Table 12.6
Bargaining deviation of output from Nash for the United States, six models (Percent of output, squared)

Model subscribed to by fiscal authority	Model subscribed to by central bank					
	MCM	EPA	LIVERPOOL	VAR	OECD	LINK
MCM						
Model representing reality						
MCM	0.0000	−59.5359	−3.3015	−0.8955	−0.7769	0.3922
EPA	0.0000	−14.7524	−4.7557	−0.9084	−2.6506	0.3527
LIVERPOOL	0.0000	56.7256	−4.1237	−0.4141	−3.7979	0.0981
VAR	0.0000	−523.7030	19.4213	0.5721	23.4202	0.3050
OECD	0.0000	−167.1917	3.1471	−0.3496	5.5709	0.2955
LINK	0.0000	−39.6906	−2.2010	−0.5970	−0.5179	0.2615
EPA						
Model representing reality						
MCM	0.1820	0.0000	2.2172	−1.0387	−0.1331	0.4006
EPA	−0.0453	0.0000	1.9856	−1.0471	−1.4099	0.3598
LIVERPOOL	−0.3402	0.0000	0.5388	−0.4683	−2.4152	0.0992
VAR	2.7129	0.0000	1.8277	0.5829	15.7758	0.3179
OECD	0.7960	0.0000	1.6971	−0.4262	3.9688	0.3035
LINK	0.1213	0.0000	1.4782	−0.6925	−0.0887	0.2671
LIVERPOOL						
Model representing reality						
MCM	50.1388	3.3076	0.0000	−2.0165	3.5228	5.2102
EPA	−91.2320	−8.2383	0.0000	−1.8812	4.4540	60.0257
LIVERPOOL	−239.1370	−19.8738	0.0000	−0.6291	3.2547	103.4688
VAR	1716.8079	140.5773	0.0000	−0.7352	−13.0870	−677.0562
OECD	467.7173	37.8559	0.0000	−1.3059	−1.4013	−170.6083
LINK	33.4259	2.2051	0.0000	−1.3444	2.3485	3.4735

VAR

Model representing reality						
MCM	−3.7632	−7.3951	1.0681	0.0000	−6.9008	0.4449
EPA	−3.7628	−7.2433	0.9708	0.0000	−6.7959	0.4040
LIVERPOOL	−1.6396	−2.9431	0.2859	0.0000	−2.8143	0.1185
VAR	1.7315	1.5439	0.7045	0.0000	1.8933	0.2973
OECD	−1.6417	−3.7025	0.7724	0.0000	−3.3390	0.3227
LINK	−2.5088	−4.9301	0.7120	0.0000	−4.6005	0.2966

OECD

Model representing reality						
MCM	−3.0297	−2.7101	−24.2659	−2.1235	0.0000	0.4210
EPA	−7.6446	−6.2426	−30.5411	−2.1107	0.0000	0.3807
LIVERPOOL	−9.8404	−7.7028	−22.1624	−0.9020	0.0000	0.1091
VAR	58.1969	44.7276	88.4326	0.8226	0.0000	0.3019
OECD	13.2340	9.9596	9.2135	−0.9660	0.0000	0.3106
LINK	−2.0198	−1.8067	−16.1773	−1.4157	0.0000	0.2806

LINK

Model representing reality						
MCM	−0.3985	−0.4362	−0.3838	0.0000	−0.3879	0.0000
EPA	−0.3403	−0.3728	−0.3278	0.0000	−0.3265	0.0000
LIVERPOOL	−0.0663	−0.0732	−0.0640	0.0000	−0.0557	0.0000
VAR	−0.5318	−0.5782	−0.5114	0.0000	−0.5767	0.0000
OECD	−0.3571	−0.3899	−0.3437	0.0000	−0.3627	0.0000
LINK	−0.2656	−0.2908	−0.2558	0.0000	−0.2586	0.0000

Table 12.7
Bargaining deviation of the current account from Nash for the United States, six models
(Percent of output, squared)

Model subscribed to by fiscal authority	Model subscribed to by central bank					
	MCM	EPA	LIVERPOOL	VAR	OECD	LINK
MCM						
Model representing reality						
MCM	0.0000	−38.1586	2.8309	0.2885	2.5903	−0.0697
EPA	0.0000	−58.3521	3.9471	0.3746	3.7227	−0.0817
LIVERPOOL	0.0000	41.0303	−1.0575	0.0361	−1.5452	−0.0540
VAR	0.0000	−25.3826	1.0420	0.0453	1.1980	0.0082
OECD	0.0000	−4.7922	1.3285	0.2059	0.9327	−0.0719
LINK	0.0000	8.2388	0.1919	0.0777	−0.0579	−0.0371
EPA						
Model representing reality						
MCM	0.2302	0.0000	−0.3832	0.3264	1.6446	−0.0705
EPA	0.3432	0.0000	−0.4467	0.4226	2.3813	−0.0825
LIVERPOOL	−0.2019	0.0000	−0.3125	0.0474	−1.0737	−0.0556
VAR	0.1338	0.0000	0.0519	0.0484	0.7998	0.0087
OECD	0.0512	0.0000	−0.4030	0.2361	0.5468	−0.0732
LINK	−0.0313	0.0000	−0.2102	0.0906	−0.0742	−0.0379
LIVERPOOL						
Model representing reality						
MCM	162.3616	13.4997	0.0000	0.4432	−2.2411	−70.4505
EPA	238.2319	19.7654	0.0000	0.5437	−3.0799	−102.0375
LIVERPOOL	−122.2898	−9.9462	0.0000	0.2204	0.6033	46.1229
VAR	85.8599	7.0450	0.0000	−0.0003	−0.7259	−34.3171
OECD	46.0028	3.9335	0.0000	0.3970	−1.1663	−23.3604
LINK	−13.9147	−1.0673	0.0000	0.1861	−0.2465	3.2320

VAR

Model representing reality						
MCM	1.1438	2.0580	−0.2026	0.0000	1.9666	−0.0840
EPA	1.4746	2.6224	−0.2413	0.0000	2.5142	−0.0999
LIVERPOOL	0.1979	0.5167	−0.1384	0.0000	0.4511	−0.0579
VAR	0.1563	0.2132	0.0161	0.0000	0.2218	0.0069
OECD	0.8430	1.5954	−0.1999	0.0000	1.5037	−0.0831
LINK	0.3303	0.6592	−0.1003	0.0000	0.6127	−0.0418

OECD

Model representing reality						
MCM	6.7191	5.2621	15.2626	0.6297	0.0000	−0.0774
EPA	9.6064	7.5065	20.9612	0.8092	0.0000	−0.0915
LIVERPOOL	−3.7471	−2.8477	−4.0377	0.1223	0.0000	−0.0562
VAR	2.9969	2.3103	4.9133	0.0804	0.0000	0.0076
OECD	2.5472	2.0374	7.9775	0.4706	0.0000	−0.0780
LINK	−0.0447	0.0001	1.7072	0.1872	0.0000	−0.0397

LINK

Model representing reality						
MCM	0.0481	0.0531	0.0464	0.0000	0.0408	0.0000
EPA	0.0501	0.0555	0.0484	0.0000	0.0401	0.0000
LIVERPOOL	0.0701	0.0765	0.0675	0.0000	0.0723	0.0000
VAR	−0.0196	−0.0213	−0.0188	0.0000	−0.0221	0.0000
OECD	0.0657	0.0721	0.0633	0.0000	0.0620	0.0000
LINK	0.0389	0.0425	0.0374	0.0000	0.0382	0.0000

variables. The reason the central bank and fiscal authority agreed to the change in the policy mix, when the first believed the MCM and the second the OECD model, is that both thought it would improve the current account. But as seen in table 12.7, such a change, according to the LIVERPOOL or LINK models, *worsens* the current account. This conclusion will probably not alarm those who do not put much faith in either of these two models. But such readers should recognize the possibility that the fiscal authority will subscribe to, say, the LIVERPOOL model and the central bank to the VAR; in this case the coordination plan (monetary and fiscal contraction) will again worsen welfare as judged by the other four models.

Of course, the proper strategy, if the true model could be discovered, would be simply for both policymakers to optimize subject to that model. The point here is that when policymakers subscribe to different models, one cannot make the blanket pronouncement that coordination must improve welfare.

Of the 216 (6^3) possible combinations in table 12.3, 180 ($216 - 6^2$) involve disagreement between the policymakers and, therefore, bargaining. Of the 180, welfare is improved by bargaining in 105 cases and worsened in 54 cases. (In 21 cases the effect is not perceptible: zero to four decimal places.) However, in 60 ($2 \times 6 \times 5$) of these cases, one agency or the other has the true model, so that a nonnegative welfare change is guaranteed. Of the 120 ($6 \times 5 \times 4$) cases in which the agencies' models differ not only from each other but also from the true model, welfare is perceptibly improved in 61 and worsened in 54.

When all eleven available models are used (the TAYLOR model is omitted because it reports no results for the current account), there are 1,331 (11^3) possible combinations. Of the 1,210 ($1331 - 11^2$) that involve disagreement and bargaining, welfare is perceptibly improved in 728 cases and worsened in 390. Of the 990 ($11 \times 10 \times 9$) cases in which three distinct models are involved, welfare is perceptibly improved in 556 cases and worsened in 390. To analyze the sensitivity of the results to the target optimizing, I tried redoing the analysis with a target level of GNP assumed to be 25 percent above the baseline. When all eleven models are used, 559 of the cases involving three distinct models show perceptible welfare gains from bargaining and 291 show losses. I also tried a target level of GNP assumed to be 5 percent below the baseline. Here 512 of the cases involving three distinct models show welfare gains and 280 show losses.[17] It may not be a coincidence that coordination does, after all, produce welfare gains in a majority of cases. A convex combination of two sets of parameter estimates—even such a strange nonlinear "convex combination" as comes out of the coordination mathematics—may be closer to the true answer, and on average closer to any third set of parameter estimates, than either is individually. But insofar as there are possible gains from coordination of this kind, the agencies might better realize them by bargaining over the correct model rather than over the policies.

12.3 Extensions

Many extensions have been left for future research, even after the same issues that have been investigated here for domestic policymaking are repeated for international policymaking. Different objective functions could be tried. The more complete time profile of multiplier effects reported in the Brookings simulations could be used for the exercises in which the policymakers are viewed as taking turns in real time. It would be interesting to compare the results of two possible kinds of cooperation among policymakers: the Nash bargaining solution versus maximization of joint welfare based on a model with parameter values determined by averaging the estimates of the two.

More ambitious modeling is possible. One alternative is to allow the structure of the models to be endogenous with respect to the policy regime chosen (cooperative or noncooperative). Another possiblity is to study the Nash equilibrium in which the policymaker is uncertain which model is correct, or is uncertain which model the *other* player believes in. Another alternative is to study a Stackelberg equilibrium in which one policymaker is able to choose its preferred point on the other's reaction curve. It would be interesting to compare a naive Stackelberg equilibrium, in which the first authority assumes that the other's actions are based on the same model as its own, with the "rational expectations" Stackelberg equilibrium, in which the first authority realizes that the other will react on the basis of its own model, even though that model is different from the model that the first authority itself believes to be correct. Other alternatives include having the policymakers update their parameter estimates each period to reflect new information in a Bayesian manner, evaluating institutional arrangements like balanced budget amendments, monetary rules, or fixed exchange rates that might substitute for coordination, and applying the game theory concepts of repeated games and precommitment.

13

International Macroeconomic Policy Coordination When Policymakers Do Not Agree on the True Model

International policy coordination was perhaps the fastest-growing research topic in the field of open-economy macroeconomics in the mid-1980s.[1] The topic owes its success to the happy marriage of the mathematical techniques of game theory and the practical problem of coordination that in the mid-1980s became of central concern to international policymakers.

Virtually all of the previous coordination literature has made the automatic assumption that policymakers agree on the true model of how the world macroeconomy behaves.[2] As a consequence, it has reached a very strong conclusion: in general, countries will be better off if they coordinate policies than they would be in the Nash noncooperative equilibrium in which each government sets its policies while taking those of the others as given.[3] The empirical literature is as yet less fully developed than the theoretical literature; but it too has claimed gains from coordination that, though small, are necessarily positive.[4]

The assumption that policymakers agree on the true model has little, if any, empirical basis. Different governments subscribe to different economic philosophies. If one wishes to think of actors as perpetually processing new information in a Bayesian manner, so that their models over time would converge on any given reality in the limit, then one must admit that the speed of convergence is sufficiently slow, or else that reality is changing sufficiently rapidly, that policymakers have not been able to reach agreement on the true model. Nor is there much prospect of their doing so in the foreseeable future.

Professional economists are not much more able to agree on the correct macroeconomic model than policymakers. A concrete illustration was offered by the exercise in which a group of economists working under the auspices of the Brookings Institution asked those responsible for twelve

With Kate Rockett, originally published in *American Economic Review* 78, 3 (June 1988): 318–40. Reprinted with permission.

leading econometric models of the world economy to simulate the effects of some carefully specified policy changes.[5] The predictions of the models varied widely as to both the magnitude and the sign of the effects on output, inflation, exchange rates, and current account balances, among trading partners and even in the country carrying out the policy change. (See tables 11.2 and 11.3.) At best, no more than one of the models can be right, and it seems unlikely that even one of them is exactly right.

Lack of knowledge as to the true model helps explain a troublesome fact. While support for the proposition that coordination would improve welfare is widespread, proponents do not generally agree on the nature of the Pareto-improving package of policy changes that is called for in any particular set of circumstances. Some call for coordinated expansion, some for coordinated discipline, some for coordinated shifts in the mix between monetary and fiscal policy, and so forth.[6] Disagreement, even within one country, as to where the economy currently sits relative to the desired values of the target variables is responsible for some of the disagreement on the desirable coordinated policy changes, but disagreement as to the correct model is also a significant factor. As William Branson (1986, p. 176) says, "With this range of disagreement on economic analysis, how are the negotiators to reach agreement? The topic is one for the National Science Foundation, not a new Bretton Woods." Martin Feldstein (1983) argues similarly.

One implication of the lack of agreement on the true model is, of course, that "more research needs to be done." But the implications for any policy coordination that might take place in the meantime are considerably more interesting than this familiar platitude.

This chapter makes three points relevant when policymakers disagree on the model. First, such policymakers will in general be able to find a package of coordinated policy changes that each believes will improve its country's welfare relative to the suboptimal Nash noncooperative equilibrium.[7] Second, and in striking contrast to the standard result when policymakers know the true model, the package of coordinated policy changes often turns out to reduce welfare, as judged by some true model of reality, rather than to raise it. For example, using ten models from the Brookings simulations as models which could represent the views of the U.S. government, the views of other industrialized countries, or the true world macroeconomy, we find that out of 1,000 possible combinations, monetary coordination perceptibly improves U.S. welfare in only 546 cases, and improves the welfare of the other industrialized countries in only 539 cases. Third, the gains to one country from unilaterally discovering the true model and adjusting its policy accordingly, are usually much greater than the potential gains from coordination. We find, as have others, that the gains from coordination turn out to be very small even when the odds are stacked in its favor by assuming that both parties know the true model.

Sections 13.1 and 13.2 analyze a very simple game where two countries, the United States and "Europe" (shorthand for the non-U.S. OECD) must decide how to set their money supplies so as to come as close as possible to their desired levels of two target variables: income and the current account (internal balance and external balance). Section 13.1 makes the two points theoretically, that the two central banks will in general be able to agree on a coordinated policy package that each thinks leaves its country in a better position, and that the package might in fact leave them in a worse position. Section 13.2 uses the multipliers from the ten models in the Brookings simulation to provide a dramatic illustration of the points.

In section 13.3 each government is given a second policy instrument, government expenditure, to use in addition to monetary policy, and a third target variable, inflation, to pursue in addition to income and the current account. Again we see that the governments will in general find a coordinated policy package that they expect to improve welfare, but that it often has the opposite effect in reality. We conclude in section 13.4 by mentioning extensions of the framework to deal with the policymaker's uncertainty regarding the true model, or the other player's model, or both.

13.1 The Theory of Monetary Coordination with Disagreement

Here we assume that each country is interested in two target variables: its own output, denoted y for the United States and y^* for Europe (expressed in log form and relative to their optimum values), and its current account balance, denoted x and x^*, respectively (expressed as a percentage of GNP and again relative to their optima). Each government seeks to minimize a quadratic loss function.

$$W = y^2 + \omega x^2 \tag{1}$$

$$W^* = y^{*2} + \omega^* x^{*2}, \tag{2}$$

where ω and ω^* denote the relative weights placed on external balance versus internal balance.

We assume a general framework in which the targets are linearly related to the available policy instruments, which in this section are limited to the countries' money supplies, m and m^*, respectively (in log form). We denote the parameters as perceived by the U.S. authorities by a "us" subscript.

$$y = A_{us} + C_{us}m + E_{us}m^*, \tag{3}$$

$$x = B_{us} + D_{us}m + F_{us}m^*. \tag{4}$$

We denote the parameters perceived by the European government by an "e" subscript.

$$y^* = G_e + I_em + K_em^*, \tag{5}$$

$$x^* = H_e + J_em + L_em^*. \tag{6}$$

Since each country has only a single instrument but two targets, it cannot unilaterally achieve its targets. We begin by considering the Nash noncooperative equilibrium. To ascertain U.S. behavior, we differentiate equation (1) with respect to m, using equations (3) and (4) and holding m^* constant. It follows that the U.S. reaction function is

$$m = M + Nm^*, \tag{7}$$

where $\quad M = -\dfrac{A_{us}C_{us} + \omega B_{us}D_{us}}{C_{us}^2 + \omega D_{us}^2}$,

and $\quad N = -\dfrac{E_{us}C_{us} + \omega F_{us}D_{us}}{C_{us}^2 + \omega D_{us}^2}$.

To ascertain European behavior we differentiate equation (2) with respect to m^*, using equations (5) and (6) and holding m constant. The European reaction function is

$$m^* = Q + Rm, \tag{8}$$

where $\quad Q = -\dfrac{G_eK_e + \omega^*H_eL_e}{K_e^2 + \omega^*L_e^2}$

and $\quad R = -\dfrac{I_eK_e + \omega^*J_eL_e}{K_e^2 + \omega^*L_e^2}$.

We solve equations (7) and (8) for the Nash equilibrium.

$$m^n = \frac{M + NQ}{1 - NR}, \tag{9}$$

$$m^{*n} = \frac{Q + MR}{1 - NR}. \tag{10}$$

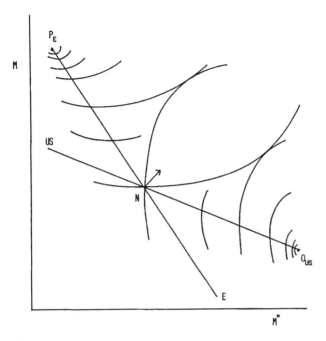

Figure 13.1
The Nash competitive equilibrium.

Figure 13.1 shows the two policymakers' reaction functions, equations (7) and (8). The optimum point as perceived by the U.S. policymakers is a point O_{us} on its reaction function. Concentric indifference curves radiate from O_{us}. These curves are vertical wherever they intersect the reaction function, because m is chosen so that its marginal benefit given m^* is zero. Similarly the optimum point as perceived by the European policymaker is a point P_e, and its concentric indifference curves are horizontal wherever they intersect its reaction function.

We have drawn the European reaction curve as steeper than the U.S. curve. One might expect the effects that are largest in absolute value to be the positive effects of money on domestic output: C in equations (3)–(4) for the United States and K in equations (5)–(6) for the non-U.S. OECD.[8] It would follow that, unless the welfare weight ω on the current account is large, the absolute value of the slope of the U.S. reaction function is less than one when the U.S. money supply is on the vertical axis, and vice versa for the European reaction function.

The possibilities for the sign of the slope are more diverse. If monetary expansion is thought to be transmitted negatively to trading partners

$(E < 0)$, presumably via a depreciation of the currency and improvement in the trade balance of the expanding country as in the Mundell-Fleming model, then the slope is positive: $N > 0$. If monetary transmission is thought to be positive on the other hand $(E > 0)$, then the slope is ambiguous: when the welfare weight ω on the current account is small, the slope is negative, but when ω is large, or when the transmission multiplier E is small (relative not only to the own multiplier C, but also to the current account multipliers D and F), the slope is again positive. (We are assuming that D and F, the effects of m and m^* on the domestic current account, are of opposite signs by symmetry.)

The same analysis holds for the foreign reaction function (for example, if $I < 0$ then most plausibly $R > 0$), though it must be remembered that even if any given model is symmetric, the two reaction functions could easily have opposite slopes. For example one country might believe that transmission is negative and the other that it is positive. In figure 13.1 we have drawn the functions downward sloping: a foreign expansion is transmitted positively to the domestic country and so the domestic government reacts by contracting.

The Nash equilibrium N is determined as the intersection of the two reaction functions. At N the indifference curves cannot be tangent, but must intersect, since their respective slopes are infinity and zero. It follows that the Nash equilibrium is perceived as Pareto-inefficient. Both policymakers think they would be better off if they could agree to move to a point within the "lens" determined by the two indifference curves that intersect at N.

As we have drawn the graph, each country would like to expand but is afraid to do so on its own, presumably because of adverse implications for the current account. But they can agree to expand simultaneously, moving northeastward in the graph to higher levels of perceived welfare. Such joint reflation is the kind of international coordination that has been urged on Germany and Japan by the United States under two different administrations: in 1977–78, in the form of the "locomotive theory," and in 1986 in the form of coordinated discount rate cuts.[9]

If an efficient mechanism of coordination exists, the countries will move, not just northeastward, but specifically to one of the points on the contract curve, where the two countries' indifference curves are tangent. There is no strong reason to choose any particular point. Nor, for that matter, is there reason to think that any Pareto-improving solution can necessarily be enforced. But we follow much of the literature in considering the Nash-bargaining solution, defined as the point where the product of the two

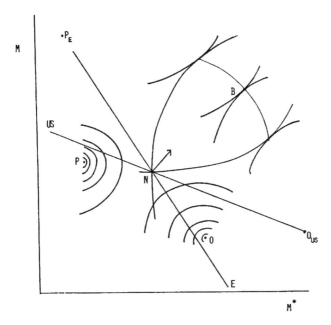

Figure 13.2
Policy coordination between the U.S. and Europe.

countries' perceived welfare gains, compared to the perceived welfare at
the Nash noncooperative solution, is maximized:[10]

$$\text{Max}[W_{us}(m, m^*) - W_{us}(m^n, m^{*n})][W_e^*(m, m^*) - W_e^*(m^n, m^{*n})] \qquad (11)$$

subject to equations (1)–(6). One would differentiate with respect to m
and m^* to find the bargaining solution (m^b, m^{*b}), a point such as B in figure
13.2.

Once we recognize that the two policymakers have different models of
the world, we must recognize that one, or both, will be wrong. To evaluate
whether the bargaining solution B is superior to the noncooperative solution (m^n, m^{*n}) not just in perception but also in reality, we would have to
know the true parameter values, the output and current account functions
(3)–(6) without the subscripts:

$$y = A + Cm + Em^* \qquad (12)$$

$$x = B + Dm + Fm^* \qquad (13)$$

$$y^* = G + Im + Km^* \qquad (14)$$

$$x^* = H + Jm + Lm^*. \qquad (15)$$

We would then plug m^b and m^{*b} into equations (12)–(15), and in turn plug the target variables into the loss functions (1) and (2), to see whether the bargaining solution in fact improves welfare.

In the standard case where the policymakers both know the correct model, coordination must necessarily improve welfare for each country, or else its government would not have agreed to go along. In our case, coordination *may* improve welfare. For example, if the true model is very close to that believed by the U.S. authorities, then the true iso-welfare map will be very similar to the perceived indifference curves shown in figure 13.1, and U.S. welfare will indeed be higher at B than N. But this need not be the case.

The true optimum policy combination to maximize U.S. welfare is given by differentiating (1) with respect to m (as in the derivation of (7) but without the subscripts), and with respect to m^*, and solving simultaneously:

$$m^0 = \frac{M(E^2 + \omega F^2) - N(AE + \omega BF)}{(E^2 + \omega F^2) + N(CE + \omega DF)}, \tag{16}$$

$$m^{*0} = -\frac{AE + \omega BF}{E^2 + \omega F^2} - \frac{CE + \omega DF}{E^2 + \omega F^2} m^0. \tag{17}$$

If the true optimum point O is not at O_{us} but rather is as shown in figure 13.2, with the new set of true iso-welfare curves drawn, then the move from N to B could very well be in the wrong direction, resulting in a reduction in U.S. welfare. Similarly if the true optimum policy combination from the viewpoint of European interests is not at P_e but rather at P as shown in figure 13.2, then coordination could reduce European welfare as well.

It is worth considering momentarily the case when the two policymakers are seeking to maximize the identical objective function, and disagree *only* about the proper model. An example, where they were the monetary and fiscal authority within the same country, was considered in the preceding chapter.[11] Our two propositions would still hold: (1) the two policymakers will in general be able to agree on a package of coordinated policy changes that each thinks will improve the (same) country's welfare relative to the Nash noncooperative solution, and (2) the package agreed to in bargaining could in fact worsen welfare as easily as improve it. While in chapter 12, conflict and coordination arise solely from different perceptions, and in the conventional literature they arise solely from different objectives, in this chapter both factors are present.

13.2   Coordination with Ten International Econometric Models

How important for coordination is the issue of conflicting models likely to be in practice? Is the case in which bargaining reduces welfare as judged by the true model merely a pathological counterexample, or is it a likely occurrence? In what follows we use the international simulation results of the macroeconometric models in the Brookings exercise to get an idea of what might actually happen if governments coordinate.

The models were asked to show the effects of four experiments, among others: an increase in the U.S. money supply, an increase in the non-U.S. OECD money supply, an increase in U.S. government expenditure, and an increase in non-U.S. OECD government expenditure. In each case the instructions were to hold the other policy instruments constant. Though twelve models participated, some did not report effects on current account balances, which we need along with effects on output levels. The ten that we can use here are the Federal Reserve Board's Multi-Country Model (MCM), Patrick Minford's Liverpool Model (LIVPL), the Sims-Litterman Vector Auto-Regression Model (VAR), the OECD's Interlink Model (OECD), the Project Link Model (LINK), the McKibbin-Sachs Global Model (MSG), the EEC Commission's Compact Model (EEC), the Haas-Masson smaller approximation of the MCM model (MINIMOD), the Economic Planning Agency model (EPA), and the Wharton model (Wharton). These models are quite representative of the range of econometric models actually in use, including as they do models both large and small in size, structural and nonstructural in approach, Keynesian and neoclassical in philosophy, backward-looking and forward-looking in expectations formation, public-sector and private-sector in function, and non-American and American in authorship.

Table 11.3 reports the effects of monetary expansion on several macroeconomic variables according to each of the twelve models. The simulations showed effects over six years, but ours is a static framework; we use only the effect in the second year. The models all agree that a monetary expansion raises domestic output, but they agree on little else. There is a surprising amount of disagreement, in particular, on whether a monetary expansion improves or worsens the current account and, in turn, on whether it is transmitted negatively or positively to the rest of the world. The reasons for this and other disagreements in the simulations are examined elsewhere.[12] It suffices to repeat that disagreements with respect to both the sign and magnitude of effects are common among honorable economists, and are common even within subsets of models that are supposedly similar in orientation, let alone among policymakers.

The first half of table 13.1 reports multipliers for output and the current account calculated in the form that we need: as a percentage of GNP per one percent change in the money supply. To save space in this and other tables below, we report numbers for only four of the models: MCM, VAR, OECD and LINK. Numbers are reported for all ten models in Frankel (1991b), an appendix to Frankel, Erwin, and Rockett (1992). Only the qualitative outcome of calculations regarding coordination will be reported here for all ten models.

Computing the policymakers' reactions requires knowing not only the perceived policy multipliers, but also the target optima and the welfare weights. We adopt the same target values as Oudiz and Sachs (1984): current accounts of zero for the United States and two percent of GNP for the non-U.S. OECD, and GNP gaps of zero for both regions. The baseline values of both variables, specified as part of the Brookings simulation exercise, were below target as of 1985. Thus policymakers will seek to increase both output and the current account. The targets, together with the baseline values for the variables and any set of policy multipliers from table 13.1, imply corresponding values for the constant terms A, B, G, and H in equations (3)–(6).[13]

The choice of welfare weights ω and ω^* is necessarily more arbitrary, even, than the choice of target optima. Oudiz and Sachs chose the values that the weights would have had to have held for countries to have produced the values of output, inflation, and the current account actually observed in the 1980s, assuming a Nash noncooperative equilibrium. For lack of a better alternative, we adopt the set of weights calculated by Oudiz and Sachs for the EPA model, and apply it uniformly regardless of model. It would be of questionable benefit to replicate their methodology separately with each model; our welfare comparisons require a common objective function. On the other hand, setting a common set of weights for all models has the drawback that the Nash solution may lie very far from the baseline for certain combinations of models. Often, in our simulations, such large moves to the Nash point resulted in a loss in welfare which was recovered in a similarly large move to the coordination point. In general, our experiment may bias our results a little toward gains from coordination because often all the models agreed on the move from the remote non-cooperative point. In order to test the sensitivity of our results to the chosen weights, we repeated the experiment two more times, using different weights. The alternative weights were obtained by using Oudiz and

Table 13.1
Money and fiscal multipliers
(for three targets in each country)

From a (1 percent) increase in:	Percentage effect on income		Effect on current account (as percentage of GNP)		Effect on percentage inflation rate	
	U.S. M	Eur. M	U.S. M	Eur. M	U.S. M	Eur. M
Effect on United States						
MCM	0.3750	0.0000	−0.0198	0.0006	0.1000	−0.0500
VAR	0.7500	0.3000	0.0311	−0.0634	0.1000	−0.1750
OECD	0.4000	0.0250	−0.0537	0.0147	0.1750	−0.0250
LINK	0.2500	0.0250	−0.0380	0.0225	−0.1000	0.0000
Effect on Europe						
MCM	−0.1750	0.3750	−0.0090	0.0090	−0.1500	0.1500
VAR	0.1000	0.1750	0.1169	0.1192	0.0250	−0.1250
OECD	0.0750	0.2000	0.0178	−0.0091	−0.0250	0.0750
LINK	−0.0250	0.2000	0.0083	−0.0077	−0.0250	−0.1500

From an increase (equal to 1 percent of GNP):	Percentage effect on income		Effect on current account (as percentage of GNP)		Effect on percentage inflation rate	
	U.S. G	Eur. G	U.S. G	Eur. G	U.S. G	Eur. G
Effect on United States						
MCM	1.8000	0.5000	−0.4217	0.2019	0.4000	0.2000
VAR	0.4000	0.3000	−0.0127	−0.0659	−0.9000	−0.1000
OECD	1.1000	0.1000	−0.3628	0.0843	0.6000	0.2000
LINK	1.2000	0.2000	−0.1647	−0.1621	0.5000	0.0000
Effect on Europe						
MCM	0.7000	1.4000	0.0912	−0.0737	0.4000	0.3000
VAR	−0.0000	0.5000	−0.0183	0.1559	0.0000	−0.3000
OECD	0.4000	1.5000	0.2583	−0.1564	0.3000	0.7000
LINK	0.1000	1.2000	0.0420	−0.1349	0.0000	0.1000

Sachs's methodology, pegging the Nash equilibrium to the baseline, for two models: the OECD and LIVPL models, respectively. The odds in favor of coordination changed little.[14]

If the U.S. policymaker can believe any of the ten models and the non-U.S. (henceforth "European") policymaker can believe any of the ten models, then there are $10 \times 10 = 100$ possible combinations, each implying a different Nash noncooperative equilibrium. For each combination we computed the values of the two countries' variables of interest in the Nash noncooperative equilibrium: the money supply, the perceived output and current account, and the perceived welfare function. All but one of the sixteen cases we report called for expansion from the baseline by one country or the other.[15]

Our main interest lies in the move from the noncooperative to the bargaining equilibrium, shown in table 13.2. To take one example, if the U.S. policymaker believes in the MCM model and the European policymaker believes in the OECD model, then they can agree to expand further their money supplies simultaneously (0.37 percent and 1.59 percent, respectively). They each believe that this policy package will result in higher output with little adverse effect on their current accounts. This is the often-mentioned case in which the Nash equilibrium is too contractionary. But besides the case of simultaneous expansion (six combinations of models in this table), every other case is possible as well: European expansion with U.S. contraction (seven combinations), U.S. expansion with European contraction (two combinations), and simultaneous contraction (one combination).

Without knowing the true model, we cannot determine whether any given policy package actually improves welfare. But we can get a good idea of the possibilities by trying out each of the models as a candidate for the true model. The sixteen cells in tables 13.3 and 13.4 correspond to the same sixteen combinations as table 13.2. But within each cell we report the effect that the corresponding coordination package of table 13.2 would have under each of the four models; thus there are $4^3 = 64$ combinations in all.[16]

Table 13.3 shows the actual effect of coordination on U.S. welfare and table 13.4 the effect on European welfare. Whenever one or the other policymaker turns out to have had the right model, his country does gain from coordination. Otherwise he would not have agreed to the package. For example the joint monetary expansion that they agree on when the U.S. policymaker believes the MCM model and the European policymaker believes the OECD model is seen to raise U.S. welfare if the MCM model is the true one (table 13.3) and to raise European welfare if the OECD

Table 13.2
The cooperative bargain[a]

Model subscribed to by the United States		Model subscribed to by Europe			
		MCM	VAR	OECD	LINK
MCM					
Bargaining Change in Policy					
M_{eur}[b]		0.240	2.020	1.590	0.710
M_{us}		−0.137	−0.441	0.367	0.253
Perceived Change in Targets					
Europe	Y	0.114	0.309	0.346	0.136
	CA	0.003	0.189	−0.008	−0.003
United States	Y	−0.051	−0.165	0.138	0.095
	CA	0.003	0.010	−0.006	−0.005
Perceived Gain for					
Europe		0.0001	0.0066	0.0011	0.0002
United States		0.0000	0.0002	0.0002	0.0001
VAR					
Bargaining Change in Policy					
M_{eur}		−5.199	25.185	−32.772	−4.129
M_{us}		−8.652	−17.173	32.898	8.394
Perceived Change in Targets					
Europe	Y	−0.436	2.690	−4.087	−1.036
	CA	0.031	0.995	0.875	0.102
United States	Y	−8.049	−5.325	14.842	5.057
	CA	0.061	−2.130	3.099	0.522
Perceived Gain for					
Europe		0.0092	0.3216	0.2415	0.0090
United States		0.3333	0.4323	3.2174	0.4100
OECD					
Bargaining Change in Policy					
M_{eur}		0.389	14.490	3.837	2.142
M_{us}		−0.533	−8.940	2.356	1.820
Perceived Change in Targets					
Europe	Y	0.239	1.642	0.944	0.383
	CA	0.008	0.682	0.007	−0.001
United States	Y	−0.204	−3.214	1.038	0.782
	CA	0.034	0.693	−0.070	−0.066
Perceived Gain for					
Europe		0.0004	0.1611	0.0078	0.0015
United States		0.0010	0.0933	0.0128	0.0064
LINK					
Bargaining Change in Policy					
M_{eur}		0.388	35.304	4.975	3.479
M_{us}		−0.851	−29.058	5.112	4.525

Table 13.2 (cont.)

Model subscribed to by the United States		Model subscribed to by Europe			
		MCM	VAR	OECD	LINK
Perceived Change in Targets					
Europe	Y	0.294	3.272	1.378	0.583
	CA	0.011	0.811	0.045	0.011
United States	Y	−0.203	−6.382	1.402	1.218
	CA	0.041	1.898	−0.082	−0.093
Perceived Gain for					
Europe		0.0006	0.6101	0.0161	0.0038
United States		0.0010	0.3590	0.0251	0.0141

a. For this and all subsequent tables, changes in instruments and targets are expressed in percent, and changes in utility are expressed in percent-squared GNP.
b. For this and all subsequent tables, the "eur" subscript refers to European variables, and the "us" subscript refers to the United States' variables.

Table 13.3
True gains from coordination for the United States

Model subscribed to by the United States	Model subscribed to by Europe			
	MCM	VAR	OECD	LINK
MCM				
Model Representing Reality				
MCM	0.0000	0.0002	0.0002	0.0001
VAR	0.0001	0.1068	−1.0427	−0.5630
OECD	0.0047	0.0313	0.0004	−0.0024
LINK	0.0019	0.0596	0.0119	0.0041
VAR				
Model Representing Reality				
MCM	−2.1398	1.0677	6.0012	1.5986
VAR	0.3333	0.4323	3.2174	0.4100
OECD	−2.5239	1.6538	6.3684	1.7626
LINK	−1.0564	1.3516	2.4973	0.7067
OECD				
Model Representing Reality				
MCM	−0.0127	−0.1063	0.0362	0.0301
VAR	0.2994	−0.6632	−3.5351	−2.4221
OECD	0.0010	0.0933	0.0128	0.0064
LINK	−0.0008	0.3912	0.0357	0.0203
LINK				
Model Representing Reality				
MCM	−0.0138	−1.4439	0.0337	0.0341
VAR	0.6384	−5.2320	−6.3935	−5.3937
OECD	0.0088	−1.1929	−0.0491	−0.0470
LINK	0.0010	0.3590	0.0251	0.0141

Table 13.4
True gains from coordination for Europe

Model subscribed to by the United States	Model subscribed to by Europe			
	MCM	VAR	OECD	LINK
MCM				
Model Representing Reality				
MCM	0.0001	1.9596	0.2717	0.0974
VAR	−0.1516	0.0066	−2.0826	−1.0593
OECD	−0.0120	0.3715	0.0011	−0.0050
LINK	−0.0127	0.4272	0.0119	0.0002
VAR				
Model Representing Reality				
MCM	0.0092	31.7840	−4.1226	−0.9188
VAR	11.2505	0.3216	1.2862	−3.0464
OECD	−0.1383	4.0254	0.2415	0.0886
LINK	0.0729	6.0950	0.3258	0.0090
OECD				
Model Representing Reality				
MCM	0.0004	16.0344	0.4762	0.2004
VAR	0.1519	0.1611	−6.4749	−4.2203
OECD	−0.0153	2.2176	0.0078	−0.0054
LINK	−0.0222	3.1398	0.0185	0.0015
LINK				
Model Representing Reality				
MCM	0.0006	39.3135	0.4532	0.2078
VAR	0.5566	0.6101	−10.6004	−8.6072
OECD	−0.0124	4.6683	0.0161	−0.0104
LINK	−0.0252	7.3543	0.0271	0.0038

model is the true one (table 13.4). It also turns out to raise both countries' welfare if the LINK model is the true one. But it turns out to *reduce* welfare if the VAR model is the correct one (also the LIVPL and MSG models). The reader who does not believe in one of the latter three models might not be concerned with that result. But such a reader should instead be concerned with the result that when the U.S. policymaker, for example, believes in the LIVPL model and the European policymaker in the VAR model, coordination will reduce welfare according to each of the other models.[17]

It must be noted that it is the countries' failure to perceive the true model, not their failure to agree with each other per se, that alters the standard conclusion regarding coordination. The case for coordination is not necessarily any stronger if the countries agree on one model and it turns out to be the wrong model. On the other hand, the point in this chapter is something stronger than simply "bad models lead to bad policies." In domestic policymaking, we are often fairly confident that we know the *sign* of policy effects and are uncertain only about the magnitude. Though it follows from such uncertainty that policymakers should be more timid about policy changes, there will still at least be some small change that will move the economy closer to its desired targets (Brainard, 1967). In international policymaking, however, we are uncertain even as to the sign of policy effects, such as monetary transmission between countries. For this reason, even a small step in the direction of a coordinated policy change may lower welfare.

Altogether there are $10^3 = 1000$ combinations counting those not shown in the tables. Coordination turns out to result in gains for the United States in 546 cases, as against losses in 321 cases and no perceptible effect (to four decimal places) in 133 cases. For Europe there are gains in 539 cases, as against losses in 327 cases and no effect in 134 cases. These figures in a sense overstate the odds in favor of successful coordination, in that by construction each country's welfare is improved (or at least not worsened) in 1/10 of the combinations, those in which the policymaker has the same model as the true one. If we take only the $10 \times 9 \times 9 = 810$ combinations where neither country is correct, the proportion of losses is higher. For the United States there are gains in 419 cases, as against losses in 286 cases and no effect in 105. For Europe there are gains in 408 cases, losses in 298, and no effect in 104.

The results thus suggest that the danger that coordination will worsen welfare rather than improve it is more than just a pathological counterexample. One cannot, under conditions where policymakers subscribe to different models, make the blanket pronouncement that coordination as it is conventionally defined must improve welfare.

It would be helpful to know whether the incidence of gains vs. losses from coordination can be associated with any particular pattern in the policymakers' perceptions. Such knowledge might allow us to devise alternative concepts of cooperation that would be more likely to improve welfare.

In our framework, losses may occur because countries make errors on the sign of the multipliers, so they adjust their instruments in the wrong direction from the true utility-improving direction. On the other hand, losses may also occur if countries are correct about the sign of the multipliers, but perceive monetary policy to be less effective than it is in reality. In this case, they may adjust their instruments in the direction of the true coordination point, but adjust the instruments too much. This may result in a loss in welfare if "overshooting" is severe. A simple remedy for the second type of loss would be to make smaller moves to reduce losses due to the incorrect magnitude effect, leaving only sign errors. In our simulations, overshooting turns out to be the cause of the losses from coordination in only 25 out of the 189 cases in which coordination results in losses for both countries. The primary reason for losses in our simulations is, then, moves in the wrong direction. Given the diversity of signs in the models we included in our simulations, this is not surprising. Based on our simulations, smaller policy moves would not much improve the case for coordination.

Another modification might be to coordinate only in those cases where the countries agree on the model they wish to use. Even assuming such agreement is possible, as noted above there is no reason why it should necessarily improve the incidence of gains from coordination, since agreeing on the model does not necessarily improve the chances that the chosen model is correct. However, for the subset of cases where the two countries do agree on a single model, the incidence of gains does happen to be somewhat higher for our simulations. The United States gains in 65 percent of the cases, while Europe gains in 59 percent of the cases.[18]

While our results indicate that coordination may frequently result in losses, we have said nothing of the magnitude of the losses or gains to cooperation. Specifically, it would be interesting to know whether there is an argument for cooperation based on the magnitude of the potential gains even in the best case when countries cooperate using the correct model. Oudiz and Sachs (1984), Oudiz (1985), Carlozzi and Taylor (1985), Hughes Hallett (1985), Canzoneri and Minford (1986), and others who have estimated the gains from coordination have described them as small, even when positive as they must be in the conventional framework. But how small is "small"?

In order to obtain a sense of how large or small the gain or loss to cooperation might be, we need a standard by which to judge these changes in welfare. We choose as a standard the gain to a single policymaker, who may previously have believed an incorrect model, of discovering the true model and unilaterally adjusting his policies accordingly while staying within the Nash noncooperative equilibrium.

Table 13.5 shows the gains to the United States from a unilateral switch to the correct model by the United States. If the United States already has the correct model, the gains are zero. Otherwise, the gains are substantial. There is no *guaranteed* gain in utility to the United States when it switches to the correct model, as is illustrated in the table by the occasional negative gains of a unilateral switch to the correct model. For example, if Europe

Table 13.5
Gains to unilateral switch to true model for the United States under Nash noncooperative solution

Model subscribed to by the United States		Model subscribed to by Europe			
		MCM	VAR	OECD	LINK
MCM					
Model Representing Reality					
MCM	(0.0000)[a]	0.0000	0.0000	0.0000	0.0000
VAR	(0.4323)	0.6069	0.0139	0.2412	0.3328
OECD	(0.0128)	0.0011	−0.0000	0.0008	0.0007
LINK	(0.0141)	0.0001	0.0008	0.0003	0.0001
VAR					
Model Representing Reality					
MCM	(0.0000)	0.0964	0.0131	0.0920	0.0716
VAR	(0.4323)	0.0000	0.0000	0.0000	0.0000
OECD	(0.0128)	0.1019	0.0198	0.0946	0.0748
LINK	(0.0141)	0.0447	0.0169	0.0389	0.0322
OECD					
Model Representing Reality					
MCM	(0.0000)	0.0009	0.0000	0.0006	0.0006
VAR	(0.4323)	0.4995	0.0137	0.2008	0.2750
OECD	(0.0128)	0.0000	0.0000	0.0000	0.0000
LINK	(0.0141)	0.0001	0.0009	−0.0000	0.0000
LINK					
Model Representing Reality					
MCM	(0.0000)	0.0004	0.0001	0.0003	0.0003
VAR	(0.4323)	0.5358	0.0179	0.2107	0.2899
OECD	(0.0128)	0.0001	−0.0003	0.0001	0.0000
LINK	(0.0141)	0.0000	0.0000	0.0000	0.0000

a. Gains to coordination to the United States assuming that all countries believe the same correct model.

were to believe the OECD model, the United States would do better if it could play the OECD model as well, even if it knew that the LINK model were correct. In these cases, the United States essentially loses bargaining power to Europe if it switches to the true model. But in most cases the gains from a unilateral switch are positive.

We show in parentheses in the left-hand column of the table numbers representing the gains to cooperation under the assumption that all countries believe the same correct model, to bias the case in favor of coordination. In many cases, the gains to cooperation as shown are small compared to the gains to the unilateral switch to the correct model. As can be seen from Table 7 in the original paper (omitted here to save space), this is true of European gains when Europe makes the unilateral switch to the correct model as well. The gains from a unilateral switch to the correct model are particularly large when a country erroneously believes the VAR model (or when the VAR is correct but the country erroneously believes any of the others).

13.3   International Coordination of Monetary and Fiscal Policy Together

In this section we give each country a second tool, government expenditure—g for the United States and g^* for Europe. We must add a third target variable for each country; otherwise each will be able to attain its optimal point regardless what the other country does. We choose the inflation rate. Now twenty-four multipliers are relevant from each model: the effects of m, m^*, g, and g^* on U.S. output, current account, and inflation and European output, current account, and inflation.

Table 11.1 reports the effects of fiscal expansion according to all twelve models. Table 13.1 reports the twenty-four multipliers for each of the four models. There is not as much disagreement regarding fiscal policy as monetary policy. A domestic fiscal expansion in most of the models is transmitted positively to the other country, via a domestic current account deficit. But a few models have fiscal or monetary expansion reducing the domestic price level rather than raising it.

We again assume that each country seeks to minimize a quadratic loss function. Rather than repeating our earlier points in algebraic form, we turn directly to the simulation results. As before, the weights and target optima are taken from Oudiz and Sachs (1984). The inflation target is zero for both the United States and Europe. Thus policymakers will seek to reduce inflation, as well as to increase output and the current account.

Table 13.6 reports the Nash-bargaining solution. For one example, when the United States subscribes to the LIVPL model and Europe to the EPA model, the resulting package of coordinated policy changes takes exactly the form urged by many economists in the 1980s: a U.S. fiscal contraction, accompanied by a fiscal expansion in the rest of the OECD and monetary expansion all around.[19] This package is considered desirable because it would depreciate the dollar and reduce the U.S. current account deficit (and European and Japanese surplus) without causing a large world recession.[20] But most other possible kinds of policy packages occur as well, as can be seen in the table.[21]

Table 13.6
The cooperative bargain (monetary and fiscal policies)

Model subscribed to by the United States		Model subscribed to by Europe			
		MCM	VAR	OECD	LINK
MCM					
Bargaining Change in Policy					
M_{eur}		−0.177	9.980	−55.755	0.869
M_{us}		1.259	4.010	−41.170	3.330
G_{eur}		0.061	−2.892	0.052	−0.217
G_{us}		−0.157	−3.969	5.845	−0.955
Perceived Change in Targets					
Europe	Y	−0.311	0.712	−11.830	−0.265
	CA	−0.032	1.292	1.285	0.010
	P	−0.260	−0.277	−1.365	−0.235
United States	Y	0.220	−7.048	−4.891	−0.579
	CA	0.053	1.015	−1.675	0.294
	P	0.084	−2.254	1.021	−0.136
Perceived Gain for					
Europe		0.0001	0.0326	0.0002	0.0059
United States		0.0002	0.0001	0.0001	0.0001
VAR					
Bargaining Change in Policy					
M_{eur}		−258.885[a]	43.693	207.547	−1.779
M_{us}		18.120	−17.723	−82.630	−7.732
G_{eur}		39.164	−13.529	−27.962	−1.911
G_{us}		63.959	−11.088	−46.589	3.121
Perceived Change in Targets					
Europe	Y	−0.652	−0.890	−25.266	−2.144
	CA	0.460	1.231	−10.996	0.339
	P	−4.218	−1.846	−15.918	0.269
United States	Y	−26.743	−8.678	−26.732	−5.658
	CA	13.579	−2.287	−13.287	−0.041
	P	−14.363	2.014	0.143	−3.079
Perceived Gain for					
Europe		0.0001	0.0002	0.0000	0.0002
United States		0.0000	0.0001	0.0001	0.0003
OECD					
Bargaining Change in Policy					
M_{eur}		213.120	47.154	−90.252	1.746
M_{us}		95.318	−20.088	22.653	11.040
G_{eur}		−38.388	−20.510	11.924	1.035
G_{us}		−23.054	−4.444	−19.374	−3.387
Perceived Change in Targets					
Europe	Y	−6.642	−4.012	−6.215	0.976
	CA	1.785	0.157	−5.653	−0.204
	P	−3.068	−0.244	−4.800	−0.434

Table 13.6 (cont.)

Model subscribed to by the United States		Model subscribed to by Europe			
		MCM	VAR	OECD	LINK
United States	Y	14.257	−13.796	−13.314	0.838
	CA	3.144	1.654	5.493	0.749
	P	−10.157	−11.463	−3.019	0.063
Perceived Gain for					
Europe		0.0333	0.0000	0.0002	0.0001
United States		0.0001	0.0001	0.0000	0.0000
LINK					
Bargaining Change in Policy					
M_{eur}		7.556	147.227	257.973	1.516
M_{us}		1.262	−53.522	−3.350	−1.796
G_{eur}		−2.858	−55.997	−28.432	1.206
G_{us}		−0.219	−6.757	−3.605	−1.704
Perceived Change in Targets					
Europe	Y	−1.542	−7.586	7.253	1.630
	CA	0.247	2.688	1.117	−0.263
	P	−0.001	−2.942	−1.552	−0.057
United States	Y	−0.331	−29.008	−4.400	−2.264
	CA	−0.305	−2.619	1.920	0.586
	P	−0.236	1.974	−1.467	−0.652
Perceived Gain for					
Europe		0.0003	0.0004	0.0001	0.0002
United States		0.0001	0.0001	0.0001	0.0001

a. See note 17.

Tables 13.7 and 13.8 show the true gains from coordination for the United States and Europe, respectively. Again we find that coordination necessarily improves U.S. welfare if the U.S. model turns out to be the correct one, and European welfare if the European model turns out to be the correct one, but that otherwise welfare can go down. Of the total 1,000 combinations of all ten models, the United States has gains in 494 cases, losses in 398, and no perceptible effect in 108. Europe has gains in 477 cases, losses in 418, and no effect in 105. If we take only the 810 combinations where neither country is correct, bargaining results in U.S. gains in 432 cases and losses in 357, and for Europe gains in 408 cases and losses in 376. Thus the odds for successful coordination appear to be no better when policymakers can take advantage of the monetary-fiscal mix than when the degree of monetary ease alone is at stake.

Table 13.7
True gains from coordination for the United States
(Monetary and fiscal policies)

Model subscribed to by the United States	Model subscribed to by Europe			
	MCM	VAR	OECD	LINK
MCM				
Model Representing Reality				
MCM	0.0002	0.0001	0.0001	0.0001
VAR	−2.6394	10.6400	236.3649	−5.8930
OECD	−0.4994	−2.3167	14.8283	−0.0695
LINK	−0.5952	6.3941	25.8278	−1.7681
VAR				
Model Representing Reality				
MCM	−74.7859	198.0402	402.5238	13.1769
VAR	0.0000	0.0001	0.0001	0.0003
OECD	−25.1592	158.5107	373.6036	5.5733
LINK	−21.5520	39.1031	122.9517	10.4207
OECD				
Model Representing Reality				
MCM	−11.3838	29.9578	0.9014	0.0322
VAR	−268.2709	12.5137	347.2785	3.0793
OECD	0.0001	0.0001	0.0000	0.0000
LINK	−23.2350	−8.0046	−5.7921	−0.0567
LINK				
Model Representing Reality				
MCM	1.5302	233.1126	−125.2759	−1.2435
VAR	−6.7995	122.1154	−942.2249	8.2880
OECD	0.9647	119.0264	−43.4986	0.2318
LINK	0.0001	0.0001	0.0001	0.0001

13.4 Extensions with Uncertainty

So far we have made the simplest assumptions to examine the topic at hand. Some readers of earlier versions of this chapter suggested that, in a world in which different models abound, it is not sensible to assume that each policymaker acts as if he knows with certainty to which model his opponent subscribes or even which model he himself considers to be correct. We now briefly consider extensions in each of these two directions in turn.

To begin with, we retain the assumption that each policymaker believes in his own model with certainty, but we allow for uncertainty regarding the other's model. A reason for such uncertainty regarding the other's model

Table 13.8
True gains from coordination for the Europe
(Monetary and fiscal policies)

Model subscribed to by the United States	Model subscribed to by Europe			
	MCM	VAR	OECD	LINK
MCM				
Model Representing Reality				
MCM	0.0001	−3.3306	−5.6736	−3.1598
VAR	−2.5132	0.0326	333.6467	−8.2613
OECD	0.1306	13.3216	0.0002	0.7635
LINK	0.0093	43.8440	44.4689	0.0059
VAR				
Model Representing Reality				
MCM	0.0001	6.2655	270.6773	−4.8492
VAR	217.4242	0.0002	209.1031	25.7900
OECD	−367.2546	327.4278	0.0000	1.2868
LINK	−973.6363	327.6573	980.1376	0.0002
OECD				
Model Representing Reality				
MCM	0.0333	17.3204	176.5559	12.6783
VAR	−549.5166	0.0000	241.4204	−29.8594
OECD	142.8152	199.9979	0.0002	1.4537
LINK	289.0842	313.7216	119.2115	0.0001
LINK				
Model Representing Reality				
MCM	0.0003	141.2746	−696.8871	−0.7884
VAR	−7.2841	0.0004	−1276.6437	−10.8551
OECD	16.4437	828.7074	0.0001	−1.7457
LINK	16.7499	1143.2227	−1016.8853	0.0002

might be that several models might be believed by different policymakers within the other country's government. The model which will actually be used in setting policy is the unknown outcome of a political process within the other country. The policymaker will set his policies so as to maximize expected welfare, a weighted average of the economic consequences of each of the policy settings that the foreign government would choose under each of the possible models to which it might subscribe. The foreign government's policy settings in turn will depend, not just on its model, but also on its beliefs about what the first country's model, and therefore its actions, might be.

The U.S. central bank chooses m_j to minimize

$$\sum_{i=1}^{10} \pi_{ij}^* W_i(m_j, m_i^*),$$

where π_{ij}^* is the U.S. estimate of the probability that Europe believes in model i given that the United States believes model j and m_i^* is the money supply Europe will pick if it believes in model i. If the U.S. central bank believes in, for example, model i, then the first-order condition is similar to equation (7), but with the foreign money supply replaced by a weighted average of the various possibilities.

$$m_1 = M_1 + N_1 \sum_{i=1}^{10} \pi_{i1}^* m_i^* \tag{7'}$$

or

$$m_1 = M_1 + N_1(\underline{\pi_1^{*\prime}} \underline{m^*}),$$

where $\underline{\pi_1^{*\prime}}$ is the row vector π_{i1}^* and $\underline{m^*}$ is the column vector of m_i^* (each for $i = 1, \overline{10}$, assuming ten possible models).

Similarly the European central bank chooses m_k^* to minimize

$$\sum_{i=1}^{10} \pi_{ik}^* W_i^*(m_i, m_k^*),$$

where π_{ik} is the European estimate of the probability that the United States believes in model i given that Europe believes model k,[22] and m_i is the money supply the United States will pick if it believes in model i. If the European central bank believes in, for example, model 2, then the first-order condition is

$$m_2^* = Q_2 + R_2(\underline{\pi_k^\prime} \underline{m}), \tag{8'}$$

where $\underline{\pi_k^\prime}$ is the row vector of π_{ik} and $\underline{m}$ is the column vector of m_i. We have one version of equation (7') for each of the ten models in which the U.S. central bank might believe, giving

$$\underline{m} = \underline{M} + \underline{N}(\underline{\pi^*} \underline{m^*}) \tag{7''}$$

and similarly for Europe,

$$\underline{m^*} = \underline{Q} + \underline{R}(\underline{\pi} \underline{m}), \tag{8''}$$

where $\underline{\pi}^*$ is the (10 × 10) matrix of the π_j^*,

$\underline{\pi}$ is the (10 × 10) matrix of the π_k,

$\underline{M}$ and $\underline{Q}$ are the (10 × 1) vector forms of M_i and Q_i,

and $\quad \underline{N}$ and $\overline{\underline{R}}$ are (10 × 10) diagonal matrices with the N_i and R_i on the diagonal. Substituting and solving,

$$\underline{m} = [\underline{I} - \underline{N}\pi^*\underline{R}\pi]^{-1}[\underline{M} + \underline{N}\pi^*\underline{Q}], \tag{9'}$$

$$\underline{m}^* = [\underline{I} - \underline{R}\pi\underline{N}\pi^*]^{-1}[\underline{Q} + \underline{R}\pi\underline{M}], \tag{10'}$$

where $\underline{I}$ is the (10 × 10) identity matrix.

Equations (9')–(10') represent the 10 × 10 computable noncooperative solutions for the 10 × 10 combinations of models in which the two policy-makers could believe. As a concrete example we try putting equal weight on each of our ten Brookings models: $\pi_i = \pi_i^* = 1/10$ ($i = 1, 10$). The bargaining solution remains the same as before, assuming that an enforcement mechanism is designed such that each policymaker must reveal his model as part of the cooperative bargain. As before we calculate in each case the gain or loss in welfare entailed in the move from one equilibrium to the other, where the true effect of any given pair of money supplies is judged by each of the ten models in turn.

The simulations indicate that the noncooperative point when each country believes its own model with certainty but averages over the possible models followed by the foreign country, is quite similar to the noncooperative point under certainty.[23] As in the earlier sections, the interesting question, under the assumption that each player averages to estimate the other's model, is the effect of coordination. Coordination under averaging improves U.S. welfare in 600 cases out of the total 1,000 combinations, against 398 losses and 2 cases with no significant change in welfare. For Europe, welfare improves in 643 cases, falls in 355 cases and has no significant change in 2 cases.

The second extension relaxes the assumption that each policymaker acts as if he were certain as to the correct model. We assume rather that policy-makers assign weight to the possibility that each of the ten models may be true, and choose their policies so as to maximize expected welfare. Due to linearity the policymaker acts as if he is playing by a weighted-average "compromise model." To preserve some disagreement about models, we could assume that each puts primary weight on a favorite model of his own, but also puts some weight on the other models (perhaps with larger weight on the favorite model of the other player, on the theory that he must have access to some independent information). Here we consider, instead, the simple case of uniform weights. As a result, each will be playing by the same "compromise" model. If heavier weight were placed on particular models, the solution would lie between the results shown here and the solution under certainty.

The noncooperative solution under averaging by both policymakers over the possible correct models lies farther from the noncooperative solution under certainty (as in section 13.2) than does the noncooperative solution when each policymaker averages over the other's model (as in the first extension). In this case, all the multipliers change, not just the foreign multipliers, so a larger move would be expected.

As before, the main interest is in characterizing the move to the cooperative point. But two types of cooperation are possible. In the first case, the cooperative point is the Nash-bargaining solution given that each country believes the compromise model. If this type of cooperation is compared to the noncooperative averaging solution, there is a true gain for Europe in more than half the cases, but a loss for the United States in the majority of cases: the United States gains in 200 cases, but loses in 800 cases, while Europe gains in 600 cases and loses in 400 cases.[24]

The second type of coordination would suppose that the two countries stubbornly continue to believe their own favorite models, but for the sake of compromise, the two countries agree simply to average over the possible correct models and play either noncooperatively or cooperatively. If this concept of cooperation is used, both countries gain in more cases than they lose. If the noncooperative averaging point is compared to the noncooperative point under certainty, the move results in gains for the United States in 568 cases and losses in 432 cases, while the move results in gains for Europe in 513 cases and losses in 487 cases. The probable reason that averaging usually raises welfare is the statistical principle that the average of ten numbers is closer to the individual numbers, on average, than the individual numbers are to each other. The principle does not apply directly, because each policymaker's having a better estimate of the "true" parameters does not necessarily imply that the noncooperative equilibrium will be better, but it seems to work here.

These extensions are more elaborate models of the Nash noncooperative equilibrium. None offers an evident reason for altering our conclusion that the bargaining solution is as likely to reduce welfare as to improve it. More definitions of cooperation should be investigated, however, including exchange of information over time to allow learning regarding the correct model. The scope for useful international cooperation remains wide, provided it is defined more broadly than in the conventional bargaining sense explored in the first sections of this chapter.

Acknowledgments

The authors would like to thank the Sloan Foundation and the Institute for International Studies at the University of California-Berkeley for research support, and to thank Ralph Bryant, Dale Henderson, and many seminar participants for useful comments.

14

International Nominal Targeting (INT): A Proposal for Overcoming Obstacles to Monetary Policy Coordination

The central theorem about the economic gains from international policy coordination, which has strong implications for the design of the international monetary system, is that if countries in general set their policies jointly they will be better able to attain their economic objectives than if they set them independently. The alternative noncooperative equilibrium, in which each country independently sets own policies, taking the policies of the others as given, is the Nash noncooperative equilibrium. The coordination theorem appears to be a strong argument for policymakers to set up the machinery for regular meetings and cooperative setting of macroeconomic policies, and the entire issue has been a popular research topic in the academic community.

After September 1985, when the finance ministers of the Group of Five (G5) countries struck their Plaza Accord, international coordination became popular in the policymaking community as well. Although the agreement at the Plaza concerned only the exchange value of the dollar, it formalized the process of cooperation, which was broadened to include the rest of macroeconomic policy management at the Tokyo Summit meeting of the Group of Seven (G7) leaders in May 1986.

As international coordination caught on among policymakers, however, some academic economists turned skeptical, beginning with public commentary by Feldstein (1983, 1988). They came up with a variety of obstacles to coordination, points that invalidate the universality of the theorem that coordination must always leave countries better off. These obstacles fell into three categories: the enforcement of compliance with any given agreement, the inflation-fighting credibility of monetary policy, and uncertainty.

Originally published in *Global Disequilibrium in the World Economy*, ed. Mario Baldassarri, John McCallum, and Robert Mundell (The Macmillan Press Ltd., and St. Martin's Press, 1992). Reprinted with permission.

This chapter begins with a review of the obstacles to successful coordination. It then takes the more constructive route of offering a modest proposal for the form that successful coordination might take. The proposal is for an international version of targeting nominal GNP (or aggregate demand) that I call international nominal targeting (INT).[1] It is designed to have a better chance of overcoming the three kinds of obstacles to coordination than the system established by the G7 leaders at Tokyo. A key element of the proposal is that it could begin with nations' sacrificing only a very small amount of national macroeconomic sovereignty—that is, with very wide bands around the target. Trust and confidence in the institution could build slowly, and then nations could progress to higher degrees of coordination if they so desired.

The essence of the argument for the need for coordination is the existence of international externalities or spillover effects. Imagine they did not exist—that is, each country were unaffected by changes in other countries. Then the decentralized, noncooperative solution for obtaining economic objectives would be optimal, and there would be little role for international meetings or a supranational institution to coordinate policies, just as there would be little role for government intervention in the domestic economy if domestic markets functioned competitively and without externalities. If, for example, floating exchange rates insulated each country from others' disturbances, there would be no need for coordination. Since this sort of insulation does not exist, spillover occurs, and so, says the theory, coordination is preferable to noncooperation.[2]

One cannot know, however, whether or what kind of coordination is desirable without first knowing the nature of the externalities. Is the Nash noncooperative equilibrium too contractionary because of a proclivity toward beggar-thy-neighbor policies? Then joint expansion is called for. (This was the logic of the "locomotive theory" that gave rise to the 1978 Bonn Summit meeting.[3]) Or is the existing equilibrium overly inflationary? In that case, joint discipline is called for. (This was the apparent motivation underlying the founding of the European Monetary System—EMS). Perhaps the problem is "competitive appreciation." Each country seeks by its policy mix to raise real interest rates, attract capital inflows, and appreciate its currency, thereby reducing the consumer price index for any given level of output and employment. Or perhaps it is "competitive depreciation" (as was feared at Bretton Woods in 1944 on the basis of the experience of the 1930s). If either of the last two such externalities is important, it points to a need for coordination schemes that give more emphasis to exchange rate stability than does the proposal developed in this chapter such as the schemes of McKinnon (1983, 1985), Williamson (1983), and Williamson and Miller (1987). If the problem is overly contractionary or expansionary monetary policy, however, then a switch toward a regime of greater exchange rate stability would likely exacerbate the problem by increasing the international transmission of disturbances.

One premise of the INT proposal is that the most relevant externalities concern the overall degree of expansion of macroeconomic policies—that is, monetary and fiscal policies are too tight or too loose. The plan does not address the proper *mix* of monetary and fiscal policy or the resulting real interest rate.[4]

Some people object that a plan for using monetary policy to target nominal GNP would have done little to prevent the major disequilibrium that arose in the early 1980s, that is, the U.S. budget and trade deficits. I agree with Feldstein (1983), however, that this disequilibrium was not a failure of coordination—the U.S. government did not pursue the policies it did as a result of insufficient expansion by its trading partners. Indeed, until after 1985, the administration did not even want Europe and Japan to expand. No international bargain would have brought about a U.S. fiscal correction. Only a recognition by the Administration and Congress of the link between their fiscal policies and the trade deficit, together with the political will necessary to make difficult budget choices, would have done so. By the same token, neither INT nor any other proposals for coordination should now be allowed to distract attention from the point that the most important policy changes to be made in the 1990s can be made unilaterally by the United States.[5]

14.1   Obstacles to International Policy Coordination

As already mentioned, the obstacles to implementing a successful regime of macroeconomic policy coordination are of three sorts: enforcement, the need for time-consistent inflation-fighting, and uncertainty. Put positively, one wants compliance, credibility, and certainty. In this section, I deal in turn with each and related topics.

Problems of Enforcement and the G7 Indicators

Difficulties of enforcement and credibility have received the most attention from economists. Even when a coordination package guarantees that each member country will be better off than it would be in the noncooperative equilibrium, a country will be able to do better still if it unilaterally deviates from the agreement. If the agreement calls for joint expansion, for example, an individual country may be tempted to hold back somewhat and let its partners bear the burden of expansion, that burden being a trade deficit or a depreciation of the currency.

Saying a country will be able to do better by deviating from the agreement refers at best to the short run, and holds only under the assumption that the other countries keep their policies as agreed. In future periods, those other countries will presumably retaliate by also abandoning the agreement. Economists have probably overemphasized the difficulties of enforcement.[6]

Norms for behavior—"peer pressure" in the language of U.S. Treasury official David Mulford after the Tokyo Summit (quoted in Funabashi, 1988, p. 131), or the formation of "reputations" in the language of economic theory—may be sufficient to enforce compliance with an agreement, provided the agreement meets two conditions. (1) It must specify explicitly what is required of each party in terms of observable economic variables. Since each party has an incentive to cheat, it is hard enough to enforce a clear-cut agreement; enforcement may be hopeless if the parties have not even spelled out what is required of them. (2) The constraints embodied in the agreement must be specified in such a way that unilateral cheating in any given period would give a country a short-term gain that is small relative to the potential future loss (when the cooperative agreement breaks down) of the gains over the Nash noncooperative equilibrium. If these two conditions are met, it is unlikely that one country will cheat just because it can gain a bit more over the cooperative equilibrium.

At the Tokyo Summit of May 1986, it was decided that the finance ministers of the G5 countries (thenceforth, the G7 countries) would focus in their meetings on a set of ten "objective indicators": the growth rate of GNP, the interest rate, the inflation rate, unemployment, the ratio of the fiscal deficit to GNP, the current-account and trade balances, the money growth rate, international reserve holdings, and exchange rates.[7]

The list was further discussed and somewhat trimmed down at subsequent G7 meetings. By the time of the Venice Summit in June 1987, it had apparently been reduced to six indicators: growth, inflation, trade balances, government budgets, monetary conditions, and exchange rates.[8] Nevertheless, a new variable was soon added to the list. The U.S. Secretary of the Treasury told the annual meeting of the International Monetary Fund (IMF) in October 1987 that "The United States is prepared to consider utilizing, as an additional indicator in the coordination process, the relationship among our currencies and a basket of commodities, including gold."

And at the Toronto Summit of June 1988: "The G7 countries welcomed the addition of a commodity price indicator and the progress made toward refining the analytical use of indicators" (*IMF Survey*, September 26, 1988, p. 292).

At no time did the G7 members make any pretense that they would rigidly commit themselves to specific numbers for the indicators—not in the sense that sanctions would be imposed on a country if it deviated far from the values agreed upon. The plan did, however, include the understanding that "appropriate remedial measures" would be taken whenever there develops significant deviations from the "intended course." This language seemed to suggest that the indicators were not intended to be mere national forecasts and that the system was intended to include some substantive bargaining over policies, rather than be simply an exchange of information. Thus the G7 system can be viewed as an attempt at small-scale coordination, sacrificing just a little national macroeconomic sovereignty, a necessary stage for building confidence before moving on to more binding forms of coordination.

The G7 list of indicators, be it six or ten, was not, however, especially well suited to workable coordination as described above. It is difficult to imagine a G7 meeting applying moral censure to one of its members for, say, having experienced a higher rate of real growth or a lower rate of inflation during the year than had been agreed on in the previous meeting.

The main problem with the list is that it is too long to be practical. When each country has six or ten indicators but only two or three policy instruments, it is virtually certain that the indicators will give conflicting signals. Thus, the national authorities will feel little constraint on their setting of policy instruments. Frenkel, Goldstein, and Masson (1990, p. 22) note that one argument for choosing a single indicator is that when multiple indicators send conflicting signals, authorities can hide behind the confusion. They also observe that multiple indicators can encourage "overcoordination." Setting a single indicator allows each country to retain some degree of freedom in setting its monetary and fiscal policies. In this light, a serious coordination scheme might *begin* in the 1990s by setting only one indicator and progress to commitments to multiple variables only when and if sufficient political consensus and confidence has developed to justify more sacrifice of sovereignty.

Another problem with the G7 indicators is that they are kept secret. It is difficult to reconcile optimistic statements about the amount of substantive coordination already taking place with the fact that G7 meetings do not publicly announce the agreed targets for the indicators. How can any pressure (be it moral suasion, embarrassment, effect on long-term reputation, or outright sanctions) be brought to bear on countries that stray from targets that have not been made public?

To take an example, in the Baker-Miyazawa Agreement reached in San Francisco in September 1986, the Japanese apparently agreed to a fiscal expansion in exchange for a promise from the US Treasury Secretary that he would stop "talking down" the dollar, plus the usual US promise to cut the budget deficit. In the months that followed, each side viewed the other as not fully living up to the agreement. (The episode is described in Funabashi, 1989.) But it was difficult for anyone to verify the extent of compliance because the precise terms of the original agreement had not been made public.

Indeed, the G7 guards the values of the indicators with even more secrecy than central banks guard their foreign exchange market interventions. Theory says that the success of a target zone is *enhanced* when speculators are made aware of the boundaries.[9] Why then does the G7 keep them secret? A possible answer is that the members do not want to lose face if their economic variables subsequently break outside the target band. This answer fits well with the suspicion that the G7 in fact reach no substantive agreements at their meetings but nevertheless find it politically useful to issue communiqués, the public announcements being sufficiently vague that each member can interpret them to its own advantage.[10]

Thus, the need to monitor performance criteria to enforce compliance with any coordination agreement suggests two conclusions about the G7 system: (1) it would be better for the agreement to focus on one variable than on six or ten or eleven; and (2) the targets for the variable should be made public.

What variable should be targeted? Below, I develop further desirable characteristics by which to evaluate the candidates.

Problems of Inflation-Fighting Credibility

A number of the problems that arise in international policymaking occur in the context of domestic policymaking as well. One of them is the need to set monetary policy so as to keep the public's expectations of inflation low. One way that monetary policymakers can do this is to precommit themselves to rules of monetary discipline. To be effective, that commitment must be credible or, in modern theoretical parlance, "dynamically consistent."[11]

Macroeconomic policymaking is always a trade-off between the advantages of rules and of discretion. In the past, writers concerned with either of the two problems often simplistically assumed away the other. If the aim is to maximize economic welfare (a function of output and inflation) for a given period only, ignoring long-run implications for expected inflation, discretion can be shown to be unambiguously superior to rules. After all, how can one possibly gain by agreeing to limit beforehand the ability to respond to developments in the economy? If, on the other hand, one ignores the possibility of short-run disturbances, rules can be shown to be unambiguously superior to discretion in a long-run equilibrium. Macroeconomic policy cannot affect output in the long run anyway, and precommitment to a nominal anchor can reduce expected inflation and thereby reduce actual inflation.

It should be clear by now that neither extreme in the "rules vs. discretion" debate represents the complete answer. If the political system's policy-making process is allowed to optimize on a purely short-run basis, the outcome will be overexpansion. Thus, some degree of longer-term commitment to resisting inflationary temptations is indicated, even if it is a decision to insulate the central bank from the political process rather than to adhere formally to a nominal anchor or rule.[12] Yet in a world where new disturbances do come along, it is important that the government retain at least some ability to respond to stabilize the economy. The solution is commitment of *some* degree, but less than 100 percent, to some nominal anchor.[13]

Coordination and Inflation in the Long Term

An important critique of international coordination is the point made by Kenneth Rogoff (1985b): if governments set up the machinery for joint welfare maximization period by period, as they did at the Bonn Summit of 1978, the cooperative equilibrium in each period is likely to entail more expansion than would otherwise be present. Countries may find this joint expansion advantageous within any given period, but in the long run it will undermine governments' inflation-fighting credibility and result in a higher inflation rate for a given level of output. In the Rogoff view, renouncing the machinery of coordination is one of the ways that governments can credibly precommit themselves to less inflationary paths.

It is important to realize that the introduction of longer-term issues of credibility, time inconsistency, and precommitment can just as easily run in favor of coordination as against it. If the perceived externality or shortcoming of the Nash noncooperative equilibrium is that it is overly expansionary, then the coordination equilibrium, even if arrived at period by period, will entail less expansion, not more. This is sometimes argued to be the basis underlying the European Monetary System. The rhetoric originally used by Helmut Schmidt and Valéry Giscard d'Estaing in proposing the EMS in the late 1970s suggested that they were doing so because the United States was neglecting its duty of supplying to the world the public good of a stable, noninflating currency. Ten years later, many observers of the EMS (for example, Giavazzi and Pagano, 1988) decided that its success lay precisely in giving inflation-prone countries such as Italy and France a credible nominal anchor for their monetary policies. Commitment to exchange rate parity or a band vis-à-vis a hard-currency country such as Germany constitutes precisely the sort of time-consistent, low-inflation policy sought by those who worry that central bankers left to their own discretion will be overly expansionary.

The case of the EMS does, however, offer an asymmetry. It is an accepted fact that Germany—whether because of its history or for some other reason—places very heavy weight on price stability. Thus, the weaker-currency countries can import inflation-fighting credibility by pegging themselves to the greater mark area.[14] In contrast, there is no presumption that the United States (the natural "Stackelberg" leader) has as much inflation-fighting credibility as do Germany and Japan. Thus proponents of worldwide coordination cannot automatically presume that year-by-year coordination would lower the average world inflation rate, rather than raise it.

The Choice of a Nominal Anchor

The implication of the credibility issue is that a scheme for coordination is more likely to produce long-run gains if it has national governments committed not just to each other period by period but also, in some degree, to a nominal anchor for a longer term. The G7 list of indicators includes four nominal variables: money, the price level, the price of gold, and the exchange rate. In the remainder of the chapter I develop grounds for choosing the nominal variable on which coordination should focus, and argue that the optimal one is nominal GNP, a variable that does not even appear on the G7 list.

Chapter 15 considers the choice of nominal anchor formally, though only in the context of a small country's unilateral choice of regime. (Some references considering the two-country problem are cited in the fourth note of the introduction to part III of this volume.)

I make no judgment on the desirable degree of precommitment to a nominal target, in the context of either domestic or international policy-making, except that it is greater than zero and less than infinity.[15] The important point is that nominal GNP (or nominal demand) makes a more suitable target than the four nominal variables in the G7 list.

The general argument has been made well by others.[16] In the event of disturbances in the banking system, in the public's demand for money, or in other mechanisms that affect the demand for goods, a policy of holding nominal GNP steady insulates the economy: neither real income nor the price level need be affected. In the event of disturbances to supply, such as the oil price increases of the 1970s, the change can be divided equally between an increase in the price level and a fall in output. (For some countries, equal shares is roughly the split that a discretionary policy would choose anyway).[17] In general, fixing nominal GNP will not give *precisely* the right answer unless the objective function puts precisely equal weights on inflation and real growth. If the choice is among the available nominal anchors, however, nominal GNP will give an outcome characterized by the greatest stability of output and the price level.

As demonstrated at the beginning of chapter 15, a nominal GNP target strictly dominates a money supply target, in the sense of minimizing a quadratic loss function, regardless of how important inflation-fighting credibility is. Chapter 15 goes on to show that a nominal GNP target also dominates an exchange rate or price-of-gold target (unless extraordinarily high weight is placed on the objective of stabilizing the exchange rate or price of gold). It is also likely to dominate a simple price level target of the sort adopted by New Zealand and Canada in the early 1990s.

An example illustrates the pitfalls of a predetermined money growth target. In late 1982, the U.S. Federal Reserve, citing large velocity shifts, decided to allow $M1$ to break well outside of the previously announced target zone. From the second quarter of 1982 to the second quarter of 1986, $M1$ grew 10.3 percent per year, leading some observers to suggest that the Federal Reserve was following a general policy of targeting nominal GNP. The monetarists were furious. For four years, they decried the betrayal of the money growth rule and warned that a major return of inflation was imminent. In retrospect, however, nobody can doubt that the Federal Reserve chose the right course. Even with the recovery that began in 1983 and continued through the four years and beyond, nominal GNP grew at 8.0 percent per year—more slowly than the money supply. Thus, velocity declined at 2.3 percent per year, in contrast to its past historical pattern of increasing at roughly 3 percent a year. If the monetary authorities had followed the monetarist prescription of rigidly precommitting themselves to a money growth rate suggested by the preceding history—say, 3 percent—and velocity had followed the same path, then nominal GNP would have grown much less—at only 0.7 percent a year in the example. In fact, this number is an upper bound. With lower inflation than occurred, velocity would almost certainly have fallen even more than it did, and the recession of 1981–82 would have lasted another five years!

Problems of Uncertainty

The argument that nominal GNP dominates such variables as the money supply as a candidate for a nominal anchor applies even more strongly to international economic policy than to domestic policy. The reason is that uncertainty, though it is a problem for policymakers in a closed economy, is an even greater problem in an open economy.

Before a country can enter negotiations with other countries on coordinated policy changes, it needs to know three things: (1) What is the initial position of the domestic economy relative to the optimum values of the target variables? (2) What are the correct weights to put on the various possible target variables? (3) What effect will each unit change in the domestic and the foreign macroeconomic policy variables have on the target variables, that is, what is the correct model of the world economy?

These three elements follow simply from the algebraic expression for the following economic objective function:[18]

$$W = (1/2)(y^2 + w_x x^2 + w_p p^2) \tag{1}$$

$$W^* = (1/2)(y^{*2} + w_x^* x^{*2} + w_p^* p^{*2}) \tag{1a}$$

where W is the quadratic loss to be minimized, y is output (expressed in log form and relative to its optimum), x is the current account (expressed as a percentage of GNP and relative to its optimum), p is the inflation rate, w_x is the relative weight placed on the current account objective, w_p is the relative weight placed on the inflation objective, and an asterisk, (*), denotes the analogous variables for the foreign country.

There are two policy instruments: the money supply, m (in log form), and government expenditure, g (as a percentage of GNP). For the home country, the marginal welfare effects of changes in these policy variables are then given by

$$dW/dm = (y)y_m + w_x(x)x_m + w_p(p)p_m \tag{2}$$

$$dW/dg = (y)y_g + w_x(x)x_g + w_p(p)p_g \tag{3}$$

$$dW/dm^* = (y)y_{m^*} + w_x(x)x_{m^*} + w_p(p)p_{m^*} \tag{4}$$

$$dW/dg^* = (y)y_{g^*} + w_x(x)x_{g^*} + w_p(p)p_{g^*} \tag{5}$$

and in the foreign country:

$$dW^*/dm = (y^*)y_m^* + w_{x^*}^*(x^*)x_m^* + w_{p^*}^*(p^*)p_m^* \tag{2a}$$

$$dW^*/dg = (y^*)y_g^* + w_{x^*}^*(x^*)x_g^* + w_{p^*}^*(p^*)p_g^* \tag{3a}$$

$$dW^*/dm^* = (y^*)y_{m^*}^* + w_{x^*}^*(x^*)x_{m^*}^* + w_{p^*}^*(p^*)p_{m^*}^* \tag{4a}$$

$$dW^*/dg^* = (y^*)y_{g^*}^* + w_{x^*}^*(x^*)x_{g^*}^* + w_{p^*}^*(p^*)p_{g^*}^* \tag{5a}$$

where the policy multiplier effect of money on output is given by y_m, the effect of money on the current account by x_m, and so on. To solve for the optimum, one can set these derivatives equal to zero, with the target variables y, x, and so on first expressed as linear functions of the policy variables m and g. For the Nash noncooperative equilibrium (in which each country takes the other's policies as given), only equations (2), (3), (4a), and (5a) are needed for the solution. Each country ignores the effect that its policies have on the other country, so equations (4), (5), (2a), and (3a) do not enter the model. Indeed, this is precisely the reason the noncooperative equilibrium is suboptimal. These cross-country effects enter only in the determination of the cooperative solution.

Before deciding on a policy change, policymakers must at least know the sign of the corresponding derivative. Equation (2), like all the eight derivatives above, neatly illustrates the three kinds of uncertainty. The first is uncertainty about the initial position of y, x, and p.[19] Position uncertainty, in turn, breaks down into three parts: (1) uncertainty about the current value of the target variable in question;[20] (2) uncertainty over the baseline forecast—how the target variables are likely to move during the forthcoming period (usually a year or more) in the absence of policy changes;[21] and (3) uncertainty about the optimum value of the target variable.[22]

The point is clear. Policymakers' estimates of the current values of y, x, or p in their own countries could easily be off by several percentage points in either direction, enough to flip the signs of the corresponding three terms—any one of which could change the sign of the derivative of the objective function—in each of equations (2) through (5). Thus, it is entirely possible that the country could ask its partners to expand, or agree to a partner's request that it itself expand, when these changes would, in fact, move the economy in the wrong direction.

To take one historical example, in the late 1970s, U.S. policymakers, looking at the available economic data, concluded that the problem of the time was insufficient growth in the world economy. This assumption was the basis of the 1978 Bonn Summit Agreement for coordinated expansion with Japan and Europe (Germany in particular). By the end of the decade, the consensus had become that the top priority in fact was fighting inflation, not promoting real growth. A natural way of interpreting the view—widely held in Germany at least—that the result of the Bonn-coordinated expansion turned out to have been detrimental is that unanticipated developments, particularly the large increase in oil prices associated with the sudden Iranian crisis of 1979, moved the world economy to a highly inflationary position where expansion was no longer called for.[23]

The second sort of uncertainty present in the equations is uncertainty regarding the proper weights, w_x and w_p, to put on the target variables in the objective function.[24] This problem is even greater than the problem of assigning optimal values to the target variables. In a society in which the relative weights that individual actors place on inflation (or the current account) vary from zero to infinity, the likelihood is very high that any given government is using weights that differ from the "correct" ones that would follow from any given criterion. One can see from the equations that, for example, putting insufficient weight on fighting inflation has the same effect as underestimating the baseline inflation rate; thus, the coordinating policymaker may ask his trading partners to adopt expansionary policies when contractionary policies are in fact called for. This is precisely the mistake that, by 1980, some people concluded had been made by the United States. From the viewpoint of the Republicans who were elected to the presidency that year or the Social Democrats who came to power in Germany two years later (or the Conservatives who had been elected in the United Kingdom the year before), the policymakers who had agreed to coordinated "reflation" at the Bonn Summit of 1978 had put insufficient weight on the objective of price stability.

The third sort of uncertainty pertains to the policy multipliers, the derivatives y_m, y_g, and so on in equations (2) to (5a), which reflect the effect on the target variables of changes in the money supply and government expenditure. Any given government is likely to be using policy multipliers that differ substantially from the "true" ones and that may even be incorrect in sign. Consider the tremendous variation in multipliers according to different schools of thought and even according to different estimates in the models of mainstream macroeconomists. They cannot all be correct.[25]

Chapter 11 illustrated in some detail the potential range of multiplier estimates. The variation in the estimates was large, not just in magnitude but also in sign. Chapter 13 considered what would happen if policymakers proceeded with coordination efforts but used conflicting models of the world. Considering 10 possible models and the resulting 1,000 combinations that represent the beliefs of U.S. policymakers, the beliefs of non-U.S. policymakers, and reality, monetary coordination was found to result in gains for the United States in 546 cases, losses in 321 cases, and no effect on the objective functions in 133 cases. Coordination resulted in gains for the rest of the OECD in 539 cases, losses in 327, and no effect in 134.

Thus, a cooperative package of policy changes that each country thinks will benefit it could, ex post, easily turn out to make things worse. The baseline level of output may differ from what is expected, the optimum level (of, for example, potential output) may vary from the anticipated level, or a foreign monetary expansion may turn out to have an effect on domestic output that is different than expected.

Moreover, uncertainty greatly complicates the enforcement problem. Recall the earlier conclusion that to enable compliance to be monitored, the agreement must involve the explicit setting of observable performance criteria. Two comments must now be made. First, policymakers often do not have direct control over the variables referred to here as "their policies." Central banks cannot determine the money supply precisely because it may be subject to disturbances within the banking system or in the wider economy's demand for money. Nor can specific policymakers in international negotiations determine their country's fiscal policies precisely. For this reason, it can be difficult to hold policymakers accountable if policy variables deviate from the cooperative bargain.

Second, ex ante uncertainty means that some countries will face an especially great temptation to cheat because they turn out ex post to lose a lot from abiding by the agreement (a lot relative to unilaterally violating the agreement and perhaps also relative to never having made it to begin with). In such circumstances, the short-run gains from abrogating may outweigh the longer-term gains from continued cooperation.

Thus, for the parties to be held accountable, the variables to which they commit their countries must, to the maximum extent possible, be both observable and under the control of government authorities—in particular, under the control of those authorities involved in the international negotiations. Otherwise, the national authorities can always claim that a failure to

satisfy a performance criterion was beyond their control.[26] It is not, however, essential that the variables be under the precise short-run control
of the authorities, especially if compliance with the agreement is to be
checked, say, once a year at an annual IMF review, or at summit meetings
of the heads of state, or twice a year at meetings of the finance ministers.
It is essential only that there be an unambiguous sign to the relationship
between the policy instruments that *are* under direct control and the variable to which the parties commit themselves, and that the lags in the
relationship not be too long. When the variable begins to deviate seriously
from the agreed-on range, the policymakers should begin to adjust their
policy instruments accordingly. Then they can be held accountable at the
end of the year for any large deviations from the agreement.

The next condition on the variables to which policymakers must commit
themselves pulls in the opposite direction. The variables specified by the
agreement must be tied closely enough to the target variables in the ultimate objective function that if there is an unexpected disturbance in one of
the economic relationships (or if one of the multipliers turns out to be
different from what was expected), the country will not be drastically
harmed. If, for example, a country commits itself to a specific number for its
monetary base or the money supply, and subsequent shifts in the money
multiplier or velocity translate that number into a severe and needless
recession, the country will be sorely tempted to break its commitment.
Just imagine if the Federal Reserve's short-lived public commitment in the
early 1980s to a regime of a low and stable M1 growth rate had been made
as part of an international agreement. Would the American public have
accepted prolonging the 1981–82 recession for another four years for the
sake of an international agreement predicated on an erroneous forecast of
velocity?

There must be a similar clear link between the variables that one party
commits itself to and the *other* countries' target variables. If one partner
sticks to its money growth targets, another country will not be much
impressed if the continued commitment turns out to be disadvantageous
to itself, for example, because a disturbance moves it to the overly
inflationary side of full employment or because the partner's money
growth turns out to be transmitted negatively rather than positively.

The Choice of Indicators: A Reprise

As noted earlier, the G7 list of indicators is too long to be useful for
enforcing an agreement. Could it be winnowed down to a practical num-

ber? There seems little point in doing so since no item on the list is a good candidate to be the single variable on which negotiation under a future coordination regime would focus.

1. Real output, employment, inflation, and the trade balance are less directly affected by policy instruments than is nominal GNP; moreover, focusing exclusively on any one of them would destabilize the others.

2. The money supply is more under the control of the authorities (at least on an annual basis), but is much less directly linked to target variables; it is one unambiguous step further away from the two fundamental target variables of real output and price level than is nominal GNP. (That step is the existence of shifts in velocity, as discussed above and demonstrated in chapter 13). Furthermore, as shown above, the effects of money on all three target variables (output, price level, and trade balance) in the other country are completely ambiguous in sign. Thus, the money supply is an even less suitable choice of focus for international coordination than for domestic policymaking.

3. Fiscal policy is more easily linked to the foreign target variables (or would be if the structural deficit were used as indicator). But it is less directly under the control of the policymakers than is the money supply. Among the G7 countries, the inability to control the budget deficit was most striking in the case of the United States in the 1980s. Feldstein (1987, pp. 23–24) suggests why the United States will never be able to participate in serious international bargaining over fiscal policy: "A primary reason why such macroeconomic policy coordination cannot work as envisioned is that the United States is constitutionally incapable of participating in such a negotiation. The separation of powers in the American form of government means that the Secretary of the Treasury cannot promise to reduce or expand the budget deficit or to change tax rules. This power does not rest with the President or the Administration but depends on legislative agreement between the President and the Congress."

4. Exchange rate policy is, of course, a very large topic. But one can easily note some difficulties with the exchange rate being the single indicator that G7 countries commit themselves to stabilizing in policy coordination agreements. If, say, the dollar/deutsche mark rate begins to stray outside the announced target zone, which of the two governments should suffer sanctions or a loss in reputation? The "$n - 1$ problem" might mean that one country—presumably the United States—would have to sit out, which is not what is wanted. Countries could commit themselves to certain targets for their foreign exchange intervention, or more generally to monetary

and fiscal policies that in theory would determine the exchange rate. But, as already noted, the link from macroeconomic policies to the exchange rate is fraught with even greater uncertainty than the link to output and inflation.

One must raise the question of whether the exchange rate has as great a claim as the other target variables to appearing directly in the objective function. In the second part of chapter 15, the exchange rate is added to the objective function along with output and the price level. It is shown that the penalty for stabilizing the exchange rate is being saddled with a monetary policy that destabilizes the overall price level relative to what happens with a regime of stabilizing nominal GNP. Thus, to opt for a fixed exchange rate regime one must put tremendous weight on the exchange rate objective. (One must be prepared to argue that a 10 percent fluctuation in the exchange rate causes greater trouble than a 10 percent fluctuation in the price level.) The only other way out is to assume that when the regime changes, much of the disturbance in the exchange rate equation will disappear rather than having to be accommodated by the money supply.[27]

5. Of the remaining three indicators on the G7 list (the interest rate, international reserves, and the price of gold), the price of gold is the only one that has been proposed as a candidate for the sole variable around which countries should coordinate. Proponents of a central role for gold do not seem to appreciate that shifts in the demand function for gold and in the other economic relationships that link it to the target variables are even more destabilizing than shifts in the demand for money or the demand for foreign exchange, and that they are likely to remain so in the future. The case for the superiority of nominal GNP over the price of foreign exchange holds equally for the price of gold. In a world where there are frequent shifts in demand among money, foreign currency, and gold, stabilizing any one of these variables means allowing the shifts to be transmitted more forcefully to the rest of the economy.

This does not mean that the price of gold (or of other minerals or agricultural commodities) is not a useful indicator in the sense of being a good early warning signal of the likely future course of the overall price level, which is the true target variable.[28] In this sense, such prices belong with the money supply, the interest rate, the yield curve, and many other leading indicators on the list of variables that policymakers may want to monitor on a short-term basis in attempting to hit their targets, whether under a regime of coordination, decentralized national policymaking with some commitment to a nominal anchor, or complete discretion.

In short, if coordination is to go beyond the stage of rhetoric to a small-scale commitment, which means some degree of international commitment to a single variable, then nominal GNP (or nominal demand) dominates each of the indicators that the G7 have apparently discussed as the natural candidate for that variable.

14.2 How International Nominal GNP Targeting (INT) Would Work

The INT framework laid out in Frankel (1988a, 1988b) is a very simple one. The G7 ministers would focus their negotiations not on the ten or eleven indicators currently on their list but on nominal demand (defined as nominal GNP minus the balance on goods and services). At each meeting the national authorities would: (1) commit themselves, without any obsessively great degree of firmness, to target growth rates (or ranges) for the level of nominal GNP for five years into the future, and (2) commit themselves, with a specific target range such as ± 2 percent, to targets for their countries' levels of nominal demand for the coming year.

In the first stage, for example, the 1990s, there would be no explicit enforcement mechanism. But the targets would be publicly announced, and if a country's growth rate of nominal demand turned out to have erred significantly in one direction or the other, the fact would be noted disapprovingly at the next G7 meeting. (This does not happen under the current system). If this first stage was successful, a future stage might add another variable or two to the list, or countries might even commit themselves firmly to specific policy responses if a level of nominal demand begins to stray from the year's target.

A plan that called for targeting nominal GNP, rather than nominal demand, might be more readily and more widely understood and thus might stand a better chance of succeeding politically. The advantage of focusing on nominal demand is that when the cooperative equilibrium entails expansion, countries need to be discouraged from the temptation to accomplish the growth of output through net foreign demand (for example, through protectionist trade measures) as opposed to domestic demand. In some years, the cooperative equilibrium might entail contraction rather than expansion, and then a nominal GNP target could be preferable to a nominal demand target. But it is usually thought that the political pressure for protectionist trade remedies is greater in recessions than in expansions, a fact that points to nominal demand as the superior choice.[29]

Monetary Policy or Fiscal Policy?

Countries could attain their nominal GNP or nominal demand targets through any of several routes. One possibility is the Williamson and Miller (1987) blueprint, which assigns fiscal policy in each country the responsibility for attaining a nominal demand target (and assigns monetary policy in each country responsibility for the exchange rate).[30] At least one serious problem could arise, however, with explicitly specifying fiscal policy as the instrument with which countries are expected to attain their agreed nominal demand targets. If an economy strays from the target, the authorities will claim that it is not politically possible to adjust fiscal policy quickly. Such claims will be completely credible—in fact, they will generally be true. Thus, an agreement is more likely to stick if monetary policy, rather than fiscal policy, is specified as the policy instrument countries are expected to use.

Even if fiscal policy is assumed to be no more subject to lags and political encumbrances than monetary policy, there is another reason for assigning monetary policy to the nominal demand target. If countries also pursue trade balance targets (and it seems that they do, whether or not they should), then the classic assignment problem is relevant. The general rule is to assign responsibility for the trade balance target to the policy instrument that has a relatively greater effect on it (Mundell, 1962). I agree with Boughton (1989) that under modern conditions of floating exchange rates, which work to decrease the effectiveness of monetary policy and to increase the effectiveness of fiscal policy with respect to the trade balance, following that rule means assigning fiscal policy to the trade balance target and monetary policy to the domestic target.

Consideration of Specific Instruments

What is the precise instrument of monetary policy that should be adjusted when nominal demand drifts away from the target? The monetary base or level of unborrowed reserves would be better than the broader monetary aggregates because the central bank controls the former more directly. For the same reason, the short-term interest rate is a likely instrument.

Working in the context of closed-economy policymaking, McCallum (1988b, p. 15) has suggested a specific feedback rule that might do well here. His proposal is that for each percentage point by which nominal GNP falls short of its target in a given quarter, the monetary base be expanded an additional 0.25 percent over the next quarter. He also suggests setting a trend growth rate in the target of 3 percent per year and subtracting from this the average growth rate of the base velocity over the preceding four years to derive the current target. An alternative possibility in the context of coordination is to replace the 3 percent target with a number to be negotiated for each member of the G7 each year, with a planned long-run tendency of 3 percent.

The central bank would be better able to hit its annual nominal demand target if it was allowed to respond to information in addition to the most recent monthly figure for nominal demand itself. Ben Friedman (1984, pp. 183–84), for example, shows that indicators such as the money supply and the stock of credit can be used to increase the accuracy of predictions of deviations from a nominal income target. One could add many other leading indicators including a number from the current G7 list. Perhaps it would be best to leave the means of attaining the nominal demand target up to the national authorities, rather than requiring that they follow a particular rule such as McCallum's.

On the other hand, it would be desirable to go beyond proofs such as those in chapter 15, which demonstrate the superiority of targeting nominal GNP only when one knows the policy multipliers and takes as given the ability of the authorities to hit their targets. The evident next step is to try out the INT proposal, using simulations of one or more econometric models of the world macroeconomy, to see how it fares relative to other proposals.

Acknowledgments

I thank Julia Lowell for highly efficient research assistance and Ralph Bryant, Doug Purvis, and John Williamson for comments and suggestions.

15

The Stabilizing Properties of a Nominal GDP Rule for Monetary Policy

This chapter makes a theoretical case in favor of a commitment to a nominal GDP target on the part of the monetary authorities, as compared to three other popularly proposed targets—the money supply, the price level, and the exchange rate. Bean (1983) and West (1986) show conditions under which a nominal GDP rule stabilizes output more effectively than does a money rule. But in their framework, it would not make sense for the monetary authorities to adopt *any* rule, if the alternative were the ability to use discretion to respond to new disturbances. This chapter carries the analysis further, not just by adding the exchange rate rule to the list of candidates, but also by adopting the framework of time consistency, in which one can weigh the advantages of rules in general against the advantages of discretion.[1] We begin by examining the general argument for rules versus discretion.

The high inflation rates of the 1970s swung a majority of analysts of monetary policy away from a focus on the merits of giving the authorities full discretion to respond to unforeseen disturbances in the economy, and toward a new appreciation of the gains from imposing a credible pre-commitment or rule on monetary policy. A commonly heard metaphor is "tying the hands" of the monetary authorities. The inflation-reducing gain comes from convincing workers and others that because the central bank will not be able to inflate even if it wants to, they should expect a low inflation rate and so should settle for low wages. But the commitment must be credible or, in modern terminology, dynamically consistent.

15.1 Nominal Anchors

In practical policy terms, a regime of credible precommitment generally means singling out a particular nominal anchor, a nominal variable that the

Forthcoming in *Journal of Money, Credit and Banking* 27, 2 (May 1995).

central bank pledges to keep close to a constant or predetermined path. The nominal variable is usually neither a policy instrument that the government controls directly, like unborrowed reserves, nor a policy goal that enters the ultimate political objective function, like the inflation rate, but is rather an intermediate target. The reason for specifying and publicly announcing a single observable intermediate target—rather than some more complicated feedback rule that is a function of instruments, goals, or other observed variables—is presumably that it enables a skeptical public to monitor what the central bank is doing, and to evaluate whether it is fulfilling its proclaimed policy.[2]

Two competing candidates for the nominal anchor had attracted the most political support in the United States by the end of the 1970s, particularly among the more enthusiastic proponents of rigid commitment. The monetarists favored a preannounced target path for M1 (or perhaps some other monetary aggregate), while the supply-siders and gold bugs, among others, favored a fixed price for gold or a basket of commodities. The monetarist prescription became the official policy of the Federal Reserve in the period 1979–82. It was subsequently abandoned on grounds considered quite sensible by most: the velocity of M1 underwent such a large shift in the period 1982–86 that a continued rigid adherence to the monetarist money growth rule would have been extremely restrictive. There is no reason to think that this large shift was a one-time phenomenon. Those who favor some degree of precommitment to a nominal target now look elsewhere for a candidate.

Commitment to the price of gold or other commodities is often considered impractical, and has not been tried since the days of the gold standard. It is pointed out that shifts in the demand for gold, judging from the variability of the price of gold during the period that it has been market-determined, appear to be even larger than shifts in the demand for money. Fixing the price of gold would needlessly transmit these disturbances to the money supply, and thereby to the rest of the economy.

Other candidates for nominal anchor have been proposed besides the money supply and the price of gold. Some historically inflation-prone European countries have sought to precommit credibly to a noninflationary monetary policy by adopting the exchange rate vis-à-vis the German mark or the European Currency Unit as their nominal anchor, an option that is particularly attractive for a relatively small open economy where exchange-rate uncertainty is also regarded as undesirable for its own sake. (See, e.g., Giavazzi and Pagano, 1988, and Romer, 1993.) Even for the United States, there is support for commitment to an exchange-rate target, though usually with a wide band (Williamson, 1983; Williamson and Miller, 1987). Ronald McKinnon has proposed a "gold standard without gold," in which exchange rates would be fixed among the dollar, yen, and mark, with a worldwide nominal anchor imposed so as to prevent worldwide inflation.[3]

This chapter reaches no judgment on the desirable degree of precommitment to a nominal target. But it shows that, given precommitment to a nominal target, nominal GDP makes a more suitable target than do the four other nominal variables that have been proposed: the money supply, the price of gold, the general price level, and the exchange rate.

The general argument in a closed-economy context has been made well by others.[4] In the event of disturbances in the banking system, disturbances in the public's demand for money, or other disturbances affecting the demand for goods, a policy of holding nominal GDP steady insulates the economy; neither real income nor the price level need be affected. In the event of disturbances to supply, such as the oil price increases of the 1970s, the change is divided equiproportionately between an increase in the price level and a fall in output. For some countries, this is roughly the split that a discretionary policy would choose anyway. In general, fixing nominal GDP will not give precisely the right answer, depending on the weights on inflation and real growth in the objective function. But if the choice is among the available nominal anchors, nominal GDP gives an outcome characterized by greater stability of output and the price level.

This chapter seeks to break new ground in that it uses the time-consistency approach to monetary policy in an open economy with three sources of disturbances (supply shocks, money or goods demand shocks, and exchange rate shocks), and evaluates the nominal GDP regime in comparison to alternative regimes in which the money supply, exchange rate, price of gold, or price level are chosen for the nominal anchor.[5] Section 15.2 begins by showing that a nominal GDP target strictly dominates a money supply target, in the sense that it minimizes a quadratic loss function, regardless of how important inflation-fighting credibility is. Section 15.3 shows that a nominal GDP target also dominates an exchange-rate or price-of-gold target under certain plausible restrictions. (For example, we must rule out that extraordinarily high weight is placed directly on the objective of stabilizing the exchange rate or price of gold.) The final section offers empirical estimates of the variances of the supply, velocity, and exchange-rate disturbances, including an allowance for correlation between the latter two, to show over how wide a range of parameters the nominal GDP rule dominates.

15.2   A Comparison of Discretion and Four Alternative Rules

We compare five possible policy regimes: (1) full discretion by national policymakers, (2) a rigid money supply rule, (3) a rigid nominal GDP rule, (4) a rigid price level rule, and (5) a rigid exchange rate (or price-of-gold) rule. The approach, incorporating the advantages of both rules and discretion, follows Rogoff (1985a), Fischer (1991), and Persson and Tabellini (1990), who in turn follow Kydland and Prescott (1977) and Barro and Gordon (1983).

In the case of each of the possible nominal anchors, proponents sometimes have in mind a target zone system. The assumption of a rigid rule makes the analysis simpler. It must be acknowledged from the outset, however, that attaining a target precisely would in practice be difficult in the case of the money supply rule, and impossible in the case of the nominal GDP rule. A target zone would be more realistic.[6]

Throughout, we assume an aggregate supply relationship:

$$y = \bar{y} + b(p - p^e) + u, \tag{1}$$

where y represents output, y^* potential output, p and p^e the actual and expected price levels (or they could be the actual and expected inflation rates), respectively, and u a supply disturbance, with all variables expressed as logs.[7] The upward-sloping relationship between price level and output is shown in figures 15.1 and 15.2.

The Closed-Economy Objective Function

We begin with an objective function that includes output and the price level, but not the exchange rate, import prices, or the trade balance; we call this the case of a closed economy. The loss function is simply

$$L = ap^2 + (y - ky^*)^2, \tag{2}$$

where a is the weight assigned to the inflation objective, and we assume that the lagged or expected price level relative to which p is measured can be normalized to 0.[8] We impose $k > 1$, which builds in an expansionary bias to discretionary policymaking. Substituting equation (1) into equation (2) gives

$$L = ap^2 + [\bar{y}(1 - k) + b(p - p^e) + u]^2. \tag{3}$$

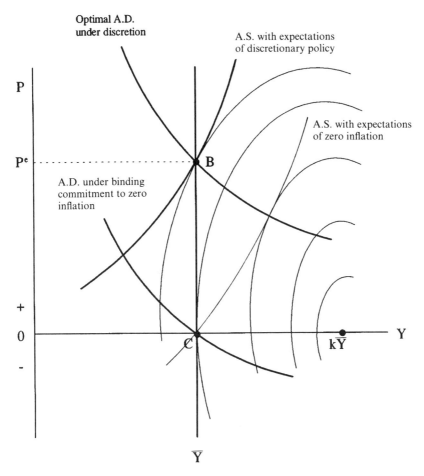

Figure 15.1
Rules (C) versus discretion (B) with no disturbances.

Regime 1: Discretionary policy
Under full discretion, the policymaker in each period chooses aggregate demand so as to minimize that period's L, with p^e given.

$$(1/2) \, dL/dp = ap + [\bar{y}(1 - k) + b(p - p^e) + u]b = 0. \tag{4}$$

$$p = [-\bar{y}(1 - k)b + b^2 p^e - bu]/[a + b^2]. \tag{5}$$

Under rational expectations,

$$p^e = Ep = -\bar{y}(1 - k)b/a. \tag{6}$$

Solving (5) for the price level,

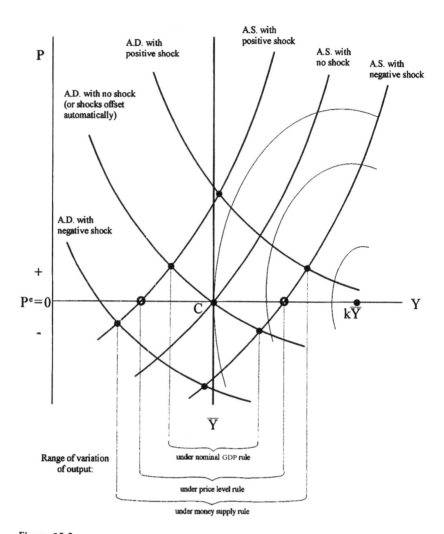

Figure 15.2
Alternative rules with supply and demand disturbances.

$$p = -\bar{y}(1 - k)\,[b/a] - ub/[a + b^2]. \tag{7}$$

From equation (2), the expected loss function then works out to

$$EL = (1 + b^2/a)[\bar{y}(1 - k)]^2 + [a/(a + b^2)]\,\mathrm{var}(u). \tag{8}$$

The first term in equation (8) represents the inflationary bias in the system, while the second represents the effect of the supply disturbance after the authorities have chosen the optimal split between inflation and output. Point B in figure 15.1 illustrates the inflationary bias that results from discretion when $k > 1$.

Regime 2: Money rule
To consider alternative regimes, we must be explicit about the money market equilibrium condition. (In regime 1, it was only implicit that the money supply m was the variable that the authorities were using to control demand.) Money supply is equal to money demand:

$$m = p + y - v, \tag{9}$$

where v represents velocity shocks. We assume v is uncorrelated with u.

If the authorities precommit to a fixed money growth rule to reduce expected inflation in long-run equilibrium, then they must give up on affecting y. The optimal money growth rate is the one that sets Ep at the target value for p, namely, 0. They are aiming for point C in figure 15.1. Thus they will set the money supply m at Ey, which in this case is $\bar{y}$. The aggregate demand equation thus becomes

$$p + y = \bar{y} + v. \tag{10}$$

Combining with the aggregate supply relationship in equation (1), the equilibrium is given by

$$y = \bar{y} + (u + bv)/(1 + b), \quad p = (v - u)/(1 + b). \tag{11}$$

Substituting into (2), the expected loss function is

$$EL = (1 - k)^2\bar{y}^2 + \{(1 + a)\,\mathrm{var}(u) + [a + b^2]\,\mathrm{var}(v)\}/(1 + b)^2. \tag{12}$$

The first term is smaller than the corresponding term in the discretion case, because the precommitment eliminates expected inflation. The second term is probably larger, however, because the authorities have given up the ability to respond to money-demand or goods-demand shocks that impinge on velocity. Whether discretion or a money rule is better depends on how big the shocks are and how big a weight, a, is placed on inflation fighting.

Regime 3: Nominal GDP rule
In the case of a nominal GDP rule, the authorities vary the money supply in such a way as to accommodate velocity shocks. Equation (10) is replaced by the condition that $p + y$ is constant. The solution is the same as in regime 2, but with the v disturbance dropped. Thus the expected loss collapses from equation (12) to

$$EL = (1 - k)^2 \bar{y}^2 + [(1 + a)/(1 + b)^2]\operatorname{var}(u). \tag{13}$$

This unambiguously dominates the money rule case.

Figure 15.2 adds disturbances to the preceding figure. It is clear that the nominal GDP rule, by holding the A.D. (aggregate demand) curve steady, narrows the range of variation of p and y, relative to the money rule. Without knowing $\operatorname{var}(u)$ or a, it is still not possible to say that the rule dominates discretion. It is quite likely, especially if the variance of u is substantial, that an absolute commitment to a rule would be unwisely constraining. Hence the argument for a target zone rather than a single number, and for subjecting the central banker to a mere diminution of reputation for missing the target rather than to a firing squad. But we have established a case that, to whatever extent the country chooses to commit to a nominal anchor, nominal GDP dominates the money supply as the candidate for anchor.

Regime 4: Price level rule
Under a price level rule, the authorities set monetary policy so that the price level is not just 0 in expectation, but is 0 regardless of later shocks. Equation (3) reduces to

$$L = [\bar{y}(1 - k) + u]^2.$$

The expected loss function is

$$EL = [\bar{y}(1 - k)]^2 + \operatorname{var}(u). \tag{14}$$

A comparison of equations (13) and (14) shows that the price level rule is dominated by the nominal GDP rule if $[(1 + a)/(1 + b)^2] < 1$. This condition, equivalent to $a/b < 2 + b$, does not automatically hold. We shall argue below that the condition $a/b < 1$ is not a very difficult one to satisfy, however, from which easily follows the necessary condition for the nominal GDP rule to dominate the price level rule.

The Open-Economy Objective Function

We now turn to consider a likely objection to choosing nominal GDP as the focus of monetary policy in an open economy—namely, that it neglects the exchange rate. Setting monetary policy so as to stabilize the exchange rate will not look attractive unless the exchange rate enters the objective function, perhaps indirectly via the consumer price index or the trade balance. Here we confront the argument head on, and include the exchange rate directly in the loss function along with output and the price level; we call this the case of the open economy. Thus we replace equation (2) with

$$L = ap^2 + (y - k\bar{y})^2 + cs^2, \tag{2'}$$

where s is the spot exchange rate measured relative to some equilibrium or target value and c is the weight placed on exchange rate stability per se. We are implicitly assuming that policymakers wish to minimize long-term swings of the exchange rate around its average value, rather than short-term uncertainty in the exchange rate.

There is no point in specifying an elaborate model of the exchange rate. All the empirical results say that most of the variation in the exchange rate cannot be explained, even ex post, to say nothing of prediction, by measurable macroeconomic variables, and thus can only be attributed to an error term that we here call e. But we must include the money supply in the exchange rate equation; otherwise, we do not allow the authorities the possibility of affecting the exchange rate. Our equation is simply

$$s = m - y + e. \tag{15}$$

We assume that e is uncorrelated with the supply disturbance u, but below will allow it to be correlated with the velocity v.[9]

Though we interpret s as the spot price of foreign currency, it could also be interpreted in what follows as the spot price of gold. It is hard to see why the price of gold should enter directly into the objective function, more so than the exchange rate; but this simply biases our results in favor of the position of the gold bugs.

From equation (9),

$$s = p - v + e. \tag{16}$$

We assume that the same aggregate supply relationship holds as before—equation (1)—and so can write the loss function (2') as

$$L = ap^2 + [(1 - k)\bar{y} + b(p - p^e) + u]^2 + c(p - v + e)^2. \tag{17}$$

We proceed as before to consider possible regimes.

Regime 1: Discretion
Minimizing L,

$$(1/2)\, dL/dp = ap + [y^*(1 - k) + b(p - p^e) + u]b + c(p - v + e) = 0.$$

This gives:

$$p = [-\bar{y}(1 - k)b + b^2 p^e - bu + c(v - e)]/[a + b^2 + c]. \tag{18}$$

The rationally expected p is given by $p^e = Ep$:

$$p^e = -(1 - k)b\bar{y}/(a + c). \tag{19}$$

Substituting into equation (19) yields

$$p = -(1 - k)\bar{y}[b/(a + b)] + [c(v - e) - bu]/[a + b^2 + c]. \tag{20}$$

The expected loss function is

$$EL = [(1 - k)\bar{y}]^2 (a + b^2 + c)/(a + c)$$
$$+ \{(a + c)\,\mathrm{var}(u) + c(a + b^2)[\mathrm{var}(v) + \mathrm{var}(e)]\}/(a + b^2 + c). \tag{21}$$

Regime 2: Money rule
As when we considered a money rule with the simpler objective function, the authorities set m at $\bar{y}$ to achieve 0 expected inflation. Thus equation (10) applies, and the same solution, equation (11), for y and p also applies. Substituting the solution for p from equation (11) into equation (16), we get the exchange rate:

$$s = e - [(u + bv)/(1 + b)]. \tag{22}$$

The additional exchange rate term is the only difference from (12) in the expected loss function:

$$EL = [\bar{y}(1 - k)]^2 + [(1 + a + c)/(1 + b^2)]\,\mathrm{var}(u)$$
$$+ [(a + b^2 + cb^2)/(1 + b)^2]\,\mathrm{var}(v) + [c]\,\mathrm{var}(e). \tag{23}$$

Again the comparison with discretion depends on the various parameter magnitudes.

Regime 3: Nominal GDP rule
When the monetary authorities are able to vary m so as to keep $p + y$ constant, the velocity shocks, v, drop out. The expected loss function becomes

$$EL = [\bar{y}(1 - k)]^2 + [(1 + a + c)/(1 + b)^2]\,\text{var}(u) + c\,\text{var}(e). \qquad (24)$$

As before, the nominal GDP rule unambiguously dominates the money rule.

In practice e shocks in the exchange rate equation are very large, and dwarf u shocks in the aggregate supply equation, as we document below. (The exchange rate often moves 10 percent in a year, without corresponding movements in the money supply or other observable macroeconomic variables. Similar movements of real output are hard to imagine.) If the weight c on the s target is substantial, then the last term in the expected loss equation may be important.

Regime 4: Exchange rate (or gold) rule
Again, the authorities cannot affect y in long-run equilibrium. But now it is the exchange rate that they peg in such a way that $Ep = 0$, which from equation (16) is $s = 0$. The ex post price level is then given by

$$p = v - e. \qquad (25)$$

From equation (1),

$$y = \bar{y} + b(v - e) + u. \qquad (26)$$

From equation (2),

$$EL = (a + b^2)\,\text{var}(v - e) + [y^*(1 - k)]^2 + \text{var}(u). \qquad (27)$$

Assume, to begin with, that v and e are uncorrelated, so that $\text{var}(v - e)$ can be replaced with $\text{var}(v) + \text{var}(e)$. The coefficient on $\text{var}(e)$ is $(a + b^2)$, as compared to the coefficient c in the expected loss under the nominal GDP rule (equation (24)). We made the point above that, in practice, e shocks dwarf u shocks. Reasoning on this basis, even if v shocks are also small and $a = c$ (the objective function puts no greater weight on a 10 percent fluctuation of the price level than on a 10 percent fluctuation of the exchange rate), an extremely conservative assumption, the expected loss from fixing s is greater than the expected loss from fixing nominal GDP. The reason is that under an exchange rate rule e shocks are allowed to affect the money supply and therefore the overall price level. Once we allow for v shocks (which are in between u and e shocks in magnitude, as we will see below), the case for nominal GDP targeting is even stronger. One would have to put extraordinarily high weight on the exchange rate objective to prefer an exchange rate rule.

Under the secondary interpretation of s as the price of gold rather than the price of foreign exchange, the e shocks are likely to be at least as large, and the argument for it receiving heavy weight directly in the objective function even more difficult to make. In short, the nominal GDP rule seems likely to dominate all of the other candidates for nominal target—the money supply, the exchange rate, the price of gold, and the price level.

15.3 Estimates of Actual Disturbance Variances (including an Allowance for Correlation between Two)

The foregoing analysis was predicated on the assumption of zero correlation among the three kinds of disturbances: supply shocks, money-demand or goods-demand shocks, and exchange-rate shocks. In the case of supply shocks, this assumption will be retained. Although it is not difficult to think of reasons why supply shocks might be either positively or negatively correlated with exchange-rate shocks or velocity shocks, one has no a priori sense of a strong correlation of either sign. One could extend the empirical analysis offered here to allow for such a correlation, but to do so would require making it dependent on one or another set of details of model specification. The approach throughout this chapter is to keep the model as simple and general as possible.[10]

The assumption that velocity shocks, v, and exchange rate shocks, e, are uncorrelated, however, may be too strong to sustain seriously, as it is likely that they are in fact positively correlated. An upward shift in the U.S. demand for money such as that which occurred in the early 1980s will cause an appreciation of the dollar (even in the absence of changes in the money supply or real income). Indeed, McKinnon (1984, 1988) believes that shifts in countries' money demands are the dominant source of fluctuations in exchange rates.

In the derivations above, we did not actually use the assumption that v and e shocks were uncorrelated until after equation (27). Thus that equation, representing the loss function for the exchange rate rule, remains unchanged, as does equation (24), representing the loss function for the nominal GNP rule. The difference between the two is

$$\text{Diff } EL = \{(a + b^2)\,\text{var}(v - e) + \text{var}(u)\}$$
$$- \{c\,\text{var}(e) + [(1 + a + c)/(1 + b)^2]\,\text{var}(u)\}. \tag{28}$$

The nominal GDP rule dominates the exchange-rate rule if this difference is positive; but now we must allow for the covariance between v and e when computing $\mathrm{var}(v - e)$. (The comparison between the nominal GNP rule and the money rule, showing how the latter always dominates so long as $\mathrm{var}(v)$ is positive, remains valid.) This section of the chapter describes an estimation of this difference for four countries over the last twenty years: the United States, Germany, Japan, and the United Kingdom. Details of the calculation methods and results are available in an appendix.[11]

The variable definitions are as follows:

y = log of real GDP (seasonally adjusted),

p = log of implicit GDP deflator,

m = log of M1 money supply,[12] and

s = log of the IMF's MERM-weighted exchange-rate index (period average) expressed as the price of foreign currency.

The equations specified earlier for money demand and the exchange rate, equations (9) and (15) respectively, were so simple as to be parameter free; thus the disturbance terms v and e can be computed directly, with no estimation required. Their variances are given for each of the four countries in table 15.1. As claimed in the preceding section, the magnitude of the exchange-rate disturbances is many times greater than the magnitude of the velocity disturbances. But for the cases of Germany and the United Kingdom, there is a fairly high positive correlation between these two disturbances, so that $\mathrm{var}(v - e)$ is substantially less than $\mathrm{var}(v) + \mathrm{var}(e)$.

It is impossible to compute the supply disturbances without taking a stand on at least one parameter, b, the elasticity of supply with respect to (unexpected) changes in the price level. We repeat equation (1):

$$y - \bar{y} = b(p - p^e) + u. \tag{1}$$

Table 15.1
Estimated variances of disturbances
1974:1 to 1989:4

		U.S.	Germany	Japan	United Kingdom
Velocity shock	v	.00612	.00521	.00323	.04219
Exchange rate shock	e	.02065	.01138	.01794	.07477
Supply shock[a]	u	.00061	.00043	.00015	.00080
Covariance of v and e		.00025	.00676	.00053	.04251

a. These are the "temporary supply shocks," estimated as the residuals in a regression of the output gap on the unexpected change in the price level.

Two of the techniques we tried for estimating the log of potential GDP, $\bar{y}$, were a fitted quadratic trend and a five-year centered moving average. The expected log price level was estimated with an ARIMA process. Regression estimates of equation (1) are available in the appendix.[13] In one sense the estimates were relatively robust with respect to which method of estimation was used for $\bar{y}$: for each country, the standard error of the regression, representing the magnitude of the u shocks, was in roughly the same range regardless of which estimation method was used. In particular, var(u) was always far smaller than var(e), and smaller than var(v) as well, as claimed in the preceding section.

In another sense, however, the estimates of equation (1) were not robust: the estimates of the coefficient b varied depending on how $\bar{y}$ was estimated. Our preferred method, the five-year moving average, produced a statistically significant value of 1.36 for the United States but lower values for the other countries, and was not statistically significant for the United Kingdom.

The sign of the criterion expression—equation (28)—is far more sensitive to the parameter b in the case where we allow for v and e to be correlated than it was in the preceding section. The magnitude of the elasticity of the supply relationship is perhaps the most controversial question in macroeconomics, so I am reluctant to assert a choice among the possible estimates. Instead, we follow an approach that allows the reader to choose b.

We proceed, as in the preceding section, to stack the odds in favor of the exchange-rate rule by assuming that the objective function gives a weight to the exchange rate that might be as large as the weight given to the price level. Thus we assume that $c = a$ (a very conservative assumption, especially for a country like the United States where internationally traded goods are a relatively small share of the economy). The difference in the expected loss under a nominal GDP rule and an exchange-rate rule is then solely a function of the parameters a and b, given our estimates of var($v - e$) and var(e), and given that an estimate of var(u) follows from equation (1) and any given parameter choice for b. In the appendix we consider for each country a whole range of possible values for a (from 0 to 6) and a similar range for b, and show in tables the value of the criterion expression for each combination.

We first consider the case where v and e shocks are uncorrelated. For all countries the nominal GDP rule dominates the exchange-rate rule, for all values of a and b, as claimed in the preceding section.

We next allow for the correlation of v and e shocks. For the cases of the United States and Japan, it is again true that the nominal GDP rule dominates the exchange-rate rule, for all values of a and b. For Germany and the United Kingdom, however, the answer depends on a and b. To help evaluate these two cases, figures 15.3 and 15.4 show possible values of a on the horizontal axis and b on the vertical axis, and plot the boundary that indicates the region where a nominal GDP rule dominates an exchange rate rule.

A pattern is evident in the results: the relative attractiveness of the nominal GDP rule depends directly on the magnitude of b relative to a. The parameter b is to be interpreted as the loss in output (in percent) that the economy would have to suffer for each percentage point reduction in inflation. The point estimate of b that emerged in the computation of the supply shocks was 1.4 for the United States and 1.1 for Japan.[14] In this vicinity, a sufficient condition for the nominal GDP rule to dominate the exchange-rate rule for the case of the United Kingdom is the simple condition that $b/a > 1$. Under regime 4 in the closed economy case, we saw that this condition was also a sufficient one for the nominal GDP rule to dominate the price level rule.

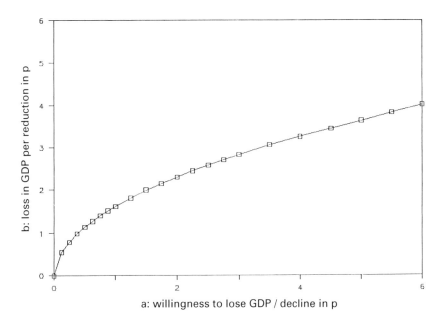

Figure 15.3
German nominal GDP policy frontier. In area above line, nominal GDP rule dominates exchange rate rule.

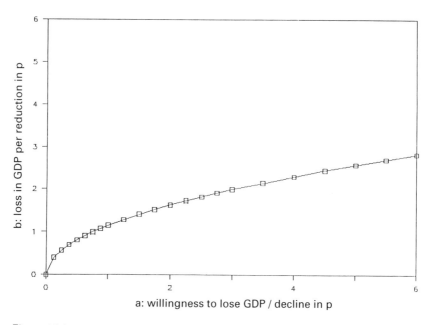

Figure 15.4
U.K. nominal GDP policy frontier. In area above line, nominal GDP rule dominates exchange
rate rule.

The reader can decide whether he or she believes that $b/a > 1$, by
conducting a simple thought experiment. If it were possible, hypotheti-
cally, to double output permanently at the cost of doubling inflation
(starting from the position where optimal discretion produces an inflationary steady-state, presumably the norm for most countries), would the output gain be worth the cost? Most economists do not believe that the
short-run costs of inflation ("shoe-leather costs" of trips to the bank, confusion of relative price signals, uncertainty, and so forth) are very high. The
argument against inflating consists rather of the long-run considerations,
which the adoption of any nominal anchor (money supply, nominal GDP,
exchange rate, or price of gold) is explicitly designed to address. It follows
that a in the objective function is thought to be less than b, and we are in
the upper-left triangular half of the graphs. The conclusion is that the
nominal GDP rule again dominates, not just for the United States but for
many other countries as well.

To the extent that the particular choice for b differs from the OLS
estimate on which table 15.1 is based, one might be concerned that the
preceding analysis has overstated the magnitude of the supply disturbances

in an important respect. For a given value of b, the entire discrepancy from equation (1), $(y - \bar{y}) - b(p - p^e)$, was assigned to the disturbance term u (with the quadratic-trend method used for estimating $\bar{y}$). Given that the uncertainty surrounding the proper estimate of b derives largely from uncertainty surrounding the measure of $\bar{y}$, however, it might seem that part of the discrepancy should be assigned to $\bar{y}$ rather than to u.

As a check on the sensitivity of the results to the method of estimating the supply shocks, we repeat the analysis without depending on the quadratic trend method of estimating $\bar{y}$. For any given value of b, we first compute $y - b(p - p^e)$. The breakdown between $\bar{y}$ and u is then estimated by an ARIMA process. In this way, u is constructed as the unforecastable component of shifts in the supply relationship. When the value of the loss function is computed, the boundary of parameter values indicating the attractiveness of the different regimes lies just where it did with the earlier estimation method (to within the degree of precision of the calculations).[15] The velocity and exchange-rate shocks are so much larger than the supply shocks that the estimation method has a negligible effect on the results. Thus the nominal GDP rule still seems to dominate.

15.4   Concluding Remarks

It must be admitted that the analysis in this chapter has made a number of simplifying assumptions, some of which might bias the results in favor of nominal GDP targeting.[16] Topping the list of desirable extensions is a more sophisticated model of the economy, allowing for the difficulty of hitting targets precisely because of lags between the realization of nominal GDP and its measurement, and allowing for even longer lags between changes in monetary policy and their effects on realized nominal GDP. Such problems exist for the other candidates for nominal anchor as well, but they are considerably smaller for the money supply, and perhaps nonexistent for the exchange rate.

Once the importance of lags is admitted into the model of the economy, an appropriate way to allow for the difficulty of hitting the targets precisely would be to consider a more practical form of the nominal GDP proposal: The authorities precommit to a target band of specified width. I would propose that the authorities precalculate the width of the announced band so that, given the estimated distribution of disturbances, they can expect to keep nominal GDP within the band 95 percent of the time. (This would probably have to be a fairly wide band.) In this way, the public can effectively monitor the authorities' record, by statistically testing with observed data the hypothesis that their commitment is sincere and that any observed deviations from the target are due to chance.

The other possible nominal anchors could also be interpreted with target zones of whatever width corresponds to 95 percent confidence. In some cases, such as the money supply target, the width would be considerably narrower than in the case of the nominal GDP target.

How the authorities can best attain the target for nominal GDP or other variables then becomes an optimal feedback problem. Some have analyzed this issue (e.g., Feldstein and Stock, 1994; McCallum, 1987, 1988a, b). But it remains as an important subject for future research to combine the question, considered in this chapter, of which choice of nominal anchor would maximize the objective function, with the question of how to attain the target.

Acknowledgments

I would like to thank Menzie Chinn, currently an Assistant Professor at U.C. Santa Cruz, for help with the statistical calculations at the end of the chapter. A complete appendix explaining them is available in U.C. Berkeley Economics Working Paper 91-166. I would also like to thank Julia Lowell and Torsten Persson for comments, and the Institute for Business and Economic Research at U.C. Berkeley for research support in 1990–91.

Notes

Introduction to Part I

1. The conclusion that portfolio effects should be small crops up in several contexts. In the context of the large differential observed between the average rate of return in the equity market and the interest rate, it leads to the "equity premium puzzle": expected-utility maximization implies that the premium should be small. (The journal editor for this paper, Lawrence Summers, thought this puzzle the most interesting implication of the findings, but the author stubbornly resisted the editor's recommendation to rewrite the paper to focus on it. The "equity premium puzzle" soon thereafter became a major "hit" for Mehra and Prescott, 1985.) In the context of the term structure of interest rates, the same conclusion implies that the expectations hypothesis should hold approximately (as mentioned in note 10 in chapter 1 and shown in chapter 2 here). In the context of observed systematic differences in expected rates of return across countries, it implies that the exchange risk premium is not sufficiently large and variable to be the explanation (Krugman, 1981; Frankel, 1982b; and note 19 in chapter 1, and chapter 4 here).

2. The current state-of-the-art tests of international asset-pricing models, including such authors as Dumas (1994) and Ferson and Harvey (1994), are reviewed in the introduction to the book in which Engel (1994) appears (Frankel, 1994).

Chapter 1   Portfolio Crowding-Out, Empirically Estimated

1. The OLS method has been used by Friedman (1983, 1985a), and the simultaneous-equation method by Friedman (1977b), Roley (1982), and Masson (1978), among others.

2. Examples of regressions in inverted form are Fair and Malkiel (1971) and Modigliani and Sutch (1966, 1967).

3. Note that this is not exactly the same as the stronger proposition that the ex post returns on the two assets are always the same. Their ex post returns can have independent components, as long as these components are uncorrelated with the returns on the market portfolio. If the individual asset is a small proportion of the market portfolio, as it is for an individual equity or bond, then that component of its return that is uncorrelated with the returns on other assets is diversifiable and will have no effect on demand for the asset.

4. Brainard and Tobin (1968) impose a priori values on the parameters outright. All these papers run simulations on the chosen parameter values to see the effects of changes in government debt, etc. They also emphasize a low degree of aggregation: separate asset-demand functions are estimated for households, banks, etc.

5. The choice to express returns relative to a numeraire is not restrictive. We could generalize equation (1) slightly to

$$\mathbf{x}_t = \mathbf{A} + \tilde{\mathbf{B}}E\begin{bmatrix} \mathbf{r}_{t+1} \\ \dots \\ r_{t+1}^d \end{bmatrix},$$

where $\tilde{\mathbf{B}}$ is $G - 1$ by G. Then when we invert,

$$E\begin{bmatrix} \mathbf{r}_{t+1} \\ \dots \\ r_{t+1}^d \end{bmatrix} = -\tilde{\mathbf{B}}^{-1}\mathbf{A} + \tilde{\mathbf{B}}^{-1}\mathbf{x}_t,$$

we need subtract only the last row from each of the others to get an equation of the precise form as equation (2). In what follows, we use only equation (2) anyway.

6. Thus, we are ruling out slow adjustment of actual portfolios toward desired portfolios. Lags of this sort are used by Brainard and Tobin (1968), Smith and Brainard (1976), Friedman (1977b, 1983), Backus et al. (1980), Backus and Purvis (1980), and Roley (1982).

7. Bosworth (1985) discusses the approaches that have been taken to measuring the cost of funds that is relevant for firms' investment decisions, an average of the rates of return on equity and corporate bonds and of corporate income taxes.

8. The validity of the technique depends on the assumption that the asset-demand function (1) holds exactly. If asset demands are determined by the optimal portfolio *plus other factors*, or if there are measurement errors in the data, the estimates will be biased and inconsistent.

9. Data appendices are available in NBER Working Paper no. 1205, Frankel and Dickens (1983), and Frankel (1985a). This chapter measures rates of return on a level basis, whereas Frankel and Dickens (1983) and Frankel (1985a) measure them on a logarithmic basis, which is more consistent with the finance theory when investors have constant relative risk aversion.

10. It is possible to reject statistically such economically interesting hypotheses as the proposition that short-term bonds and long-term bonds are perfect substitutes and the proposition that federal bonds are perfect substitutes for corporate bonds. The former is the "expectations hypothesis" of the term structure of interest rates, tested by Modigliani and Sutch (1966, 1967) and Masson (1978); the latter is the proposition tested by Fair and Malkiel (1971). The test results for these hypotheses, based on the estimates from table 1.1, are reported in NBER Working Paper no. 1205. They are omitted here under the logic that, once mean-variance optimization by risk-averse investors is assumed (as it is in the next section), perfect substitutability is ruled out automatically.

11. Frankel and Dickens (1983) and chapter 3 here give further references on CAPM. Whereas this chapter develops a technique to *impose* the hypothesis of mean-variance optimization in order to test other hypotheses, those papers use the same technique to *test* the hypothesis of mean-variance optimization itself.

12. In the one-period maximization framework, the assumption that returns are normally distributed is sufficient to imply that investors look only at the mean and variance. The assumption of quadratic utility would be an alternative way to do it, but that assumption is

unrealistic, and we shall need to assume a normal (or some other) distribution anyway in order to do our maximum likelihood estimation. Two similar formulations are Friend and Blume (1975, equation (5)) and Friedman and Roley (1979, equation (20′)).

13. The utility function will have a constant coefficient of relative risk aversion if it is a power function:

$$U(W) = \frac{1}{1-\rho} W^{1-\rho}$$

The one-period maximization problem considered here presumes separability of the portfolio and saving decisions. The solution will give the same answer as the general intertemporal maximization problem if the utility function is further restricted to the logarithmic form, the limiting case as ρ goes to 1.0, or if expected returns in future periods are independent of this period's return. See Merton (1973, pp. 877–78).

14. The complete MLE results with ρ unconstrained are reported in NBER Working Paper no. 1205, Frankel and Dickens (1983), and (using log returns) in chapter 3 here. The estimated standard errors may not be trustworthy, but a likelihood ratio test is valid, and it is unable to distinguish different values of ρ.

15. As Blanchard and Plantes (1977, p. 770) show, "the 'similarity' between two assets, i.e., a positive correlation, is clearly far from implying substitutability between them." However, there does turn out to be a one-to-one correspondence between positive signs for the off-diagonal elements in table 1.2 and negative signs for the off-diagonal elements in table 1.3.

16. Details regarding the construction of the test-statistics are given in appendix 3 to NBER Working Paper no. 1205.

17. The same would be true of the debt of state and local governments, perhaps more so because it is clearer that they have to pay off their debt eventually. Corporate debt is different because, with a given real capital stock, every dollar of corporate debt reduces the equity of the firm by one dollar.

18. The system of asset demand functions (1) does not constitute a complete model of the determination of the levels of interest rates or bond prices. One would need to combine it with, for example, the assumption of a stochastic process for the asset supplies and assumptions of rationality and stability for expectations. Expectations of future debt would in theory affect today's asset prices through expectations of capital losses.

19. This point was made in the context of international differences in expected rates of return in Frankel and Engel (chapter 4 in this volume, note 11). Small portfolio effects, on the same order of magnitude as those estimated here, are also implied by the variance-covariance estimates in Friedman (1983, 1985a), properly interpreted.

Chapter 2   A Comment on Debt Management

1. This is the approach followed by Smith and Brainard (1976), Backus and Purvis (1980), Backus et al. (1980), and Friedman (1978, 1985b).

2. Example of regressions in inverted form include Fair and Malkiel (1971) and Modigliani and Sutch (1966, 1967).

3. Citations include Friedman (1977b), Roley (1982), and Masson (1978).

4. For example, many of the authors cited in note 1 have thought it necessary to impose a priori some element of their own beliefs on the estimates.

5. Examples of this approach include Roley (1979) and the studies by Ben Friedman.

6. One example of this approach is Bodie, Kane, and McDonald (1983), who estimate expected returns as a univariate autoregressive process.

7. The technique has also been applied by Friedman (1985a, 1986). Friedman and Kuttner (1988) give declining weight to observations with longer lags.

8. References are Froot and Frankel (1989) and Froot (1989), respectively. Friedman (1986) uses survey data on long-term interest rates, stock prices, and inflation rates to help estimate directly investors' reactions to expected rates of return.

9. The portfolio effects calculated when the variances are estimated from options prices are considerably smaller, in proportion to the variances.

10. In any case, Mehra and Prescott (1985), working within the paradigm of intertemporal optimization, come to the same conclusion regarding the implausibly small magnitude of the risk premium.

Chapter 3   Portfolio Shares as "Beta Breakers"

1. Tobin (1958). Tobin (1983) confirms that his original work "was intended primarily as a contribution to positive macroeconomics rather than to management science" (p. 236).

2. Two common early references are Black, Jensen, and Scholes (1972) and Blume and Friend (1973).

3. Stambaugh (1982) and Nordhaus and Durlauf (1982).

4. Gibbons (1982) and Shanken (1983).

5. A few studies, such as Friend and Blume (1975), have looked at actual portfolios held by households, but not in time series form.

6. Residents of the San Francisco Bay Area are already familiar with Beta Breakers.

7. Cheng and Grauer (1980) have criticized the standard tests on these grounds.

8. From equation (4) it follows that the expected return on asset i *relative* to a numeraire asset d is the same linear combination of the covariances with the other assets' relative returns. Such equations can also be derived from first principles of mean/variance optimization on the part of the investor. Chapter 1 in this volume does this, in vector form.

9. The error term in the regression equation is the expectational error that investors make in predicting what rates of return will turn out to be. The assumption that expectations are rational means that the error is uncorrelated with all available information, in particular with the asset supplies x.

10. We chose the sixth asset, short-term bills and deposits, as "numeraire." Returns on each of the other five were computed relative to the sixth. The share of the portfolio allocated to the sixth asset is omitted from the x's, since it is simply one minus the sum of the other five. See chapter 1 in this volume for the appropriate algebra. The data are described in appendix 3A.

11. Appendix 3 in Frankel and Dickens (1983) describes the nonlinear MLE program used, a modified form of a program written by Paul Ruud to use the Berndt et al. (1974) algorithm.

12. We can impose a more reasonable value on ρ, like 2, and use the MLE technique to estimate the parameters subject to this constraint. Such estimates are reported in chapter 1 in this volume.

Chapter 4   Do Asset-Demand Functions Optimize over Real Returns?

1. The field was pioneered by Kouri (1976, 1977), Solnik (1974), and Grauer, Litzenberger and Stehle (1976). The results were formulated in a manner simple enough for direct use in macroeconomic models by Dornbusch (1983), with an amendment by Krugman (1981). Other contributions include Adler and Dumas (1976, 1983), Frankel (1979), Fama and Farber (1979), Garman and Kohlhagen (1980), Stulz (1981), and Hodrick (1981).

2. Examples are Roll and Solnik (1977), Cornell and Dietrich (1978), Kouri and de Macedo (1978), de Macedo (1982), and Dornbusch (1980). For references to the standard CAPM tests, and for a well-known critique of them, see Roll (1977).

3. Examples of studies that attempt to relate returns to asset supplies without imposing all constraints of mean-variance optimization are Dooley and Isard (1983), and Frankel (1982a).

4. Frankel (1982b, 1983) treat only the exchange rates as stochastic. The 1983 paper differs further from this chapter by restricting the assets to two: marks and dollars. The 1982b paper differs from this chapter by *imposing* the optimization hypothesis, and thus obtaining more efficient estimates of the parameters, rather than *testing* the hypothesis. Among previous studies of the optimal portfolio, Kouri and de Macedo (1978), de Macedo (1980), and de Macedo, Goldstein and Meerschwam (1982) have allowed for stochastic price levels. Among joint tests of market efficiency and risk-neutrality, Frenkel and Razin (1980) and Engel (1982) have allowed for stochastic price levels.

5. Among theoretical models, some like Grauer, Litzenberger, and Stehle (1976), Fama and Farber (1979), and Frankel (1979) assume that all investors consume a common basket of goods; others, like Solnik (1974), assume that investors of each country consume only their own goods; while still others, like Kouri (1976) and Dornbusch (1983), allow investors of each country to consume baskets that include foreign goods but that are more heavily weighted toward their own goods. The last framework is adopted in Frankel (1982b, 1983). Since data on asset supplies are available only in aggregate form, not broken down by holder, differing asset-demand functions have to be aggregated before they can be estimated. When all investors share the same source of uncertainty, the exchange rate, this can be done, using data on the distribution of wealth, as in those two papers. When prices of national goods are stochastic as well, as in this chapter, the aggregation is not possible.

6. As always, omitted variables or measurement errors would render the estimates biased and inconsistent. These considerations justify, at a minimum, special care in the calculation of the asset supply variables, described in the data appendix available in Frankel (1982b). Very briefly the net supply of assets denominated in a country's currency is calculated as the cumulation of that country's government debt, corrected for three factors: (1) debt issued in foreign currency, (2) foreign exchange intervention by the country's central bank

(inferred from data on international reserve holdings by correcting for valuation changes), and (3) foreign exchange intervention in the domestic currency by *other* countries' central banks (a factor often neglected in empirical studies).

7. The assumption that returns are normally distributed is sufficient to imply that investors look only at the mean and variance. The normality assumption might be justified by an appeal to a continuous-time diffusion process observed at discrete intervals. In any case it is necessary to assume some specific distribution for the maximum likelihood estimation.

8. We do not impose the other constraint,

$$\beta^{-1}\alpha = \rho \operatorname{cov}_t(z_{t+1}, r^{\$}_{t+1}),$$

because it is not feasible to do so econometrically. The constraint offers only five over-identifying restrictions anyway, whereas we already have twenty-five from our constraint on the coefficient matrix (twenty-four when ρ is not constrained).

9. An alternative approach would be to derive the maximizing system in terms of six absolute returns, rather than five relative returns:

$$\begin{bmatrix} r_{t+1} \\ \cdots \\ r^{\$}_{t+1} \end{bmatrix} = r^0_t \begin{bmatrix} l \\ \cdots \\ 1 \end{bmatrix} + \rho \Sigma \begin{bmatrix} x_t \\ \cdots \\ 1 - x'_t l \end{bmatrix} + u_{t+1},$$

where Σ is the variance-covariance matrix of the errors u_{t+1} made in predicting the absolute returns r_{t+1}, as opposed to the errors ε_{t+1} made in predicting the relative returns z_{t+1}. The advantage would be that because Σ is six-by-six, we would have more overidentifying restrictions. The disadvantage is that the intercept term ($r^0 \equiv \lambda W/F_1$, where λ is the Lagrangian shadow-price of wealth), though constant across equations, is not constant across time. A separate value of r^0_t could be estimated for each point in time, but the large-sample properties of such an estimator are unclear. Subtracting the last row from each of the others eliminates r^0_t. Collecting terms in x_t then restores us to equation (6). For example, the first entry, $\Sigma_{DMDM} - \Sigma_{DM\$} - \Sigma_{DM\$} + \Sigma_{\$\$}$, is the same as the first entry in Ω. The lost row of Σ seems a small price to pay.

10. The idea of estimating asset-demand equations by drawing the link between the matrix of coefficients of the expected returns and the variance-covariance matrix of the actual returns is not entirely new. See, for example, Parkin (1970) and Wills (1979).

11. The estimates in table 4.2 appear implausibly low. For example, a shift of 1 percent of the portfolio from U.S. dollars to Canadian dollars raises the expected relative returns that Canadian assets must pay by only 0.00037 percent (0.037 basis points)! The low magnitude of the coefficients is an artifact of the mean-variance optimization hypothesis, as Krugman (1981) points out, not of the estimation procedure. The reader is invited to take his own estimates of the coefficient of relative risk-aversion and the variance of the exchange rate and note how small their product is. The fact that such calculations give estimates of the coefficient that are very different than those in table 4.1, is of course the reason that our test rejects the constraint of mean-variance optimization.

12. See, for example, Roll (1977) and the references cited there.

13. If optimizing residents of different countries consume different baskets of goods, then they will use the variances of different quantities to measure risk, and the aggregation in this paper will be invalid. As in Frankel (1982b), we can disaggregate according to seven areas of residence: the six countries whose currencies are used here, and the rest of the world. Residents of each area are assumed to evaluate returns in terms of a weighted average of

the six countries' prices, with prices assumed non-stochastic when denominated in the currency of the producing country and weights determined by that area's consumption shares. A likelihood ratio test then again rejects the constraint of mean-variance optimization. The likelihoods are 1,043 unconstrained and 987 constrained with $\rho = 2.0$. We are indebted to Tony Rodrigues for these calculations.

14. However, if the coefficient of risk-aversion ρ is close to 1.0, then the intertemporal complications vanish, as mentioned in note 8. As a further bonus, the need to distinguish among investors according to their consumption basket, discussed in notes 5 and 14, also vanishes. (See Adler and Dumas (1983) or Krugman (1981).) The likelihood ratio test, not surprisingly, also rejects the mean-variance optimization hypothesis when ρ is constrained to 1.0.

15. One might legitimately wonder how we can assume the *second* moments of the returns constant over time while criticizing earlier studies for assuming the *first* moments constant over time. Could shifts in the variance-covariance matrix explain our results? Arnold (1983) uses our technique with the sample period divided in four subperiods to allow the variance-covariance matrix to change over time. He obtains the same answer we do: a rejection of the constraint of mean-variance optimization.

Chapter 5   The Constrained Asset Share Estimation (CASE) Method

1. For example, chapter 3 in this volume.

2. Ferson, Kandel, and Stambaugh (1987) estimate the constant-variance version for stock portfolios. Bodurtha and Mark (1991), Bollerslev, Engle, and Wooldridge (1987), and Engel and Rodrigues (1989) estimate a version that allows for changing conditional second moments.

3. The ARCH process does not allow second moments to vary freely. It is analogous to estimating the first moments by an ARIMA process, in which this period's expectation is related to recent realizations, rather than by the CASE technique, in which expectations can vary freely.

4. See, for example, Fama and French (1988) and Poterba and Summers (1988) for evidence on the predictability of stock-market returns, and Bollerslev (1987) and Bollerslev, Engle, and Wooldridge (1988) for evidence on the predictability of conditional variances of excess returns. These findings coupled with the results of Hansen and Richard (1987), who show that the conditionally and unconditionally mean-variance efficient frontiers are generally different, suggest that such variation in conditional moments is important for tests of MVE.

5. Note that the N asset shares, $\lambda_{t,1} \ldots \lambda_{t,N}$ are perfectly collinear because they sum to 1. This does not pose a problem for the estimation of equation (7), however, because the equations do not include a constant term.

6. If there are N assets, the computation involves a parameter matrix of dimension $N(N-1)/2 \times N(N-1)/2$ that must be repeatedly inverted. Engel and Rodrigues (1993) offer a Wald test version of the CASE test that is less difficult computationally. We apply it in section 5.4 below.

It is easy to demonstrate that, if the returns on the industry portfolios are computed using the asset shares as weights, then the MVE model of equations (1) or (2) holds for returns on industry portfolios.

7. On the other hand, we would not want to include together the suppliers of intermediate products and the producers of final output in the same industry. When steel prices rise, the cost of producing autos increases so that it is possible that steel producers' profits rise when auto manufacturers' profits decline.

8. The 99 percent critical value is 159.32.

9. The only prior belief we have about the coefficients is that the return on asset j is likely to be positively related to the share of asset j in the total portfolio. If we think of the market portfolio as composed only of stocks, then in equilibrium investors will demand a higher return from a given stock portfolio the more of it they are required to hold. Table 5.2 shows that in eight out of the eleven regressions this own-coefficient is negative (and significantly negative for industries 2 and 7). It is not significantly positive in any of the regressions.

10. Under the MVE restrictions, constraining ρ to be 0 lowers the log-likelihood value by 1.1.

11. To save space we do not report these results.

12. The comparable Wald test for the eleven-asset aggregation yields a statistic distributed as χ^2_{10} equal to 22.76. This also rejects the MVE restrictions at the 99 percent level. These particular tests reject easily even though they restrict only the diagonal elements of the return covariance matrix.

13. Equation (11) imposes symmetry on the portfolio balance model. Testing the GARCH-MVE against a version of the portfolio balance model in which the constant term in equation (11) is allowed to be asymmetric produces an LM statistic of 335.15. This is drawn from a chi-square (62 d.f.) distribution and is highly significant.

14. An LM test for that proposition is distributed chi-square (28 d.f.), and takes on a value of 359.0, rejecting the null extremely strongly.

15. More accurately, the ARCH-MVE does not significantly improve on the risk-neutral model, but the GARCH-MVE model does.

16. Similar results were found, however, when money, bonds, and real estate were allowed into the portfolio (chapters 1 and 3 in this volume) and when foreign assets were allowed (Frankel, 1982b, and chapter 4 in this volume).

Introduction to Part II

1. The model has in turn been used by Boughton and Branson (1991) and Trivedi and Varangis (1994).

2. We are indebted to Stephen Grubaugh and Scott Sumner for correcting a major data error in this chapter, as explained in note 1 in chapter 7.

Chapter 6   Expectations and Commodity Price Dynamics

1. Furthermore, the higher interest rate implies a fall in real money demand in the long run. With no jump in the current level of the money supply (as opposed to its growth rate), the long-run equilibrium path of the price level must shift up discretely (in addition to becoming steeper) in order to reduce the equilibrium real money supply. In the exchange rate literature, for example, Frenkel (1976), this is sometimes called the "magnification effect." See equation (17) below.

2. The model is qualitatively unchanged if we adopt other interpretations of μ such as the rate of change of $\bar{p}_m$ or $\bar{p}$ defined below. See Obstfeld and Rogoff (1984) or Engel and Frankel (1984a).

3. The description of $i - \mu$ as the real interest rate is loose, because i is the short-term interest rate while μ is the expected long-term inflation rate. However, the model is again qualitatively unchanged if we substitute the expected short-term inflation rate $\dot{p}^e$. See, for example, Obstfeld and Rogoff (1984).

4. The assumption that output is fixed means that the excess demand referred to in equations (1) and (2) must be coming out of inventories or else going unmet (unfilled orders). It would be preferable to have manufactured output endogenously determined by demand: $y_m = d$ (and $y = y_m + \bar{y}_c$). Once again, the model is not qualitatively altered by such an extension. See the appendix to Dornbusch (1976).

5. Unfortunately, argues Moalla-Fetini (1991), the overshooting phenomenon disappears in this case of periodic stock exhaustion of a seasonal agricultural commodity (or in the case of finite-horizon stock exhaustion of a depletable natural resource).

Chapter 7   Commodity Prices, Money Surprises, and Fed Credibility

1. It is remarkably easy, in doing empirical work, to make mistakes, even when one tries to be careful and conscientious. I discovered this in writing "Commodity Prices, Money Surprises, and Fed Credibility." Some of the data points were erroneously recorded one day earlier than intended. We did not discover the mistake until after publication, when two researchers, Stephen Grubaugh and Scott Sumner, seeking to reproduce our results, requested our data, which we had supplied to the *Journal of Money, Credit, and Banking* data bank, and found the problem. They ran the tests on the corrected data, and obtained results that their published comment was kind enough to describe as "qualitatively similar to those reported by Frankel and Hardouvelis [and providing] even stronger evidence in favor of the 'policy anticipations hypothesis'..." (Grubaugh and Sumner, 1989, p. 407). The tables shown here substitute their results for ours. We are grateful for their permission to do this. Several lessons were learned in this experience. One of them is the importance of replication and of sharing data.

2. Bordo (1980) shows empirically that prices of raw goods respond more quickly to monetary growth than do prices of manufactured goods.

3. The positive reaction of interest rates to the weekly money announcements has been documented by Grossman (1981), Roley (1983), Urich and Wachtel (1981), Urich (1982), Naylor (1982), Cornell (1982), Hardouvelis (1984a), and Shiller, Campbell, and Schoenholtz (1983). A negative reaction in the price of foreign exchange has been found by Engel and Frankel (1983, 1984b), Cornell (1982), and Hardouvelis (1984a) and in the equity markets by Pearce and Roley (1983).

4. For present purposes of studying the money announcement phenomenon, it is not necessary to rule out a risk premium or storage costs that can change from week to week, or even that change before and after October 1979. It is necessary only to rule out that they change at 4:10 P.M. on Friday afternoons. Hardouvelis (1984b) offers one piece of evidence that indeed they do not.

5. As noted in the preceding chapter, there is a problem with assuming that commodity prices cp_t move proportionally to the general price level in the long run. If storage costs are

positive, equation (2) implies that the expected rate of change of cp_t is greater than the nominal interest rate i_t. Yet the expected rate of change of p_t must be less than the nominal interest rate most of the time if the real interest rate is to be positive, as it is believed to be. The implication seems to be that commodity prices in the long run increase relative to manufactures prices. There are three possible solutions to the problem. Rather than repeat them, we refer the reader to the preceding chapter (the paragraph following equation (15)).

6. When the exchange rate appears in place of cp_t, the foreign interest rate appears in place of $-sc$.

7. If commodity prices (or the exchange rate via import prices) enter the CPI with weight β, it can be easily shown that equation (7) generalizes to

$$\Delta cp_t = \left[\left(1 + \frac{1}{\theta\lambda} \right) \middle/ \left(1 + \frac{\beta}{\theta\lambda} \right) \right] \Delta\bar{p}_t.$$

8. The proposition that Money Market Services numbers do in fact represent market expectations, and that these expectations are rational, is supported in Grossman (1981) and in Engel and Frankel (1983), by a demonstration that one cannot use exchange rates or interest rates on the morning of the announcement, or relevant lags, to improve on the survey number as a predictor of what the money announcement will be.

9. The price is the price of the nearest maturing futures contract. The data on opening (9:00 A.M. E.S.T.) and closing (3:00 P.M. E.S.T.) prices are taken from the *Wall Street Journal*. The data for cattle and feeders are from the Chicago Mercantile Exchange; for cocoa and (world) sugar from the New York Coffee, Sugar, and Cocoa Exchange; for gold and silver from the New York Commodity Exchange, and for foreign currencies and Treasury bills from the International Money Market at the Chicago Mercantile Exchange. Corn, soybeans, and wheat are from the Chicago Board of Trade. Whenever a futures contract was traded during the same month that it matured, we skipped to the next maturing contract. Whenever the month of the maturing contract changed, we made sure that the change did not occur between Friday close and Monday close. We did not use cash price data because they are not available at precise times before and after the 4:10 money announcements. The reaction in the futures price presumably incorporates a small positive interest rate effect beyond the reaction in the spot price of equation (8). Given that the interest rate is known to react positively to the money announcements, the use of futures contracts biases our results slightly *away* from our findings of a negative reaction in the post-1979 period.

10. On a few occasions, the Fed did not announce the money supply until Monday. In that case we used the change in market price in the Tuesday open from the Monday close. When Friday or Monday was a market holiday, we used the preceding market close or the next market opening, respectively.

11. See, for example, chapter 5 in Frankel (1993), or the other papers mentioned in note 3. Such results were also reported in the original version of this paper.

12. One cannot rule out this possibility a priori. For example, in a model with risk, gold and silver might be considered the only effective hedge against hyperinflation; their relative prices might rise permanently in response to an increase in inflationary fears. However, table 7.1 shows that the tendency of their prices to move in the opposite direction from the money surprise is even stronger than that for the other commodities, with the exception of sugar.

13. The sum of squared residuals in table 7.1 varies considerably from one commodity to the next, indicating that the stacked regression may suffer from heteroskedasticity. A correction for heteroskedasticity reduces the coefficient estimate and its standard error slightly. Significance levels are about the same. The results are reported in the working paper version: Frankel and Hardouvelis (1983).

14. The overshooting theory tells us that the commodity prices will come back, gradually over time, as the entire price level of the economy adjusts to excess supply. This counter-movement should not in theory show up in one day of trading. Some market observers claim, however, that prices in fact overshoot by far more than is rational.

15. "Domestic Financial Developments in the Second Quarter of 1980," *Federal Reserve Bulletin* 66 (August 1980), 629. The dates were chosen ex ante to demarcate this transitional period, not ex post to get the significant regression results reported for the other two subsamples.

Chapter 8   Expected Inflation from the Interest Rate Term Structure

1. While this chapter and Fama's work can both be interpreted as assuming how nominal interest rates are determined as a function of expected inflation, in order to obtain a measure of expected inflation, there is an older literature that assumes how expected inflation is determined, in order to estimate the effect of expected inflation on nominal interest rates. For example, Modigliani and Shiller (1973) assume that expected inflation is determined as a distributed lag of actual inflation in order to estimate the effect on nominal interest rates. Pyle (1972) and Gibson (1972) assume that expected inflation is accurately reflected in survey data in order to estimate the effect on nominal interest rates; Gibson finds a greater effect for the one-year term than for the six-month term, supporting the approach of this chapter. Carlson (1977) and Cargill (1976) point out problems with the survey data. But when they correct the problems, regressions by Cargill (1976) and Cargill and Mayer (1980) of the nominal interest rate against the expected inflation rate show a significance level that rises almost monotonically with the term of the Treasury security used, again supporting the approach of this chapter.

2. Tests on the data set used in this chapter (1959–79) rejected the Fisher hypothesis, that is, the hypothesis that nominal interest rates fully reflect expected inflation. For brevity, the results are not reported.

3. *Wall Street Journal*, November 2, 1978, p. 2.

4. This interpretation relies on the assumption that the target rate of monetary growth follows a random walk. Deviations of the money supply from the target are not ruled out, provided they either are transitory or have expectation zero. We could, of course, measure the rate of monetary growth directly. Transitory deviations of the actual week-to-week or month-to-month money supply figures from the Federal Reserve Board's targets are large, however. The "underlying trend" could be estimated by a distributed lag or ARIMA process extending back over an interval of time, but if the necessary interval were long relative to the frequency with which the Fed changed its target, then the procedure would not be accurate.

5. The rational value of δ, the speed of adjustment, turns out to depend positively on the responsiveness of the rate of price change to goods demand and negatively on the responsiveness of money demand to income and the interest rate.

6. In order for equation (3) to hold as an arithmetic average (rather than as a geometric average), and in order to enable us to work generally with linear equations, all rates are defined logarithmically:

$i_0^\tau \equiv \log(1 + \text{current } \tau\text{-maturity interest rate})$

$i_t \equiv \log(1 + \text{instantaneous interest rate at time } t)$

$\pi_0 \equiv \lim_{\tau \to \infty} [\log(\text{price level at time } \tau) - \log(\text{current price level})]/\tau.$

For small rates, the log of one plus the rate is numerically close to the rate itself, which justifies the reference in the text to i as "the interest rate," etc.

7. Hicks (1939) first argued that lenders require a liquidity premium for longer-term maturities to compensate for risk regarding future short-term rates. Pesando (1978) accepts the joint hypothesis that (1) the bond market is efficient and (2) the variation in long-term bond rates is due solely to expectations effects, suggesting that if there is a liquidity premium structure, it must be time-invariant. However, Sargent (1969), Roll (1970), and Cargill (1975) reject versions of this joint hypothesis.

McCulloch (1975) presents evidence that the liquidity premium curve is independent of the level of interest rates and suggests a monotonically increasing functional form. Modigliani and Sutch (1966, 1967) develop a more general model in which lenders demand a liquidity premium in order to commit themselves to a term different from their "preferred habitat"; a priori, the liquidity premium could have any shape, though it would presumably be smooth.

8. Henceforth, we drop the subscript on the time series variables $\pi^e, i, i^{\tau 1}$, and $i^{\tau 2}$.

9. Referring to $i - \pi^e$ as the "real interest rate" is loose terminology because i is the instantaneous nominal interest rate and π is the long-term expected inflation rate.

10. Abstracting from the possible liquidity premium, the real interest rate gap $(i - \pi^e - \bar{r})$ is proportional to the spread between the short-term and long-term interest rates. This implication of (6) can also be seen graphically in figure 9.1 (in the next chapter) by "similar triangles." I am indebted to Shanta Devarajan for the graphical point.

11. Since the theory of course does not work perfectly, the question arises as to how to get an optimal estimator by using the entire term structure, rather than just two points. If we could ignore the existence of the liquidity terms, then one strategy would be to fit, at each point in time, a least-squares line through the points; the R^2s would then be tests of the validity of the theory. Given the existence of the liquidity terms, they would have to be estimated at the same time as the expected inflation time series. This extension is left for the future: See chapter 9 in this volume.

12. Within the context of the macroeconomic model specified in the appendix, β is not only the speed with which the real interest rate adjusts to its long-run equilibrium value, but is also the speed with which the output level and price level adjust to their respective equilibrium values (though the equilibrium price level is a moving target, expected to increase at rate π^e).

13. Some studies using price expectations survey data support this possibility. Carlson (1977), Mullineaux (1978), and Figlewski and Wachtel (1981) use data from the Livingston price survey to test the hypothesis that the expected inflation rate has been an unbiased estimator of actual inflation, and they obtain generally negative results. An examination of the time series indicates that the underprediction was concentrated in the latter part of the period, particularly in 1972–74. Supply shocks, particularly the OPEC oil price increase, are the obvious suspects in assigning responsibility for the unexpected increase in inflation. The removal of wage-price controls is another possibility.

14. I am obligated to Stephen McNeese for access to the Livingston data.

15. The difference is even greater when the measures based on the three-month to twelve-month term spread or one-year to ten-year term spread are used.

16. It can be shown within the context of the model developed in the appendix that the measure of expected long-run inflation is closer to the expected one-year inflation rate than is the current one-year interest rate (even if suitably normalized for the liquidity premium and long-run real rate of interest), and is *closer still* to the expected five-year inflation rate.

17. As already noted, the description of $i - \pi^e$ as the "real interest rate" is not quite proper, since i is short-term and π^e is long-term. But the model would be unchanged if the interest and inflation rates were specified to be of the same term—for example, the short term:

$$y - \bar{y} = -\psi \left(i - \frac{dp}{dt} - r \right).$$

We simply substitute (A.3) and solve for $(y - \bar{y})$:

$$y - \bar{y} = -\frac{\psi}{1 - \psi\rho}(i - \pi^e - r).$$

This equation is the same as (A.1), with γ defined as $\psi/(1 - \psi\rho)$.

Chapter 9 Future Inflation Extracted from the Entire Yield Curve

1. The other two indicators were the exchange rate and the price of a basket of commodities. See Johnson (1988) and Lown (1989).

2. One could in fact derive Mishkin's equation (equation (1) below, with a coefficient constrained to 1) from assumptions somewhat less restrictive than a constant real interest rate. If the real interest rate varied over time, but was the same for the short-term interest rate and long-term interest rate, then it would drop out of the term differential. (We are grateful to Angelo Melino for pointing this out.)

3. It is common to reject statistically the hypothesis that long-term interest rates offer unbiased forecasts of expected future short-term interest rates. Many researchers have interpreted this finding as evidence against the expectations hypothesis of the term structure of interest rates, and evidence in favor of a time-varying risk premium, in contradiction to the assumption we make here. A second group, on the other hand, has interpreted the finding as evidence of systematic errors in expectations formation (Shiller, Campbell, and Schoenholtz, 1983; Mankiw and Summers, 1984), or of the pitfalls of econometric tests in small samples (Froot, 1989; Lewis, 1991). In adopting the expectations hypothesis, we take our inspiration from this second group. (For a survey of work on the term structure, see Shiller, 1990, or chapter 10 in this volume.)

4. Mishkin points out that when Irving Fisher originally suggested the "Fisher effect," whereby the expected inflation rate becomes incorporated into the nominal interest rate, it was as something that takes place in the long run, not the short run.

5. The overnight federal funds rate used in the second column of table 9.1 is quoted on the accurate basis of a 365-day year. Most interest rate studies use the federal funds rate as it is. We also tried the regressions with the rate computed on a standard 360-day basis; the statistics were unchanged, to the first two decimal places.

6. For equation (4) to hold as an arithmetic average (rather than as a geometric average), and to enable us to work generally with linear equations, all rates are defined logarithmically. For small rates, the log of 1 plus the rate is numerically close to the rate itself, which justifies the reference in the text to i as "the interest rate," etc.

7. The existence of these liquidity premia provides a possible explanation for those occasions when the term structure is observed to be nonmonotonic even though the expected future path of the short-term interest rate is monotonic in our model.

8. If the model held perfectly, then it might seem that the OLS regressions that are estimated at each point in time would fit the yield curve perfectly. But of course they do not. (The R^2s, averaged across all time series observations, is .37.) How should one think about the error term in such a regression? The easiest interpretation of the error term at a given maturity is that it is a small time-varying liquidity premium (left after a constant average premium for each term is subtracted from the interest rate series), which is assumed to be independent of the term of maturity. Under the assumption of such regression errors, our measure extracted from the entire length of the yield curve will be a best linear unbiased estimate. In particular, it will be a better estimate of the true steepness than a measure extracted from two points close together.

9. Although technically we have a "generated regressors" problem (e.g., Murphy and Topel, 1985), we believe that this method of estimating the slope of the term structure is more accurate than the conventional two-point procedure.

10. The results are not very sensitive to the value of δ.

11. Results in the NBER Working Paper version (no. 3751, June 1991) were reported in two forms: with interest rates expressed in level form, because that is the way Mishkin and most other authors do it, and then with interest rates expressed as the log of 1 plus the interest rate, because that is the form best suited to the expectations hypothesis for the term structure of interest rates—equation (4)—and for the rest of the model that follows. We find very similar results regardless of which form is used.

12. The corrected t-statistic on the coefficient shift in table 9.1 is 1.27 (not reported there). The regressions on the simple spreads in the first two columns show the same pattern: the fall in the constant term between the two subperiods is statistically significant, but the increase in the coefficient is not.

Chapter 10   The Power of the Yield Curve to Predict Interest Rates

1. For surveys of the subject, see Shiller (1990) or Mishkin (1992).

2. One might apply the term "rational expectations methodology" to make clear how demanding the definition is. Investors could be "rational" (meaning that they could eventually figure out the structure of the universe if it were stable) and yet, because of incomplete information (the real structure of the economy is in fact changing), be unable to anticipate the pattern of interest rates, in a given finite sample period. The orthodox methodology, however, implicitly assumes that they can.

3. Fama (1984) for the two-month–one-month T-bill spread.

4. Grieves and Marcus (1990), as well as references therein, and Jones (1992).

5. For a survey of the now popular application of the ARCH models to the term structure question, see part 4 of Bollerslev, Chou, and Kroner (1992).

6. Chapter 1 argues that it would have to be as large as 110.3.

7. For example, chapters 1–3.

8. Often the Fed targets the overnight interest rate rather than the short-term T-bill rates that we have focused on, as in the 1970s until its October 1979 change in operating procedures, and again during the last decade. The arguments regarding the EHTS, the observed bias, and its possible explanations are unaffected by this difference, however.

9. Ederington and Huang (1991) explore this point.

Introduction to Part III

1. There appeared to be somewhat more agreement on the effects of a fiscal expansion. Even in this case, however, as well-grounded a model as the McKibbin-Sachs global model changed its mind on the sign of transmission, in a revision of the model subsequent to the version examined here. See McKibbin and Sachs (1991).

2. For an authoritative study, see Canzoneri and Henderson (1991).

3. The last section of the article only begins to address the possibility of policymakers taking into account their own uncertainty. Ghosh and Masson (1994) have modeled policymakers learning about the true model. Holtham and Hughes Hallett (1987, 1992) suggest that policymakers engage only in "strong" bargains. Frankel, Erwin, and Rockett (1992) reply.

4. The analysis of nominal income targeting in two-country models is pursued by Funke (1991), Leder (1992), and Frankel and Funke (1993). One example of a comprehensive study of cooperation under uncertainty is Ghosh and Masson (1994).

5. With Warwick McKibbin's help, I attempted a rudimentary start at applying the McKibbin-Sachs global model to this problem in Frankel (1991). Other models are used extensively to study other regimes in Bryant, Hooper, and Mann (1993).

6. More recently, a neo-Keynesian school has given much-needed micro-foundations to such stickiness: Akerlof and Yellen (1985), Ball and Romer (1989, 1990), Mankiw (1985), and Yellen (1984). Surveys are provided by Blanchard (1990), Gordon (1990b), and Romer (1993a).

Chapter 11   Ambiguous Policy Multipliers

1. Also omitted are some so-called supply-side effects, such as the possibility that a balanced-budget reduction in tax rates and government expenditure would stimulate output and appreciate the currency. Such effects do not seem to be incorporated into any of the twelve models involved in the Brookings simulation exercise.

2. See, for example, Henderson (1983) and the references cited there.

3. It is certainly possible to get reversals of sign. For example, in some models a fiscal expansion can be contractionary if expectations of future debt sufficiently drive up expected future short-term interest rates and current long-term interest rates, and therefore crowd out investment. The LIVERPOOL model appeared to show this effect for the case of a U.S. expansion in earlier work (Minford 1984, pp. 100, 114, 133).

4. Citations for the two-country Mundell-Fleming model are Mundell (1964), Mussa (1979), and Swoboda and Dornbusch (1973). Girton and Henderson (1976) was possibly the first two-country version of the portfolio-balance model, with the degree of substitutability between domestic and foreign bonds filling in for the Mundell-Fleming model's degree of capital mobility.

5. To abstract from the valuation effect of exchange rate changes on the trade balance, in equation (5) import demand can be assumed to have a price elasticity of one.

6. In the limiting case of perfect capital mobility ($k = \infty$) and an exogenous foreign interest rate (small country), the interest rate is fixed and so these effects vanish.

7. The standard Mundell-Fleming result of negative transmission of monetary policy can also be reversed through a reversal of the trade balance. This occurs if net capital inflows respond to expected future depreciation, which, in turn, depends negatively on the current level of the spot rate relative to its equilibrium level, as indicated in equation (6). Because discussion of this effect is not very common in the theoretical literature on international transmission, it is postponed to the following section.

8. On the other hand, the modern theory of saving says that only if the currency depreciation is perceived as a *temporary* decline in real income or, in the case of a permanent decline, if the rate of time preference rises with a fall in welfare, will intertemporally optimizing consumers react by reducing saving. See Obstfeld (1982) and Svensson and Razin (1983).

9. See, for example, Branson and Buiter (1983, pp. 256–58).

10. Of course, models do exist in which prices rise so quickly that there is no effect on output even in the short run. At the opposite extreme, a few of the large econometric models represented in the Brookings simulations show that an expansion actually *reduces* prices in the short run. This may result from highly procyclical productivity and the (more questionable) assumption that prices are determined as a markup over current unit labor costs. Alternatively, in a monetary expansion prices may fall if capital costs (interest rates) are reflected in markup pricing. In chapter 5 of Bryant et al. (1988) Hickman identifies such an effect in the LINK and WHARTON models for the United States, and it appears dominant in the LINK simulation results for France, Italy, and Canada.

11. Sachs (1980, p. 737), and Argy and Salop (1977, pp. 2–12, 1979, 228). However, if real wages are rigid in Europe and nominal wages are rigid in the United States, U.S. monetary policy *can* be transmitted positively. Argy and Salop (1977, pp. 6–10), and Oudiz and Sachs (1984, pp. 13–14).

12. Fitoussi and Phelps (1986, pp. 496–502) identify a fifth way that the traditional positive transmission of U.S. fiscal expansion to European output can be reversed in sign: higher world real interest rates have negative supply effects. One example is that higher real interest rates induce imperfectly competitive firms to increase their price markups, because they are less eager than before to "invest" in market share. Another example, relevant when wages are indexed to the CPI, is that higher real interest rates depress the capital goods sector.

13. Oudiz and Sachs (1984, pp. 7, 9, 22) find the asymmetry present in the MCM and EPA models and attribute it to the slopes of the LM curve and the importance of dollar assets in the world portfolio. Yoshitomi (1984, pp. 34–37, 62) explains that the asymmetry in the EPA model is due to the slopes of the LM curve and the degree of bond substitutability.

14. In the VAR results originally presented at the conference (and subsequently retracted by the authors) a fiscal expansion in either country produced a current account deficit in the other country. In a U.S. fiscal expansion, the ROECD current account worsened slightly in the second year even though the U.S. current account also worsened. This outcome would almost be tantamount to a claim that the entire world's current account worsened! Such results suggest limitations to the usefulness of using nonstructural models to answer questions about the likely effects of changes in policy. Cooley and LeRoy (1985) consider this methodological issue.

15. Marston (1984, p. 136), however, specifically describes Minford's exchange rate effect on supply as coming from imported inputs, not labor costs. (Neither wages nor imported inputs appear explicitly in the model.)

16. The WHARTON model also shows the ROECD CPI declining in response to a fiscal expansion originating in either country, presumably because of a combination of markup pricing and procyclical productivity, as mentioned in note 10.

17. Oudiz and Sachs (1984, pp. 20–22) report that monetary expansion worsens the domestic current account in the EPA model as well as in the MCM model (for the United States, Japan, or West Germany). Yoshitomi (1984, pp. 347–50, 396) confirms this property of the EPA model.

18. The U.S. and non-U.S. current accounts move in the same direction in the VAR model as well. In a well-specified two-country model such results would be impossible. (Since the simulation results include only the larger countries, the total U.S. and ROECD current accounts could conceivably change vis-à-vis excluded country groups like OPEC.)

19. Although, for most models, the nominal interest rate has already started back up by the second year.

20. In models of perfect capital mobility, the ex ante decrease in demand for dollar assets, which leads to the depreciation of the currency, is not the same thing as an ex post decrease in the net capital account balance. But if perfect capital mobility ties the domestic interest rate to the foreign interest rate, that means the trade balance must improve even more (by enough so that the higher transactions demand absorbs all the increased money supply, with no help from lower interest rates except through large-country effects).

21. Yoshitomi (1984) emphasizes the importance of regressive exchange rate expectations in potentially reversing the direction of capital flows. Among the other models that now incorporate the regressive exchange rate expectations of Dornbusch (1976) are the MCM model (Haas and Symansky 1984) and MINIMOD. The MSG model, Minford (1984, pp. 90, 97), and Taylor (1985b, p. 56), make the assumption that efficient market arbitrage drives the interest differential to the rationally expected rate of depreciation, but only MSG shows the exchange rate overshooting that is required if regressive expectations are to be rational.

22. I am indebted to Gerald Holtham and Warren Trepeta for this point.

Chapter 12   Conflicting Models and Coordination between Policymakers

1. This is not to make the naive mistake of thinking that policymakers put complete faith in the models of the macroeconomists at their own agencies, or that the latter necessarily have access to the latest data and thoughts of the former. But policymakers, at best, base

their thinking on models—whether developed by government, academic, or corporate institutions—similar to those in the Brookings modeling exercise. (For example, British macroeconomic policy under Prime Minister Margaret Thatcher may have been based on a model closer to the LIVERPOOL model, which appears in this exercise, than to any models previously existing at the U.K. Treasury or Bank of England.) Policymakers, more likely, base their thinking on models that conform even less to one another or to truth than do the models of macroeconomists.

2. For example, Marris (1985).

3. Sachs (1985), for example, has argued on these grounds that the U.S. monetary-fiscal mix in the early 1980s might have been optimal given the objective function.

4. One of many examples from the 1980s is Bergsten and others (1982). The alleged gains from coordinated expansion by Europe, Japan, and the United States were also the basis of the locomotive theory that led to the 1978 Bonn summit meeting.

5. Some of the conflicting possibilities arise from uncertainty over what variables should enter the objective function and where the economy currently is relative to the optimum, rather than uncertainty over the correct model or parameter values. The economist could plausibly argue that such questions can be answered only by the political process.

6. Some authors, such as Canzoneri and Gray (1985), set up their theory in a framework general enough to encompass all the possible positive or negative effects. The direction in which policies must be moved to reap gains from coordination can be viewed as a function of the parameter values, the latter presumably to be filled in later by the econometrician.

7. In the appendix to Frankel (1986c), the NBER Working Paper version of this chapter, the monetary authority is assumed to care about one variable (internal balance or external balance) and the fiscal authority to care about the other. This is the classic "assignment problem." But when each authority has only a single target variable, the optimum is attained in the Nash equilibrium and the question of a separate cooperative equilibrium does not arise. In chapter 13, policymakers compete or cooperate both because of conflicting perceptions, as in this chapter, and because of conflicting targets, as in the standard literature.

8. If the second target variable were the exchange rate instead of the trade balance, the ambiguous effect of a fiscal expansion discussed previously could change negative slopes to positive. If it were the price level, the negative effect of a monetary expansion in the LINK model or of a fiscal expansion in the VAR model could have the same implication. In any case, the points to be made here, particularly that coordination need not improve welfare, require only that the parameter values differ; they need not differ enough to give opposite-signed slopes.

9. There is a potential issue of stability, considered in the original version of this chapter. If the policymakers are thought of as taking turns reacting to each other according to equations (4) and (5), will they actually reach the Nash equilibrium point? Stability requires that the absolute value of the slope of $CB1$ exceed the absolute value of the slope of $FA2$. If the condition is satisfied, a second question arises of whether convergence to equilibrium will be slow or rapid.

10. For example, Oudiz and Sachs (1984, pp. 36–37). When speaking of the product of the gains, I mean them to be positive. And I rule out side payments.

11. It is as easy to program the computer to do 1,728 combinations as to do fewer. But the output is too much to present in a table.

12. Table 13.1 reports the multipliers for only four of the 11 models. The multipliers for the complete set of models are reported in table 1 of the originally published version of this paper, and are in any case the same as those reported earlier in table 11.3 except that the effects of a 4 percent increase in the money supply have now been divided by four.

13. Choosing the target optimums around which x and y are measured is equivalent to choosing the constant terms A and B.

14. The reason I do not use their weights for the MCM case is that the reported weight on the U.S. current account is zero.

15. A complete Bayesian analysis would have agents ascribe only part of the observed discrepancy to the error terms and part to a revision of the parameter values. But the premise of this chapter is that it is realistic to assume that policymakers revise their models to a negligible extent.

16. Only 12 out of 36 combinations exhibit technical instability (most of them models in which the monetary authority is acting on the basis of either the MCM or VAR models). Another 5 out of 36, though technically stable, require more than 20 iterations to converge.

17. I also tried putting equal weights on the two targets. Of the cases involving three distinct models, 461 show gains and 328 show losses.

Chapter 13   International Macroeconomic Policy Coordination

1. Hamada (1976) is generally credited with the birth of the topic in its modern analytic form (though under the assumption of fixed-exchange rates). More recent contributions include Canzoneri and Gray (1983), Miller and Salmon (1985), Rogoff (1985b), and Buiter and Marston (1985). For introductions to the literature and further references, see Cooper (1985) or Fischer (1988).

2. We have become aware since this paper was written of some papers on coordination that do allow for policymakers to be uncertain as to the true model: Atish Ghosh (1986), Swati Ghosh (1987), Nouriel Roubini (1986), Holtham (1986), and Holtham and Hughes Hallett (1987).

3. There are two important qualifications to the generality of the proposition that coordination improves welfare under the standard assumption that policymakers know the true model. The first is that if policymakers have enough independent instruments to reach their optimum target goals regardless of one anothers' actions, then coordination is moot. The second is that Rogoff (1985b) and Kehoe (1986) have shown that if coordination reduces governments' ability to precommit to anti-inflationary policies credibly to their own peoples, then it can reduce welfare. The present paper is a counterexample along very different lines.

4. Oudiz and Sachs (1984), Carlozzi and Taylor (1985), Oudiz (1985), Ishii, McKibbin, and Sachs (1985), Hughes Hallett (1985), and Canzoneri and Minford (1986).

5. See Bryant et al. (1988). Chapter 11 in this volume discusses the disagreements among the twelve models.

6. Some of the authors in the coordination literature decline to take any position at all on whether the problem with the Nash noncooperative equilibrium is that it is too contractionary or too expansionary, etc. They leave it for econometricians to fill in the correct parameter values at some later date.

7. One's intuition is that players who disagree about the model will find it harder to agree on a package of joint policy changes (e.g., Cooper, 1986). The correct way to interpret this intuition may be that, even if there exists a bargaining solution that is believed to be Pareto-superior to the noncooperative solution, it will be harder for the players to agree on a mechanism to enforce the bargaining solution if they do not share a common view of the world.

8. This holds in the ten econometric models considered in the following section except the LIVPL and MSG models for the United States, and LIVPL, MSG, Wharton, and EPA models for Europe.

9. Often, it has been private economists, and the governments of smaller countries, who have urged such coordinated expansion; for example, Bergsten et al. (1982).

10. In a related exercise, Holtham and Hughes Hallett (1987, p. 26) show that the results change little when definitions of the bargaining equilibrium other than the Nash solution are used.

11. In equations (3) and (4) here, one could simply redefine m^* as fiscal policy, and let $y^* \equiv y$, $x^* \equiv x$, and $\omega^* \equiv \omega$. As long as the two policymakers have different parameter estimates, there will still be scope for coordination. One difference is that in figure 13.2 the true optimal points P and O would coincide.

12. The positive effect of a monetary expansion on the current account via currency depreciation is offset by a negative effect via higher income. In the Mundell-Fleming model the positive effect on the current account must dominate, to match the net capital outflow that results from lower interest rates, giving negative transmission abroad. But in more modern models the net capital flow may be reversed, in response to perceived overshooting of the exchange rate. The theoretical literature contains many other ways of reversing the Mundell-Fleming transmission results as well. (See Mussa, 1979, or, for an optimizing approach, Svensson and van Wijnbergen, 1986.) On the models used in the Brookings simulations, see chapter 11 in this volume.

13. Our objective functions (1) and (2), like those of Oudiz and Sachs, and others, pertain only to welfare in the current period. They thus neglect any dynamic effects such as the effect current expansion has on next period's inflationary expectations and therefore on next period's welfare. Propositions stated here about the desirability of changes in the levels of policy *variables* could be reinterpreted as propositions about the desirability of changes in policy *rules*, using dynamic models with rational expectations. See Taylor (1985b). But the question of whether governments should coordinate policies is usually in practice intended to refer to regular meetings in which representatives discuss the current setting of their money supplies and other variables rather than a one-time "global constitutional convention" in which they discuss whether to adopt strict monetarist rules versus, for example, nominal income targeting. Most of the ten models used here to represent policymakers' beliefs, with the exception of the MSG and Taylor models, are designed to predict the effects of changes in policy variables rather than changes in policy rules.

14. After testing for sensitivity to the choice of weights, we also tested for sensitivity to the choice of targets. The total count for true gains and losses for the two countries were:

		U.S.	Europe
OECD weights;	gains	507	479
$\omega = 1/11.8$	losses	322	349
$\omega^* = 1/244.0$	zeroes	171	172
LIVPL weights;	gains	421	471
$\omega = 1/.26$	losses	302	267
$\omega^* = 1/2.4$	zeroes	277	262
Original weights;	gains	538	537
target level of U.S.	losses	338	340
GNP = 95 percent of baseline	zeroes	124	123
Original weights;	gains	484	465
target level of European	losses	272	291
GNP = 95 percent of baseline	zeroes	244	244

15. The numbers for all 100 cases are reported in Frankel (1991b).

16. The diagonal entries of the three-dimensional matrix are the cases in which both policymakers have the correct model. These calculations correspond conceptually to those in Oudiz and Sachs (1984) for the MCM and EPA models.

17. The most bizarre combination occurs when the United States believes the LIVPL model and Europe believes the OECD model (not shown). Under this combination, the Nash non-cooperative equilibrium entails a mutually destructive increase in the European money supply of almost 100 percent and decrease in the U.S. money supply of over 100 percent (!). Evidently the problem is that the LIVPL model shows European monetary expansion raising U.S. output much more than does U.S. monetary expansion, as can be seen in table 11.3. There is no reason why the Nash solution for the money supply specified in equations (9) and (10) need be positive. One need only plug in the multiplier values from table 13.1 to see how negative money supplies are possible. Presumably, in practice, U.S. policymakers would begin to doubt a linear model and its prediction that European monetary expansion would have such a powerful expansionary effect on U.S. output, long before they relied on it to the extent of reducing the U.S. money supply to zero.

18. Holtham and Hughes Hallett (1987, p. 25), looking only at those cases where the two countries agree on the (perhaps wrong) model, confirm our finding: judged by the correct model, only slightly more than half the cases result in gains.

19. Examples include Blanchard and Dornbusch (1984), Layard et al. (1986), and Marris (1985).

20. Table 8 in Frankel (1986b) shows that according to the MSG model this change in the monetary/fiscal mix, though increasing non-U.S. output 0.1 percent and having the desired effect on the current accounts, would in fact reduce U.S. output 0.7 percent There are several other combinations in the table where this same change in mix results from coordination, all of them involving the LIVPL model; but none of them shows quite the expected effects on the target variables.

21. As in the experiment of coordination of monetary policy alone, there are a few cases of absurdly large changes, in particular the two combinations with the MSG and MCM models. The explanation, again, is that these changes offset absurdly large changes implied by the move from the baseline to the Nash equilibrium.

22. The probabilities, π_j^* and π_k, are conditional probabilities, given the beliefs of the United States (j) or Europe (k). These conditional probabilities are formed using Bayes rule from some underlying probability distribution over models which is known by both countries' policymakers.

23. The tables showing the results for a subset of the models are reported in Frankel (1988a). They are omitted here to save space.

24. Again the tables are reported in Frankel (1988a).

Chapter 14   International Nominal Targeting (INT)

1. The INT proposal appears in brief form in Frankel (1988a) and in a longer version in Frankel (1988b).

2. The standard formulation of the theorem contains a second technical qualification for the optimality of coordination. Each country must have more economic objectives (such as trade balance equilibrium, output equal to the full employment level, and zero inflation) than it has independent policy instruments (such as monetary and fiscal policy). If each has as many instruments as targets, then each can offset the actions of the others so as to attain its optimum and issues of conflict and cooperation among countries do not arise. In practice, countries seldom feel that they have enough freedom to be able to attain their optimum positions.

3. The history of the Bonn Summit and the other annual meetings of the leaders of the G7 countries is given in Putnam and Bayne (1987).

4. Such questions are described by the next section of this chapter in its review of the obstacles to coordination (except in the discussion of inflation-fighting credibility, which applies only to questions of overall economic expansion).

5. Such thoughts are supported by the findings in Frankel and Rockett (1988) and in Frankel (1988b) and (1988a) that the gains from coordination would often be smaller than the gains from the United States' discovering the true model and unilaterally adjusting its policies accordingly.

6. Kenen (1987, pp. 31–36) thinks so. Holtham and Hughes Hallett (1987, p. 130) agree: "Economists have perhaps focused on moral hazard problems because of their interesting logical character rather than because of their empirical importance. It seems likely that uncertainty and model disagreement are greater obstacles to international cooperation."

7. The story of the Tokyo Summit is recounted in both Putnam and Bayne (1987) and Funabashi (1987).

8. This list did not appear in the official communique but rather in comments to the press by U.S. Assistant Secretary of the Treasury David Mulford. Funabashi (1987, especially p. 130) offers a fascinating account of the machinations of the G7 mechanism from 1985 to 1987.

9. See Krugman (1988) for the application of the latest "smooth pasting" technology to this problem.

10. It is clear from Funabashi (1987) that the various members held differing views as to which indicators were most important, what responses were called for if indicators strayed from the agreed-on path, and how binding the agreement should be. It is also clear that each was able to interpret the Plaza and Louvre Agreements afterwards so as to reflect its own views.

11. A "dynamically consistent" or "time-consistent" regime is one that manages to prevent the monetary authorities from breaking their own commitment to monetary discipline where they otherwise might have an incentive to do so in the future. For surveys of the rules-versus-discretion debate and the implications of the time-consistency literature, see Barro (1986), Fischer (1991), and Rogoff (1987).

12. Milton Friedman has had more influence on this issue than one human being is usually able to have, and justifiably so. Nevertheless, two aspects of his campaign against the Federal Reserve Board have long been puzzling. First, his argument against discretion in monetary policymaking is largely based on the analysis in Friedman and Schwartz (1963) that the Federal Reserve made the Depression of the 1930s much worse than it otherwise would have been by "allowing" the M1 money supply to fall. Yet in recent decades he has campaigned for the Federal Reserve to do precisely what he accuses it of doing in the 1930s: set a firm target for the monetary base, rather than for M1. The second, even more puzzling aspect is that Friedman and his fellow monetarists claim to believe that U.S. money growth would be slower and more stable if monetary policy were placed more under the control of the democratic political process, via the Treasury or the U.S. Congress, than under the control of elitist central bankers such as Paul Volcker. It is particularly ironic that when a member of the monetarists' Shadow Open Market Committee finally became undersecretary of the Treasury for monetary affairs in the early 1980s, his view that the money growth rate was dangerously high was overruled by the Treasury and the White House, who sought to pressure the Federal Reserve for faster money growth in the period leading up to the 1984 election.

13. Rogoff (1985a) shows that some intermediate degree of commitment to a target is optimal for monetary policy.

14. There is a close analogy here with the idea in Rogoff (1985a) that if a particular individual—say, Paul Volcker—is known to have extreme aversion to inflation, then the country can gain by appointing him as central banker, even if the country's objective function puts less weight on fighting inflation. His tight-money credibility will reduce the public's expectations of inflation and in long-run equilibrium will produce a lower level of actual inflation for any level of output.

15. Analogously, I take as given by the political process the degree of commitment to coordination.

16. Tobin (1980), Gordon (1985), Hall (1985), Taylor (1985a) and McCallum (1987, 1988a, b), for example, argue in favor of targeting nominal GNP in the closed-economy context. The idea also has proponents in the United Kingdom: Bean (1983), Meade (1984) and Brittan (1987). Miller and Williamson (1988, pp. 7–10) propose targeting nominal demand as part of their blueprint for exchange-rate target zones.

17. Switzerland can be given as an example of a country that chose to take the adverse supply shock of 1974 almost entirely in the form of lost income and employment in order to restore price stability. Sweden was a country that chose to take it almost entirely in the form of inflation, in order to preserve output and employment. The United States fell in between.

18. The specification here is a function of the three target variables. One could as easily have more or fewer.

19. Uncertainty about the position of the economy in the absence of policy changes is the same thing as uncertainty about the disturbance terms in the model of the economy, such as the disturbances in chapter 15. That chapter, though it considers uncertainty in an open

economy (in the sense that the exchange rate enters the objective function), deals only with a country's unilateral policymaking problem. In this section, I am considering the problems that uncertainty creates for coordination per se.

20. This uncertainty is a genuine concern. Mankiw and Shapiro (1986) find that the standard deviation from the preliminary estimate of the real growth rate to the revised final number is 2.2 percentage points.

21. Kenen and Schwartz (1986) have studied the accuracy of current-year forecasts in the IMF *World Economic Outlook* for the last fifteen years. They find that the root mean squared error among the G7 countries is 0.773 percentage points for real growth and 0.743 percentage points for inflation. These prediction errors, although relatively small, are large enough to reverse the signs of the derivatives of the welfare function equations (2) to (5). Errors would presumably be much larger for the horizons of two years or so that are probably most relevant for policymaking. Many major international econometric models show that the effects of monetary and fiscal policy peak in the second year for output and not until much later for the price level or current account.

22. Economists disagree about the correct estimates of, for example, the natural rate of unemployment and the level of potential output.

23. Another unexpected development in the late 1970s was the downward shift in the demand for money in the United States. This disturbance, like the oil shock, meant that the planned growth rate of money turned out to be more inflationary than expected.

24. One way to obtain estimates for these weights is to follow Oudiz and Sachs (1984), who assume that as of 1984, policymakers were optimizing their objective functions in a Nash equilibrium and infer the welfare weights they must have had in order to produce the observed outcomes for output, inflation, and the current account. The estimates turn out to be very sensitive to such things as the model of the economy that the policymakers are assumed to have used. To equate the inferred weights with the actual rates, as Oudiz and Sachs do, requires not only that the policymakers were indeed seeking to optimize in a Nash equilibrium in that particular year but also that they knew the correct model, the correct weights, and the correct position of the economy relative to the optimum.

25. The German view that the 1978 Bonn Summit entailed joint "reflation" that was, in retrospect, inappropriate was used above to illustrate, alternatively, uncertainty about the baseline forecast (the unanticipated oil shock of 1979) and uncertainty about the objective function (the proper weight to be placed on inflation versus growth). A third possible interpretation is model uncertainty: the Germans believe that the slope of their aggregate supply curve turned out to be steeper than they, or at least the Americans, thought it would at the time. This interpretation is plausible if one believes that the German labor market is characterized by a high degree of real wage rigidity, as was pointed out by Branson and Rotemberg (1980).

26. It is for this reason that when the International Monetary Fund (IMF) negotiates a letter of intent with the finance minister of a borrowing country, the "performance criteria" that are agreed on tend to be variables directly under the control of the authorities, such as the growth rate of the monetary base, rather than variables that are harder to control, such as the broad money supply, let alone the ultimate target variables such as inflation.

27. Miller and Williamson (1988) and Williamson (1983, pp. 54–55) do precisely this; they assume that there is a large "fad" component to exchange rate fluctuations under the current floating regime, and that it would disappear under their target zone proposal. The idea is not absurd. But it certainly stacks the deck in an empirical comparison of the two regimes.

28. Indeed, there is reason to think that the prices of gold and other commodities react instantaneously to changes in expectations regarding whether monetary policy will be tight or loose in the future (chapters 6 and 7).

29. Besides subtracting from total GNP that part going to the foreign sector (the trade balance) it might also be a good idea to subtract the part going to inventories, as suggested by Gordon (1985).

30. The Williamson-Miller blueprint also specifies that the G7 should set the *average* level of their interest rates so as to attain a target for the *aggregate* level of their GNPs. This part of their plan is similar to the first part of my proposal. It is my second part—cooperative yearly setting of each country's nominal demand target, to be attained primarily through monetary policy—that differs the most from the Williamson-Miller plan (in addition to my setting exchange rate stability aside as a separable issue). For attempts to evaluate empirically the stabilizing properties of the blueprint plan, see Miller and Williamson (1988) and Frenkel, Goldstein, and Masson (1990, pp. 33–49).

Chapter 15   The Stabilizing Properties of a Nominal GDP Rule

1. A time-consistent or dynamically consistent regime is one that manages to prevent the monetary authorities in the future from breaking whatever commitment to monetary discipline they have proclaimed, where they otherwise might have an incentive to do so. For surveys of the rules versus discretion debate and the implications of the time-consistency literature, see Barro (1986), Fischer (1991), Rogoff (1987), and Persson and Tabellini (1990).

2. Surprisingly, the phenomenon whereby the authorities proclaim a simple target range for an intermediate variable, so that the public can monitor its degree of commitment, has not been definitively modeled (though Levine, 1991, has addressed this issue). Under standard assumptions, there is little theoretical justification for an intermediate target, as Friedman (1977a, 1984) pointed out some years ago. This chapter takes as given that, if the authorities make a commitment, it is to a single nominal variable.

3. In the scheme of McKinnon (1984), dubbed a world monetarist standard, the worldwide nominal anchor was to be the total of the three countries' money supplies (valued at the fixed exchange rates). In McKinnon (1988), the anchor is to be a worldwide price index.

4. Tobin (1980), Gordon (1985), Hall (1985), Taylor (1985a), McCallum (1987, 1988a, b) and Hall and Mankiw (1994), for example, argue in favor of targeting nominal GNP in the closed-economy context. U.K. proponents include: Vines, Maciejowski, and Meade (1983), Meade (1984), and Brittan (1987), in addition to Bean (1983). Some have developed international variants of nominal GNP targeting, such as Williamson and Miller (1987, pp. 7–10), who propose targeting nominal demand as part of their "blueprint" for exchange-rate target zones. But theoretical analysis in the open economy is still quite limited. Chapter 14 in this volume proposes nominal GNP targeting in the context of international policy coordination. (For these purposes, I use GDP and GNP interchangeably.)

5. The inspiration is the observation the case for nominal GNP targeting has previously only taken into account disturbances in money demand or goods demand, not in supply, and that it has not been shown superior in an open economy (Dornbusch and Frankel, 1988, pp. 175–76).

6. Rogoff (1985a) warns that the welfare ranking among the candidate variables for rigid targeting need not be the same as the welfare ranking among the candidate variables for partial commitment.

7. We assume that expectations are formed rationally. Some may prefer to think that, because of the existence of contracts, these expectations are formed well in advance of the period in which actual inflation and output are determined. It should also be noted that, if the parameter b is thought to depend on the variance of the price level, then our results could be vulnerable to the famous Lucas (1976) critique.

8. Bean (1983) and West (1986) use a quadratic objective function that includes only output. But clearly inflation must be added to the objective function if one wants to be able to consider the advantages of precommitting to a nominal target or rule.

9. This chapter thus generalizes the argument made in the appendix to Frankel (1989b).

10. Warwick McKibbin and I made a start, using the McKibbin-Sachs global model, which is specified in far more detail than the simple model analyzed here, to compare nominal GDP targeting to other regimes. All disturbances are allowed to be correlated. Preliminary results bear out the stabilizing properties of nominal GDP targeting (Frankel, 1991a).

11. Written by Menzie Chinn, and available in Frankel and Chinn (1991).

12. Repeating the analysis with M2 produced similar results.

13. This approach to estimating potential output and the supply shocks is referred to as the "transitory supply shock" approach in the appendix, because it implies that the u shocks are transitory.

14. The estimate of b was lower and less significant for the United Kingdom and Germany. Gray and Spencer (1990) have estimated b to be in the range of 1.5–2.4 for the United States, and Ball, Mankiw, and Romer (1988) estimate an upper bound of 5.6. The equation is more often estimated in inverse form, with inflation as the dependent variable. Such a coefficient estimate, when inverted so as to be comparable with b, is 4.4 in Adams and Coe (1990, table 8B, pp. 273, 277), 5.0–5.9 in Gordon (1990a, table 3, p. 29), and 4.0–4.5 in Schultze (1986, table 1-1, p. 8). (The inflation equations are estimated from U.S. data, 1965–88, 1954–87, and 1953–83, respectively). The appendix in Frankel and Chinn (1991) discusses this literature, and presents its own estimates of the coefficient from equations in which inflation is the dependent variable: 2.7–2.9 for the United States, and somewhat less for other countries.

15. Again, the results are available in an appendix. This approach to computing the supply shocks is referred to there as the "permanent supply shock" approach, because the ARIMA process entails the conclusion that the u disturbances have a unit root.

16. Argy (1991) identifies a number of circumstances, such as when contracts are indexed or when the nominal income target is missed, when nominal income targeting has little if any advantage. Among the others who raise the issue of the attainability of the target are Hilton and Moorthy (1990).

References

Adams, Charles, and David Coe. 1990. A systems approach to estimating the natural rate of unemployment and potential output for the United States. *IMF Staff Papers* 37, 2 (June): 232–93.

Adler, Michael, and Bernard Dumas. 1976. Portfolio choice and the demand for foreign exchange. *American Economic Review* 66, 2 (May): 332–39.

Adler, Michael, and Bernard Dumas. 1983. International portfolio choice and corporation finance: A survey. *Journal of Finance* 38 (June): 925–84.

Agell, Jonas, and Mats Persson. 1992. Does debt management matter? Part I in *Does Debt Management Matter?*, ed. J. Agell, M. Persson, and B. Friedman. FIEF Studies in Labor Markets and Economic Policy. Oxford: Oxford University Press.

Akerlof, George, and Janet Yellen. 1985. A near-rational model of the business cycle with wage and price inertia. *Quarterly Journal of Economics*, 100, 5 (suppl.): 823–38.

Argy, Victor. 1991. Nominal income targeting: A critical evaluation. Research Department Working Paper 91/92, October. Washington D.C.: International Monetary Fund.

Argy, Victor, and J. Salop. 1979. Price and output effects of monetary and fiscal policy under flexible exchange rates. *IMF Staff Papers* 26, 2 (June): 224–56.

Arnold, Bruce. 1983. Variable coefficients and the mean-variance optimization hypothesis: Continuing the search for the exchange risk premium. Thesis, Princeton University.

Backus, David, William Brainard, Gary Smith, and James Tobin. 1980. A model of U.S. financial and nonfinancial economic behavior. *Journal of Money, Credit, and Banking* 12: 239–93.

Backus, David, and Douglas Purvis. 1980. An integrated model of household flow-of-funds allocations. *Journal of Money, Credit, and Banking* 12: 400–21.

Balduzzi, Pierluigi, Giuseppe Bertola, and Silverio Foresi. 1993. A model of target changes and the term structure of interest rates. NBER Working Paper no. 4347. Cambridge, Mass.: National Bureau of Economic Research, April.

Ball, Lawrence, N. Gregory Mankiw, and David Romer. 1988. The new Keynesian economics and the output-inflation tradeoff. *Brookings Papers on Economic Activity* 1: 1–65.

Ball, Lawrence, and David Romer. 1989. Are prices too sticky? *Quarterly Journal of Economics* 104, 3 (August): 507–24.

Ball, Lawrence, and David Romer. 1990. Real rigidities and the non-neutrality of money. *Review of Economics Studies* 57: 183–203.

Barro, Robert. 1977. Unanticipated money growth and unemployment in the United States. *American Economic Review* 67, 2 (March): 101–15.

Barro, Robert. 1978. Unanticipated money, output and the price level in the United States. *Journal of Political Economy* 86, 4 (August): 549–80.

Barro, Robert. 1986. Recent developments in the theory of rules versus discretion. *Economic Journal* 96 (Suppl.): 23–37.

Barro, Robert, and David Gordon. 1983. A positive theory of monetary policy in a natural rate model. *Journal of Political Economy* 91, 4 (August): 589–610.

Bean, Charles. 1983. Targeting nominal income: An appraisal. *Economic Journal* 93 (December): 806–19.

Bergsten, C. Fred et al. 1982. *Promoting World Recovery: A Statement on Global Economic Strategy by Twenty-Six Economists from Fourteen Countries.* Washington, D.C.: Institute for International Economics, September.

Berndt, E., B. Hall, R. Hall, and J. Hausman. 1974. Estimation and inference in nonlinear structural models. *Annals of Economic and Social Measurement* 3: 635–65.

Black, F., M. Jensen, and M. Scholes. 1972. The capital asset pricing model: Some empirical tests. In *Studies in the Theory of Capital Markets,* ed. M. Jensen 79–121. New York: Praeger.

Blanchard, Olivier Jean. 1990. Why does money affect output? A survey. In *Handbook of Monetary Economics,* vol. 2, ed. B. Friedman and F. H. Hahn. Amsterdam: Elsevier Science Publishers, B.V.

Blanchard, Olivier, and Rudiger Dornbusch. 1984. U.S. deficits, the dollar, and Europe. *Banca Nazionale del Lavoro Quarterly Review* 148 (March): 89–113.

Blanchard, Olivier, and Mary Kay Plantes. 1977. A note on gross substitutability of financial assets. *Econometrica* 45: 769–71.

Blinder, Alan, and Robert Solow. 1973. Does fiscal policy matter? *Journal of Public Economics* 2: 314–37.

Blume, Marshall, and I. Friend. 1973. A new look at the capital asset pricing model. *Journal of Finance* 28 (March): 19–33.

Bodie, Zvi, Alex Kane, and Robert McDonald. 1983. Why are real interest rates so high? NBER Working Paper no. 1141. Cambridge, Mass.: National Bureau of Economic Research, June.

Bodurtha, James, and Nelson Mark. 1991. Testing the CAPM with time-varying risks and returns. *Journal of Finance* 46: 1485–1505.

Bollerslev, Tim. 1986. Generalized autoregressive conditional heteroskedaticity. *Journal of Econometrics* 31: 307–27.

Bollerslev, Tim. 1987. A conditionally heteroskedastic time-series model for speculative prices and rates of return. *Review of Economics and Statistics* 69: 542–47.

Bollerslev, Tim, Ray Chou, and Kenneth Kroner. 1992. ARCH modelling in finance: A review of the theory and empirical evidence. *Journal of Econometrics* 52: 5–59.

Bollerslev, Tim, Robert Engle, and Jeffrey Wooldridge. 1988. A capital asset pricing model with time-varying covariances. *Journal of Political Economy* 96: 116–31.

Bordo, Michael. 1980. The effects of monetary change on relative commodity prices and the role of long-term contracts. *Journal of Political Economy* 88 (December): 1088–1109.

Bosworth, Barry. 1985. Taxes and the economic recovery. *Brookings Papers on Economic Activity* 1: 1–38.

Bosworth, Barry, and Robert Lawrence. 1982. *Commodity Prices and the New Inflation*. Washington, D.C.: Brookings Institution.

Boughton, James. 1989. Policy assignment strategies with somewhat flexible exchange rates. In *Exchange Rate Regimes and Macroeconomic Policy*, ed. B. Eichengreen, M. Miller, and R. Portes, 125–54. London: Academic Press, for Centre for Economic and Policy Research.

Boughton, James, and William Branson. 1991. Commodity prices as a leading indicator of inflation. In *Leading Economic Indicators*, ed. K. Lahin and G. E. Moore, 305–38. Cambridge, U.K.: Cambridge University Press.

Brainard, William. 1967. Uncertainty and the effectiveness of policy. *American Economic Review* 57 (May): 411–25.

Brainard, William, and James Tobin. 1968. Pitfalls in financial model building. *American Economic Review* 58 (May): 99–122.

Branson, William. 1986. The limits of monetary coordination as exchange rate policy. *Brookings Papers on Economic Activity* 1: 175–88.

Branson, William, and Willem Buiter. 1983. Monetary and fiscal policy with flexible exchange rates. In *Economic Interdependence and Flexible Exchange Rates*, ed. J. Bhandari and B. Putnam, 251–85. Cambridge, Mass.: MIT Press.

Branson, William, and Julio Rotemberg. 1980. International adjustment with wage rigidity. *European Economic Review* 13, 3 (May): 309–37.

Brittan, Samuel. 1987. *The Role and Limits of Government*. Rev. ed. London: Wildwood House.

Bryant, Ralph. 1987. Intragovernmental coordination of economic policies: An interim stocktaking. In *International Monetary Cooperation: Essays in Honor of Henry C. Wallich*, Paul Volcker et al., 4–15. Essays in International Finance no. 169. Princeton, N.J.: Princeton University, December.

Bryant, Ralph, Peter Hooper, and Catherine Mann. 1993. *Evaluating Policy Regimes*. Washington D.C.: Brookings Institution.

Bryant, Ralph, Dale Henderson, Gerald Holtham, Peter Hooper, and Steven Symansky, eds. 1988. *Empirical Macroeconomics for Interdependent Economies*. Washington, D.C.: Brookings Institution.

Calvo, Guillermo. 1978. On the time consistency of optimal policy in a monetary economy. *Econometrica* 46: 1411–28.

Campbell, John, and Robert Shiller. 1987. Cointegration and tests of present value models. *Journal of Political Economy* 95: 1062–68.

Campbell, John, and Robert Shiller. 1989. Yield spreads and interest rate movements: A bird's eye view. *Review of Economic Studies* 58, 195 (May): 495–514.

Canzoneri, Matthew, and JoAnna Gray. 1985. Monetary policy games and the consequences of non-cooperative behavior. *International Economic Review* 26 (October): 547−64.

Canzoneri, Matthew, and Dale Henderson. 1991. *Monetary Policy in Interdependent Economies: A Game-Theoretic Approach*. Cambridge, Mass.: MIT Press.

Canzoneri, Matthew, and Patrick Minford. 1986. When policy coordination matters: An empirical analysis. Discussion Paper no. 119. London: Centre for Economic Policy Research, July.

Cargill, Thomas. 1975. The term structure of interest rates: A test of the expectations hypothesis. *Journal of Finance* 30 (June): 761−71.

Cargill, Thomas. 1976. Anticipated price changes and nominal interest rates in the 1950s. *Review of Economics and Statistics* 58 (August): 364−67.

Cargill, Thomas, and Robert Mayer. 1980. The term structure of inflationary expectations and market efficiency. *Journal of Finance* 35 (March): 57−70.

Carlozzi, Nicholas, and John Taylor. 1985. International capital mobility and the coordination of monetary rules. In *Exchange Rate Management under Uncertainty*, ed. J. Bhandari, 186−211. Cambridge, Mass.: MIT Press.

Carlson, John. 1977. A study of price forecasts. *Annals of Economic and Social Measurement* 6 (Winter): 27−56.

Chambers, Robert, and Richard Just. 1981. Effects of exchange rate changes on U.S. agriculture. *American Journal of Agricultural Economics* 63: 32−46.

Chambers, Robert, and Richard Just. 1982. An investigation of the effect of monetary factors on U.S. agriculture. *Journal of Monetary Economics* 9: 235−47.

Cheng, Pao, and Robert Grauer. 1980. An alternative test of the capital asset pricing model. *American Economic Review* 70, 4 (September): 660−71.

Cooley, R., and S. LeRoy. 1985. Atheoretical macroeconometrics: A critique. *Journal of Monetary Economics* 16: 283−308.

Cooper, Richard. 1985. Economic Interdependence and coordination of economic policies. In *Handbook of International Economics*, vol. 2, ed. R. Jones and P. Kenen. Amsterdam: North-Holland.

Cooper, Richard. 1986. International cooperation in public health as a prologue to macroeconomic cooperation. *Brookings Discussion Papers in International Economics* no. 44. Washington, D.C.: Brookings Institution, March.

Corden, W. Max. 1983. The logic of the international monetary nonsystem. In *Reflections on a Troubled World Economy*, ed. F. Machlup and H. Muller-Groeling, 59−74. London: Macmillan.

Cornell, Bradford. 1982. Money supply announcements, interest rates, and foreign exchange. *Journal of International Money and Finance* 1 (August): 201−8.

Cornell, Bradford. 1983. Money supply announcements and interest rates: Another view. *Journal of Business* 56 (January): 1−24.

Cornell, Bradford, and J. Kimball Dietrich. 1978. The efficiency of the market for foreign exchange under floating exchange rates. *Review of Economics and Statistics* 60, 1 (February): 111−20.

Cox, W. 1985. The behavior of Treasury securities: Monthly 1942–1984. *Journal of Monetary Economics* 16: 227–50.

Dooley, Michael, and Peter Isard. 1983. The portfolio-balance model of exchange rates and some structural estimates of the risk premium. *IMF Staff Papers* 30, 4 (December): 683–702.

Dornbusch, Rudiger. 1976. Expectations and exchange rate dynamics. *Journal of Political Economy* 84: 1161–76.

Dornbusch, Rudiger. 1980. Exchange rate economics: Where do we stand? *Brookings Papers on Economic Activity* 1: 143–94.

Dornbusch, Rudiger. 1983. Exchange risk and the macroeconomics of exchange rate determination. In *The Internationalization of Financial Markets and National Economic Policy*, ed. R. Hawkins, R. Levich, and C. Wihlborg, 3–27. Greenwich: JAI Press.

Dornbusch, Rudiger, and Jeffrey Frankel. 1988. The flexible exchange rate system: Experience and alternatives. In *International Finance and Trade in a Polycentric World*, ed. S. Borner, 151–97. London: Macmillan. Reprinted as chap. 1 of *On Exchange Rates*, Jeffrey Frankel, 5–39. Cambridge, Mass.: MIT Press, 1993.

Dumas, Bernard. 1982. Discussion of international portfolio diversification: Short-term financial assets and gold. In *Exchange Rate Theory and Policy*, ed. John Bilson and Richard Marston, 232–36. Chicago: University of Chicago Press.

Dumas, Bernard. 1994. A test of the international CAPM using business cycle indicators as instrumental variables. In *The Internationalization of Equity Markets*, ed. J. Frankel, 23–50. Chicago: University of Chicago Press.

Ederington, Louis, and Chao-Hsi Huang. 1991. Parameter uncertainty and the rational expectations model of the term structure. Mimeo, University of Oklahoma, October.

Engel, Charles. 1984. Testing for the absence of expected real profits in the forward exchange markets. *Journal of International Economics* 17 (November): 299–308.

Engel, Charles. 1994. Tests of CAPM on an international portfolio of bonds and stocks. In *The Internationalization of Equity Markets*, ed. J. Frankel, 149–83. Chicago: University of Chicago Press.

Engel, Charles, and Jeffrey Frankel. 1983. Why money announcements move interest rates: An answer from the foreign exchange market. *Proceedings of Sixth West Coast Academic/ Federal Reserve Economic Research Seminar*. San Francisco: Federal Reserve Bank of San Francisco. Reprinted as chap. 5 of *On Exchange Rates*, Jeffrey Frankel, 117–34. Cambridge, Mass.: MIT Press, 1993.

Engel, Charles, and Jeffrey Frankel. 1984a. The secular inflation term in open-economy Phillips curves: A comment on Flood. *European Economic Review* 24: 161–64.

Engel, Charles, and Jeffrey Frankel. 1984b. Why interest rates react to money announcements: An explanation from the foreign exchange market. *Journal of Monetary Economics* 13 (January): 31–39.

Engel, Charles, Jeffrey Frankel, Kenneth Froot, and Anthony Rodrigues. 1995. The constrained asset share estimation (CASE) method: Testing mean-variance efficiency of the U.S. stock market. Forthcoming in *Journal of Empirical Finance* 2. (Appears as chapter 5 in this volume.)

Engel, Charles, and Anthony Rodrigues. 1989. Tests of international CAPM with time-varying covariances. *Journal of Applied Econometrics* 4: 119–38.

Engel, Charles, and Anthony Rodrigues. 1993. Tests of mean-variance efficiency of international equity markets. *Oxford Economics Papers* 45, 3 (July): 403–21.

Engle, Robert. 1982. Autoregressive conditional heteroscedasticity with estimates of the variance of United Kingdom inflation. *Econometrica* 50: 987–1007.

Engle, Robert, David Lilien, and Russell Robins. 1987. Estimating time-varying risk premia in the term structure: The ARCH-M model. *Econometrica* 55: 391–407.

Engle, Robert, and Victor Ng. 1990. An examination of the impact of volatility shocks on the short end of the term structure based on a factor-ARCH model for Treasury bills. Mimeo, University of Michigan Business School.

Evans, Martin D. D., and Karen K. Lewis. 1994. Do stationary risk premia explain it all? Evidence from the term structure. *Journal of Monetary Economics* 33, 2 (April): 285–318.

Fair, Ray, and Burton Malkiel. 1971. The determination of yield differentials between debt instruments of the same maturity. *Journal of Money, Credit, and Banking* 3: 733–49.

Fama, Eugene. 1970. Multi-period consumption-investment decisions. *American Economic Review* 60: 163–74.

Fama, Eugene. 1975. Short-term interest rates as predictors of inflation. *American Economic Review* 65 (June): 269–82.

Fama, Eugene. 1984. The information in the term structure. *Journal of Financial Economics* 13 (December): 509–28.

Fama, Eugene. 1990. Term-structure forecasts of interest rates, inflation and real returns. *Journal of Monetary Economics* 25: 59–76.

Fama, Eugene, and Robert Bliss. 1987. The information in long-maturity forward rates. *American Economic Review* 77, 4 (September): 680–92.

Fama, Eugene, and André Farber. 1979. Money, bonds, and foreign exchange. *American Economic Review* 69, 4 (September): 639–49.

Fama, Eugene, and K. French. 1988. Permanent and temporary components of stock prices. *Journal of Political Economy* 96: 246–73.

Fama, Eugene, and K. French. 1992. The cross-section of expected stock returns. *Journal of Finance* 47: 427–65.

Feldstein, Martin. 1983. The world economy. *The Economist* (June 11), 43–46.

Feldstein, Martin. 1988. Distinguished lecture on economics in government: Thinking about international economic coordination. *Journal of Economic Perspectives* 2, 2 (Spring): 3–13.

Feldstein, Martin, and James Stock. 1994. The use of monetary aggregates to target nominal GNP. In *Monetary Policy*, ed. N. Gregory Mankiw, 7–69. Chicago: University of Chicago Press.

Ferson, Wayne, and Campbell Harvey. 1994. An exploratory investigation of the fundamental determinants of national equity market returns. In *The Internationalization of Equity Markets*, ed. J. Frankel, 59–138. Chicago: University of Chicago Press.

Ferson, W., S. Kandel, and R. Stambaugh. 1987. Test of asset pricing with time-varying expected returns and market betas. *Journal of Finance* 42: 201–20.

Figlewski, Stephen, and Paul Wachtel. 1981. The formation of inflationary expectations. *Review of Economics and Statistics* 63 (February): 1–10.

Fischer, Stanley. 1977. Long-term contracts, rational expectations, and the optimal money supply rule. *Journal of Political Economy* 85: 191–205.

Fischer, Stanley. 1980. Dynamic inconsistency, cooperation, and the benevolent dissembling government. *Journal of Economic Dynamics and Control* 2: 93–107.

Fischer, Stanley. 1988. International macroeconomic policy coordination. In *International Economic Cooperation*, ed. M. Feldstein, 11–43. Chicago: University of Chicago Press.

Fischer, Stanley. 1991. Rules versus discretion in monetary policy. In *Handbook of Monetary Economics*, vol. 2, ed. B. Friedman and F. Hahn. Amsterdam: North-Holland.

Fisher, Irving. 1930. *The Theory of Interest*. New York: Macmillan.

Fitoussi, J. P., and Edmund S. Phelps. 1986. Causes of the 1980s slump in Europe. *Brookings Papers on Economic Activity* 2: 487–513.

Frankel, Jeffrey. 1979. The diversifiability of exchange risk. *Journal of International Economics* 9 (August): 379–93. Reprinted in *On Exchange Rates*, Jeffrey Frankel. Cambridge, Mass.: MIT Press, 1993.

Frankel, Jeffrey. 1981. Estimation of portfolio-balance functions that are mean-variance optimizing: The mark and the dollar. International Finance Discussion Paper no. 188. Washington, D.C.: Federal Reserve Board, September. Revised 1982.

Frankel, Jeffrey. 1982a. A test of perfect substitutability in the foreign exchange market. *Southern Economic Journal* 49 (October): 406–16.

Frankel, Jeffrey. 1982b. In search of the exchange risk premium: A six-currency test assuming mean-variance optimization. *Journal of International Money and Finance* 1 (December): 255–74. Also in *Exchange Rate Economics*, Vol. 2 of *International Library of Critical Writings in Economics*, ed. R. MacDonald and M. Taylor. Hants, U.K.: Edward Elgar Publishing, 1992.

Frankel, Jeffrey. 1982c. A technique for extracting a measure of expected inflation from the interest rate term structure. *Review of Economics and Statistics* 64: 135–42. (Appears as chapter 8 in this volume.)

Frankel, Jeffrey. 1984. Commodity prices and money: Lessons from international finance. *American Journal of Agricultural Economics* 66: 560–66.

Frankel, Jeffrey. 1985a. Portfolio shares as "beta-breakers": A test of CAPM. *Journal of Portfolio Management* 11, 4 (Summer): 18–23. (Appears as chapter 3 in this volume.)

Frankel, Jeffrey. 1985b. Portfolio crowding-out empirically estimated. *Quarterly Journal of Economics* 100: 1041–65. (Appears as chapter 1 in this volume.)

Frankel, Jeffrey. 1986a. Ambiguous macroeconomic policy multipliers, in theory and in twelve econometric models. In *Empirical Macroeconomics for Interdependent Economies*, ed. Ralph Bryant, Dale Henderson, Gerald Holtham, Peter Hooper, and Steven Symansky. Washington, D.C.: Brookings Institution. (Appears as chapter 11 in this volume.)

Frankel, Jeffrey. 1986b. International macroeconomic policy coordination when policy-makers disagree on the model. NBER Working Paper no. 2059. Cambridge, Mass.: National Bureau of Economic Research, October.

Frankel, Jeffrey. 1986c. The sources of disagreement among international macro models and implications for policy coordination. NBER Working Paper no. 1925. Cambridge, Mass.: National Bureau of Economic Research, May.

Frankel, Jeffrey. 1988a. Obstacles to international macroeconomic policy coordination. *Studies in International Finance* 64 (December). Princeton: Princeton University Press. First appeared as International Monetary Fund Working Paper 87-29, April 1987.

Frankel, Jeffrey. 1988b. To coordinate or not coordinate? A proposal for policy coordination: International nominal targeting (INT). In *International Payments Imbalances in the 1980s*, ed. N. Fieleke, 234–39. Boston: Federal Reserve Bank of Boston.

Frankel, Jeffrey. 1989a. International financial integration, relations among interest rates and exchange rates, and monetary indicators. In *International Financial Integration and the Conduct of U.S. Monetary Policy*, ed. C. Pigott, 17–49. New York: Federal Reserve Bank of New York. Reprinted in *International Finance*, D. Das, 333–59. London: Routledge, 1993.

Frankel, Jeffrey. 1989b. International nominal targeting: A proposal for overcoming obstacles to policy coordination. Special issue of *Rivista di Politica Economica* 79, 12 (December): 257–94. Also in *Global Disequilibrium in the World Economy*, ed. M. Baldassarri, J. McCallum, and R. Mundell. New York: St. Martin's Press, 1992. (Appears as chapter 13 in this volume.)

Frankel, Jeffrey. 1990. Obstacles to coordination, and a consideration of two proposals to overcome them: International nominal targeting (INT) and the Hosomi Fund. In *International Policy Coordination and Exchange Rate Fluctuations*, ed. W. Branson, J. Frenkel, and M. Goldstein. Chicago: University of Chicago Press. First appeared as NBER Working Paper no. 2849. Cambridge, Mass.: National Bureau for Economic Research, 1989, February.

Frankel, Jeffrey. 1991a. The obstacles to macroeconomic policy coordination in the 1990s and an analysis of international nominal targeting (INT). In *International Trade and Global Development: Essays in Honor of Jagdish Bhagwati*, ed. K. A. Koekkoek and L. B. M. Mennes, 211–36. London: Routledge.

Frankel, Jeffrey. 1991b. A note on internationally coordinated policy packages intended to be robust under model uncertainty. Economics Working Paper 91-167, University of California at Berkeley, May.

Frankel, Jeffrey. 1993. *On Exchange Rates*. Cambridge, Mass.: MIT Press.

Frankel, Jeffrey. 1994. The internationalization of equity markets: Introduction. In *The Internationalization of Equity Markets*, ed. J. Frankel, 1–20. Chicago: University of Chicago Press. First appeared as NBER Working Paper no. 4590. Cambridge, Mass.: National Bureau for Economic Research, 1993.

Frankel, Jeffrey, and Menzie Chinn. 1991. Appendix to "The stabilizing properties of a nominal GNP rule in an open economy." Economics Working Paper 91-166, University of California at Berkeley, May. Revised February 1993.

Frankel, Jeffrey, and William Dickens. 1983. Are asset-demand functions determined by CAPM? NBER Working Paper no. 1113, April. Cambridge, Mass.: National Bureau of Economic Research. Revised as IBER Finance Working Paper no. 140, University of California at Berkeley, June.

Frankel, Jeffrey, and Charles Engel. 1984. Do asset-demand functions optimize over the mean and variance of real returns? A six-currency test. *Journal of International Economics* 17 (December): 309–23. (Appears as chapter 4 in this volume.)

Frankel, Jeffrey, Scott Erwin, and Katharine Rockett. 1992. International macroeconomic policy coordination when policymakers do not agree on the true model: Reply. *American Economic Review* 82, 4 (September): 1052–56.

Frankel, Jeffrey, and Norbert Funke. 1993. A two-country analysis of international targeting of nominal GNP. Special issue of *Rivista de Politica Economica* 83, 3 (April): 69–106, ed. M. Di Matteo.

Frankel, Jeffrey, and Gikas Hardouvelis. 1983. Commodity prices, overshooting, money surprises, and Fed credibility. NBER Working Paper no. 1121. Cambridge, Mass.: National Bureau of Economic Research, May.

Frankel, Jeffrey, and Gikas Hardouvelis. 1985. Commodity prices, money surprises, and Fed credibility. *Journal of Money, Credit, and Banking* 17, 4 (November): 425–38. (Appears as chapter 7 in this volume.)

Frankel, Jeffrey, and Cara Lown. 1991. An indicator of future inflation extracted from the steepness of the interest rate yield curve along its entire length. NBER Working Paper no. 3751. Cambridge, Mass.: National Bureau of Economic Research, June. Reprinted in *Quarterly Journal of Economics* 109, 2 (May 1994): 517–30.

Frankel, Jeffrey, and Katharine Rockett. 1988. International macroeconomic policy coordination when policymakers do not agree on the true model. *American Economic Review* 78, 3 (June): 318–40. (Appears as chapter 12 in this volume.)

Frenkel, Jacob. 1976. A monetary approach to the exchange rate: Doctrinal aspects and empirical evidence. *Scandinavian Journal of Economics* 78: 200–24.

Frenkel, Jacob, and Morris Goldstein. 1986. A guide to target zones. *IMF Staff Papers* 33, 4 (December): 633–73.

Frenkel, Jacob, Morris Goldstein, and Paul Masson. 1990. The rationale and effects of international economic policy coordination of economic policies: Scope, methods, and effects. In *International Policy Coordination and Exchange Rate Fluctuations*, ed. W. Branson, J. Frenkel, and M. Goldstein, 9–59. Chicago: University of Chicago Press.

Frenkel, Jacob, and Assaf Razin. 1980. Stochastic prices and tests of efficiency of foreign exchange markets. *Economics Letters* 6: 165–70.

Friedman, Benjamin. 1977a. The inefficiency of short-run monetary targets for monetary policy. *Brookings Papers on Economic Activity* 2: 293–335.

Friedman, Benjamin. 1977b. Financial flow variables and the short-run determination of long-term interest rates. *Journal of Political Economy* 75: 661–89.

Friedman, Benjamin. 1978. Crowding out or crowding in? Economic consequences of financing government deficits. *Brookings Papers on Economic Activity* 3: 593–641.

Friedman, Benjamin. 1984. The value of intermediate targets in implementing monetary policy. In *Price Stability and Public Policy*, 169–91. Kansas City: Federal Reserve Bank of Kansas City.

Friedman, Benjamin. 1985a. Crowding out or crowding in? Evidence on debt-equity substitutability. NBER Working Paper no. 1565. Cambridge, Mass.: National Bureau of Economic Research, February.

Friedman, Benjamin. 1985b. The substitutability of debt and equity securities. In *Corporate Capital Structures in the United States*, ed. B. Friedman. Chicago: University of Chicago Press. First appeared as NBER Working Paper no. 1130. Cambridge, Mass.: National Bureau for Economic Research, 1983, May.

Friedman, Benjamin. 1985c. Portfolio choice and the debt-to-income relationship. *American Economic Review* 75, 2 (May): 338–43.

Friedman, Benjamin. 1986. Implications of government deficits for interest rates, equity returns, and corporate financing. In *Financing Corporate Capital Formation*, ed. B. Friedman. Chicago: University of Chicago Press.

Friedman, Benjamin. 1992. Debt management policy, interest rates, and economic activity. Part II in *Does Debt Management Matter?* ed. J. Agell, M. Persson, and B. Friedman. FIEF Studies in Labor Markets and Economic Policy. Oxford: Oxford University Press.

Friedman, Benjamin, and Kenneth Kuttner. 1988. Time-varying risk perceptions and the pricing of risky assets. Mimeo, National Bureau of Economic Research.

Friedman, Benjamin, and Vance Roley. 1979. A note on the derivation of linear homogeneous asset demand functions. NBER Working Paper no. 345. Cambridge, Mass.: National Bureau of Economic Research, May.

Friedman, Milton. 1968. The role of monetary policy. *American Economic Review* 68 (March): 1–17.

Friend, Irwin, and Marshall Blume. 1975. The demand for risky assets. *American Economic Review* 65, 5 (December): 900–22.

Friedman, Milton, and Anna Schwartz. 1963. *A Monetary History of the United States.* Princeton, N.J.: Princeton University Press, for the National Bureau of Economic Research.

Froot, Kenneth. 1989. New hope for the expectations hypothesis of the term structure of interest rates. *Journal of Finance* 44: 283–305.

Froot, Kenneth. 1990. Short rates and expected asset returns. Unpublished paper, Harvard Business School and National Bureau of Economic Research.

Froot, Kenneth, and Jeffrey Frankel. 1989. Forward discount bias: Is it an exchange risk premium? *Quarterly Journal of Economics* 104: 139–61.

Funabashi, Yoichi. 1988. *Managing the Dollar: From the Plaza to the Louvre.* Washington, D.C.: Institute of International Economics.

Funke, Norbert. 1991. International monetary policy coordination: A classification and evaluation of recent concepts in a stochastic two-country model. Kiel Advanced Studies Working Paper No. 215, Kiel Institute of World Economics, Germany.

Garman, Mark, and Steven Kohlhagen. 1980. Inflation and foreign exchange rates under production and monetary uncertainty. Unpublished paper, University of California at Berkeley, June.

Ghosh, Atish. 1986. International policy coordination in an uncertain world. *Economic Letters* 21: 271–6.

Ghosh, Atish, and Paul Masson. 1988. International policy coordination in a world with model uncertainty. *International Monetary Fund Staff Papers* 35, 2 (June): 230–58.

Ghosh, Atish, and Paul Masson. 1994. Economic cooperation in an uncertain world. Oxford and Cambridge: Blackwell.

Ghosh, Swati. 1987. International policy coordination when the model is unknown. M. Phil. thesis, Oxford University, London.

Giavazzi, Francesco, and Alberto Giovannini. 1988. *Limiting Exchange Rate Flexibility: The European Monetary System.* Cambridge, Mass.: MIT Press.

Giavazzi, Francesco, and Marco Pagano. 1988. The advantage of tying one's hands: EMS discipline and central bank credibility. *European Economic Review* 32 (June): 1055–82.

Gibbons, M. 1982. Multivariate tests of financial models: A new approach. *Journal of Financial Economics* 10: 3–27.

Gibson, William. 1972. Interest rates and inflationary expectations: New evidence. *American Economic Review* 62 (December): 854–65.

Giovannini, Alberto, and Philippe Jorion. 1989. The time variation of risk and return in the foreign exchange and stock markets. *Journal of Finance* 44, 2 (June): 307–25.

Girton, Lance, and Dale Henderson. 1976. Financial capital movements and central bank behavior in a two-country, short-run portfolio-balance model. *Journal of Monetary Economics* 2: 33–61.

Gordon, Robert. 1985. The conduct of domestic monetary policy. In *Monetary Policy in Our Times*, ed. A. Ando, H. Eguchi, R. Farmer, and Y. Suzuki, 45–81. Cambridge, Mass.: MIT Press.

Gordon, Robert. 1987. Productivity, wages, and prices inside and outside of manufacturing in the U.S., Japan, and Europe. *European Economic Review* 31, 3 (April): 685–739.

Gordon, Robert. 1990a. U.S. inflation, labor's share, and the natural rate of unemployment. In *Economics of Wage Determination*, ed. H. Konig, 1–34. New York: Springer-Verlag.

Gordon, Robert J. 1990b. What is new-Keynesian economics? *Journal of Economic Literature* 28 (September): 1115–75.

Grauer, F. L. A., R. H. Litzenberger, and R. E. Stehle. 1976. Sharing rules and equilibrium in an international capital market under uncertainty. *Journal of Financial Economics* 3, 3: 233–56.

Gray, J. A., and D. E. Spencer. 1990. Price prediction errors and real activity: A reassessment. *Economic Inquiry* 28, 4 (October): 658–81.

Grieves, Robin, and Alan Marcus. 1990. Riding the yield curve: A reprise. NBER Working Paper no. 3511. Cambridge, Mass.: National Bureau of Economic Research, November.

Grossman, Jacob. 1981. The "rationality" of money supply expectations and the short-run response of interest rates to monetary surprises. *Journal of Money, Credit, and Banking* 13 (November): 409–24.

Grossman, Sanford, and Robert Shiller. 1982. Consumption correlatedness and risk measurement in economies with non-traded assets and heterogeneous information. *Journal of Financial Economics* 10 (July): 195–210.

Grubaugh, Stephen, and Scott Sumner. 1989. Commodity prices, money surprises, and Fed credibility: A comment. *Journal of Money, Credit, and Banking* 21, 3 (August): 407–8.

Haas, R., and S. Symansky. 1984. Assessing dynamic properties of the MCM: A simulation approach. International Financial Discussion Paper no. 214. Washington, D.C.: Federal Reserve Board of Governors.

Hall, Robert. 1985. Monetary policy with an elastic price standard. *Price Stability and Public Policy.* Kansas City: Federal Reserve Bank of Kansas City.

Hall, Robert, and N. Gregory Mankiw. 1993. Nominal income targeting. In *Monetary Policy*, ed. N. Gregory Mankiw, 71–93. Chicago: University of Chicago Press.

Hamada, Koichi. 1976. A strategic analysis of monetary interdependence. *Journal of Political Economy* 84 (August): 77–99.

Hansen, Lars, and Robert Hodrick. 1983. Risk-averse speculation in the forward foreign exchange market: An econometric analysis of linear models. In *Exchange Rates and International Macroeconomics*, ed. Jacob Frenkel. Chicago: University of Chicago Press.

Hansen, Lars, and S. Richard. 1987. The role of conditioning information in deducing testable restrictions implied by dynamic asset pricing models. *Econometrica* 55: 587–614.

Hansen, Lars, and Kenneth Singleton. 1983. Stochastic consumption, risk aversion, and temporal behavior of asset returns. *Journal of Political Economy* 91: 249–65.

Hardouvelis, Gikas. 1984a. Reserve announcements and interest rates: Does monetary policy matter? Mimeo, Barnard College, Columbia University, October.

Hardouvelis, Gikas. 1984b. Market perceptions of Federal Reserve policy and the weekly monetary announcements. *Journal of Monetary Economics* 14 (September): 225–40.

Hardouvelis, Gikas. 1988. The predictive power of the term structure during recent monetary regimes. *Journal of Finance* 43, 2 (June): 339–56.

Harvey, Campbell. 1989. Time-varying conditional covariances in tests of asset pricing models. *Journal of Financial Economics* 24: 289–317.

Helliwell, J., and T. Padmore. 1985. Empirical studies of macroeconomic interdependence. In *Handbook of International Economics*, Vol. 2, ed. Ronald Jones and Peter Kenen, 1007–51. Amsterdam: North-Holland.

Henderson, Dale. 1983. Canadian post-war balance of payments and exchange rate experience: Comment. In *The Canadian Balance of Payments: Perspectives and Policy Issues*, ed. D. Purvis, 222–37. Montreal: Institute for Research on Public Policy.

Hess, Patrick, and James Bicksler. 1975. Capital asset prices versus time series models as predictors of inflation. *Journal of Financial Economics* 2 (December): 341–60.

Hicks, J. R. 1939. Value and Capital. London: Oxford University Press.

Hilton, Spence, and Vivek Moorthy. 1990. Targeting nominal GNP. In *Intermediate Targets and Indicators for Monetary Policy: A Critical Survey*. New York: Federal Reserve Bank of New York.

Hodrick, Robert. 1981. International asset pricing with time-varying risk premia. *Journal of International Economics* 11 (November): 573–77.

Holtham, Gerald. 1986. International policy coordination: How much consensus is there? *Brookings Discussion Papers in International Economics* 50 (September). Washington, D.C.: Brookings Institution.

Holtham, Gerald, and Andrew Hughes Hallett. 1987. International policy coordination and model uncertainty. In *Global Macroeconomics: Policy Conflict and Cooperation*, ed. R. Bryant and R. Portes, 128–84. London: Macmillan.

Holtham, Gerald, and Andrew Hughes Hallett. 1992. Policy coordination under uncertainty: The case for some disagreement (A comment on Frankel and Rockett). *American Economic Review* 82, 4 (September): 1043–51.

Hughes Hallett, Andrew. 1985. How much could international coordination of economic policies achieve? An example from U.S.–E.E.C. policymaking. Discussion Paper no. 77. London: Centre for Economic Policy Research.

Hughes Hallett, Andrew. 1989. What are the risks in coordinating economic policy internationally? In *Exchange Rates and Open Economy Macroeconomics*, ed. R. MacDonald and M. Taylor. Oxford and Boston: Blackwell.

Ibbotson Associates. 1986. *Stocks, Bonds, Bills and Inflation: 1986 Yearbook*. Chicago: Ibbotson Associates.

Ishii, Naoko, Warwick McKibbin, and Jeffrey Sachs. 1985. The economic policy mix, policy cooperation, and protectionism: Some aspects of macroeconomic interdependence among the United States, Japan, and other OECD countries. *Journal of Policy Modeling* 7: 533–72.

Johnson, Manuel. 1988. Current perspectives on monetary policy. *Cato Journal* 8: 253–60.

Joines, Douglas. 1977. Short-term interest rates as predictors of inflation: Comment. *American Economic Review* 67 (June): 476–77.

Jones, David, and V. Vance Roley. 1983. Rational expectations and the expectations model of the term structure: A test using weekly data. *Journal of Monetary Economics* 12 (September): 453–65.

Jones, Irwin. 1992. Can a simplified approach to bond portfolio management increase return and reduce risk? *Journal of Portfolio Management* (Winter): 70–76.

Jorion, Philippe, and Frederic Mishkin. 1991. A multi-country comparison of term structure forecasts at long horizons. *Journal of Financial Economics* 29: 59–80.

Kehoe, Patrick. 1986. International policy cooperation may be undesirable. Research Department Staff Report no. 103. Minneapolis, Minn.: Federal Reserve Bank of Minneapolis, February.

Kenen, Peter. 1987. Exchange rates and policy coordination. *Brookings Discussion Paper in International Economics* no. 61. Washington, D.C.: The Brookings Institution, October.

Kenen, Peter, and Stephen Schwartz. 1986. An assessment of macroeconomic forecasts in the International Monetary Fund's World Economic Outlook. International Economics Working Paper no. G-86-04. Princeton: Princeton University, December.

Kouri, Pentti. 1976. The determinants of the forward premium. Seminar Paper no. 62, Institute for International Economic Studies. Stockholm: University of Stockholm, August.

Kouri, Pentti. 1977. International investment and interest rate linkages under flexible exchange rates. In *The Political Economy of Monetary Reform*, ed. R. Aliber. London: Macmillan.

Kouri, Pentti, and Jorge de Macedo. 1978. Exchange rates and the international adjustment process. *Brookings Papers on Economic Activity* 1: 111–50.

Krugman, Paul. 1981. Consumption preferences, asset demands, and distribution effects in international financial markets. NBER Working Paper no. 651. Cambridge: National Bureau of Economic Research, March.

Krugman, Paul. 1988. Target zones and exchange rate dynamics. NBER Working Paper no. 2481. Cambridge, Mass.: National Bureau of Economic Research, January.

Kydland, F., and E. Prescott. 1977. Rules rather than discretion: The inconsistency of optimal plans. *Journal of Political Economy* 85 (June): 473–91.

Laursen, S., and L. Metzler. 1950. Flexible exchange rates and the theory of employment. *Review of Economics and Statistics* 32: 281−89.

Layard, R., G. Basevi, O. Blanchard, W. Buiter, and R. Dornbusch. 1986. Europe: The case for unsustainable growth. *CEPS Discussion Papers 8/9.* Brussels: Center for European Policy Studies, February.

Leder, Dorothea. 1992. The stabilizing effects of pure and of mixed monetary policy strategies on the world economy. Berlin, Germany.

Levine, Paul. 1991. Should rules be simple? Discussion Paper no. 515. London: Centre for Economic Policy Research, March.

Lewis, Karen. 1991. Was there a "peso problem" in the U.S. term structure of interest rates: 1979−1982? *International Economic Review* 32, 1 (February): 159−73.

Lown, Cara. 1989. Interest rate spreads, commodity prices, and the dollar: A new strategy for monetary policy? *Federal Reserve Bank of Dallas Economic Review* (July): 13−26.

Lucas, Robert E., Jr. 1972. Expectations and the neutrality of money. *Journal of Economic Theory* 4 (April): 103−24.

Lucas, Robert E., Jr. 1973. Some international evidence on output-inflation tradeoffs. *American Economic Review* 63 (June): 326−34.

Lucas, Robert E., Jr. 1976. Econometric policy evaluation: A critique. In *The Phillips Curve and Labor Markets*, Vol. 5, Carnegie-Rochester Conference Series, ed. K. Brunner and A. Meltzer, 19−46. Reprinted in Robert E. Lucas, *Studies in Business Cycle Theory*. Cambridge, Mass.: MIT Press, 1981.

de Macedo, Jorge. 1982. Portfolio diversification across currencies. In *The International Monetary System under Flexible Exchange Rates*, ed. R. Cooper, P. Kenen, de Macedo, J., and V. Ypersele, 69−100. Cambridge, Mass.: Ballinger.

de Macedo, Jorge, J. Goldstein, and D. Meerschwam. 1984. International portfolio diversification: Short-term financial assets and gold. In *Exchange Rate Theory and Practice*, ed. J. Bilson and R. Marston, 199−232. Chicago: University of Chicago Press.

Mankiw, N. Gregory. 1985. Small menu costs and large business cycles: A macroeconomic model of monopoly. *Quarterly Journal of Economics* 100: 529−39.

Mankiw, N. Gregory. 1986. The term structure of interest rates revisited. *Brookings Papers on Economic Activity* 1 (Spring): 61−110.

Mankiw, N. Gregory, and Jeffrey Miron. 1986. The changing behavior of the term structure of interest rates. *Quarterly Journal of Economics* (May): 211−26.

Mankiw, N. Gregory, and Matthew Shapiro. 1986. News or noise: An analysis of GNP revisions. *Survey of Current Business* (May): 20−25.

Mankiw, N. Gregory, and Lawrence Summers. 1984. Do long-term interest rates overreact to short-term interest rates? *Brookings Papers on Economic Activity* 1 (Spring): 223−42.

Markowitz, H. M. 1952. Portfolio selection. *Journal of Finance* 7: 77−91.

Marris, Stephen. 1985. *Deficits and the Dollar: The World Economy at Risk.* Policy Analyses in International Economics no. 14. Washington, D.C.: Institute for International Economics, December.

Marston, Richard. 1984. Comment on "The effects of American policies—A new classical interpretation." In *International Economic Policy Coordination*, ed. W. Buiter and R. Marston, 134–38. Cambridge: Cambridge University Press.

Masson, Paul. 1978. Structural models of the demand for bonds and the term structure of interest rates. *Economica* 45: 363–77.

McCallum, Bennett. 1987. The case for rules in the conduct of monetary policy: A concrete example. *Federal Reserve Bank of Richmond Economic Review* (September–October): 10–18.

McCallum, Bennett. 1988a. The role of demand management in the maintenance of full employment. NBER Working Paper no. 2520. Cambridge, Mass.: National Bureau of Economic Research, February.

McCallum, Bennett. 1988b. Robustness properties of a rule for monetary policy. In *Money, Cycles, and Exchange Rates*, ed. K. Brunner and B. McCallum. *Carnegie-Rochester Conference Series on Public Policy* 29 (Autumn): 173–203.

McCulloch, J. Huston. 1975. An estimate of the liquidity premium. *Journal of Political Economy* 83 (February): 95–119.

McKibbin, Warwick, and Jeffrey Sachs. 1988. Coordination of monetary and fiscal policies in the industrial economies. In *International Aspects of Fiscal Policies*, ed. Jacob Frenkel, 73–120. Chicago: University of Chicago Press.

McKibbin, Warwick, and Jeffrey Sachs. 1991. *Global Linkages: Macroeconomic Interdependence and Cooperation in the World Economy*. Washington, D.C.: Brookings Institution.

McKinnon, Ronald. 1984. *An International Standard for Monetary Stabilization*. Washington, D.C.: Institute for International Economics.

McKinnon, Ronald. 1988. Monetary and exchange rate policies for international financial stability. *Journal of Economic Perspectives* (Winter): 83–103.

Meade, James. 1984. A new Keynesian Bretton Woods. *Three Banks Review* (June).

Mehra, Rajnish, and Edward Prescott. 1985. The equity premium: A puzzle. *Journal of Monetary Economics* 15: 145–61.

Merton, Robert. 1973. An intertemporal capital asset pricing model. *Econometrica* 43: 867–87.

Miller, Marcus, and Mark Salmon. 1985. Dynamic games and the time inconsistency of optimal policy in open economies. *Economic Journal* 85 (suppl.): 124–37.

Miller, Marcus, and John Williamson. 1988. The international monetary system: An analysis of alternative regimes. Discussion Paper no. 266. London: Centre for Economic and Policy Research, July. Also in *European Economic Review* 32, 5 (June): 1031–48.

Minford, Patrick. 1984. The effects of American policies—A new classical interpretation. In *International Economic Policy Coordination*, ed. W. Buiter and R. Marston, 84–126. Cambridge: Cambridge University Press.

Mishkin, Frederic. 1981. The real rate of interest: An empirical investigation. In *The Costs and Consequences of Inflation. Carnegie-Rochester Conference Series on Public Policy* 15: 151–200.

Mishkin, Frederic. 1988. The information in the term structure: Some further results. *Journal of Applied Econometrics* 3: 307–14.

Mishkin, Frederic. 1990a. What does the term structure tell us about future inflation? *Journal of Monetary Economics* 25: 77–95.

Mishkin, Frederic. 1990b. The information in the longer-maturity term structure about future inflation. *Quarterly Journal of Economics* 105: 815–28.

Mishkin, Frederic. 1990c. Does correcting for heteroscedasticity help? *Economics Letters* 34: 351–56.

Mishkin, Frederic. 1991. A multi-country study of the information in the term structure about future inflation. *Journal of International Money and Finance* 19: 2–22.

Mishkin, Frederic. 1992. Yield curve. In *New Palgrave Dictionary of Money and Finance*. New York: Stockton Press.

Moalla-Fetini, Rakia. 1991. Commodity price dynamics and the overshooting hypothesis. Chapter from Ph.D. thesis, Department of Agricultural and Natural Resource Economics, University of California, Berkeley.

Modigliani, Franco, and Robert Shiller. 1973. Inflation, rational expectations, and the term structure of interest rates. *Economica* 40 (February): 12–43.

Modigliani, Franco, and Richard Sutch. 1966. Innovations in interest rate policy. *American Economic Review* 56 (May): 178–97.

Modigliani, Franco, and Richard Sutch. 1967. Debt management and the term structure of interest rates: An empirical analysis of recent experience. *Journal of Political Economy* 75 (August): 569–89.

Mullineaux, Donald. 1978. On testing for rationality: Another look at the Livingston price expectations data. *Journal of Political Economy* 86 (April): 329–36.

Mundell, Robert. 1962. The appropriate use of monetary and fiscal policy under fixed exchange rates. *IMF Staff Papers* 9 (March): 70–77.

Mundell, Robert. 1964. A reply: Capital mobility and size. *Canadian Journal of Economics and Political Science* 30: 421–31. Also in R. Mundell. *International Economics*, R. Mundell. New York: Macmillan, 1968.

Murphy, Kevin, and Robert Topel. 1985. Estimation and inference in two-step econometric models. *Journal of Business and Economic Statistics* 3: 370–79.

Mussa, Michael. 1975. Adaptive and regressive expectations in a rational model of the inflationary process. *Journal of Monetary Economics* 1 (October): 423–42.

Mussa, Michael. 1979. Macroeconomic interdependence and the exchange rate regime. In *International Economic Policy: Theory and Evidence*, ed. R. Dornbusch and J. Frenkel, 160–204. Baltimore: Johns Hopkins University Press.

Naylor, John. 1982. Do short-term interest rate expectations respond to new information on monetary growth? *Southern Economic Journal* 48 (January): 754–63.

Nelson, Charles, and G. Schwert. 1977. Short-term interest rates as predictors of inflation: On testing the hypothesis that the real rate of interest is constant. *American Economic Review* 67 (June): 478–86.

Ng, L. 1991. Tests of the CAPM with time-varying covariances: A multivariate GARCH approach. *Journal of Finance* 46: 1507–21.

Nichols, Donald, David Small, and Charles Webster, Jr. 1983. Why interest rates rise when an unexpectedly large money stock is announced. *American Economic Review* 73 (June): 383–88.

Nordhaus, William. 1994. Policy games: Coordination and independence in monetary and fiscal policies. *Brookings Papers on Economic Policy* 2: 139–216.

Nordhaus, William, and Steve Durlauf. 1982. The structure of social risk. Cowles Foundation Discussion Paper no. 648. New Haven: Yale University, September.

Obstfeld, Maurice. 1982. Aggregate spending and the terms of trade: Is there a Laursen-Metzler effect? *Quarterly Journal of Economics* 96: 251–70.

Obstfeld, Maurice, and Kenneth Rogoff. 1984. Exchange rate dynamics with sluggish prices under alternative price-adjustment rules. *International Economic Review* 25: 159–74.

Okun, Arthur. 1975. Inflation: Its mechanics and welfare costs. *Brookings Papers on Economic Activity* 2: 351–401.

Oudiz, Gilles. 1985. European policy coordination: An evaluation. Discussion Paper no. 81. London: Centre for Economic Policy Research, October.

Oudiz, Gilles, and Jeffrey Sachs. 1984. Macroeconomic policy coordination among industrial economies. *Brookings Papers on Economic Activity* 1: 1–76.

Parkin, Michael. 1970. Discount house portfolio and debt selection. *Review of Economic Studies* 37 (October): 469–97.

Pearce, Douglas, and V. Vance Roley. 1983. The reaction of stock prices to unanticipated changes in money: A note. *Journal of Finance* 38 (September): 1323–33.

Persson, Torsten, and Guido Tabellini. 1990. *Macroeconomic Policy, Credibility, and Politics.* Chur, Switzerland: Harwood Academic Publishers.

Pesando, James. 1978. On the efficiency of the bond market: Some Canadian evidence. *Journal of Political Economy* 86 (December): 1057–76.

Phelps, Edmund. 1967. Phillips curves, expectations of inflation and optimal employment over time. *Economica* 34 (August): 254–81.

Phelps, Edmund. 1968. Money-wage dynamics and labor market equilibrium. *Journal of Political Economy* 76 (August): 678–711.

Phelps, Edmund. 1970. *Microeconomic foundations of employment and inflation theory.* New York: Norton.

Poterba, James, and Lawrence Summers. 1988. Mean reversion in stock returns: Evidence and implications. *Journal of Financial Economics* 22: 27–59.

Putnam, Robert, and Nicholas Bayne. 1987. *Hanging Together: The Seven-Power Summits.* 2d ed. Cambridge, Mass.: Harvard University Press.

Pyle, David. 1972. Observed price expectations and interest rates. *Review of Economics and Statistics* 54 (August): 275–80.

Rogoff, Kenneth. 1985a. The optimal degree of commitment to an intermediate monetary target. *Quarterly Journal of Economics* 100 (November): 1169–89.

Rogoff, Kenneth. 1985b. Can international monetary policy coordination be counterproductive? *Journal of International Economics* 18 (February): 199–217.

Rogoff, Kenneth. 1987. Reputational constraints on monetary policy. In *Bubbles and Other Essays*, ed. K. Brunner and A. Meltzer. *Carnegie-Rochester Conference Series on Public Policy* 26 (Spring): 141–82. Supplement to *Journal of Monetary Economics*.

Roley, V. Vance. 1979. A theory of federal debt management. *American Economic Review* 69: 915–26.

Roley, V. Vance. 1982. The effect of federal debt-management policy on corporate bond and equity yields. *Quarterly Journal of Economics* 97 (November): 645–68.

Roll, Richard. 1970. *The Behavior of Interest Rates: An Application of the Efficient Market Model to U.S. Treasury Bills*. New York: Basic Books.

Roll, Richard. 1977. A critique of the asset pricing theory's test: Part 1: On past and potential testability of the theory. *Journal of Financial Economics* 4: 129–76.

Roll, Richard, and Bruno Solnik. 1977. A pure foreign exchange asset pricing model. *Journal of International Economics* 7, 2 (May): 161–80.

Romer, David. 1993a. The new Keynesian synthesis. *Journal of Economic Perspectives* 7, 1 (Winter): 5–22.

Romer, David. 1993b. Openness and inflation: Theory and evidence. *Quarterly Journal of Economics* 108, 4 (November): 869–903.

Roubini, Nouriel. 1986. International policy coordination and model uncertainty. Unpublished paper, Harvard University.

Sachs, Jeffrey. 1980. Wages, flexible exchange rates, and macroeconomic policy. *Quarterly Journal of Economics* 94: 731–47.

Sachs, Jeffrey. 1985. The dollar and the policy mix, 1985. *Brookings Papers on Economic Activity* 1: 117–85.

Sargent, Thomas. 1969. Commodity price expectations and the interest rate. *Quarterly Journal of Economics* 83 (February): 127–40.

Sargent, Thomas. 1971. A note on the 'Accelerationist Controversy.' *Journal of Money, Credit, and Banking* 3: 721–25.

Sargent, Thomas. 1973. Rational expectations, the real rate of interest and the natural rate of unemployment. *Brookings Papers on Economic Activity* 2: 429–72.

Sargent, Thomas, and Neil Wallace. 1975. 'Rational' expectations, the optimal monetary instrument, and the optimal money supply rule. *Journal of Political Economy* 83, 2: 241–54.

Sargent, Thomas, and Neil Wallace. 1976. Rational expectations and the theory of economic policy. *Journal of Monetary Economics* 2: 169–83.

Schuh, Edward. 1974. The exchange rate and U.S. agriculture. *American Journal of Agricultural Economics* 56: 1–13.

Schuh, Edward. 1976. The new macroeconomics of agriculture. *American Journal of Agricultural Economics* 58: 802–11.

Schultze, Charles. 1986. *Other Times, Other Places*. Washington, D.C.: Brookings Institution.

Shanken, Jay. 1983. Multivariate tests of the zero-beta CAPM. Unpublished paper, University of California at Berkeley, June.

Sharpe, William F. 1964. Capital asset prices: A theory of market equilibrium under conditions of risk. *Journal of Finance* 19: 277–93.

Shiller, Robert. 1982. Consumption, asset markets, and macroeconomic fluctuations. In *Economic Policy in a World of Change*, ed. K. Brunner and A. Meltzer, 203–38. Carnegie-Rochester Conference Series on Public Policy 17. Amsterdam: North-Holland.

Shiller, Robert. 1990. The term structure of interest rates. In *Handbook of Monetary Economics, Volume 1*, ed. B. Friedman and F. Hahn, 627–74. Amsterdam: North-Holland.

Shiller, Robert, John Campbell, and Kermit Schoenholtz. 1983. Forward rates and future policy: Interpreting the term structure of interest rates. *Brookings Papers on Economic Activity* 1 (Spring): 173–217.

Smith, Gary, and William Brainard. 1976. The value of a priori information in estimating a financial model. *Journal of Finance* 31: 1299–1322.

Solnik, Bruno. 1974. An equilibrium model of the international capital market. *Journal of Economic Theory* 8, 4: 500–24.

Stambaugh, Robert. 1982. On the exclusion of assets from tests of the two-parameter model: A sensitivity analysis. *Journal of Financial Economics* 10: 237–68.

Stevens, G., R. Berner, P. Clark, E. Hernandez-Cata, H. Howe, and S. Kwack. 1984. *The U.S. Economy in an Interdependent World: A Multi-Country Model*. Washington, D.C.: Federal Reserve Board of Governers.

Stulz, Rene. 1981. A model of international asset pricing. *Journal of Financial Economics* 9 (December): 383–406.

Svensson, Lars, and Assaf Razin. 1983. The terms of trade account and the current account: The Harberger-Laursen-Metzler effect. *Journal of Political Economy* 91: 97–125.

Svensson, Lars, and Sweder van Wijnbergen. 1986. International transmission of monetary policy. NBER Summer Institute paper. Cambridge: National Bureau of Economic Research, August.

Swoboda, Alexandre, and Rudiger Dornbusch. 1973. Adjustment, policy, and monetary equilibrium in a two-country model. In *International Trade and Money*, ed. M. Connolly and A. Swoboda, 229–61. London: Allen and Unwin.

Taylor, John. 1980. Aggregate dynamics and staggered contracts. *Journal of Political Economy* 88, 1 (February): 1–23.

Taylor, John. 1985a. What would nominal GNP targeting do to the business cycle? *Carnegie-Rochester Conference Series on Public Policy* 22: 61–84.

Taylor, John. 1985b. International coordination in the design of macroeconomic policy rules. *European Economic Review* 28 (June–July): 53–81.

Thomas, S. H., and M. R. Wickens. 1993. An international CAPM for bonds and equities. *Journal of International Money and Finance* 12, 2 (August): 390–412.

Tobin, James. 1958. Liquidity preference as behavior towards risk. *Review of Economic Studies* 67, 8 (February): 65–86.

Tobin, James. 1961. Money, capital and other stores of value. *American Economic Review* 51: 26–37.

Tobin, James. 1963. An essay on the principles of debt management. In *Fiscal and Debt Management Policies*, Commission on Money and Credit. Englewood Cliffs, N.J.: Prentice-Hall.

Tobin, James. 1969. The general equilibrium approach to portfolio balance theory. *Journal of Money, Credit, and Banking* 1: 15−29.

Tobin, James. 1980. Stabilization policy ten years after. *Brookings Papers on Economic Activity* 1: 19−72.

Tobin, James. 1983. Liquidity preference, separation, and asset pricing. *Zeitschrift Für Betriebswirtschaft* 53, 3 (March): 236−38.

Tobin, James, and Willem Buiter. 1976. Long-run effects of fiscal and monetary policy on aggregate demand. In *Monetarism*, ed. Jerome Stein, 273−309. Amsterdam: North-Holland.

Trivedi, Pravin, and Panos Varangis. 1994. Commodity prices and macroeconomic shocks in G-5 countries. Indiana University.

Urich, Thomas, and Paul Wachtel. 1981. Market responses to the weekly money supply announcements in the 1970s. *Journal of Finance* 36 (December): 1063−72.

Van Duyne, Carl. 1979. Macroeconomic effects of commodity disruptions in open economies. *Journal of International Economics* 9: 559−82.

Vines, D., J. Maciejowski, and J. E. Meade. 1983. *Demand Management*. London: George Allen.

Von Furstenberg, George. 1981. Incentives for international currency diversification by U.S. financial investors. *IMF Staff Papers* 28: 477−94.

West, Kenneth. 1986. Targeting nominal income: A note. *Economic Journal* 96 (December): 1077−83.

Williamson, John. 1983. *The Exchange Rate System*. Washington, D.C.: Institute for International Economics.

Williamson, John, and Marcus Miller. 1987. Targets and indicators: A blueprint for the international coordination of economic policy. *Policy Analyses in International Economics* 22 (September). Washington, D.C.: Institute for International Economics.

Wills, Hugh. 1979. Inferring expectations. Unpublished paper, London School of Economics.

Yellen, Janet. 1984. Efficiency wage models of unemployment. *American Economic Review* 74: 200−205.

Yoshitomi, M. 1984. The insulation and transmission mechanisms of floating exchange rates analyzed by the EPA World Econometric Model. In *EPA World Economic Model*, ed. Yoshitomi et al. Tokyo: Economic Planning Agency.

Index